I0048442

The CSR International Research Compendium

Volume 3: Society

Paperback edition first published in 2015
by Kaleidoscope Futures
16B North End Road, Golders Green, London NW11 7PH, UK

Copyright © 2015
Wayne Visser, Ileana Magureanu, Karina Yadav
Kaleidoscope Futures and CSR International

All rights reserved. No part of this publication may be reproduced, stored in a retrieval system, or transmitted, in any form or by any means, electronic, mechanical, photocopying, recording or otherwise, except as permitted by the UK Copyright, Designs and Patents Act 1988, without the prior permission of the publisher.

Cover photography and design by Wayne Visser and Kaleidoscope Futures.

ISBN 978-1-908875-21-1

The CSR International Research Compendium

Volume 3: Society

Human Rights | Labour practices | Consumer-oriented CSR
Communication | Consumer Social and Environmental
Responsibility | Community Involvement and Contribution |
Community Development

Summaries of the Best Research from 2009 to 2014

Wayne Visser

Ileana Magureanu

Karina Yadav

Contents

CONTENTS

Acknowledgements and Disclaimers

We would like to express our heartfelt gratitude to everyone who has volunteered their time and efforts to compile the CSR International monthly Research Digests between 2009 and 2014. Their work is greatly appreciated and we look forward to continuing to collaborate, as well as to welcome new CSR enthusiasts into our virtual research team.

Our thanks also goes to the researchers and the research organisations authoring the reports, surveys and papers compiled in the current compendium.

This is the third in a series of three volumes of the CSR International Research Compendium. It covers society-related research sourced from publicly available research publications, which we have summarised. The research summaries originally appeared in our Research Digests, which have been produced and made available to the public since our free, knowledge sharing platform was launched in 2009.

The authors of each research publication are cited and readers are encouraged to refer to the original document to fully comprehend the findings. Each research publication also indicates which Research Digest it originally appeared in. These monthly Digests are prepared by CSR International as a voluntary service to its freely subscribed members.

The views expressed in the research summaries in this Compendium in no way reflect those of CSR International, nor does CSR International endorse or vouch for the quality or accuracy of any third party research included.

All the proceeds for the book will go to the ongoing resourcing of CSR international, a nonprofit organisation run by volunteers.

Introduction

When I founded CSR International in 2008 and officially launched the organisation as a social enterprise in London in March 2009, I had two main objectives:

1. To create a focal point for the community of professionals, students and enthusiasts who are deeply concerned about the world's social and environmental problems and profoundly inspired by the potential of business to contribute to the solutions; and
2. To be an incubator for CSR 2.0 inspired, knowledge-based solutions, through research-related projects and by constantly challenging the theory and practice of corporate social responsibility to be more effective.

As I look back over the past six years, I am satisfied that we have remained true to our original vision. Today, we have a database of over 7,000 members who have registered on our website or subscribed to our monthly newsletter. We also have more than 15,000 Twitter followers, and an active presence on Facebook and LinkedIn.

Through our virtual internship program, we have given over 500 CSR champions the opportunity to volunteer (usually for 3 months) to do research and publish book reviews, blogs, sustainability report profiles and other outputs on the CSR International website. Recently, we reached out to our membership to ask them about their vision for CSR in 2020. They identified 10 key trends, to be published in a research report in 2015.

CSR International has also been steadfast in promoting the concept of CSR 2.0, which I established as a new framework in 2008. CSR 2.0 strives to move beyond defensive, charitable, promotional and strategic CSR to transformative CSR, based on the principles of creativity, scalability, responsiveness, glocality and circularity. Applied research on CSR 2.0 has been written up in my books *The Age of Responsibility* (2010) and *CSR 2.0* (2014), as well as numerous journal papers and media articles.

CSR International also worked with Hexagon Consultores to develop an online CSR 2.0 Self-Assessment Diagnostic Tool, which professionals and consultants can be trained.on and accredited to use with their companies and clients.

In terms of research projects, in 2010 we published *The World Guide to CSR*, an analysis and profiling of corporate sustainability and responsibility practices in 5 regions and 58 countries, bringing together the research of 87 contributors. In 2015, a sequel will be published called *The World Guide to Sustainable Enterprise*, which will cover more than 100 countries and appear in four regional volumes.

Besides all of this activity and these accomplishments, the most consistent thread – and arguably the greatest service we have provided – has been the monthly Research Digests. This continues a tradition I started in 2003 of summarising key findings from the best research, which I first did on behalf of KPMG and then for the Cambridge Institute for Sustainability Leadership.

Now, for the first time, we are bringing together all of the research summaries since 2009 into three thematic volumes: on Governance, Environment, and Society. This third volume alone profiles more than 400 research publications relating to society, from over 180 authors and over 280 organisations. I believe this will serve as an invaluable resource for CSR researchers and professionals everywhere.

I must express my heartfelt thanks and gratitude to my co-editors. Karina Yadav served as Research Associate and Managing Director at CSR International from 2011 to 2013 and Ileana Magureanu, our Research Director and compiler of this volume, has been active in the organisation since 2012. Between them, Karina and Ileana have put together almost all of the Research Digests over the past six years, so this Compendium is the fruit of their unfailing commitment and hard work.

I invite you to write to us at info@csrinternational.org and tell us if you find our Research Digests and these Compendiums useful, so that we know whether to continue and whether to update the Volumes periodically.

Cambridge, March 2015

I.   HUMAN RIGHTS

1.1   Due Diligence

1.1.1   Applying the Guiding Principles on Business and Human Rights to the ICT Industry Version 2.0: Ten Lessons Learned

Author(s): BSR

This briefing paper has been written to provide insight for information and Communications technology (ICT) companies on how to apply the Guiding Principles on Business and Human Rights. BSR has now published the "Version 2.0" of the report, with the ten key lessons we have learned during this time added to the original text.

Key findings

Companies seeking to apply the Guiding Principles are advised to build these lessons into their human rights programs and strategies.

- The speed of innovation in the ICT industry presents a daunting practical challenge for human rights impact assessments (HRIAs).
- We have found it helpful to think in terms of categories of product, rather than individual products, which can change even during the course of an assessment.
- Convergence, mergers, and acquisitions can significantly alter the human rights risk profile of individual companies. It is important to reassess a company's human rights risk profile following a significant event.
- A tree structure (i.e. that branches out to other issue-specific policies) works well for human rights policies in the ICT industry.
- HRIAs at the level of the product, service, or technology can be especially important for ICT companies.
- Stakeholders can significantly contribute to helping identify human rights risks, but many (though not all) ICT companies consistently

undervalue them.

- Outside corporate HQ, such as at the country or business unit level, the standard of human rights expertise in a company can be very low. Training and guidance is required to embed human rights due diligence throughout a company.

- ICT companies often find themselves in positions with limited room for maneuvering on human rights; they need to think creatively about their use of leverage.

- Dialogue and discussion with key departments, executives, and managers about potential human rights scenarios are effective methods for integrating human rights into company operations—and must be used alongside refreshed management systems and processes.

- With some notable exceptions, ICT companies rarely report sufficient information on human rights, or produce low-quality reports. Innovation in reporting is a significant priority.

- Transparency around human rights means both reporting to the public and communicating with users.

Source: CSR Research Digest, Sep. 2012 (Vol. 4, No. 9)

1.1.2 Business Ethics & Human Rights

Author(s): Institute of Business Ethics

An IBE Briefing explores the link between business ethics and human rights with a brief overview of the current business and human rights landscape. It also looks at how businesses seek to respect human rights and avoid human rights violations in their business operations and relationships.

Key findings

Attention to human rights has been shown to have a positive impact on business performance through improved stakeholder relations, positive corporate reputation and brand image, and employee motivation and retention.

- 'Doing business ethically' necessarily involves respecting human rights in the course of business operations.

- A company that is wishing to be considered as ethical will need to be mindful of human rights within the responsibilities of business and consistent with local law.
- Although respecting human rights can be considered integral to a business ethics agenda, IBE research (2012) found that only half of FTSE100 companies (52%) explicitly consider human rights in their code of ethics in some way.
- The positive and negative duties to protect human rights are still firmly with national governments.
- However, trends such as globalisation and the increasing presence of multinational corporations, pressures from NGOs, and reputation risk management, has meant there are increasing expectations of business in respecting human rights.
- The Briefing explores how companies are responding to this and the mechanisms they are using to express commitment and avoid human rights violations.

Source: Governance Research Digest, Sep. 2012 (Vol. 3, No. 9)

1.1.3   Guiding Principles on Business and Human Rights

Author(s): UN Human Rights Council

The United Nations Human Rights Council has endorsed a new set of Guiding Principles for Business and Human Rights designed to provide a global standard for preventing and addressing the risk of adverse impacts on human rights linked to business activity. The Guiding Principles are the product of six years of research led by Professor Ruggie from Harvard University, involving governments, companies, business associations, civil society, affected individuals and groups, investors and others around the world.

Key findings

The new standards outline how States and businesses should implement the UN "Protect, Respect and Remedy" Framework in order to better manage business and human rights challenges.

- Under the 'State Duty to Protect,' the Guiding Principles recommend how governments should provide greater clarity of expectations and consistency of rule for business in relation to human rights.
- The 'Corporate Responsibility to Respect' principles provide a blueprint for companies on how to know and show that they are respecting human rights.
- The 'Access to Remedy' principles focus on ensuring that where people are harmed by business activities, there is both adequate accountability and effective redress, judicial and non-judicial.

Source: Social Research Digest, Jun. 2011 (Vol. 2, No. 2)

1.1.4 Applying the UN Guiding Principles on Business and Human Rights to the ICT Industry

Author(s): BSR

This briefing paper was written to provide insight for information and communications technology (ICT) companies on how to apply the UN Guiding Principles on Business and Human Rights. The report will be updated with new versions after workshops, discussions and projects with ICT companies and stakeholders.

Key findings

The key human rights question faced by companies today is this: How should companies apply the UN Guiding Principles to business strategy and operations?

- BSR recommends that businesses use the Guiding Principles to create a human rights strategy based on four features:
  - a Human Rights Policy that expresses a commitment to respect human rights and provides a focal point for internal and external communication on human rights;
  - a corporate-wide Human Rights Impact Assessment that identifies key human rights risks and prioritizes areas requiring deeper assessment;
  - a Human Rights Action Plan to eliminate abuses, mitigate or avoid risk, and capitalize on opportunities for positive impact. Implementation of the action plan should be integrated into key

> corporate functions and overseen by some type of cross-functional body;
> o report and communicate human rights impacts and how they are being addressed.

- There are a number of briefings that describe how businesses in general should implement this four-part human rights strategy.

Source: Social Research Digest, Aug. 2011 (Vol. 2, No. 4)

1.1.5 Law Firms' Implementation of the Guiding Principles on Business & Human Rights

Author(s): *Advocates for International Development*

This paper prepared by A4ID with John Sherman provides an overview of discussions conducted by leading law firms on human right issue in London in September 2011. The report discusses the issues, and analyses some of the professional legal and ethical responsibilities for lawyers that offer both challenges and opportunities for lawyers, their clients, and society.

Key findings

Law is a vital tool for international development and lawyers have a crucial role to play in the fight against poverty as gatekeepers to the institutions and processes of justice.

- The legal professional rules of conduct examined in this report do not prohibit, but instead encourage, and in certain respects require, a lawyer to advise a client on the potential human rights impact of the client's action, in order to prevent or mitigate the impact.
- However, this places a premium on the need for the firm to obtain sufficient information as early as possible to enable the firm to advise the client, or point it to where it can get further input.
- Obtaining this information from some clients may be problematic, particularly where the firm is hired simply to 'paper the deal'.
- This demonstrates the need for the firm to state its commitment to human rights clearly and publicly.
- And where the client ignores the firm's advice, and persists in engaging in conduct that is likely to impact human rights adversely, the firm faces the difficult decision of whether to terminate its representation,

consistent with Guiding Principle 19 and professional rules of conduct that require evidence of good cause, adequate prior notice and steps to minimise legal prejudice to the client.

- In order for the firm to 'show' that it is respecting human rights, it must develop appropriate processes to demonstrate that it is doing so without jeopardising legitimate client interests and professional legal obligations to preserve client confidentiality.

Source: Social Research Digest, Apr. 2012 (Vol. 3, No. 4)

1.1.6 Formula One Companies' Response to Human Rights Concerns Business & Human Rights Resource

Author(s): Business & Human Rights Resource Centre

Business & Human Rights Centre published the summary of business response to human right concerns relating to the Bahrain Grand Prix, scheduled for 20-22 April. The centre lists each company that failed to respond and summarizes human rights concerns raised by international human rights groups, human rights advocates in Bahrain, and others.

Key findings

Only 29% of firms linked to Formula One responded to Business & Human Rights Resource Centre about human rights concerns that various organizations raised relating to the Bahrain Grand Prix.

- Forty two companies or teams failed to respond.
- The usual response rate to the Resource Centre is 75% globally.
- It is 95% for South African companies, 80% for Western European and North American companies, 50% for mainland Chinese companies.
- Since 2005 the Centre has invited over 1000 company responses, to a range of human rights concerns.
- The company responses were on the whole disappointing, given the gravity of the human rights concerns raised about Bahrain, and given that last year the United Nations Human Rights Council adopted by consensus the Guiding Principles on Business and Human Rights, which confirmed that all companies have a responsibility to respect human rights.

Source: Social Research Digest, May 2012 (Vol. 3, No. 5)

1.1.7 Handbook on UN Guiding Principles

Author(s): Social Accountability International (SAI) and Interchurch Organisation for Development Cooperation (ICCO)

SAI and ICCO's Handbook offers a sixstep approach to help businesses implement the Principles in their supply chain. The Handbook sets out a six-step method for firms to implement a supply chain management system that integrates respect for human rights.

Key findings

The handbook describes steps a company should follow as well as required policies and procedures.

- The handbook is based on the Guiding Principles on Business and Human Rights, written by John Ruggie.
- It is designed to help companies operationalise these principles, which include the framework "Protect, Respect and Remedy".
- The Guide describes six steps to implement a supply chain management system that protects human rights. These steps including assessing and then remedying human rights impact.
- It also and offers practical advice on how to overcome typical human rights problems companies face in their supply chain.

Source: Social Research Digest, Jul. 2012 (Vol. 3, No. 7)

1.1.8 Guide to Human Rights for SMEs

Author(s): European Commission

The European Commission has published an introductory guide to human rights for SMEs. The report is based on the United Nations Guiding Principles on Business and Human Rights, and translates those principles into the context of European small and mediumsized enterprises.

Key findings

Having a process in place to avoid and address negative human rights impacts will help you to identify possible areas in which legal compliance on its own does not guarantee that your company is respecting human rights.

- Such a process should therefore enable you to know where and when you may need to take action that goes beyond compliance.
- The six steps you should take to understand your risks of having negative impacts on human rights and to avoid and address such impacts:
  o commit to respect human rights and embed the commitment in your business;
  o identify your human rights risks;
  o take action to avoid and address the risks you identify;
  o enable remedy for those affected, if you are directly involved in a negative impact;
  o track your progress;
  o communicate about what you are doing.

Source: Social Research Digest, Dec. 2012 (Vol. 3, No. 12)

1.1.9 Labour Rights in Unilever's Supply Chains: From Compliance Towards Good Practice

Author(s): *Oxfam International*

Oxfam International issued a report that aims to (1) assess the labour standards in Unilever's operations and wider supply chain international and locally (2) develop a set of principles and measures to guide Unilever in fulfilling their social responsibilities. The "Labour Rights in Unilever's Supply Chain: From Compliance Towards Good practice" Report is the outcome of a collaboration between Oxfam and Unilever and it aims to examine Unilever's management of labour rights and uses Viet Nam as the country case study.

Key findings

There is evidence of poor labour practices in Unilever's operations in Vietnam between 2011 and 2012

- Unilever has made a commitment to social responsibility via adopting the UNGP and has made publicly available its Code of Business Principles, a Respect, Dignity, and Fair Treatment policy.
- Yet, Human and labour rights are missing from the Unilever Sustainable Living Plan.

- Unilever Management in Vietnam was found to lack the capacity and knowledge to ensure the company's operations comply with international standards, and did not have authority to support suppliers to do so.
- Some Unilever sourcing practices were found to contribute to excessive working hours and precarious work in the supply chain.
- The risk management system, involving selfassessment and audit, is not sensitive to the vulnerability of workers.
- There are no tracking or internal reporting mechanisms covering Unilever's effectiveness in dealing with labour issues; input is not sought on this from civil society stakeholders.
- While Unilever shows a level of transparency and actively engages with stakeholders at the global level, in Viet Nam it is at an early stage.
- Phone survey reveals that workers do not have any grievance mechanism and only one in four have an assigned person and procedures to deal with them.
- At the global level, corporate policy provides a good overall framework for labour rights; however, challenges arise when it comes to implementation since the industrial relations policy of Unilever along with other multinational corporations may be country-specific and locally determined.
- Commitment towards implementation has been demonstrated via actions taken to resolve industrial relations disputes and by subsequent corporate engagement of Unilever with International Union of Food Workers (IUF).
- At the Unilever Viet Name level, there is a UVN union but employees below management level do not have opportunities to raise issues collectively with management and have no influence in collective bargaining.
- All wages pain in Unilever's own factory were well in excess of the applicable minimum wages and thus were compliant with national law and Unilever policy.
- Unilever did not meet other benchmarks of the basic needs of employees and their families, such as the Asia Floor Wage and Oxfam's estimate of monthly expenses for an adult with child.

Source: Social Research Digest, Apr. 2013 (Vol. 4, No. 4)

1.1.10 Business & Human Rights Workshop Report 2013

Author(s): CSR Europe and Econsense

The workshop on Business and Human Rights-Putting Ruggie Framework and the Guiding Principles into Practice organized by CSR Europe and Econsense released a report that aims to provide a platform for member companies to share experiences in implementing the Ruggie Framework and discussing remaining challenges and incubate solutions. The "Business and Human Workshop Report 2013" highlights the practices of 10 companies around developing a human rights policy, conducting due diligence, dealing with complaints and addressing human rights along the supply chain.

Key findings

The discussion concluded that efforts are well underway to look at human rights in a systematic way.

- The professional discussion based on 15 short presentations which covered all aspects of the UNGP to business solutions such as setting up a human rights policy, conducting due diligence, setting up effective grievance mechanisms and dealing with human rights issues in the supply chain.
- One challenge remains identifying material issues, which can be overcome through collaboration in a multi-stakeholder context
- The final panel focused on human rights in the global supply chain.
- Deutsche Telekom and Hewlett-Packard were examples of industry collaboration in the ICT sector and company programs to trace conflict minerals included
- There is a common expectation for companies to make a policy commitment, exercise due diligence and engage in remediation, outlined in the UN Guiding Principles on business and human rights.
- CSR Europe and Econsense will continue to aim to support member companies in the practical implementation of the UN Guiding Principles, the project will focus on (1) embedding human rights across departments and identifying scope for improvement of company grievance mechanisms.

Source: Social Research Digest, Aug. 2013 (Vol. 4, No. 8)

1.1.11 Who Will Be Accountable? Human Rights and Post-2015 Development Agenda

Author(s): The United Nations Human Rights

The Office of the United Nations High Commissioner for Human Rights (OHCHR) and the Center for Economic and Social Rights (CESR) jointly published a report that highlights the accountability gaps that fetter the realization of global national development goals. The "Who Will Be Accountable? Human Rights and Post-2015 Development Agenda" publication focuses on the question of accountability, understood from a human rights perspective.

Key findings

It is critical that the next generation of development goals should be developed through a meaningfully participatory process in which all voices are heard, including civil society, human rights groups, women, minorities, indigenous peoples.

- Two key weaknesses have undermined the effectiveness of the current Millenium Development Goal Framework, particularly the rights and aspirations of those living in poverty: (1) the Goals nor the plans for enforcing them have been adequately framed in human rights terms; (2) lack of robust mechanisms to hold States and others accountable for what they have done to fulfill these pledges and to answer to people suffering from poverty and destitution.
- Post-2015 agreement should include commitments to improve the collection and analysis of statistical data at global, national and local levels, including data that can help track whether development efforts are in line with human rights principles such as nondiscrimination and progressive realization.
- Agreed criteria are also needed to guide national and local tailoring if the accountability and other objectives of a post-2015 agenda are not to be undermined.
- The requirements should ensure that there is consistency with international law, as emphasized in the "Rio+20" Conference.
- National tailoring should involve the following 8 steps:

(1) Align national and other goals with the human rights treaty targets as applicable to the country concerned;

(2) Set national goals, targets, indicators and benchmarks and aim to monitor progress via participatory processes;

(3) Embed the principles of non-discrimination and equality to ensure that the most disadvantaged regions are prioritized;

(4) Address constraints where rights are not being realized and create an enabling environment for human rights fulfillment;

(5) Look for connections and gaps in the general framework, and ensure that it reflects an adequate balance of human rights and sustainable development concerns;

(6) Define a time frame with an objective assessment of the "maximum" resources" available to the country;

(7) Set targets and indicators for fiscal and policy efforts and outcomes; and

(8) Use variety of indicators and all available information (qualitative & quantitative), across full range of human rights (civil, cultural, political and social) to help monitor progress.

Source: Social Research Digest, Sep. 2013 (Vol. 4, No. 9)

1.1.12 Migrant Workers and Health – The Role of Business

Author(s): BSR

The report addresses the issue of international migration and health care laying out the steps business can and should take to begin to protect the health of migrant workers at each phase of migration. This paper identifies health issues at each phase of the migration process: pre-departure and transit, postarrival/ on-boarding, integration, and return.

<u>Key findings</u>

As health is recognized as a human right, and with migrant workers now identified as a specific group of individuals requiring protection, business should adopt and establish standards or specific procedures to promote and protect migrant worker health.

- Migrant workers face unique health risks that require solutions beyond the realm of traditional occupational health and safety.
- Some steps that businesses can undertake include:

- o mapping and identifying health risks for major migration corridors in the supply chain;
- o building health profiles for migrant workers at the pre-departure phase;
- o developing preventative health programs for migrant workers in the workplace;
- o ensuring occupational health and safety standards and procedures are communicated and enforced effectively with migrant workers;
- o taking proactive steps to ensure the availability, accessibility, and acceptability of health services in the destination country.
- Solutions will be tailored based on the migration corridor and industry in question, but business must be willing to invest the resources into understanding the risks, planning and take the steps necessary to help promote migrant worker health.
- Business can better address migrant workerrelated workplace health risks by:
  - o examining effectiveness of current training curriculum in transferring information to migrant workers
  - o assessing whether information campaigns are carried out in ways that encourage migrants to be associated with health and safety issues more proactively;
  - o ensuring information and materials on health and safety training are provided in linguistically and culturally appropriate ways.
- Business can address health issues unique to migrant workers by:
  - o providing cultural awareness training as a part of the orientation process (BSR Management Toolkit, Post Arrival Orientation) and cultural adaption sessions during the course of employment.
  - o providing robust, appropriate, and accessible counseling programs in the workplace that include peer-to-peer counseling;
  - o leveraging counseling as a means of monitoring mental health among workers;
  - o seeking resources offered by migration and mental health experts such as the IOM;
  - o supporting multi-cultural activities during leisure time such as cultural nights, food festivals, and language exchange nights.

Source: Social Research Digest, Jan. 2012 (Vol. 3, No. 1)

1.2   Human Rights Risks and Violations

1.2.1   Human Exploitation Report

Author(s): Global Witness

International NGO Global Witness has released a report detailing the connections between the illegal mining trade, human rights abuses and global technology and mining firms. The report illustrates the current picture, the background to the situation and names a number of companies who are complicit in disregarding corporate social responsibility and perpetuating the conflict.

Key findings

Few of the companies contacted as part of this research have a coherent or comprehensive plan for addressing the impact of their trade on the violence and human rights abuses in eastern DRC.

- Foreign companies who buy minerals from Eastern Democratic Republic of Congo (DRC) have a responsibility to ensure that their trade is not benefiting any of the warring parties.
- Many firms based in Europe, Asia and elsewhere have been buying minerals from comptoirs known to be trading with armed groups, apparently without adjusting their practices in light of the conflict or carrying out sufficient due diligence to ensure that their trade is not fuelling the violence.
- Companies registered in Belgium accounted for the largest proportion of cassiterite, wolframite and coltan imports from North and South Kivu in 2007-8. The main Belgian companies are Trademet, Traxys, SDE, STI and Specialty Metals.
- After these Belgian companies, the largest buyers include:
  - o the Thailand Smelting and Refining Corporation (THAISARCO), the world's fifthlargest tin-producing company owned by the large British metals company Amalgamated Metal Corporation (AMC) Group;
  - o Afrimex, a UK-registered company;
  - o MPA, the Rwanda-based subsidiary of South- African owned Kivu Resources;

- o The Malaysian Smelting Corporation Berhad (the world's fourth-largest tin-producing company).
- o Companies based in China, India, Austria, the Netherlands and Russia also imported significant volumes of these minerals.
- Some of the companies contacted as part of this research mention their intentions to tighten their due diligence procedures, but these rarely go beyond their immediate suppliers and do not provide details of independent verification or checks of the entire chain of supply.
- A recurring argument in companies' responses is that it would be extremely difficult or impractical for them to track every stage of their supply chain and obtain information about the suppliers and origin of every single component, in part because of the many sources of supplies and large number of suppliers.
- Some of the positive measures which companies mention, for example imposing tighter requirements on their direct suppliers and observing codes of conduct, will be of limited use if they are not accompanied by corresponding steps all along the supply chain.
- Most of the letters to Global Witness from trading and processing companies failed to address the specific question of how they ensure that their trade is not contributing to the conflict.
- Many referred to general standards of corporate social responsibility, but few described specific measures they were taking to identify the exact origin of their supplies.
- Some of the companies which replied to Global Witness stated that they were committed to upholding and improving due diligence policies.
- However, the policies or internal codes of conduct they refer to are fairly general and do not include specific safeguards against the mineral trade fuelling armed conflict.

Source: Governance Research Digest, Aug. 2009 (Vol. 1, No. 8)

1.2.2   Emerging Markets Human Rights Report

Author(s): Maplecroft

International risk researchers, Maplecroft, have released a report detailing the most pressing human rights risks in emerging markets, alongside information to help companies mitigate these risks. The report, focusing on the BRICS nations (Brazil, Russie, India, China and South Africa), includes a series of individual country briefings which set out detailed quantitative risk scores for thirty human rights indicators.

Key findings

Country	Areas of Improvement	Areas of Deterioration
Brazil	Internal displacement and refugees; security forces; freedom of association and collective bargaining; arbitrary arrest and detention.	Child soldiers; freedom of speech and press; human rights defenders; female rights; business integrity and corruption; reporting environment.
Russia	Extrajudicial or unlawful killings; torture; security forces; forced or involuntary labour; trafficking; freedom of association and collective bargaining.	Child labour; indigenous people's rights; business integrity and corruption.
India	Extrajudicial or unlawful killings; disappearances; kidnapping; security forces; freedom of speech and press.	Child soldiers; human rights defenders; business integrity and corruption.
China	Kidnapping; trafficking; discrimination.	Disappearances; torture; security forces; child labour.
South Africa	Extrajudicial or unlawful killings; child labour; freedom of association and collective bargaining; female rights; indigenous people's rights.	Internal displacement and refugees; child soldiers; security forces; freedom of speech and press.

Source: Governance Research Digest, Sep. 2009 (Vol. 1, No. 9)

1.2.3   Migrant Workers' Exploitation Report

Author(s): Kav LaOved

Israeli NGO Kav LaOved has published a report detailing the extent of exploitation of migrant workers in Israel's agriculture sector. The report is based on a wide review of workers' complaints, as well as visits by the researchers to agricultural communities.

<u>Key findings</u>

Migrant workers earn less than the minimum wage (which is approximately US$1,000 a month), and that 90% of migrant workers work for longer hours than permitted under Israeli law and without overtime payment.

- It is common for employers to withhold the passports of their workers - a practice that is strongly condemned by the Israeli authorities.
- It is common practice in agri-businesses to suspend leave and observes that some employers grant their workers merely one day off a month.
- In many cases, salary payments are delayed for months or sent directly to the worker's country of origin, with no indication or report of the amount deposited.
- The report also says that 10% of agricultural workers (equivalent to 2,950 individuals) have been injured since the beginning of 2009 (the agricultural accident rate in Israel is reportedly three times higher than that in industry).
- Kav LaOved's inspection reports regularly say that migrant workers are subjected to harsh living conditions and demeaning treatment.
- Many migrant workers are unable to leave their jobs for financial reasons. Having paid US$8,000 to US$10,000 (in brokerage fees) to work in Israel, migrant workers are prime material for abuse by the farmers, as they are afraid to lose their jobs and not able to pay off loans taken to cover these payment to the middle men.

Source: Social Research Digest, Dec. 2009 (Vol. 1, No. 12)

1.2.4   Forced Labour Commodity Atlas

Author(s): Verite

Verite launched its Forced Labour Commodity Atlas in an effort to raise public awareness about goods produced under forced labor conditions and modern forms of slavery. The report examines link between commodities and some of the worst forms of labor exploitation in the global economy that is coming under increasing scrutiny from stakeholders around the world.

Key findings

According to the U.S. Department of Labor (2010), bricks are among the manufactured goods most commonly produced with forced or child labor.

- They are produced with forced labor in China, India, Myanmar (Burma), Nepal, North Korea and Pakistan and child labor in Afghanistan, Argentina, Bangladesh, Brazil, Cambodia, China, Colombia, Ecuador, India, Myanmar, Nepal, North Korea, Pakistan, Peru, and Uganda.
- There have also been reports of forced labor in Afghanistan contributing to NATO building projects (Kamber 2011).
- Cattle and beef products are also among the goods most commonly produced with child or forced labor.
- Cattle ranching takes place with forced labor in Bolivia, Brazil, and Paraguay and with child labor in Bolivia, Brazil, Chad, Ethiopia, Lesotho, Namibia, Paraguay, Uganda, and Zambia.
- In addition, cotton is one of the goods most commonly produced using forced and/or child labor, with the greatest concentration of producer countries occurring in Central Asia.
- Gold, according to the U.S. Department of Labor (2010), is one of the goods most widely produced with forced or child labor.
- Forced labor in gold production is found in Burkina Faso, North Korea, Nigeria, and Peru and child labor is found in Bolivia, Burkina Faso, Colombia, DRC, Ecuador, Ghana, Guinea, Indonesia, Mali, Mongolia, Nicaragua, Niger, Peru, the Philippines, Senegal, and Tanzania.
- Tobacco is among the agricultural goods most commonly produced with child or forced labor.
- Tobacco is being produced with forced labor in Malawi and Kazakhstan and with child labor in Argentina, Brazil, Indonesia, Kazakhstan, Kenya, Kyrgyz Republic, Lebanon, Malawi, Mexico, Mozambique, Nicaragua, the Philippines, Tanzania, Uganda and Zambia.

Source: Social Research Digest, May 2011 (Vol. 2, No. 1)

1.2.5 Help Wanted: Hiring, Human Trafficking and Slavery in the Global Economy

Author(s): Verite

Verite released a major report from a year-long investigation on migrant workers. The report illustrated the prevalence of forced labor and human trafficking across multiple sectors and widespread throughout the globe.

Key findings

Human trafficking and forced labor in our modern lives and across the global economy are very alive and well.

- Migrant workers all around the world make the products we buy and harvest the food we eat.
- In many ways our economy is driven by migrants, who cross borders for jobs that can help them achieve a better life, or simply allow them to feed their family.
- No matter what product - clothes, shoes, computers, toys, furniture and food - it is likely that migrant workers were a part of making or harvesting it.
- Migrants provide the flexible workforce that keeps our just-in-time global economy humming.
- Workers will go to great lengths to snag promising jobs, no matter where they are located.
- Often prospective workers will pay sizable sums to one or more middlemen – labor brokers and moneylenders - whose practices are often exploitative and illegal.
- Often workers take out loans to pay the fees.
- In doing so, they make a simple calculation: if they work so many months at a certain rate, they will have a specific sum at the end of the contract period -enough to pay off the loan and still net significant savings.

Source: Social Research Digest, Jun. 2011 (Vol. 2, No. 2)

1.2.6 Sexual Predators and Serial Rapists at Wal-Mart Supplier in Jordan

Author(s): Institute for Global Labour and Human Rights

Institute for Global Labour and Human Rights has released a very disturbing report on sexual abuse and repeated rapes. The report documents in great detail and in the workers' own words highlighting scores of young Sri Lankan women sewing clothing for Wal-Mart and Hanes.

<u>Key findings</u>

The minimal efforts of Wal-Mart, Hanes and the other labels to monitor factory conditions at Classic have failed completely.

- Workers are threatened by management and forced to say that conditions are good.
- According to witnesses who work at Classic Fashion, scores of young Sri Lankan women sewing clothing for Wal-Mart and Hanes have suffered routine sexual abuse and repeated rapes, and in some cases even torture.
- One young rape victim at the Classic factory in Jordan told us her assailant, a manager, bit her, leaving scars all over her body.
- Women who become pregnant are forcibly deported and returned to Sri Lanka.
- Women who refuse the sexual advances of Classic's managers are also beaten and deported.
- The standard shift at Classic is 13 hours a day, six and seven days a week, with some 18 ½ hour shifts before the clothing must be shipped to the U.S.
- According to witness testimonies, workers are routinely cursed at, hit and shortchanged of their wages for failing to reach their mandatory production goals.
- The workers-who are from Sri Lanka, Bangladesh, India, Nepal and Egypt, earn a take-home wage of just 61 cents an hour.

Source: Social Research Digest, Jun. 2011 (Vol. 2, No. 2)

1.2.7   A Fair Hiring Framework for Responsible Business

Author(s): Verite

Verite's Fair Hiring Framework is a "primer" that articulates the risk to multinational companies of forced labor and resulting debt-bondage caused by labor brokerage, and identifies the places within a company's sourcing practices where brokers present a reputational and legal liability. The report assists to identify the needed changes in corporate practices and ways that brands and their suppliers can take action.

<u>Key findings</u>

While the resolution on trafficking and slavery is complicated, companies are not powerless; in fact they can and should take action to stem these egregious abuses in their supply chains.

- This Framework document lays out the key steps that companies and their suppliers can take to rid themselves of supply chain trafficking and slavery.
- What brands should do:
  - o improving codes of conduct & company policies;
  - o raising awareness & building capacity;
  - o strengthening assessments & social audits;
  - o taking corrective action;
  - o reporting & transparency;
  - o multistakeholder and multibrand engagement & partnership;
  - o public policy advocacy.
- What suppliers should do:
  - o improving codes of conduct & company policies;
  - o raising awareness & building capacity;
  - o screening & evaluating labor brokers;
  - o managing labor brokers & monitoring for ethical recruitment and hiring;
  - o ensuring good practice in human resources management;
  - o establishing effective grievance mechanisms
  - o taking corrective action.

Source: Social Research Digest, Jul. 2011 (Vol. 2, No. 3)

1.2.8 Compliance is not Enough: Best Practices in Responding to The California Transparency in Supply Chain Act

Author(s): Verite

The California Transparency in Supply Chains Act has focused company attention on the presence of human trafficking and modernday slavery in supply chains. Verité outlines the content of the Act, the sources of trafficking and forced labor risk, and what is necessary in order to address these problems adequately in supply chain production.

Key findings

Standard social compliance responses will not be adequate to reduce company risks - or worker vulnerability - to these egregious problems.

- To fully understand and prevent trafficking and slavery in the making of products requires a greater level of effort and commitment.
- Broadly credible assessments must be integrated into companies' entire legal compliance and corporate social responsibility programs and cover the entirety of the supply chain – not only the top tier.
- Migrant workers especially can be deceived by the promise of high wages and good working conditions.
- Slavery and forced labor can be perpetuated at the job site when employers keep workers trapped.
- Embedding the capacity, knowledge, and system-based approach across the entire supply chain helps companies affectively and comprehensively meet their new obligations under Bill 657.

Source: Social Research Digest, Nov. 2011 (Vol. 2, No. 7)

1.2.9 Research on Indicators of Forced Labor: Success, Challenges and Reflections on Future Engagement

Author(s): Verite

Verité has released a report on lessons learned during the research process carried out from 2008 through 2011 on the presence of indicators of forced labor. The research covers production of ten goods in seven countries: shrimp in Bangladesh; Brazil-nuts, cattle, corn, and peanuts in Bolivia; sugar in the Dominican Republic; coffee in Guatemala; rubber in Liberia; fish in Indonesia; and tuna in the Philippines.

Key findings

A mixed quantitative-qualitative research methodology proved a good model for elucidating key patterns and circumstances, while at the same time remaining flexible and adaptive to field realities as they evolved.

- Whenever possible, Verité's research teams included individuals who were from the communities in which the research took place, or were of the same ethnicity or cultural background, or had worked in the past with the communities.
- This was critical in facilitating access establishing rapport and trust, particularly in indigenous communities and with populations where mistrust of outsiders was high.
- Verité's research cast a wide net, looking at potential contributing factors to exploitative labor emanating not only from the employment relationship itself, but from the jobseeking phase, and from the external landscape of community, economy, politics, supply chain and world market.
- This approach allowed for a nuanced analysis that could form the basis for a more comprehensive set of policy solutions.
- Verité's research also highlights the need for further research on key issues, including:
  o forced labor and family dynamics;
  o patronage systems and forced labor;
  o compulsory labor in indigenous communities;
  o child labor in the production of the goods under study;
  o the complex role of debt in subjecting individuals to forced labor;
  o and determining the existence and scale of forced labor at a country level in environments of extreme poverty and lack of alternative livelihood.

Source: Social Research Digest, Oct. 2012 (Vol. 3, No. 10)

1.2.10 An Ethical Framework for Cross-Border Labour Recruitment: An Industry/Stakeholder Collaboration to Reduce the Risks of Forced Labour and Human Trafficking

Author(s): Verite and ManpowerGroup

ManpowerGroup and Verité are working together to mobilize a new, pragmatic, multistakeholder effort to combat forced labor and human trafficking in the cross-border movement of workers. The report offers a set of specific operational practices ("Standards of Ethical Practice") for recruitment firms that operate across borders.

Key findings

The framework is designed as a remedy to the current institutional fragmentation of the crossborder recruitment marketplace, where employers, recruiters, and their local and regional subcontractors may operate in different jurisdictions with limited accountability to one another, to regulators, or to workers.

- The framework creates a set of credentials and information for third parties that will help eliminate unscrupulous brokers, by:
  - allowing employers to avoid entanglement with unethical sources of labor supply;
  - providing more leverage to NGOs, labor unions, consumer groups, and other stakeholders trying to persuade employers to use ethical partners;
  - helping recruitment firms with limited geographical reach to selectively partner with ethical subcontractors in other regions;
  - supporting licensing, oversight, and law enforcement initiatives by regulators;
  - improving information and choices for workers themselves.

Source: Social Research Digest, Nov. 2012 (Vol. 3, No. 11)

1.2.11 Human Rights Risk Atlas

Author(s): Maplecroft

The Research Report by Maplecroft's Human Rights Atlas 2013 looks at how public protest and political dissent resulting from human rights violations increases the risk to businesses. The Report identifies human rights violations, political instability and business risks through an analysis of 24 human rights violations categories across 197 countries.

Key findings

Burgeoning socio-economic and political instability in growing economies is a result of increasing levels of public dissent against government.

- Accordingly, the reaction of oppressive governments exacerbates global human rights situation, which in effect, is leaving foreign investors exposed to high levels of operational, financial, legal and reputational risks.

- Growth economies with the world's worst human rights records are Pakistan (ranked 5 in the atlas), Nigeria (12), China (16), Bangladesh (18), India (19), Russia (23), Mexico (25), and the Philippines (26).
- Only recently are Egypt (24) and Indonesia (32) are classified as 'extreme risk'.
- Multinational corporations are susceptible to allegations of complicity in human rights abuses in particular countries due to their complex supply chains.
- Business investment is grounded in emerging economies and many of these countries are plagued with social tensions.
- Correspondingly, a decline in human rights risk serves as a predicament of political risk and business disruption.
- There has been a jump in human rights violations over the last six years, with the 'extreme risk' category has increasing by 60% to 32 countries.
- The increase can be attributed to three core reasons:
  - perennial crushing of protestors and political dissent;
  - rising socio-economic tensions due to uneven distribution of wealth;
  - increased digital inclusion that has jolted protest movements.
- In growing market economies, industries requiring infrastructure investments, such as energy and transportation there is are increased risks.
- Particularly, the reliance on security forces to protect assets or make land seizures through oppressive methods could result in risks of complicity and legal implications in the future.
- The risk of complicity in human rights violations by security forces is high in fragile resource wealthy countries such as DR Congo (2), Myanmar (6), Iraq (7), Nigeria (12), and Indonesia (32).

Source: Social Research Digest, Jan. 2013 (Vol. 4, No. 1)

1.2.12 Company Mechanisms for Addressing Human Rights Complaints

Author(s): CSR Europe

CSR Europe released a report that aims to enhance joint learning on the business implications of the UN Guiding Principles on Business & Human Rights ("the UNGPs") and to support companies in their implementation. The "Company Mechanism for Addressing Human Rights Complaints" Report looks at the UNGPs that set expectation on what constitutes an effective corporate mechanism for addressing human rights complaints.

<u>Key findings</u>

It is possible to equip companies with a "practical Author(s)" and to give an indication of the process requirements for an effective company grievance mechanism through providing (1) a practical interpretation of the 8 effectiveness criteria (2) an overview of how a number of companies address complaints from employees and communities.

- The UNGPs set expectations on what constitutes an effective corporate mechanism for addressing human rights complaints
- The eight effectiveness criteria introduce concepts which companies sometimes find challenging to link in practice with business processes: legitimate, predictable, accessible, equitable, transparent, rights-compatible, a course of continuous learning, based on engagement and dialogue.
- Interviews conducted through the study demonstrated that companies are at different levels of maturity in implementing an effective process for addressing complaints
- When companies deal with Human Rights Complaints
- Little is known about what constitutes an efficient and effective grievance mechanism
- It is not clear what the eight UN effectiveness criteria mean in a business contact
- Companies express strong need to learn from peers and share examples of good practices
- The analysis of ten companies reveals that there are gaps and remaining challenges could be identified:
- The companies interviewed have established a formal process to address complaints with defined roles and responsibilities at either HQ or local level; Companies perform well with regards to accessibility

- Closer look revels that details are seldom presented in external report that although companies keep a record of complaints received, how grievances are resolved at an operational level is seldom monitored
- Complaints are rarely considered as human rights issues, which relates to the wider issue for global companies of overcoming cultural differences across regions and strengthening the internal communication on international standards and human rights.
- Engaging with external stakeholders is equally important in establishing "legitimacy" of the grievance procedure.
- For global companies, the challenge remains implementing policies at a local level which have been set at the corporate level
- Companies need to have a channel through which complaints can be recorded and dealt with—internal expertise is required
- In order to address remaining challenges and to further refine the process requirement to better identify what constitutes an effective grievance mechanism, CSR Europe needs to work further to improve the MOC-A tool and make it available to interested companies.

Source: Social Research Digest, Apr. 2013 (Vol. 4, No. 4)

1.2.13 Legitimate and Meaningful: Stakeholder Engagement in Human Rights Due Diligence | Challenges and Solutions for ICT Companies

Author(s): BSR

BSR released a paper that seeks to address the challenges faced by information and communications technology (ICT) companies working to integrate rights holder engagement into their human rights due diligence, which is a part of Principle 18 of the UN Guiding Principles on Business and Human Rights (UNGPs). In particular, the report, 'Legitimate and Meaningful: Stakeholder Engagement in Human Rights Due Diligence | Challenges and Solutions for ICT Companies' focuses on who companies should engage with and how they should engage, with an emphasis on specific human rights—privacy, security, and freedom of expression—where engagement with users of ICT is especially challenging.

Key findings

Insights that are worth profiling and keeping in the forefront during future rights holder engagement:

- Identify rights holders whose rights have been violated in the past.
- Prioritize vulnerable rights holders, and zoom in on the perspectives of those whose rights face the greatest risk.
- Follow "the and not the or" of engagement by convening different types of expertise.
- Pay special attention to combining the technology expert, the human rights expert, and the location expert.
- Engage rights holders before real business decisions are made, and involve significant business decision-makers from the get-go.
- Utilize multistakeholder organizations and resources, but do not limit engagement to them.
- Offer employees close to the front lines—not just the ones at HQ— opportunities for engagement.
- Undertake engagement that anticipates events, in addition to engagement that responds to current or recent events.

Source: Governance Research Digest, Oct. 2014 (Vol. 5, No. 10)

1.2.14 Human Rights Risk Atlas 2014

Author(s): Maplecroft

Risk analysis company Maplecroft released its 7th annual Human Rights Risk Atlas. The Atlas analyses human rights risk trends in 197 countries across 31 different violations and provides the most accurate picture available of the state of global human rights.

Key findings

The Atlas reveals a 70% rise in 'extreme risk' countries since 2008 – from 20 to 34.

- Since 2008 the countries which have seen the worst deterioration of their human rights environment include: Syria (ranked 1st and most at risk), Egypt (16th), Libya (19th), Mali (22nd) and Guinea-Bissau (74th). Regionally, the Middle East and North Africa (MENA) and Africa account for the majority of this increase

- Key emerging economies to drop into the 'extreme risk' category include: Nigeria (10th), India (18th), the Philippines (27th) and Indonesia (30th)
- Factors in the 70% increase include: repression of freedom of speech; ethnic and sectarian conflicts; a lack of worker protection; and competition for land and water between local populations and industrial business usersIn 2014, the highest risk countries include: Syria (1st), Sudan (2nd), DR Congo (3rd), Pakistan (4th), Somalia (5th), Afghanistan (6th), Iraq (7th), Myanmar (8th), Yemen (9th), Nigeria (10th)
- Scandinavia is the best performing region, while UK is ranked 165th and low risk.
- In MENA, state repression of societal protests, particularly youth protests, reveals an increase in the number of 'extreme risk' countries from two to seven, and an overall change in the regional average from 4.29/10 in 2008 to 2.75/10 in 2014 (where 0 represents the worst score). In addition to Syria (1st), Egypt (16th) and Libya (19th), other 'extreme risk' countries in the region include Iraq (7th), Yemen (9th), Iran (11th) and Saudi Arabia (31st).
- In sub-Saharan Africa, ongoing ethnic and sectarian conflict has resulted in a worsening risk score – from 4.56/10 in 2008 to 3.34/10 in 2014. Sudan (2nd), DR Congo (3rd) and Somalia (5th) remain amongst the five most extreme risk countries in the world, with DR Congo still having amongst the worst records of all countries for violations of women's and girl's rights, particularly sexual violence.
- In Asia, the increase in risk is also evident, with a risk score of 3.49/10 in 2014, compared to 4.04 in 2008. The highest risk countries include Pakistan (4th), Afghanistan (6th) and Myanmar (8th). In Bangladesh (17th) and India (18th) poor legal and regulatory frameworks contribute to a lack of access to remedy and pervasive labour rights violations, which account in turn for their poor risk rating.

Source: Social Research Digest, Mar. 2014 (Vol. 5, No. 3)

1.2.15   State of World's Human Rights 2013

Author(s): Amnesty International

Amnesty International published their 2013 report that documents the state of human rights during 2012. The Foreword and the country-by-country survey of 159 individual countries and territories set out a global overview of human rights violations and abuses inflicted by those in power on those who stand in the way of their vested interests.

Key findings

Global inaction on human rights is making the world an increasingly dangerous place for refugees and migrants.

- The rights of millions of people who have escaped conflict and persecution, or migrated to seek work and a better life for themselves and their families, have been abused. Governments around the world are accused of showing more interest in protecting their national borders than the rights of their citizens or the rights of those seeking refugee or opportunities within those borders.
- In 2012 the global community witnessed a range of human rights emergencies that forced large numbers of people to seek safety, within states or across borders. From North Korea to Mali, Sudan and the Democratic Republic of the Congo people fled their homes in the hope of finding safe haven.
- Another year has been lost in Syria, where little has changed apart from the ever-increasing numbers of lives lost or ruined. Tens of thousands have died and millions have been displaced by the conflict. The world stood by while Syrian military and security forces continued to carry out indiscriminate and targeted attacks on civilians, and to subject to enforced disappearance, arbitrarily detain, torture and extrajudicially execute those deemed to oppose the government, while armed groups continue to hold hostages and to carry out summary killings and torture on a smaller scale.
- People attempting to flee conflict and persecution regularly encountered formidable obstacles trying to cross international borders. It was often harder for refugees to cross borders than it was for the guns and weapons that facilitated the violence that forced such people from their homes. However, the UN's adoption of an Arms Trade Treaty in March 2013 offers hope that shipments of weapons that may be used to commit atrocities may at last be halted.
- The European Union implements border control measures that put the

lives of migrants and asylum-seekers at risk and fails to guarantee the safety of those fleeing conflict and persecution. Around the world, migrants and asylum-seekers are regularly locked up in detention centres and in worst case scenarios are held in metal crates or even shipping containers.

- The rights of huge numbers of the world's 214 million migrants were not protected by their home or their host state. Millions of migrants worked in conditions amounting to forced labour – or in some cases slavery-like conditions – because governments treated them like criminals and because corporations cared more about profits than workers' rights. Undocumented migrants were particularly at risk of exploitation and human rights abuse.

Source: Social Research Digest, Apr. 2014 (Vol. 5, No. 4)

1.2.16 Trafficking in Persons (TIP) Report

Author(s): U.S. State Department

The U.S. State Department released its annual report that ranks governments based on their perceived efforts to acknowledge and combat human trafficking, advance reforms and target resources for prevention, protection and prosecution programs. The Trafficking in Persons (TIP) Report divides nations into four tiers based on their compliance with 11 "minimum standards for the elimination of trafficking": • Tier 1 countries include governments fully compliant with the minimum standards. • Tier 2 Countries don't fully comply, but are making significant efforts to do so. • The Tier 2 Watch List includes countries with a high number of victims, or where the numbers are significantly increasing. It also includes countries where there's insufficient evidence of acceptable efforts to improve anti-trafficking programs. • Tier 3 countries do not fully comply with the minimum standards and have not shown the U.S. they are making significant efforts to do so.

Key findings

After several years of what it says are broken promises, the U.S. government has singled out Thailand, Malaysia, Venezuela and The Gambia for taking insufficient action against human trafficking. The U.S. State

Department downgraded the four countries to Tier 3, the lowest possible ranking it gives for national responses to fighting modern day slavery.

- There is evidence of forced labor and sex trafficking in Malaysia and Thailand. Migrants from other Asian nations who seek work on farms, factories and construction sites in Malaysia are trapped and have their passports taken and wages withheld.
- In Thailand, tens of thousands of migrants from neighboring countries are being exploited in the commercial sex industry, on fishing boats or as domestic servants.
- In Venezuela, women and girls are often lured from poor interior regions to tourist centers with the promise of false job offers. When they arrive, they are often forced into prostitution.
- While the United States puts itself in the Tier 1 category, the State Department acknowledges its own problems fighting trafficking, something that hadn't been done in the report until 2010. Several new groups within the U.S. may be vulnerable to traffickers, including teens living on Native American reservations and members of the LGBT community.
- Other countries listed on Tier 3 are:
  1. Algeria
  2. Central African Republic
  3. Cuba
  4. Democratic Republic of Congo
  5. Equatorial Guinea
  6. Eritrea
  7. Guinea-Bissau
  8. Iran
  9. Kuwait
  10. Libya
  11. Mauritania
  12. North Korea
  13. Papua New Guinea
  14. Russia
  15. Saudi Arabia
  16. Syria
  17. Uzbekistan

18. Yemen
19. Zimbabwe
20. The following countries were upgraded in this year's report:
21. Afghanistan
22. Albania
23. Barbados
24. Chad
25. Chile
26. China
27. Honduras
28. Liberia
29. Maldives
30. Micronesia
31. St. Lucia
32. Seychelles
33. Sudan
34. Switzerland
35. Trinidad and Tobago

Source: Social Research Digest, Jul. 2014 (Vol. 5, No. 7)

1.2.17 ITUC Global Rights Index: The World's Worst Countries For Workers

Author(s): The International Trade Union Confederation

The International Trade Union Confederation built the world's most comprehensive data base of violations of workers' rights that covers violations in 139 countries recorded between April 2013- March 2014. The methodology of the ITUC Global Rights Index is grounded in standards of fundamental rights at work, in particular the right to freedom of association, the right to collective bargaining and the right to strike.

Key findings

In the past year, governments of at least 35 countries have arrested or imprisoned workers as a tactic to resist demands for democratic rights, decent wages, safer working conditions and secure jobs.

- In at least 9 countries murder and disappearance of workers were commonly used to intimidate workers.

- Workers in at least 53 countries have been dismissed or suspended for attempting to negotiate better working conditions.
- Laws and practices in at least 87 countries exclude certain type of workers from the right to strike.
- At a time when corporate power has never been greater, these results show that almost every country can improve its treatment of workers. Only Denmark received a perfect score of zero for respecting all 97 indicators of workers' fundamental rights:
  - 1 – Irregular violations of rights: 18 countries including Denmark and Uruguay
  - 2 – Repeated violations of rights: 26 countries including Japan and Switzerland
  - 3 – Regular violations of rights: 33 countries including Chile and Ghana
  - 4 – Systematic violations of rights: 30 countries including Kenya and the USA
  - 5 – No guarantee of rights: 24 countries including Belarus, Bangladesh and Qatar
  - 5+ - No guarantee of rights due to breakdown of the rule of law: 8 countries including Central African Republic and Somalia.
- Cambodia's labour law fails to cover many civil servants, there are undue restrictions on the right to elect union representatives, and in 2013 the government responded with lethal force to demonstrators seeking a decent wage and working conditions. This resulted in Cambodia receiving a score of 5 in the Rights Index – the worst possible rating other than for those countries where the rule of law has completely broken down.
- In the Middle East, Qatar is yet to allow unions at all for its many migrant workers, while in Latin America, Guatemala was one of the worst places to be a worker, with no guarantee of rights

Source: Social Research Digest, Aug. 2014 (Vol. 5, No. 8)

1.2.18   Profits and Poverty: The Economics of Forced Labour

Author(s): International Labour Organization (ILO)

The International Labour Organization (ILO) released a study that investigates the underlying factors that drive forced labour, of which a major one is illegal profits. The report, titled Profits and Poverty: The Economics of Forced Labour offers new knowledge of the determinants of forced labour, including a range of figures that break down profits by area of forced labour and by region.

Key findings

The power of normative pressure against those who still use or condone the use of forced labour is essential, and national legislation needs to be strengthened to combat forced labour and penalties against those who profit from it need to be strictly enforced. However, a better understanding of the socio-economic root causes and a new assessment of the profits of forced labour are equally important to bringing about long-term change.

- In the private economy forced labour generates US$ 150 billion in illegal profits per year, about three times more than previously estimated – thrives in the incubator of poverty and vulnerability, low levels of education and literacy, migration and other factors.
- More than a century after being banned in the developed world, and decades after being outlawed in the newly emerging developing world, modern forms of slavery — forced labour, human trafficking, forced sexual exploitation—still exist, and unfortunately risk growing in extent and profitability in the world today.
- Put into perspective, the 21 million victims in forced labour and the more than US$150 billion in illegal profits generated by their work exceeds the population and GDP of many countries or territories around the world. Yet this vast nation of men, women and children, along with its resources, remains virtually invisible, hidden behind a wall of coercion, threats and economic exploitation.
- While unscrupulous employers and criminals reap huge profits from the illegal exaction of forced labour, the losses incurred by the victims are also enormously significant. People in forced labour are often caught in a vicious cycle that condemns them to endless poverty. They may suffer personal trauma that will require years to overcome as they try to rebuild their lives.
- At the same time, law-abiding businesses and employers are disadvantaged by forced labour as it creates an environment of unfair competition and risks tarnishing the reputation of entire industries and

sectors.

- Governments and societies are also harmed because the profits generated by forced labour bypass national tax collection systems, and the costs involved in dealing with forced labour cases are significant.
- The impact of poverty and income shocks is central to the understanding of forced labour. Individuals living in poverty are more likely to be in forced labour and to borrow money, leading to an increase in vulnerability to forced labour or a family member being held in debt bondage.
- The choice of a specific occupation also has an impact on whether the person ends up in forced labour. Forced labour is more common in unskilled occupations in agriculture, fishing, domestic work, manufacturing and other work requiring low levels of education and skills. Informal sector workers are more vulnerable to forced labour than workers who possess enforceable employment contracts.
- Education and literacy are very important factors, both in terms of vulnerability to, and in the elimination of, forced labour. Educated individuals are less likely to be in basic forms of manual labour, and are more likely to know their rights. Literate individuals can read contracts and recognize situations that could lead to exploitation and coercion. In addition, households headed by educated persons are more likely to be better off and thus less likely to borrow, especially in the event of unforeseen income shocks.

Source: Social Research Digest, Sep. 2014 (Vol. 5, No. 9)

1.2.19 Global Report on Trafficking in Persons

Author(s): UNDOC

The United Nations Office of Drugs and Crime (UNODC) released its second report that highlights the role of organized crime in trafficking in persons, and includes an analytical chapter on how traffickers operate. The Global Report on Trafficking in Persons covers 128 countries and provides an overview of patterns and flows of trafficking in persons at global, regional and national levels, based on trafficking cases detected between 2010 and 2012 (or more recent).

Key findings

One in three known victims of human trafficking is a child, and girls and women are particularly targeted and forced into "modern slavery.

- Girls make up 2 out of every 3 child victims. And together with women, they account for 70% of overall trafficking victims worldwide.
- In some regions – such as Africa and the Middle East – child trafficking is a major concern, with children constituting 62% of victims.
- Trafficking for forced labour – including in the manufacturing and construction sectors, domestic work and textile production – has also increased steadily in the past five years. About 35% of the detected victims of trafficking for forced labour are female.
- However, no country is immune – there are at least 152 countries of origin and 124 countries of destination affected by trafficking in persons, and over 510 trafficking flows criss-crossing the world.
- There are, however, regional variations as to why people are trafficked in the first place. For example, victims in Europe and Central Asia are mostly trafficked for sexual exploitation, whereas in East Asia and the Pacific forced labour drives the market. In the Americas, the two types are detected in almost equal measure.
- The report found that most trafficking flows are interregional, and more than 6 out of 10 victims have been trafficked across at least one national border. The vast majority of convicted traffickers – 72% – are male and citizens of the country in which they operate.
- The report also highlighted that impunity remains a serious problem: 40% of countries recorded few or no convictions, and over the past 10 years there has been no discernible increase in the global criminal justice response to this crime, leaving a significant portion of the population vulnerable to offenders.

Source: Social Research Digest, Dec. 2014 (Vol. 5, No. 12)

1.2.20   Torture in 2014: 30 Years of Broken Promises

Author(s): Amnesty International

Amnesty International commissioned a new survey to gauge worldwide attitudes to torture, with some 21,000 people in 21 countries asked their views by the polling company GlobeScan. Amnesty's new 50-page briefing,

Torture in 2014: 30 Years of Broken Promises, details a shocking variety of torture techniques - with at least 27 different kinds of torture and other cruel treatment recorded during 2013-14.

Key findings

Torture "is flourishing" around the world, despite 155 countries having ratified the United Nations' Convention Against Torture - a milestone convention that Amnesty campaigned hard for in the 1970s and 1980s.

- Nearly half (44%) of respondents fear that they would be at risk of torture if taken into custody in their country.
- In Mexico this figure was far higher - nearly two-thirds (64%) feared torture in detention - while high levels of fear over torture were also recorded in Pakistan, Turkey, Kenya, Peru, South Korea, Indonesia, Greece and Brazil.
- In the UK this figure was much lower (15%), though even this means that three people in every 20 fear being tortured if they are detained by the authorities.
- Meanwhile, while the survey showed that a large majority (82%) of respondents believe there should be clear laws against torture, more than a third (36%) still thought "torture is sometimes necessary and acceptable to gain information that may protect the public". Shockingly, almost three-quarters of the respondents in China (74%) and two-thirds in Kenya (66%) thought that torture could be justified. In the UK the figure was 29%, almost one in three people.
- In Nigeria police and military personnel use torture as a matter of routine.
- In Mexico the government argues that torture is the exception rather than the norm, but in reality abuse by the police and the security forces is widespread and goes unpunished.
- In the Philippines a secret detention facility was recently discovered where police officers abused detainees "for fun".

Source: Social Research Digest, Aug. 2014 (Vol. 5, No. 8)

1.3 Gender-Related Issues

1.3.1 Women in the Boardroom: A Global Perspective

Author(s): Deloitte

The Deloitte Global Center for Corporate Governance produced a new survey of recent efforts — legislative and otherwise — to increase the participation of women in boardrooms across the globe. The survey, "Women in the boardroom: A global perspective" is in its third edition, highlights initiatives, spanning 25 countries and six continents, aimed at balancing the scales in favor of a more diverse and gender-inclusive boardroom.

Key findings

In some parts of the world, governments commit to expand opportunities for women; still others have seen the movement toward quotas as another response to the financial crisis.

- The Australian corporate governance code, known as the ASX Corporate Governance Council Principles and Recommendations, was re-issued on 30 June 2010 by the ASX
- Corporate Governance Council and now contains a number of new recommendations relating to gender diversity.
- China's corporate governance code (Code of Corporate Governance for Listed Companies in China) does not mention gender as a desirable quality or background for board candidates.
- In December 2012, the Parliament of India passed the Companies Bill that improved corporate governance practices throughout India. Chapter XI, titled Appointment and Qualifications of Directors, states that public companies must have at least one woman director.
- In New Zealand, publicly listed companies will now come under pressure to promote women to boards and management under proposed new stock exchange rules.
- The Brazilian Senate is discussing the inclusion of compulsory quotas for state and mixedcapital enterprises, which would eventually require a 40% representation of women on boards by 2022.

Source: Governance Research Digest, Mar. 2013 (Vol. 4, No. 3)

1.3.2   Women in Corporate Leadership

Author(s): Lipscomb University / InterOrganization Network

A 2011 national study led by the Lipscomb University College of Business examines the presence of women in corporate leadership. The study captured information on women directors and executive officers of public companies, based on FYE 2009 SEC filings in 14 regions of the United States.

Key findings

There is a limited presence of women in corporate leadership nationwide, proving that a gender gap still exists in the nation's executive suites and boardrooms.

- More than 91% of the 617 corporate directors in Tennessee were men at a time when women made up 48.0% of the Tennessee work force.
- Out of the 72 public corporations, 46% had no women directors at all.
- Only 12.7% of the 71 board seats for Fortune 500 companies were held by women in Tennessee, making it next to last by this measure.
- Only 1.4% of Tennessee's companies claimed 25% or more women directors, ranking next to last in this category as well.

Source: Social Research Digest, Aug. 2011 (Vol. 2, No. 4)

1.3.3   Business Ethics and Board Diversity

Author(s): Institute of Business Ethics

The latest Briefing from the Institute of Business Ethics looks at the case for board diversity. The report offers some practical advice on how to achieve a diverse board.

Key findings

Women are underrepresented in corporate boards worldwide.

- The new UK Corporate Governance Code attempts to remedy the UK situation.
- It states that: "The search for board candidates should be conducted, and appointments made, on merit, against objective criteria and with

due regard for the benefits of diversity on the board, including gender" (p13, opcit).

- Recent figures published by Cranfield School of Management show that in the UK only 13.9% of FTSE 100 board members are women (and only 8.7% of the FTSE 250(5)) – encouragingly this is up on the 12.5% figure for the past three years.

- Around one fifth of FTSE 100 boards and over half of FTSE 250 boards have no women board members at all.

- In the USA the percentage of women on top corporate boards has remained at 15% for the past five years.

- Lord Davies" Women on Boards review recommended that companies in the FTSE 100 should aim for a minimum of 25% female board member representation by 2015.

- The CBI has warned that listed companies must convince the EU that they are doing all they can to increase the number of women board members voluntarily or they will face quotas.

- Around the world, Norway has the highest proportion of women board members due to a legal requirement for there to be 40% women on the boards of publicly listed companies since 2008.

- France, Spain and Iceland have also passed legislation requiring quotas while other countries such as Australia have a „comply or explain" approach.

Source: Social Research Digest, Sep. 2011 (Vol. 2, No. 5)

1.3.4 Women Directors on Corporate Boards: From Tokenism to Critical Mass

Author(s): M. Torchia, A. Calabrò and M. Huse

The aim of the study is to test if 'at least three women' could constitute the desired critical mass by identifying different minorities of women directors (one woman, two women and at least three women). Tests are conducted on a sample of 317 Norwegian firms.

Key findings

The results suggest that attaining critical mass – going from one or two women (a few tokens) to at least three women (consistent minority) – makes it possible to enhance the level of firm innovation.

- Moreover, the results show that the relationship between the critical mass of women directors and the level of firm innovation is mediated by board strategic tasks.
- Implications for both theory and practice, and future research directions are discussed.

Source: Social Research Digest, Sep. 2011 (Vol. 2, No. 5)

1.3.5   Corporate Equality Index 2012: Rating American Workplaces on Lesbian, Gay, Bisexual and Transgender Equality

Author(s): Human Rights Campaign Foundation

The Human Rights Campaign's 2012 Corporate Equality Index chronicles a decade of progress in workplace equality. The HRC's CEI report provides an in-depth analysis and rating of large U.S. employers and their policies and practices pertinent to lesbian, gay, bisexual and transgender employees.

Key findings

2012 marks the first year of new more stringent criteria regarding transgender health benefits.

- 189 participants earned the top rating of 100%, evidence the CEI has helped transform the American workplace for the better over the past ten years.
- In the first year of the CEI a decade ago, 13 businesses achieved a top score of 100%.
- In its debut year in which 319 participants were rated, the CEI noted that most of the largest U.S. employers fell within the middle of the ratings bell curve: workplace protections on the basis of sexual orientation, domestic partner health care benefits and some internal inclusion practices were becoming more common but transgender inclusion lagged.

- Year after year, participants have successfully used the CEI guideposts and HRC Foundation staff as resources to push themselves towards the gold standards captured by the CEI criteria.
- The CEI standards have most dramatically shifted the way the largest U.S. businesses have incorporated transgender protections and benefits in the workplace.
- In 2002, only 5% of participants included "gender identity" in their non-discrimination policy.
- Today, 80% of participants have implementing this basic, yet crucial, protection for employees.
- Even among non-participants, the CEI has helped create market norms where LGBT workplace equality is essential to staying relevant among competitors.
- The evolution of workplace protections among the Fortune 500 in the past decade reflects the progress seen among participating companies in the CEI, further demonstrating the improved landscape in which LGBT employees now work.
- Eighty-six percent of the Fortune 500 include "sexual orientation" in their nondiscrimination policies and 50% include "gender identity."
- The majority of the total Fortune 500 — 60% — offer equivalent medical benefits between spouses and partners and 19% offer transgender-inclusive health care benefits, including surgical procedures.

Source: Social Research Digest, Apr. 2012 (Vol. 3, No. 4)

1.3.6 Migration of Women Workers from South Asia to the Gulf

Author(s): UN Women and V.V Giri Labour Institute

The report analyses the processes, outcomes and problems associated with the migration of women workers from South Asian countries to the Gulf region, focusing on five major sending countries in South Asia – Bangladesh, India, Nepal, Pakistan and Sri Lanka – and six major receiving countries of the Gulf region – Bahrain, Kuwait, Oman, Qatar, Saudi Arabia and United Arab Emirates. Highlighting the positive economic aspects of migration in South Asia, this report also addresses the areas where women continue to experience injustice, violence and inequality at various stages of the migration cycle.

Key findings

In the context of increasing feminisation of international migration, it is more than likely that migration of women from South Asia to the Gulf region will see an increasing trend in future.

- Both demand side (growth of the service sector and care economy) and supply side (limited job opportunities and increasing LFPR among women) factors will drive the escalation in the migration of women workers.
- The process of migration is a highly convoluted one and reflects the power relations and hierarchies in terms of gender, race and other development indicators in the global economy and society.
- Evidence from the study indicates that, with increasing migration, for both the individual migrant and the sending economies, income and welfare are likely to increase with positive multiplier effects on the households and at regional and sub-regional levels.
- In the social and political spheres, these will have enormous consequences as the ensuing empowerment of women will reshape gender and power relations at the micro and macro levels.
- However, it is also more than probable that in the near future, women migrants from South Asia will continue to encounter discrimination and exploitation at different phases of the migration cycle, in both the sending and receiving countries.
- Most of the low skilled women migrants are caught in a web of marginal existence, on account of being women and low skilled migrants working in the confines of the household where the piercing eyes of labour law do not reach.
- It must be noted, however, that the enormous increase in the scale of migration of women has evoked several positive responses from various stakeholders.
- These have to an extent attenuated the insecurities and vulnerabilities of migrant women. At the international level, a number of organisations have engaged constructively to make female migration a central issue in public debate.

- At the national level, there is increasing awareness of the need for the migration policy to be gender-sensitive and also have specialised measures and programmes directed at women migrants.

Source: Social Research Digest, Jun. 2012 (Vol. 3, No. 6)

1.3.7 Gender Equality: It's Your Business

Author(s): Oxfam

This briefing concentrates on gender equality and the responsibilities of business to uphold and promote it, recognising that business can have a positive impact on the lives and status of women as well as men, while enhancing companies' own productivity and reputation. It is intended for senior managers in global and national companies, especially those retailing and producing food and fast-moving consumer goods, and which source goods or labour in developing countries.

Key findings

Gender equality gives businesses the opportunity to hire from a wider pool of talent, gain greater insights into consumers' needs, and improve the security and quality of supply.

- Enlightened businesses are realising that enabling women's full potential delivers returns.
- For business, equal treatment of women and men means access to the most talented pool of workers, a more balanced and talented board, greater appeal to the consumer base, an enhanced corporate reputation, and even a more stable supply of basic commodities.
- Tackling gender inequality is also the right thing to do, as inequality increases women's vulnerability to poverty and suffering.
- And yet aggregate performance on gender equality in the business sector has been poor:
  - only 13 of the largest 500 corporations in the world have female CEOs;
  - women are over-represented in precarious, low-waged, or informal sectors of the economy in most countries;

o female food producers have less access than men to the resources that are crucial for efficient food production (training, inputs, extension services, and financial services).

Source: Social Research Digest, Jun. 2012 (Vol. 3, No. 6)

1.3.8   Corporate Equality Index

Author(s): Human Rights Campaign Foundation

Human Rights Campaign Foundation's 2013 Corporate Equality Index is the national benchmarking tool on corporate policies and practices related to LGBT employees. It provides an in-depth analysis and rating of large U.S. employers and their policies and practices pertinent to lesbian, gay, bisexual and transgender employees.

Key findings

Despite this patchwork of state laws, private sector employers have implemented fully inclusive nondiscrimination polices at rates that are leaps and bounds ahead of lawmakers.

- 99% of CEI-rated employers provide employment protections on the basis of sexual orientation.
- 84% of CEI-rated employers provide employment protections on the basis of gender identity or expression — the highest figure to date.
- 89% of C EI-rated employers provide medical and comprehensive health benefits such as dental, vision, dependent medical and Consolidated Omnibus Budget Reconciliation Act (COBRA)-equivalent continuation coverage.
- 65% of C EI-rated employers have complete parity in spousal and partner access to "soft" benefits (when such benefits are offered at all) such as bereavement leave, employee assistance programs, employee discounts and relocation assistance.
- 69% of CEI-rated employers offer a robust set of practices (at least three efforts) to support organizational LGBT diversity competency.

Source: Social Research Digest, Jan. 2013 (Vol. 4, No. 1)

1.3.9 Green Jobs For Women And Youth: What Can Local Governments Do?

Author(s): United Nations Development Programme

The UNDP released a report that highlights examples of policies and programmes initiated by local governments to advocate green jobs for women and youth, for the purpose of inspiring local government to consider policies that address economic, social and environmental dimensions of sustainable development in a synergetic manner. The "Green Jobs for Women and Youth: What Can Local Governments Do?" report focuses on real examples from developing countries in which local governments have introduced programmes that have created work opportunities for youth and women (between ages 14 and 24) while addressing environmental challenges as well.

<u>Key findings</u>

It is estimated that over 400 million people will join the workforce within the next decade and green jobs creation is thus seen as an opportunity to address this challenge as countries transition to green economies.

- It is estimated that over 400 million people will join the workforce within the next decade and green jobs creation is thus seen as an opportunity to address this challenge as countries transition to green economies.
- In the Global Employment Trends 2012, the ILO reported that from 2002 to 2007, women had a higher unemployment rate at 5.8% in comparison with men at 5.3% and by 2012, it increased by 0.7%age points—eliminating 13 million jobs for women.
- Women had higher unemployment rates than men in Africa, the Arab region, South and South-East Asia, and Latin America.
- Women are more limited in their choice of employment across sectors, and they continued to be segregated into particular types of occupations.
- Young women have been fundamentally affected by the global economic crisis. For example, in South Asia, for example, women account for 60% of the region's labour force.

- In Fiji, Samoa and the Solomon Islands, less than one third of the employed are women; in some cases they tend to be more employed in urban verses rural economic activities.
- Women are seen as more vulnerable than men to the effects of climate change because they represent the majority of the world's poor and are proportionally more dependent on threatened natural resources.
- Local institutions often take a central role in promoting green job opportunities in rural settings.
- Several local governments have captured green job opportunities by introducing programmes coupled with training schemes targeted specifically for women and youth.
- South Africa: The local government of Keiskammahoek, launched the Working for Water programme in 1995 to combat the devastating effects of alien species in waters on biological diversity and water security. The programme places special emphasis on creating jobs and training for unemployed women and youth.
- The Phillipines: This programme emphasizes women's empowerment and awareness-raising on gender issues. Local women are provided with leadership and management training, and supported to participate in decision-making processes at the household level as well as at project sites.
- Recommendations for local government and their role in promoting green jobs include (1) setting green job indicators (2) developing training and skills development programmes social protection labour market policies and green economic opportunities (4) mobilizing fiscal spaces and financing mechanisms (5) establishing and harnessing innovative partnerships (6) promoting green technology innovation and transfer.

Source: Social Research Digest, Jun. 2013 (Vol. 4, No. 6)

1.3.10 Lessons From The Leading Edge of Gender Diversity

Author(s): McKinsey & Company, McKinsey Quarterly

McKinsey Quarterly & McKinsey & Company released article that highlights new research, which points to four principles, which can help any to advance women to the top. The "Lessons From The Leading Edge of Gender

Diversity" Article relies on interviews with senior executives at 22 US companies.

Key findings

It is fundamental for companies and their leaders to be committed to gender-diversity process and there are four principles that can help women advance to the top.

- (1) Diversity is personal: numbers are important, but the belief in having a gender diversity workplace makes the case more powerful.
- (2) Cultures and values are at the core: gender diversity programs are half the effort. While they can provide the stepping-stones. Values last if they are lived everyday by the leadership and if gender diversity fits with that value set, almost all the people in an organization will want to bring more of themselves to work everyday.
- (3) Improvements are systematic: it is critical to identify talented women and look for the best career paths to accelerate their growth and impact. Achieving a culture that embraces gender diversity requires a multiyear transformation and the support of an HR function that is an empowered force for change.
- (4) Boards Spark Movement: research suggest that a correlation between the representation of women on boards and on top-executive teams. Leaders at many companies encourage female (and male) board members to establish relationships with potential future women leaders and to serve as their role models or sponsors.

Source: Social Research Digest, Jun. 2013 (Vol. 4, No. 6)

1.3.11 Towards Gender Equality in Turkey: A Summary Assessment

Author(s): The World Bank

The World Bank, as per request of the Executive Directors during the discussion of the Country Partnership Strategy (CPS) 2012-15, published a summary assessment report that takes note of Turkey's progress and current performance with respect to gender equality. The "Towards Gender Equality in Turkey: A Summary Assessment" report has the objective of summarizing the information and existing analytical work on gender equality in Turkey, using the framework elaborated in the World Development Report 2011.

Key findings

While Turkey has achieved major socio-economic progress in the past decade, the country lags in several important dimensions of gender equality.

- The government has made significant progress in tracking gender equity across various domains of public policy and – in part inspired by the ongoing EU accession process – additional policy initiatives are under way.
- Turkey aims to be one of the world's 10 largest economies by 2023, with per capita income targeted to reach US$ 25,000. This vision can only be achieved if Turkey addresses its gender equality challenges.
- According to the World Economic Forum Global Gender Gap Report 20112, Turkey ranks 122 out of 135 countries, second to the bottom in the category of upper-middle income countries.
- Turkey faces a large gender gap in labor force participation.
- Only 29% of Turkish women (defined as being between the ages of 15-64 years) in Turkey are active in the labor market, which is the lowest rate in the OECD.
- The Government introduced a number of specific programs, measures and policies geared to increase employability of women.
- Turkey's Industrial Strategy 2011-201421 and Small and Medium Enterprise Strategy 2011-1322 are also geared to support greater female employment.

Source: Social Research Digest, Jul. 2013 (Vol. 4, No. 7)

1.3.12 Handbook for National Human Rights Institutions on Women's Rights and Gender Equality

Author(s): The OSCE Office for Democratic Institutions and Human Rights (ODIHR)

The OSCE Office for Democratic Institutions and Human Rights (ODIHR) released a survey report to document how national human rights institutions (NHRIs) in the OSCE region address women's rights and gender equality. The "Handbook for National Human Rights Institutions on Women's Rights and Gender Equality" Report presents the results of the survey based on the responses received from 38 NHRIs in OSCE participating states and provides analysis and recommendations for action.

<u>Key Findings</u>

NHRIs should address protection needs through gathering gender-disaggregated data; training staff to work with victims of gender based discrimination and violence against women, including sexual violence; and recommending remedies for victims, among other activities.

- The ODIHR survey did not reveal any particular organizational structure as being more effective than others in protecting women's rights and promoting gender equality.
- Promotional activities should consider how messages on women's rights and gender equality can be mainstreamed into all promotional activities and should also develop targeted campaigns relevant to their national context.
- The NHRIs surveyed demonstrate impressive knowledge, skills and commitment to protecting and promoting human rights, including women's rights and gender equality.
- All relevant national, regional and international bodies should sup- port NHRIs in the important task of advancing women's rights and gender equality.

Source: Social Research Digest, Jul. 2013 (Vol. 4, No. 7)

1.3.13 Integrating Gender in Disaster Management in Small Island Developing States: A Guide

Author(s): UNDP

The United Nations Development Programme (UNDP) published a guide that outlines the vulnerability of Small Island Development States (SIDS) in the Pacific and the Caribbean and explains how gender roles and responsibilities result in differential exposure and impact of disasters. The "Integrating Gender in Disaster Management in Small Island Developing States: A Guide" focuses on Caribbean and Pacific islands, and aims to help practitioners identify and integrate gender into their decision-making and actions on the ground in every phase of disaster risk management.

<u>Key findings</u>

A gender analysis help indentify differences between men and women in terms of activities, conditions, needs, and control over resources and access to development benefits and decisionmaking.

- Three elements need to be examined
    (1) Division of labour: Men are generally involved in the productive ambit whereas women carry the reproductive task of carrying for children, elderly, and the sick and running the household.
    (2) Division of Resources: Access to capital assets and control of resources impacts an individuals household's ability to mitirgate the effects of disaster.
    (3) Needs: Practical and strategic needs differ greatly between men and women.
- Natural disasters in SIDS, are increasing in frequency and intensity due to the effects of climate change caused by global warming.
- Research indicates that the participation of women in decision-making is low in climate policy and its implemention in instruments and measures.
- Climate protection measures often fail to take into consideration the needs of large numbers of poor, women, children and elderly members of society in terms of infrastructure, energy supply, and other facilities and amenities.
- Practitioners need to be especially vigilant in ensuring that gender is taken into account in their low implementation of disaster risk reduction strategies for best outcomes possible.
- Female Poverty is a major concern for disaster management.
- The worldwide increase in women's poverty is caused by factors such as lower wages, increased worload, insufficient support systems, violence, meager opportunities for participation in decision-making and limited access to education and productive resources.
- This poverty exacerbates vulnerability in situations of crisis, particularly for women because they have access to fewer resources.

- Rural poverty also requires special consideration in the assessment of natural disasters in SIDS, because in addition to potential loss of property, rural conditions following a disaster and ability to recover may threaten food security at a household, community and national level.
- The main goal of disaster risk management (DRM) is to reduce the risk of disaster by reducing vulnerability and building resilience within communities, households and individuals.
- When gender is integrated into the Program and Project Management Cycle (PPMC), it permits disaster managers to identify and integrate important gender considerations for every stage of planning for a program or project.

Source: Social Research Digest, Sep. 2013 (Vol. 4, No. 9)

1.3.14 Global Gender Gap Index

Author(s): World Economic Forum (WEF)

World Economic Forum (WEF) released the eighth annual index that benchmarks national gender gaps on economic, political, education- and health-based criteria, and provides country rankings that allow for effective comparisons across regions and income groups, and over time. The Global Gender Gap Index report ranks 136 countries on their ability to close the gender gap in four key areas: economic participation and opportunity, political empowerment, health and survival, educational attainment, political participation and economic equality.

Key findings

86 out of 133 countries improved their global gender gap between 2012 and 2013, with the area of political participation seeing the greatest progress.

- Iceland has the narrowest gender gap in the world, followed by Finland, Norway and Sweden.
- Europe's progress towards eliminating its gender gap is polarized, with countries from Northern and Western Europe presenting a stark contrast to those from the South and East. Spain comes in 30th, having

closed 72% of its gender gap, France ranks 45th (70% closed) while Italy ranks 71st.

- The Philippines is the highest ranking country in Asia, primarily due to success in health, education and economic participation. China stays in the same position as last year. India remains the lowest-ranked of the BRICS economies, even after gaining four places.
- A number of countries in Africa fare relatively well in this year's Report, with Lesotho (16th), South Africa (17th), Burundi (22nd) and Mozambique (26th) all in the top 30. This is largely due to the participation of women in the workforce.
- The index shows four broad groups emerging.
1. The first group comprises those that have made investments in women's health and education and are now seeing a return in terms of economic and political participation.
2. In a second group are countries that are investing in these areas yet failing to exploit their additional talent pool due to prevailing social and institutional barriers.
3. In the third group are countries where significant education and health gaps are preventing women from achieving their full potential even though they fulfill an important role in the workforce, often in low-skilled labour.
4. The last group comprises countries that have large education, economic and political gaps

Source: Social Research Digest, Dec. 2013 (Vol. 4, No. 12)

1.3.15   HERproject: Health Enables Returns

Source: Social Research Digest, Aug. 2011 (Vol. 2, No. 4)

Author(s): BSR

The study seeks to provide a clear business case for investments in women's health for international companies and their supplier partners. This study includes data from HERproject programs at four factories – the factories are located in Port Said, Egypt; Ismailia, Egypt; and two in Karachi, Pakistan.

Key findings

All four of the factory programs demonstrated that HERproject represents an effective mechanism for increasing female factory workers' awareness of general and reproductive health.

- In particular, the peer education methodology used in HERproject proved effective in improving knowledge, increasing use of clinic services, and improving workers' hygiene and other behaviors.
- For example, the percentage of women responding that family planning was "good for the health of the mother" increased from 47 to 97% in the Port Said factory, and from 65 to 83% in the Ismailia factory.
- Knowledge of family planning methods also significantly increased in both factories.
- From a health needs perspective, the study found that menstruation causes significant health issues for female factory workers, including monthly effects on absenteeism, early leave, and production errors.
- Other significant health needs included personal hygiene, proper use of family planning products, nutrition, and pre-and postnatal care.
- For meeting the needs of workers, the study found that, at many factories, nurses represent untapped resources for expanded services— particularly for family planning and reproductive health.
- Nurses also can take on leadership of the peer education program.
- By increasing worker awareness and improving factory clinic staff capacity, HERproject was found to increase worker use of factory clinics and worker satisfaction with clinics.
- About 74% of female workers in the Karachi factory, compared with 34% in baseline, said they went to the factory clinic for consultation when they felt ill.

1.3.16 Women, Business and the Law 2014: Removing Restrictions to Enhance Gender Equality

Author(s): World Bank, International Finance Corporation

The World Bank Group published their third, biannual report that quantitatively compares gender-based legal differences in 143 economies. The report, "Women, Business and the Law 2014: Removing Restrictions to Enhance Gender Equality" provides insight into how laws and regulations prevent or hinder women from starting businesses, navigating the workforce and fully contributing to and sharing in the prosperity of their societies.

Key findings

While 42 economies reduced legal differences between women and men, 128 out of 143 economies studied still impose legal differences on the basis of gender in at least one of the report's key indicators.

- The report also identifies 48 law and regulatory reforms enacted between March 2011 and April 2013 that could enhance women's economic opportunities.

- In all economies, married women face more legal differentiations than unmarried women. In 25 economies, married women cannot legally choose where to live in the same way as married men, and in 29 they cannot be legally recognized as head of household in the same way as married men.

- The 2014 report covers new questions on issues such as gender differences in obtaining national identification cards; the use of quotas to increase women's representation on corporate boards, national parliaments and local governments; women's ownership rights in the marital home; and the number of women justices in supreme courts. The report also includes a new indicator, Protecting women from violence, which examines laws on domestic violence against women and the existence and scope of laws on sexual harassment.

- Economies with greater numbers of restrictions on women's work have, on average, lower female participation in the formal labor force and have fewer firms with female participation in ownership. Conversely, economies which provide a greater measure of incentives for women to work, have greater income equality.

- Every region includes economies with unequal rules for men and women, although the extent of the inequality varies widely. On average, high-income economies have fewer differences than middle- and low-income economies.

- The Middle East and North Africa have the most legal differences between men and women, followed by South Asia and Africa.

- In Africa, a notable exception is Cote d'Ivoire, which leads globally with the most gender-parity reforms during the past two years. Ivorian wives can now choose the family residence and claim tax deductions for their children or spouses in the same manner as their husbands as the result of sweeping 2013 reforms.

- Further, each spouse can now stop the other from working if they deem it against family interests, whereas prior to the 2013 reform only husbands had this ability under the law. Regionally, the most improvements in gender parity occurred in Sub-Saharan Africa.

Source: Social Research Digest, Feb. 2014 (Vol. 5, No. 2)

1.3.17 Corporate Equality Index 2014

Author(s): Human Rights Campaign Foundation

Human Rights Campaign Foundation published its eighth national benchmarking tool on corporate policies and practices pertinent to lesbian, gay, bisexual and transgender employees. The primary source of information for the Corporate Equality Index rating each business receives is the CEI survey sent every year to previous and prospective respondents.

Key findings

304 major businesses — spanning nearly every industry and geography — earned a top score of 100% and the distinction of "Best Places to Work for LGBT Equality."

- A record 299 of the Fortune 500-ranked businesses have official CEI ratings based on submitted surveys (as compared to 293 last year), with an average rating of 83.
- One hundred and twenty-five of the Fortune 500-ranked businesses achieved a 100% rating, with 13 of the top 20 Fortune-ranked businesses at this top score.
- Ninety-one percent of the Fortune 500 include "sexual orientation" in their nondiscrimination policies and 61% include "gender identity."
- The majority of the total Fortune 500 — 67% — offer equivalent medical benefits between spouses and partners and 28% offer transgender-inclusive health care benefits, including surgical procedures

Source: Social Research Digest, May 2014 (Vol. 5, No. 5)

1.3.18   Closing the Gender Gap in Japan

Author(s): The World Economic Forum in collaboration with McKinsey & Company

The World Economic Forum in collaboration with McKinsey & Company published a report that identifies priority actions for promoting gender equality in Japan. The report, Closing the Gender Gap in Japan draws on surveys of large Japanese companies to identify the measures needed to make the most of female talent.

Key findings

Japan has one of the lowest female labour participation rates among OECD countries.

- Integrating women into the economy is an efficient use of a nation's human capital endowment and important for economic growth.
- Gender parity is imperative to Japan's competitiveness and addressing long-term economic challenges brought on by an ageing workforce, low fertility and an acute talent shortage.
- The rate of female participation in Japan's labour force is only 63%, compared to 85% for men. It is one of the lowest female labour participation rates among OECD countries and 79th globally. Among the employed, 35% of women are in part-time employment, compared to 10% of men.
- Despite some improvements in recent years in terms of the economic participation of women in the workforce, Japan continues to fall behind relative to other countries, ranking 104th out of 136 countries on the Forum's 2013 Global Gender Gap Index. To close the gap and better leverage the female talent base, the report points to five areas where Japanese companies can improve their gender parity strategies. They include:
  o Visible leadership and commitment to gender parity from chief executive officers and other top leaders
  o Measurement and target setting to track gender parity goals
  o Awareness and capacity building, including training for male and female managers
  o Incentives and accountability for all managers on gender parity goals

    o   Improvements to the work environment and work-life balance.

Source: Social Research Digest, Sep. 2014 (Vol. 5, No. 9)

1.3.19 Women's Access to Justice in Afghanistan

Author(s): The US Institute of Peace

The US Institute of Peace issued a report that maps how Afghan women seek justice when their rights are violated and the barriers women face in pursuing justice or receiving a fair outcome, whether in the formal system, in community-based mechanisms, or at home. The study, ' Women's Access to Justice in Afghanistan' offers timely recommendations for finding Afghan-specific approaches to women's justice needs, as actors both inside and outside Afghanistan express concerns about how the pace and progress will be sustained as Afghanistan transitions to full economic and security leadership.

<u>Key findings</u>

Restrictions on freedom of movement, access to education, and civic participation, in addition to high rates of gender-based and domestic violence combined to make Afghanistan "the worst place in the world to be born a woman."

- After international intervention in 2002 led to the overthrow of the Taliban government, the Karzai regime installed new governance institutions such as the Ministry of Women's Affairsand the Afghan Independent Human Rights Commission with specific mission to improve women's status in Afghanistan.
- The situation for Afghan women has improved drastically in the last 12 years – particularly with regards to gains in women's health and access to education. And, though improvements have been made in regards to women's rights, the multitude of strategies initiated by Afghan and foreign NGOs toward ensuring women's full enfranchisement and rights protection have struggled to make the structural changes that many sought in the immediate aftermath of the Taliban regime.
- Some Afghan women, like writer Mujib Mashal, fear that the reversals in rights adherence already taking place in far flung regions of the country herald a possible return to the old normal – even in the most

progressive areas of the country.

- Human rights violations are not isolated incidents, but are interconnected concerns that, when unaddressed, snowball into significant legal and social problems.
- With no guarantee of legal protection, Afghanistan's women are left in a precarious and uncertain position, where seeking assistance is as likely to intensify conflict and instances of abuse as to resolve it.

Source: Social Research Digest, Oct. 2014 (Vol. 5, No. 10)

1.3.20 Women in Leadership: What Needs to Change?

Author(s): St. Paul's Institute

St. Paul's Institute published a report that explores the institutional and cultural barriers preventing many women from reaching positions of leadership. The report, Women in Leadership: What Needs to Change?, reminds us that we must challenge ourselves to fully recognise each other's humanity before we will find respect and equality for all.

Key findings

As long as we continue to teach inequality to the next generation, consciously or unconsciously, we will be perpetuating a kind of society that can only contribute to conflict in the long-term.

- We cannot continue to live in the 21st Century as though we are 'back in the day'. Little girls growing up in Britain must know that there are no ceilings, be it glass or ecclesiastical, that will prevent them from reaching whatever they perceive the top to be.
- The reality is, whether we like it or not, Britain is a diverse society. It is therefore imperative that the community in which we live see the diversity reflected in all walks of life. Sadly, we have used religion and other cultural practices to maintain the status quo.
- There's something going on in society and the way we educated our children, something in the way we parent our children, that is eking away at the ambition and the confidence of these young girls.
- The role models that we all are, in whatever walk of life we come from, is so important. We need to lift as we climb through our own organisations. We need to encourage the next generation. We need to

really, truly help them to believe that they can be all and anything that they want to be.

Source: Social Research Digest, Oct. 2014 (Vol. 5, No. 10)

1.3.21 The Glass Floor: Sexual Harassment in the Restaurant Industry

Author(s): *Restaurant Opportunities Center (ROC) United*

The US Restaurant Opportunities Center (ROC) United released a report that examines the commonality of multiple explicit behaviors that restaurant workers have been exposed to from restaurant owners, managers, and supervisors (management), from co-workers, and from customers, measured through nearly 700 surveys of people who are currently or recently worked in a restaurant, along with focus groups conducted in Houston, New York, New Orleans, and Washington, DC. The report, The Glass Floor: Sexual Harassment in the Restaurant Industry, also presents data compiled and analyzed from the Equal Employment Opportunity Commission, the Bureau of Labor Statistics, the Current Population Survey, and the American Community Survey to gain a broad understanding of the conditions impacting sexual harassment in the restaurant industry.

Key findings

Laws that allow employers to pay tipped workers below the minimum wage lead to increased sexual harassment in the workplace. Female restaurant workers who virtually live off tips are in a "uniquely vulnerable position."

- Some state laws permit employers to pay hourly wages as low as $2.13 to employees who carry out services that are customarily tipped by customers — such as bar and wait staff — "creating an environment in which a majority female workforce must please and curry favor with customers to earn a living."
- "Glass floor," a term coined by ROC, refers to a system that exacerbates the already poor job security of low-wage workers by layering on a sexualized atmosphere. If workers feel expendable at their workplace, they are more likely to ignore sexual harassment.

- Workers earning tipped subminimum wage are twice as likely to experience sexual harassment than those making a standard minimum wage.
- The United States is the only industrialized democracy that has a two-tiered minimum wage. According to the U.S. Department of Labor, only seven states and the territory of Guam require employers to pay the minimum wage before tips.
- Tipped workers in states where subminimum wage is permissible are three times as likely to be told to wear sexier or more revealing clothing than those where such payment practices are barred.
- The restaurant industry is the single largest source of sexual harassment complaints. Many incidents are ignored or go unreported because of fear of retaliation by customers — not tipping — or their employers.

Source: Social Research Digest, Oct. 2014 (Vol. 5, No. 10)

1.3.22 Violence against women: an EU-wide survey. Main results report

Author(s): FRA, the European Union Agency for Fundamental Rights

FRA, the European Union Agency for Fundamental Rights issued the results of a the first of its kind survey on violence against women across the 28 Member States of the European Union (EU), based on interviews with 42,000 women across the EU, who were asked about their experiences of physical, sexual and psychological violence, including incidents of intimate partner violence ('domestic violence'). The Violence against women survey also included questions on stalking, sexual harassment, and the role played by new technologies in women's experiences of abuse.

Key findings

Violence against women undermines women's core fundamental rights such as dignity, access to justice and gender equality.

- For example, one in three women (33 %) has experienced physical and/or sexual violence since the age of 15.
- One in five women (18 %) has experienced stalking; every second woman (55 %) has been confronted with one or more forms of sexual

harassment. Given this, violence against women cannot be seen as a marginal issue that touches only on some women's lives.

- Yet the scale of violence against women is not reflected by official data. Women generally do not report to the police, and they also do not report to a number of other services that could support them, including victim support organisations.

- In this regard, it is clear that the needs and the rights of women – for example under the Victims Directive, which explicitly refers to victims of gender-based violence – are currently not being met in practice.

- In response, significant efforts need to be made at the EU and Member State levels to create a climate where women can report incidents of abuse, and where these reports will be taken seriously and followed up so that women receive the support they need and, where appropriate, can get justice. Currently, the fact that so many incidents are not reported means that many offenders can act with impunity.

- Future EU strategies on equality between women and men could build on the survey's findings to address key areas of concern with respect to women's experiences of violence. Examples could include new or newly recognised forms of violence against women, such as stalking or abuse through the medium of new technologies, as well as aspects of violence that are under-reported by women to the police and victim support organisations.

Source: Social Research Digest, Nov. 2014 (Vol. 5, No. 11)

1.3.23 The Global Gender Gap Report 2014

Author(s): *World Economic Forum*

World Economic Forum issued its 9th edition of the Index that benchmarks national gender gaps of 142 countries on economic, political, education- and health-based criteria, allowing for time-series analysis on the changing patterns of gender equality around the world and comparisons between and within countries. The Global Gender Gap Report 2014 emphasizes persisting gender gap divides across and within regions.

Key findings

The gender gap for economic participation and opportunity now stands at 60% worldwide, having closed by 4% from 56% in 2006.

- The gender gap is narrowest in terms of health and survival with a gap standing at 96% globally, with 35 countries having closed the gap entirely.
- Despite all this, it is the only subindex which declined over the course of the past nine years.
- The educational attainment gap is the next narrowest, standing at 94% globally. Here, 25 countries have closed the gap entirely
- While the gender gap for economic participation and opportunity lags stubbornly behind, the gap for political empowerment, the fourth pillar measured, remains wider still, standing at 21%, although this area has seen the most improvement since 2006.
- Iceland continues to be at the top of the overall rankings in The Global Gender Gap Index for the sixth consecutive year.
- Finland ranks in second position, and Norway holds the third place in the overall ranking.
- Sweden remains in fourth position and Denmark gains three places and ranks this year at the fifth position.
- Northern European countries dominate the top 10 with Ireland in the eighth position and Belgium (10) Nicaragua (6), Rwanda (7) and Philippines (9) complete the top 10.

Source: Social Research Digest, Dec. 2014 (Vol. 5, No. 12)

1.4   Social Dialogue and Civil Rights

1.4.1   Whistleblowing Among Young Employees: A Life Course Perspective

Author(s): J.M. Stansbury, B. Victor

This study examines the extent to which young employees are inclined or disinclined to blow the whistle on misconduct observed within the workplace. The authors use data from the 2003 US National Business Ethics

Survey. 1,417 respondents took part, and of these, 314 reported having observed organisational misconduct.

Key findings

Respondents who were both young and had short organizational tenure were substantially less likely than other respondents to report misconduct that they observed in the workplace to an authority.

- Young and short-tenured employees will be more likely to agree that their supervisors reward employees who get good results even if they use questionable ethical practices.
- Young and short-tenured employees will be more likely to agree that their coworkers show respect for employees who get good results.
- Agreeing that reporting ethics concerns will cause one to be seen as a troublemaker by management negatively predicts whistleblowing.
- Agreeing that reporting ethics concerns will cause one to be seen as a snitch by coworkers negatively predicts whistle-blowing.
- Agreeing that one's supervisors reward employees who get good results even if they use questionable ethical practices negatively predicts whistle-blowing.
- Agreeing that one's coworkers show respect for employees who get good results even if they use questionable ethical practices negatively predicts whistle-blowing.
- Agreeing that reporting ethics concerns will cause one to be seen as a snitch by coworkers partially mediates the relationship between newness to the workforce and whistle-blowing.
- Agreeing that one's supervisors reward employees who get good results even if they use questionable ethical practices partially mediates the relationship between newness to the workforce and whistle-blowing.
- Young and new employees assimilate into the group in part by adopting and enforcing the group's norms, so that whistle-blowing becomes not an exceptional and heroically individualistic act, but rather a normal part of the maintenance of the social system.
- Ethics and compliance offices concerned about their ability to detect misbehavior that threatens the organization or its stakeholders may wish to devote efforts not only to formulate training that introduces

new employees to the organization's standards and systems, but also to enhance new employees' social bonding with others.

Source: Governance Research Digest, Jun. 2009 (Vol. 1, No. 6)

1.4.2 OBS Annual Report 2013: Violations of the right of NGOs to funding - from harassment to criminalization

Author(s): International Federation for Human Rights

The Annual report 2013 of the Observatory for the Protection of Human Rights Defenders, a joint programme of the World Organization Against Torture (OMCT) and International Federation for Human Rights (FIDH), provides a global review of the violations of NGOs' right to funding via various forms of restrictions imposed by States. The "OBS Annual Report 2013: Violations of the right of NGOs to funding—from harassment to criminalization" Report provides its analysis through illustrative cases from 35 countries.

Key Findings

Although the right to access funding is a fundamental condition for freedom of association, and is itself universally recognized right embedded in numerous international and regional instruments—many States are guilty of placing abusive restrictions on this right.

- Access for NGOs defending human rights is a universal right.
- Limitations or denial of the right to freedom of association constitute the most radical restriction on access to funding.
- Restriction on access to funding can have an impact on the conditions for the establishment or management of an NGO, which should be guaranteed without any interference or pressure from authorities.
- The right of NGOs to access funding is violated either/or (1) indirectly by restricting the ability of defenders to operate openly in the framework of an NGO (2) directly through legislation, regulations or administrative practices that explicitly restrict or obstruct access to funding.
- Smear campaigns related to the issue of funding for NGOs pervert and destroy the concept of solidarity or international cooperation to the

detriment of the movement in defense of human rights and advancement of democratic tenets.

- In some countries, the authorities impose a system of prior authorization for the establishment of an association or even prohibit or criminalize unregistered NGOs.

- The absence of legal status blocks access to funding and the situation is more serious in countries where unregistered NGOs are heavily penalized either through fines or imprisonment.

- The reasons provided by authorities to justify denying the right to freedom of association including access to funding are based on ambiguous concepts and may include reasons on a discriminatory criteria, for example, on the nationality of defenders.

- Recommendations to address this issue: For the states includes ensuring that any limitation on the right to freedom of association is consistent in it entirety with Article 22 of the ICCPR.

- Other recommendations are provided for (1) access to funding and taxation system (2) donors (states, organizations and foundations) (3) NGOs affected by funding restrictions (4) human rights institutions, bodies and agencies.

Source: Social Research Digest, Jun. 2013 (Vol. 4, No. 6)

1.4.3 The Right to Information and Privacy: Balancing Rights and Managing Conflicts

Author(s): World Bank Institute

World Bank Institute has lately published a report 'The Right to Information and Privacy: Balancing Rights and Managing Conflicts'. The paper examines legislative and structural means to better define and balance the rights to privacy and information.

Key findings

The right to privacy and the right to information are both essential human rights in the modern information society.

- For the most part, these two rights complement each other in holding governments accountable to individuals.

- But there is a potential conflict between these rights when there is a demand for access to personal information held by government bodies.

- Where the two rights overlap, states need to develop mechanisms for identifying core issues to limit conflicts and for balancing the rights.

Source: CSR Research Digest, Apr. 2011 (Vol. 3, No. 4)

1.4.4   Strengthening Institutions for Worker Empowerment

Author(s): Verité Works

The inaugural report of the Verité Works series focuses on the organisations' capacity-building work in China. A key focus of this research is its attention to the importance of civil society organizations in supporting the improvement of working conditions, not just in China but worldwide.

Key findings

Integral to Verité's approach to improving working conditions worldwide is collaboration and partnership with local institutions in assessing workplaces; training workers, managers and other stakeholders; and conducting in-depth research.

- A number of significant violations remain resistant to attempts at improvement in Chinese workplaces, in spite of widespread implementation of Codes of Conduct.
- The most persistent violations include the creation of obstacles to the empowerment of workers and legal restrictions on their ability to associate freely; widespread violations of working hour standards and laws, resulting in excessive overtime and endemic underpayment of workers' wages – by a minimum of 15%; and non-payment of benefits, including social security and health coverage, among others.
- Local civil society organizations (CSOs) are critical to imbuing labour assessments and remedial programs with a nuanced, deep and accurate understanding of local conditions.
- CSOs are also vital to ensuring that workers have local, independent voices supporting and advocating for their interests over the long term.
- In China the number and diversity of CSOs is growing, but still small relative to the scale of the social challenges facing the country.

- The community of civil society organizations that does exist lacks institutional capacity in the areas of labour standards and corporate social responsibility.
- The few labour-oriented organizations that operate in China are hampered by limited capacity to deliver the types of programs that are critical to sustaining systemic improvements in labour protections.

Source: Social Research Digest, Jan. 2009 (Vol. 1, No. 1)

1.4.5 Press Freedom in Australia 2013

Author(s): Media Alliance

Media Alliance released its annual report into press freedom in Australia. The report 'Power, Protection & Principles: The State of Press Freedom in Australia 2013' calls for laws to protect whistle-blowers who turn to the media to expose corruption and wrongdoing and criticises comments made by public servants about their reluctance to process freedom of information applications, among others.

Key findings

Media regulations were tightened with a heavy-handed emphasis on improving "media standards" in Australia.

- By March 2013, at least five members of the Media, Entertainment & Arts Alliance were facing criminal convictions, fines and/or jail terms if they maintained their ethical responsibilities and refused to disclose the identity of their confidential sources. It is unprecedented in Australia that so many journalists are simultaneously in this position.
- Subpoenaing journalists is being used by big businesses and the wealthy to trace whistleblowers and the source of leaks.
- Federal attorney-general Mark Dreyfus introduced the Public Disclosure Bill 2013 to federal parliament in March this year; a Senate inquiry into the bill is expected to report in June. The bill aims to implement the government's 2010 response to a report by the House of Representatives Standing Committee on Legal and Constitutional Affairs, Whistleblower Protection: a comprehensive scheme for the Commonwealth public sector.
- The "Deed of Agreement" introduced by the Department of Immigration

and Citizenship (DIAC)ssets out the arrangements for the Media Entity's visit to an immigration detention centre or immigration detention facility, and sets out the access rules, visitation procedures, media content restrictions, and subsequent editing requirements."

- The excessive use of non-publication orders across various legal jurisdictions continues to indicate a willingness to muzzle the media and shroud the operation of the justice system with a veil of secrecy.

Source: Social Research Digest, Jan. 2014 (Vol. 5, No. 1)

1.4.6 World Trends in Freedom of Expression and Media Development

Author(s): UNESCO

UNESCO, in partnership with an advisory group of 27 international experts from civil society and academia and with the support of the Government of Sweden spearheaded a study that analyses trends in media freedom worldwide since 2007 from four angles: freedom, pluralism, independence and the safety of journalists. The study, World Trends in Freedom of Expression and Media Development, hails the opportunities that new technologies have opened up, empowering individuals through unprecedented ways to access, produce and share media content across multiple platforms.

Key findings

There is a clear trend of adopting Freedom of Information (FOI) or access to information laws even as there appears to be growing recognition that information control has become an increasingly important aspect of both global conflicts and local disputes.

- A slow trend towards decriminalization of defamation has been partly offset by the increasing use of civil defamation, with disproportionate fines and damages, particularly against some media that are critical of powerful individuals or groups. In regions that have experienced democratic transitions, progress towards greater press freedom has lost momentum in some cases, and press freedom laws have not always been effectively implemented.
- National security, anti-terrorism and anti-extremism laws have been

used in some cases to limit legitimate debate and to curtail dissenting views in the media, while also underwriting expanded surveillance, which may be seen to violate the right to privacy and to jeopardize freedom of expression.

- Direct and self-censorship remain challenges to journalists worldwide, even as a trend towards private sector censorship as well as the privatization of censorship has emerged, with the increasing importance of technology companies and other intermediaries in the media ecosystem.

- Expanding diversity of news media content, the internet, digitalization and online-search capacities have enabled more people to participate in information production and news flows.

- The combined impact of the global financial crisis and technological disruption has led to divergent trends with respect to advertising revenue and its impact on the news industry worldwide amid the migration of news online, although television has remained the dominant focus of advertising spending worldwide.

- Although there has been some improvement in representation of women in the news industry and in media content in some parts of the world, women remain significantly underrepresented and continue to often be stereotypically portrayed.

- Overall numbers of women in news employment have increased over the past six years, but gender imbalances in the institutional media remain acute in the upper echelons of management, and gains are not distributed evenly across regions.

- Although there are some regional trends towards news organizations adopting gender equality policies, implementation mechanisms are often weak or non-existent.

- The past six years have seen both a rise in the killings of journalists and a significant increase in international awareness of the issue. Analysis of condemnations of journalist killings by the UNESCO Director-General between 2007 and 2012 shows an upward trend in the number of journalist killings, with nearly 30% of the 430 occurring in 2012, driven by conflict in two countries.

- Targeted attacks on women journalists are lower than their proportion in newsrooms, but appear to have increased in parallel with the multiplying of platforms for expression.

- Politically motivated killings remain endemic, and at least 75% of the journalists whose killings were condemned by the UNESCO Director-General in 2010 and 2011 had been targeted for murder. The period has reportedly seen an increasing trend concerning imprisonment of journalists and social media producers, and a declining trend in the number of journalists reported to have gone into exile each year. Citizen journalists have become targets alongside their professional counterparts.

Source: Social Research Digest, Jul. 2014 (Vol. 5, No. 7)

1.4.7 USCIS Ombudsman's 2014 Annual Report

Author(s): United States Citizenship and Immigration Services (USCIS)

United States Citizenship and Immigration Services (USCIS) released this year's Ombudsman Annual Report, detailing the accomplishments and challenges the agency faces across the spectrum of U.S. immigration. The Ombudsman's 2014 Annual Report, the second from Ombudsman Maria Odom, who was appointed in September 2012, proves to be especially forthright, revealing statistics about the agency that have never before been published.

Key findings

- The Provisional Unlawful Presence Waiver program holds out the promise of an effective solution to a longstanding challenge in family immigration. In January 2014, USCIS issued new guidance crucial to ensuring the success of the Provisional Waiver program.
- While this guidance addresses the most pressing stakeholder concerns, other aspects of the provisional waiver process remain problematic, such as denials where USCIS found the applicant inadmissible for fraud or a willful misrepresentation without a full examination of the information contained in the record or without first affording the applicant the opportunity to respond.
- There is no appeal available for a denial of a provisional waiver.
- Stakeholders continue to report concerns regarding the quality and consistency of adjudications of high-skilled petitions. There are ongoing issues with the application of the preponderance of the evidence legal standard and gaps in agency policy.

- Stakeholders cite redundant and unduly burdensome RFEs, and data reveal an RFE rate of nearly 50% in one key high-skilled visa category. Employers continue to seek the Ombudsman's assistance to resolve case matters and systemic issues in high-skilled adjudications.
- The Immigrant Investor program has presented USCIS with significant challenges due to many variables, including the complexity of projects, the financial arrangements with investors, and the attribution of job creation to the investment.
- The new adjudications unit and updated policy guidance usher in a new era for this increasingly popular investment and job-creating program.

Source: Social Research Digest, Sep. 2014 (Vol. 5, No. 9)

1.4.8 Why Care About Faith?

Author(s): World Economic Forum

The Global Agenda Council on the Role of Faith (2012-2014) collected a series of essays, highlighting the practical aspect of faith and how to engage with faith actors in long-term and effective partnerships. The aim of 'Why Care About Faith?' is to showcase the "value-added of faith" when it comes to tackling global challenges and dealing with emerging trends at the regional and international level.

Key findings

Regardless of one's personal opinion of faith, here are three reasons why engaging with people's beliefs is important and can improve the state of the world.

- Partnerships: The world's challenges cannot be solved by any one state or non-state actor. To address common concerns, all need to come together and work through global communities founded on a shared moral and ethical understanding. World faiths represent global identities and communities based on deep, shared values. Important foundations like the "Golden Rule" of reciprocity and respect are shared among all major belief systems and offer a practical basis for how to cooperate with the "other" – the individual or institution whose perspective and interests are different from one's own. Working within and between global faith communities, there is a substantial and mostly unrealized potential to address issues that affect all societies.

- Reach and effectiveness: Communities and organizations based on religion and shared beliefs are present throughout the world. They are often significant providers of essential health, education and community services – indeed, in many countries, particularly in the global South, they are the main sources of such social good, sometimes more so than the government itself. This capacity for service delivery, coupled with the moral and ethical leadership exercised by religious leaders, is a powerful means of enhancing social welfare and promoting change in attitudes and practices.

- Transformation of conflict: Conflict and tension corrupt human relationships on local, national and global scales. Arbitration alone does not offer a moral imperative to forgive, compromise and seek the other party's good, and a conflict not transformed is a conflict postponed. A shared understanding of religious identities and values can be instrumental in prevention or resolution of conflict. Often, a transformation of the heart in favour of resolving conflicts is the precondition to sustainable peace.

- Attempts to achieve a more resilient and dynamic economy and system of governance are challenged by deficits in legitimacy, an erosion of trust and the risk of violent conflict. Of course, religion can also contribute to the problem, but the best of faith can defeat the worst of religion. For societies to be civil, states to be stable and for economies to flourish, faith is essential.

Source: Social Research Digest, Dec. 2014 (Vol. 5, No. 12)

1.5 Minorities' and Indigenous Peoples' Rights

1.5.1 Freeport-McMoRan Copper & Gold, Inc.: An Innovative Voluntary Code of Conduct to Protect Human Rights, Create Employment Opportunities, and Economic Development of the Indigenous People

Author(s): S. P. Sethi, D. B. Lowry, E. A. Veral, H. J. Shapiro and O. Emelianova

The article examines the activities of one mining company, Freeport-McMoRan Copper & Gold, Inc., which has taken a radically different approach in responding to the challenges at its mining operations in West Papua, Indonesia. The new set of challenges that the industry is facing involve treatment of indigenous people and their traditional land rights, fair treatment of workers, human rights abuses, and bribery and corruption involving local officials and political leaders.

Key findings

While cooperating with industry-based efforts of voluntary codes of conduct, Freeport also initiated a radically different response through its own voluntary code.

- The voluntary code would directly focus on issues of human rights, treatment of indigenous people on whose traditional land its mine was located; economic development and job creation and, improvements in health, education, and housing facilities, to name a few.
- Additionally, the company earmarked large sums of money and involved representatives of the indigenous people in their management and disbursement.
- The company took an even more radical action when it committed itself to independent external audits of the company's compliance with the code, and that these findings and company's responses would be made public without prior censorship by the company.
- The authors analyze the nature of corporate culture, vision and risk-taking propensities of its management that would impel the company to embark on a high risk strategy whose outcomes could not be predicted with any degree of certainty before the fact.
- The parent company also had to confront discontent among the management ranks at the mine site because of cultural differences and management styles of expatriates and local (Indonesian) managers.
- Finally, authors discuss in some detail the extensive and intensive character of a two phase audit conducted by the outside monitors, their findings, and the process by which they were implemented and reported to general public.

- Authors also evaluate the strengths and challenges posed by such audits, their importance to the company's future, and how such projects might be undertaken by other companies.

Source: Governance Research Digest, Sep. 2011 (Vol. 2, No. 5)

1.5.2 Corporate Policy on Indigenous Rights Report

Author(s): EIRIS/Center for Australian Ethical Research

A new report from EIRIS and the Center for Australian Ethical Research examines the extent to which companies engaged in extractive industries have policies that address the rights of indigenous people. The report, entitled Indigenous Rights: Risks and Opportunities for Investors, identifies several key issues for indigenous people, who account for 5% of the world's population but over 15% of the world's poor.

Key findings

250 companies have been identified as having an exposure to indigenous rights. 17% of these companies have a high risk exposure to indigenous rights issues.

- EIRIS identifies companies operating in extractive sectors (oil & gas, mining, forestry & paper and agricultural producers) and operating in one or more high indigenous rights risk countries (such as Australia, Canada, United States, New Zealand, South Africa, Sweden, Finland, Argentina, Mexico, Thailand, Zimbabwe) as a medium risk for indigenous rights exposure.
- Companies which are also subject to allegations of indigenous rights abuse within the last three years are classified as high risk exposure.
- Allegations against companies include failure to inform or consult, negative impacts on traditional ways of life, destruction of sacred sites or impacts on health through pollution.
- Few companies report on indigenous rights issues and the quality of reporting is generally poor. Whilst most companies provide a response to allegations of breaches of indigenous rights, few report voluntarily on areas of non-compliance.

- 19% of companies have a corporate-wide indigenous rights policy. Only 15% of companies have a corporate-wide policy supporting free prior informed consultation.
- Fewer than 10% of companies have a policy for involuntary resettlement.
- The reputational risk associated with abuse of indigenous rights can harm brand value, employee morale, the ability to recruit and in some cases the ability to access markets and resources.
- In consumer-facing companies, poor performance with regard to indigenous peoples may result in a boycott.

Source: Social Research Digest, Aug. 2009 (Vol. 1, No. 8)

1.5.3 State of the World's Minorities and Indigenous Peoples 2014

Author(s): Minority Rights Group International (MRG)

Minority Rights Group International (MRG) launched its annual flagship report that focuses on 'Freedom from hate' and presents compelling evidence showing that hate crime and hate speech are prevalent in all regions of the world. The report, State of the World's Minorities and Indigenous Peoples 2014 documents disheartening levels of violence, harassment and verbal abuse across the world and it also includes many examples of how hatred is being countered by legislators, politicians, journalists, and communities, by addressing the root causes.

Key findings

Hate crime towards minorities and indigenous peoples is a daily reality in many countries across the globe, but hate crime is widely ignored, under-reported and often left unchecked by governments, resulting in escalating violence against minorities.

- Targeted violence often has a purpose. Anti-migrant rhetoric in Greece or sectarian violence in India serves to consolidate the power base of extremist organizations. Negative representations of indigenous groups in Guatemala or Uganda may provide justification for further exclusion or eviction from ancestral lands.
- The impact of hatred may extend beyond discrimination to more visible

extremes, as in the Democratic Republic of Congo, where it drives the continuation of inter-ethnic conflicts. In the Central African Republic, hate speech and targeted attacks during 2013 were responsible for fomenting religious violence that has resulted in almost a million people being internally displaced.

- Hate crimes send a message not only to the individuals targeted, but also to their communities. This is especially evident in violence against minority and indigenous women, with rape and sexual assault employed as a weapon of war or an instrument of oppression to fragment and humiliate entire civilian populations.

- In South Asia, for example, Dalit women are regularly subjected to sexual violence as a result of their lower caste status – often in response to their demands for basic rights.

- The prevalence of demeaning or inflammatory language in political discourse, sermons, the media and online has very real implications for marginalized communities.

- Historical patterns of colonialism and segregation continue to be felt in some countries. In the USA migrants, Jews, African Americans and other minorities are still subject to vilification, particularly with the apparent rise of hate groups in recent years, in part due to anxieties over the country's changing demographics.

Source: Social Research Digest, Sep. 2014 (Vol. 5, No. 9)

1.5.4   Indigenous Rights Risk Report

Author(s): *First Peoples Worldwide*

First Peoples Worldwide released a report that looks at the impact of companies and government polices on native peoples worldwide. First Peoples' Indigenous Rights Risk Report analyzes 370 oil, gas and mining sites on or near Indigenous land operated by 52 U.S.-based companies.

Key findings

Global warming and land rights conflicts with industrial operations both continue to impact Indigenous people's rights and way of life.

- 35% (115) of the 330 projects assessed had high risk exposure to Indigenous community opposition or violations of Indigenous Peoples' rights, 54% (177) had medium risk exposure, and 11% (38) had low risk exposure

- The oil and gas industry had collectively higher risk exposure than the mining industry, with both a larger percentage of high risk projects and a smaller percentage of low risk projects. 37% (94) of the 257 oil and gas projects received high risk scores, compared to 29% (21) of the 73 mining projects.

- By contrast, 10% (26) of the 257 oil and gas projects received low risk scores, compared to 16% (12) of the 73 mining projects. The average risk score for oil and gas projects was 3.3, while the average risk score for mining projects was 3.1.

- This is possibly attributable to the mining industry's noticeably stronger standards related to Indigenous Peoples' rights, compared to the oil and gas industry. The International Council on Mining and Metals (ICMM) has a binding position statement on Indigenous Peoples and mining that recognizes FPIC "as a process based on good faith negotiation, through which Indigenous Peoples can give or withhold their consent to a project."

- Although only 2 of the mining companies assessed are ICMM members, many others are affiliated with ICMM's network of member associations. By contrast, the International Petroleum Industry Environmental Conservation Association (IPIECA) provides some guidance on Indigenous Peoples' rights25 and FPIC,26 but lacks a binding position statement. 7 of the oil and gas companies assessed are IPIECA members.

- The report assigned risk scores to projects, rather than companies as a whole, because most companies do not disclose financial data at the project level. Thus, the impacts of a project's risk score to the company's overall financial health cannot be accurately determined.

- Companies with high risk scores at more than 50% of their projects on or near Indigenous territories were Alpha Natural Resources (100%), Anadarko Petroleum (67%), Chevron Corporation (57%), Continental Resources (60%), Kosmos Energy (100%), Murphy Oil (89%), Royal Gold (67%), SM Energy (67%), Southern Copper (72%), Southwestern Energy (100%), Whiting Petroleum (100%), and WPX Energy (80%).

Source: Social Research Digest, Nov. 2014 (Vol. 5, No. 11)

1.5.5 The Impact of Canadian Mining in Latin America and Canada's responsibility

Author(s): Work Group on Mining and Human Rights in Latin America

The "Work Group on Mining and Human Rights in Latin America" formed four years ago by six civil society organizations from Latin America and one in the USA wrote a report that put the growing role of Canadian mining companies across Latin America under the spotlight at the Inter-American Commission on Human Rights (IACHR) in Washington. 22 large-scale projects operated by 20 companies across Argentina, Chile, Colombia, El Salvador, Guatemala, Honduras, Mexico, Panama and Peru are considered in 'The Impact of Canadian Mining in Latin America and Canada's responsibility' report.

Key findings

Canadian firms are exploiting weak legal systems in Latin American countries and Canada itself, as well as failing to respect indigenous peoples' rights, international human rights and social responsibility principles, and supposedly "protected" areas.

- Mining operations by Canadian firms across nine Latin American countries are causing "serious environmental impacts" by destroying glaciers, contaminating water and rivers, and cutting down forest, according to the report, as well as forcibly displacing people, dividing and impoverishing communities, making false promises about economic benefits, endangering people's health, and fraudulently acquiring property. Some who protest such projects have been killed or seriously wounded, it states, and others persecuted, threatened or accused of being terrorists.

- Criminal charges such as "sabotage", "terrorism", "rebellion", "conspiracy" and "incitement to commit crime" have been made against social leaders and human rights defenders who oppose and resist the development of industry.

- Canadian companies are responsible for 50% to 70% of all mining in Latin America, and the role of the Canadian government in actively supporting these projects — through legal, political, and judicial channels — is problematic. While Canada is aware of the concerns plaguing the mining industry, it continues to work to strengthen the power and legal position of its companies through diplomatic and financial pressure.

Source: CSR Research Digest, Oct. 2014 (Vol. 6, No. 10)

1.6 Children's Rights and Child labour

1.6.1 Accelerating Action Against Child Labour

Author(s): International Labour Organisation (ILO)

The International Labour Organisation (ILO) has published a report entitled 'Accelerating Action Against Child Labour', which details progress towards the ILO's 2006 Global Action Plan. The 2006 Plan set the target of eliminating the worst forms of child labour by 2016, but the report, released in May 2010, concludes that "the pace of progress is not fast enough to achieve this target."

Key findings

New global estimates presented in the report show a continued modest decline in child labour since 2006, although there are still as many as 215 million child labourers globally (equating to 13.6% of the global child population).

- The Asia-Pacific and Latin America regions, with 113 million (13.3% of the child population) and 14 million (10% of the child population) child labourers respectively, continue to make improvements.
- However, sub-Saharan Africa, where one in four children work, has seen an increase in child labour practices.
- The ILO report comments that the global economic crisis may hinder efforts to reduce child labour. The World Bank has predicted that the global economic crisis may leave an additional 64 million people in extreme poverty by the end of 2010, likely forcing increased numbers of children into work.
- The ILO cites inadequate provision of education as a primary cause of child labour.
- Whilst Africa remains the region most affected by child labour, Central

and Eastern Europe, the Middle East and South Asia are also raised in the ILO report as regions of concern.

- India is highlighted as a country of particular risk given that it has one of the largest out-ofschool child populations in the world (according to the World Bank, in 2007 over 5.5 million children of primary school age were out of school).
- Moreover, India has a significant informal economy, with 370 million informal economy workers, providing the opportunity to find work away from legal and regulatory supervision.
- Whilst the estimated number of child labourers in India has fallen from 13.3 million in 1993- 1994 to 8.6 million in 2004-2005, there remains a significant pool of potential child labourers, suggesting that the problem may become more acute in future if the government does not take measures to address it.
- Child labour is a continuing risk to businesses that have operations in or source from developing countries. Businesses are advised to monitor their supply chains to ensure that they are not complicit in child labour practices.
- Furthermore, businesses can contribute towards education programmes that take children out of work and allow them to gain the skills that may allow them to reach a higher potential in later life.
- Businesses that are found to be connected to child labour violations, as in the case of Primark in 2008, face reputational risk, the potential loss of sales and shareholder value and, in some cases, the possibility of legal action.

Source: CSR Research Digest, Jun. 2010 (Vol. 2, No. 6)

1.6.2   Child Labour Report

Author(s): Maplecroft

The risks to business relating to child labour in the BRICs countries of Brazil, Russia, India and China are increasing according to a new report released by Maplecroft. The report analyses the most recent events, reports and published raw data to offer a detailed overview of the child labour situation in the BRICs. It will enable business and investors to identify potential supply chain and investment risks arising from child labour in the world's fastest growing economies.

Key findings

Of the four countries, India has the most challenging environment for business relating to child labour, as it is ranked 1/196 countries in Maplecroft's Child Labour Index. The country has the highest number of child workers in the world.

- Estimates from national and international NGOs place the figures of child workers in India between 60 and 115 million. Latest official government figures estimate 16.4 million child labourers between the ages of 5 and 14.
- Of those, approximately two million are thought to work in "hazardous industries," including mining, ship breaking and manufacturing or are trafficked and exploited in the sex industry.
- China is rated "extreme risk" in all of Maplecroft's labour rights and protection indices with the risks for child labour, trafficking and discrimination increasing.
- Key findings of the report point towards the highest prevalence of child labour violations in the agricultural and manufacturing sectors of China.
- Human rights abuses associated with suppliers within the textile and electronic sectors are of particular concern following a recent cluster of suicides that occurred in a Foxconn factory based in the country.
- According to the report, child labour in Brazil is prevalent in the informal, agricultural and manufacturing sectors. In 2008, the ILO estimated that 58.7% of child workers between 5-14 years old worked in agriculture.
- Children working in this sector are particularly vulnerable to accidents, often involving agricultural chemicals and machinery. The latest available statistics from the Brazilian government reported that in 2006 there were 273,000 accidents involving child labourers.
- Business in Russia is not immune from the risks associated with child labour, as the country is ranked 75/196 and "high risk" in Maplecroft's Child labour Index.
- While an overall estimated figure on children working is unavailable, the Federal Labour and Employment Service (FLES) found over 10,000 child labour law violations in 2008.
- These children often received little pay and were discovered in

dangerous working conditions in the industrial and agricultural sectors. The report also states that risks associated with working conditions in Russia are growing.

Source: CSR Research Digest, Jul. 2010 (Vol. 2, No. 7)

1.6.3   Child Labour Index 2011

Author(s): Maplecroft

The Child Labour Index highlights child labour risks for business throughout all regions of the world and all stages of operation, supply and distribution. It measures the prevalence and type of child labour, as well as government efforts to combat child labour, across 196 countries.

Key findings

The elimination of child labour in supply chains is important for business operations as it decreases reputational and legal risks of companies being complicit in human rights abuses.

- It is important to do this responsibly, in order to move children out of the supply chain and into education, ensuring that they have better opportunities in the future to move out of the poverty cycle.
- Responsible management and the formulation of innovative strategies to cope with child labour dilemmas can support the right to childhood and primary education.
- For instance, IKEA, the multinational retailer, has hired a Children's Ombudsmen to oversee all aspects of its work with children.
- IKEA holds workshops for suppliers on a wide range of issues, including child labour and is partnering with UNICEF to combat child labour in the carpet-producing area of India, Uttar Pradesh. As a result of the project, more than 80,000 children have enrolled in schools.
- The clothing retailer, H&M has also initiated projects to combat child labour.
- Together with UNICEF, H&M has launched a five-year initiative to focus on the rights of children in cotton-producing regions of Southern India.
- H&M has donated US$45 million to rehabilitate child workers by providing them with educational opportunities and access to better health care and nutrition.

- Another approach has been offered by M&S which, under its pillar on 'fair partnership', has committed to a number of ethical trade and labour standard commitments to assist in the elimination of child labour in the supply chain.
- By the 2009/10, the company had extended its use of Fairtrade certified products and purchased approximately a third of the world's Fairtrade cotton; it increased Fairtrade food sales by 55% from 2006/7 and sold 7.9 million Fairtrade cotton garments; and it assisted its suppliers to develop six ethical model factories to identify and share best practice.

Source: Social Research Digest, Jun. 2011 (Vol. 2, No. 2)

1.6.4   CSR Market Assessment Quantitative Stage Report

Author(s): Unicef

Unicef produced a report that examines whether UK businesses incorporate children's rights among their main corporate social responsibility issues. The "CSR Market Assessment Quantitative Stage Report" released by UNICEF and Ipsos MORI, is qualitative and quantitative study and relies on 150 interviews conducted with medium to large companies.

Key findings

Although, more than two-thirds of UK businesses interviewed in this Report believe that responsibilities to children will become more important to UK companies in the next five years, yet, 89% do not include children's rights in their main CSR issues.

- 37% of businesses participating in the research say they know at least a little bit about Children's Rights and Business Principles
- 82% think the concept of Principles is useful in encouraging UK companies to act on the responsibilities to children.
- 96% agree their company is committed to acting on CSR.
- 91% agree the senior managers of their company recognize the business benefits that corporate responsibility can bring.
- 89% believe that their company is concerned with CSR.

- Three-quarters believe that business people in their country think CSR is important.
- 87% in the UK have a CSR policy or a set of principles or values in place.
- Two-thirds have heard of the Guiding Principles on Business and Human Rights.
- 63% claim their company is very/fairly active on its responsibilities to children.
- In the UK, the main reason companies take action on child-focused CSR is a desire to do the right thing and reflect company values.
- 73% in the UK believe that more needs to be done to assist companies to act.
- 93% believe it is appropriate for UNICEF to give companies guidance on child-focused CSR.

Source: Social Research Digest, Apr. 2013 (Vol. 4, No. 4)

1.6.5 The State of the World's Children

Author(s): UNICEF

UNICEF released a report that examines the barriers – from inaccessible buildings to dismissive attitudes, from invisibility in official statistics to vicious discrimination – that deprive children with disabilities of their rights and keep them from participating fully in society. The 2013 edition of 'The State of the World's Children' also lays out some of the key elements of inclusive societies that respect and protect the rights of children with disabilities, adequately support them and their families, and nurture their abilities – so that they may take advantage of opportunities to flourish and make their contribution to the world.

<u>Key findings</u>

Children and adults with disabilities often face a wide range of physical, social and environmental barriers to full participation in society, including reduced access to health care, education and other support services.

- They are also thought to be at significantly greater risk of violence than their peers without disabilities.
- Understanding the extent of violence against children with disabilities is an essential first step in developing effective programmes to prevent

them from becoming victims of violence and to improve their health and the quality of their lives.

- Children placed away from home need increased care and protection, and institutional cultures, regimes and structures that exacerbate the risk of violence and abuse should be addressed as a matter of urgency.
- Humanitarian crises, such as those stemming from warfare or natural disasters, pose particular risks for children with disabilities. Inclusive humanitarian response is urgently needed – and feasible.

Source: Social Research Digest, Nov. 2013 (Vol. 4, No. 11)

1.6.6 Business and Children: Mapping Interests, Managing Responsibilities

Author(s): A. Crane, B.A. Kazmi.

This paper reports on a systematic analysis of the reputational landscape constructed by the media, corporations and NGOs around business responsibilities to children. The data that informs the study comes from an extensive content analysis of media articles, corporate reports and websites, and NGO reports over the last five years.

Key findings

Seven key areas were found where businesses were found to be confronted with issues of corporate responsibility towards young people.

- Safeguarding children in terms of their physical protection is a key area where business can have a positive or negative impact on children through its core business activities. This is most evident in two areas: the physical safety of children, and their overall health and tness.
- Safety impacts occur in three main ways:
  - products that directly safeguard children (such as car safety seats and pharmaceutical products specially formulated for children);
  - products that are potentially directly dangerous for children (tobacco, adult-only pharmaceuticals, products containing dangerous chemicals);
  - and potentially hazardous locations (i.e. companies operating in construction or power generation, for example, manage sites that are potentially dangerous for young people).

- This is a challenging area for business because it appears that there is not always a clear consensus on what content, or how much, constitutes a threat to children's moral protection.
- Children are also open to exploitation through child labour. There has been a great deal of investigation into this issue in the developing world, where it is an acknowledged threat to children's education as well as their general wellbeing. It remains an under-researched issue in the developed world.
- In highly industrialized, consumerist societies, corporations and their products represent a vital conduit for children's societal engagement and success. This can either be as direct consumers, or as in uencers or subjects of family decisions. Business can have a positive or negative impact here.
- Positive social and cultural impacts include: the development of products designed specifically for children that improve their cultural life, including television programming, music, books, and other media products, as well as special family-oriented products and services.
- Negative impacts include: the problems of individualism and consumerism brought on by an overemphasis on commodity culture, the dangers of some children being priced out of socially important products and services, and even speci c exclusions by companies of children from privatized "public" spaces such as shops and malls.
- Various industries can also have a significant impact on young people's health and fitness, including healthcare companies, food and drink producers, food retailers, restaurants and food service producers.
- The authors also indentify the role of business in ensuring young people's economic wellbeing, both on an individual and family level; promoting education and employability; and issues relating to parental employment and family life.
- Many firms are attempting to make more positive impacts, through offering healthy options, providing educational programmes, and various other initiatives aiming to get children to be more active. However, such initiatives have been known to backfire when the company's priority has simply been to shift sales volume.
- The majority of companies examined in the course of this research had also engaged in corporate giving to various children's causes. Increasingly firms are seeking to engage with causes or organizations

that can be tied to their own brand, such as food companies and child nutrition projects.

- Business also has a role to play in safeguarding the moral protection of young people. For many companies, particularly those in the media, leisure and telecoms industries, this largely involves preventing the exposure of children to inappropriate content.

- Overall, the approach of companies in relation to children is usually ill-defined, fragmented and frequently reactive. Many sectors only take up issues that have been raised by the media, government or NGOs.

- Few companies have a clear and comprehensive policy towards children, yet many see young people's markets as major sources of revenue and growth.

Source: Social Research Digest, Oct. 2009 (Vol. 1, No. 10)

1.6.7   Joining the Dialogue: Vulnerable Children and Business

Author(s): CSR Asia, Aviva

At the proposal of AVIVA, a global insurer and asset management company, CSR Asia has prepared a report on how businesses within Asia are taking initiatives to improve the life of vulnerable children by enabling them to access their rights. The goal of the report Joining the Dialogue: Vulnerable Children and Business is to make businesses understand that their role in helping children is not mere acts of benevolence but to act responsibly towards whatever impact (positive or negative) their products/services have on children and thus engage in multi-stakeholder dialogue to promote and respect the rights of such children.

Key findings

The current context of business and child rights and challenges facing vulnerable children in Asia- poverty, unemployment, lack of education, exploitation.

- Perspectives on actual and potential impacts of businesses on vulnerable children through operations, supply chain and community investment:
  o Reasons for companies engaging in this issue;
  o Nature of engagement linked to their core business activities;

- o Changes created by the companies;
- o Steps taken for sustainability .
- Challenges and opportunities in the area of supporting vulnerable children (Business perspective)
- Case studies:
  - o In 2013, AVIVA reached 649,043 children through Street to School Programme
  - o Adidas group has a set Workplace Standards for all its suppliers to ensure that their workers have a safe, fair and healthy place to work and to discourage child labour.
  - o HSBC's Future First programme aims to tackle child poverty through education projects.
  - o Kuoni has taken a leading role in fighting against child exploitation in tourism.
  - o Microsoft is combating child online pornography with the help of PhotoDNA software.
  - o The Body Shop's campaign against sex trafficking of children and young people.

Source: Social Research Digest, Apr. 2014 (Vol. 5, No. 4)

II.   LABOUR PRACTICES

2.1   Market Assessment of Sustainability Consulting

2.1.1   Green Quadrant Sustainability Business Consulting 2011

Author(s): Verdantix

To help decision makers in roles such as CEO, CSO and COO this Green Quadrant report provides a detailed, fact-based comparison of the 14 sustainability business consulting firms most active in the UK market. The analysis is based on interviews with 15 buyers of consulting engagements, representing firms with combined revenues of $214 billion, supplier responses to a 45 point questionnaire, interviews with practice leaders in consultancies and desktop research.

Key findings

Only a handful of firms – Deloitte and PricewaterhouseCoopers being the most prominent – have excelled when providing major companies with corporate-wide sustainability visions.

- Deloitte and PwC enjoy the highest "capability" rating among 14 major consultancy firms with sustainability consulting arms.
- According to the report the most successful sustainability consultants excel in seven characteristics, or "secrets", of their trade.
- They are:
  - breadth of service offerings;
  - delivery of high profile projects;
  - transparency on sustainability performance;
  - longevity in the sustainability market;
  - depth of expertise in each domain;
  - investments in brand awareness;
  - long-term vision for energy and environmental trends.
- According to the data, PwC has the highest brand awareness as a

provider of sustainability business consulting services, followed by Accenture and McKinsey in second and third place.

- Furthermore, 24% of respondents named PwC as a consultant with strong sustainable business expertise.
- The study also identified Accenture, ARUP and WSP Environment & Energy as consulting firms with strong specialist expertise as well as a significant level of positive market momentum.

Source: CSR Research Digest, Dec. 2011 (Vol. 3, No. 12)

2.1.2 Global Sustainability Consultant Survey

Author(s): Green Research

This report analyzes the results of a global survey of sustainability and CSR consultants. The survey was fielded online to a global audience in February and March 2012 and it drew over 1500 responses and some 520 screened and completed questionnaires.

Key findings

Some 49% of sustainability consultants believe business conditions are somewhat or very strong today even though just 26% of them work full-time in sustainability.

- Despite such a low percentage of consultants working full-time on green issues, they generally see a bright future for their trade, with 62% expecting a strong business environment six months from now.
- Consultants working in Asia-Pacific countries are the most upbeat of all.
- Some 68% of respondents from that region see a positive business outlook over the next six months, compared to 61% of those from the U.S. and 59% from the Euro-zone.
- This optimism has drawn many newcomers to the field: 40% of consultants have been at it for less than three years.
- Consultants are more likely to work in the manufacturing sector than in any other field.
- Some 45% of consultants surveyed worked on projects in that sector last year, while 39% worked in the public or governmental sector and 33% worked in the construction sector.

Source: CSR Research Digest, May 2012 (Vol. 4, No. 5)

2.1.3 The 2011 Market Assessment of the UK Environmental Consulting Sector

Author(s): Environmental Analyst

Market research firm Environment Analyst highlights the environmental consulting market trends of 2011. The market dynamics of environmental consulting are given as well as listed the top practices in UK.

<u>Key findings</u>

The U.K. environmental consulting market contracted by 8.4% in 2010, and prospects for 2011 are relatively flat.

- In 2010 the market declined for the second consecutive year after more than two decades of constant growth, to stand at £1.23 billion ($1.98 billion).
- The environmental consultancy field suffered from declining fees as just under 1,000 jobs were lost at the top 32 firms – eight percent of their staff.
- Government austerity measures and a drop in local authority spending were largely responsible for the £113 million decline and will continue to hinder a return to growth.
- Public spending was responsible for 70% of the 2010 decline, or £79 million.
- The private sector declined less sharply, losing £34 million.
- Environment Analyst predicts 0.5% growth for 2011, but said it has spotted a few encouraging signs.
- 2011 growth is driven by capital infrastructure projects needed for stimulating the economy, along with strict legislative targets on energy, carbon and waste.
- In terms of service areas, the only offering which grew substantially during 2010 was environmental policy and strategy, which grew by 14.7%.
- The top 10 practices in the U.K. in order of market share are:
  o RPS Group
  o Halcrow Group
  o AEA
  o URS/Scott Wilson

- o Atkins
- o Mott MacDonald
- o Environmental Resources Management (ERM)
- o Jacobs Engineering
- o RSK Group
- o AMEC Environment & Infrastructure

Source: Environmental Research Digest, Jan. 2012 (Vol. 3, No. 1)

2.1.4 India Outlook: Consultancy Boom on Infrastructure and Multinational Investment

Author(s): Environmental Analyst

The latest Market Briefing from Environment Analyst provides a snapshot view of the current state of the environmental consultancy market in India, together with forecasts for future growth. The report is based on the views of 40 consultants who completed a survey in December 2011, supported by in-depth interviews conducted by Environment Analyst with those running operations in India.

Key findings

Environmental consulting firms experienced 11% average growth in India in 2010 with expectations of reaching 16.4% growth in 2011 and 17.5% in 2012.

- Albeit from a relatively small base The Indian government's twelfth five-year plan commencing in 2012/13 will see US$1trillion spent on infrastructure, $500billion of that through Public-Private Partnerships (PPP) West Bengal, Gujarat and Maharashtra offer the greatest opportunities for growth.

Source: Environmental Research Digest, Mar. 2012 (Vol. 3, No. 3)

2.1.5 Environment Consulting Study

Author(s): Environment Analyst

The recent study by Environment Analyst covers in detail the market of UK environmental consulting sector. The market analysis is based on core figures supplied by over 50 companies as well as market trends information collated from 375 environmental business managers via Market Snapshot survey conducted during March to May 2010.

Key findings

UK environmental consulting market falls by 5% but a return to growth is projected for 2010.

- Market declines for first time in two decades to £1.35 billion in 2009, shedding over 1,000 jobs.
- The headline findings also reveal the economic downturn has forced firms to sharpen their commercial skills and become more efficient, evident through rising staff utilization rates and turnover per head in 2009.
- Demand from government bodies rose by 17% in 2009, in sharp contrast to a 9.5% dip in sales to the private sector (including utilities and other corporate clients).
- There were double- digit declines in sales to the extractive, manufacturing & process industries, as well as to the finance & services and construction/property sectors.
- However, public sector demand began to weaken in 2010, with consultants reporting growth of just 1-2% in government work at the time of our market snapshot survey3, which ran from March to May 2010.
- Notwithstanding the spectre of public sector spending cuts, the overall market in the UK is forecast to grow by 1.4 % in 2010, compared with the projected GDP increase of 1.2%.
- Climate change and energy, waste management and strategic environmental/ sustainability services are expected to be the strongest growth areas for this year.
- Contaminated land no longer ranks as the number-one income generator for UK environmental consultants as it has been for the last fifteen years, with revenue shrinking by more than a fifth in 2009 to £167 million – a victim of the decimation of the housebuilding industry and fall-out from the credit crunch.
- Environmental impact assessment (EIA) & sustainable development has moved into pole position to account for just over 14% of the total sector last year, with revenues declining less steeply than in

contaminated land largely due to a more diverse client base.

- Although overall market conditions are set to improve in 2010, there are indications that many small firms will struggle for survival this year.
- Nearly half of SME survey respondents (those working for firms with revenues of less than £10 million) said their Q1 2010 performance was worse that they had budgeted for, compared with just 16% of larger firms (those with revenues greater than £10 million).

Source: CSR Research Digest, Sep. 2010 (Vol. 2, No. 9)

2.2 CSR and Sustainability Employment Prospects

2.2.1 An Examination of Perceived Corporate Citizenship, Job Applicant Attraction, and CSR Work Role Definition

Author(s): W. R. Evans and W. D. Davis

The experimental study examined how perceptions of corporate citizenship influence job applicant attraction and work role definitions. The study is driven by a need to examine whether individual differences affect the relationship between CSR and individual reactions to CSR.

Key findings

Personal values and education concerning CSR are considered as interactive factors affecting the influence of perceptions of corporate citizenship.

- Results indicate that perceived corporate citizenship had a greater impact on job applicant attraction for those individuals who received prior education regarding CSR and for those who were higher in other-regarding value orientation.
- Furthermore, perceived corporate citizenship had a positive impact on the extent to which participants defined CSR as a personal work role responsibility.
- The authors also discuss the practical implications of these results for job applicant attraction and employee socialization.

Source: Social Research Digest, Sep. 2011 (Vol. 2, No. 5)

2.2.2 Corporate Social Responsibility as an Organizational Attractiveness for Prospective Public Relations Practitioners

Author(s): S-Y. Kim and H. Park

The study explores the perceptions about corporate social responsibility (CSR) as a job attraction condition. It was conducted among the students majoring in public relations as prospective public relations practitioners.

Key findings

The results showed that the students perceived CSR to be an important ethical fit condition of a company.

- One of the significant findings is that CSR can be an effective reputation management strategy for prospective employees, particularly when a company's business is suffering.
- In examining the effect of CSR efforts on attitudinal and behavioral outcomes, person– organization fit appeared to serve as a mediator between CSR performances and organizational attractiveness.

Source: Social Research Digest, Nov. 2011 (Vol. 2, No. 7)

2.2.3 Managing Corporate Citizenship Report

Author(s): Boston College Center for Corporate Responsibility

The Boston College Center for Corporate Responsibility has released a report which examines corporate citizenship as an emerging profession and standard corporate practice. In the study which supported the report, researchers investigate the structures and systems keyed to citizenship in a broad sample of mostly North America based companies. 330 companies took part in the survey in January 2008.

Key findings

The emerging picture suggests companies will continue to formalize the corporate citizenship functions in some way. 65% of companies represented in the sample identify a department and dedicated staff (albeit often a small one) that owns and manages most corporate citizenship issues.

- No standard organizational model for corporate citizenship dominates.
- Cross-functional teams or senior-level councils are used to integrate corporate citizenship in companies at a more advanced stage of corporate citizenship.
- Corporate citizenship is not strongly linked to strategy or business plans in most companies.
- Top management identifies corporate citizenship as important but does not exercise significant leadership on the issue.
- Employees are seen as the most influential stakeholder for citizenship but inside the company are seen as the least informed.
- Boards of directors are just beginning to focus on corporate citizenship issues.
- Measurement and use of measures of corporate citizenship are weak.
- Minimal training is being done at every level regarding the relevance of citizenship to the success of the business.
- A company's size and its relative "domestic vs. global" reach influence to what extent citizenship is a priority for top executives and is integrated into management processes and systems.

Source: Social Research Digest, Mar. 2009 (Vol. 1, No. 3)

2.2.4 The State of the Corporate Responsibility Profession Report

Author(s): U.S. Chamber of Commerce Business Civic Leadership Center (BCLC) and Corporate Responsibility Officers Association (CROA)

To provide a benchmark of corporate responsibility as a profession and a field, CROA and BCLC surveyed various stakeholders, including academics, practitioners, and recognized thought leaders. The results serves as a benchmark for where the CR profession stands in 2012 as well as provides recommendations on how to mature the field's set of knowledge, skills and attributes.

Key findings

The characteristics that define a mature profession, such as an educational curriculum and a career pipeline, currently are lacking in the corporate responsibility (CR) profession.

- The study also found that while few of the CR leaders in companies today entered the field deliberately, they have paved the way for "generation 2.0" CR practitioners.
- The majority of survey respondents agreed on the following: CR remains a nascent profession lacking the distinct set of professional characteristics; the CR field lacks a deliberate career path; and the progress of the corporate responsibility officer (CRO) is continuously evolving.
- Dealing with the tough issues – creating sustained economic growth, preserving resources for future generations, increasing respect for human dignity – requires complex decision making.
- This report lays out a roadmap for embedding that kind of critical thinking into the leadership curriculum for business people everywhere.

Source: CSR Research Digest, Apr. 2012 (Vol. 4, No. 4)

2.2.5   Environmental Professionals Career and Salary Survey

Author(s): Environmental Analyst/Allen & York

The 2009 Environmental Professionals Career and Salary Survey examines how environmental organizations have coped with the economic downturn, and the salaries, bonuses and job satisfaction of professionals working in these organizations. Over 2,500 respondents participated in an online survey in Summer 2009. The records of a further 22,000 individuals working in environmental organisations were analysed in order to build the fullest possible picture of salaries.

Key findings

According to the online survey, the average basic salary across the industry is £39,500, with 39.7% earning less than £30k, and 21.7% earning more than £50k.

- Almost a quarter of all respondents reported staff redundancies as their organization's main response to the current economic downturn.
- 21% reported a freeze on pay increases as the main response, and 17% said their organization had stopped recruiting.
- Over 37% of participants felt less secure in their role than they did 12

months ago, compared with just 11% feeling more secure. As a measure of job security more widely, 46% felt less secure about environmental roles in general.

- Over 50% of participants did not receive a bonus in 2008.
- Looking forward, 64% of participants felt prospects were good or very good for the sector for the period 2010-2015.
- 50% of those working in the industry are either satisfied or very satisfied with their current job, whilst only 25% are unsatisfied or very unsatisfied.
- Over 40% of the participants felt that they had good or very good career progression prospects within their organization as opposed to almost 29% who felt they were poor or very poor.
- There is a stronger feeling that prospects are better beyond their current employer, with 58% saying they were good or very good.
- Those primarily working in the area of corporate social responsibility and sustainability earn the highest average basic salary at £45,900, whilst those in ecology and conservation earn the least, at £29,800.
- 23.7% of the survey participants received a bonus of over 5% of their basic salary in 2008.

Source: CSR Research Digest, Jan. 2010 (Vol. 2, No. 1)

2.2.6   The CR and Sustainability Salary Survey

Author(s): *Acre Resources, Acona, Flag and Ethical Performance*

The fourth CR and Sustainability Salary survey has been released by collaboration between sustainability recruitment specialists Acre Resources, corporate responsibility consultancy Acona, creative communications agency Flag and the publication Ethical Performance. It provides insight into the individuals employed in this expanding marketplace, from the types of organisations they work for, to their job functions, salaries and career backgrounds.

Key findings

The results indicate a positive outlook for the sector in regard to salary, job security and job satisfaction.

- On average, those working in the Europe (excluding the UK) earn

£69,000 followed by £68,010 for North America and £56,360 in the UK.

- Almost one quarter of respondents received basic salaries of £80,000 and upwards and 4% were rewarded with salaries in excess of £140,000.
- Over 80% of respondents felt that their job security has improved or remained the same over the past 12 months (the same as 2010) with the same number (80%) of respondents satisfied with their jobs.
- 94% of respondents would recommend a career in the sector.
- A major development over the past 12 months is the increasing number of CEOs that are engaging with sustainability.
- This coupled with the positive salary trends points to a maturing sector that's gaining in credibility and influence within the corporate structure.

Source: CSR Research Digest, Oct. 2012 (Vol. 4, No. 10)

2.2.7   CSR Professionals Survey

Author(s): Acona/Acre Resources/Ethical Performance

A new survey of UK executives working in corporate social responsibility has been carried out by CSR consultancy Acona, Acre Resources and Ethical Performance. 350 UK CSR professionals took part in the research.

Key findings

CSR professionals are 'overwhelmingly happy' with their positions, commanding significant salaries and experiencing a greater degree of job security than many of their fellow managers.

- Median salaries for in-house CSR executives stand at £45,000 to £50,000.
- Eight out of 10 respondents claiming they were happy with their current role and 97% stating that they would recommend CSR positions to other people.
- The high levels of job satisfaction are likely to be attributed to the 'deep personal interest' that many CSR executives have in environmental and ethical issues.

- Despite the onset of recession, the growing importance of CSR to many firms meant that a relatively high proportion of executives still feel secure in their roles.
- Over half of respondents said they felt just as secure now as they did a year ago, while 15% said they felt more secure.
- Only 11% of all CSR professionals have a specific professional CSR qualification.
- However, some evidence is emerging that postgraduate qualifications are becoming the norm for the more senior and better paid roles, especially in-house.
- The survey also revealed that while CSR departments can have responsibility for equality issues, they appear to be subject to much the gender pay gap as other parts of the business.
- The research found that while 62% of respondents were female, women only occupied 49% of director level roles and only a third of jobs with salaries of over £100,000.
- London and the South East were the most common work locations for respondents.
- Overall, 64% worked in London and 14% selected South East.
- 80% of consultants were based in London compared to 58% within in-house roles.
- Just over 40% of respondents having a global focus in their work and a similar percentage identifying the UK (or particular regions of the UK) as their area of operation.

Source: Social Research Digest, Apr. 2009 (Vol. 1, No. 4)

2.2.8   Green Job Security Survey

Author(s): Reuters/Acre Resources/Acona

Reuters has conducted its first Carbon Salary Survey, along with recruitment company Acre Resources and consultancy Acona. The survey polled nearly 1,200 professionals in areas such as renewable energy and greenhouse gas emissions trading.

Key findings

68% of employees in the climate change sector feel the same or more job security than they did a year ago, due to a heightened response from government and business to the threat of climate change.

- The average green collar worker makes $76,000 per year, with half of respondents receiving an annual bonus of about $11,000.
- US-based workers were the best paid, receiving salaries averaging $100,000.
- Australasia followed with $93,000, and workers in Asia earned the least at $41,500, according to the survey.
- Other findings reveal that workers in the financial and legal sectors had the highest average salary at $116,000 and annual bonus at $95,500 while employees in green marketing, PR or media were paid the least at $58,000 a year.
- The survey also indicates that men earned 18% more than women.
- Reuters also reports that the UK remains the green sector's center, with 28% of corporate headquarters located there, followed by North America at 26% and the rest of Europe at 24%.
- A common trait among respondents was a solid education, with 96% having at least one university degree, but the results showed that having green qualifications made little difference in salary.
- Those with environment-related degrees made less than $70,000 on average, while those holding more general degrees made around $85,000 annually.

Source: Social Research Digest, Jul. 2009 (Vol. 1, No. 7)

2.2.9 The evolution of the CSR manager: past, present and future

Author(s): Johan De Herdt

Johan De Herdt, under the supervision of Lars Moratis, conducted a survey amongst the members (38 participants) of Business & Society Belgium. The work on CSR 2.0 by Wayne Visser provided the starting point for the survey and the resulting report, 'The evolution of the CSR manager: past, present and future' focuses its attention to the role and competencies of the CSR manager as a potential 'shared value business modeler'.

<u>Key findings</u>

The CSR manager's function will predominantly consist of managing the stakeholder dialogue, business modeling and reporting.

- Belgian CSR managers describe a rather mature landscape consisting mainly of strategic CSR, promotional CSR but also systemic CSR.
- While the current CSR management function is characterized by a more internal focus, it is expected that in the future the CSR manager will be characterized by other competencies.
- Paramount are stakeholder management, reporting, business modeling, sound knowledge of the big sustainability themes, assessing the impact of them on the company via risk management and identifying new opportunities and new partners.
- The shared value concept can bring an important added value to the evolution of the CSR manager position.
- Competencies linked to internal orientation seem to become less important than competencies linked to external orientation.
- Reputation stays paramount and reporting is by consequence, even more important than today. Sharp materiality analysis or integrated reporting will become more important.

Source: CSR Research Digest, Dec. 2013 (Vol. 5, No. 12)

2.2.10 Environmental Education Report

Author(s): National Environmental Education Foundation

A new report by the US National Environmental Education Foundation shows that more and more companies are looking at job candidates in terms of their knowledge of environmental and sustainability themes. The report, 'The Engaged Organisation,' includes several case studies looking at the environmental education opportunities at a number of corporations, including Wal-Mart, Johnson & Johnson, Hewlett-Packard and Cisco.

<u>Key findings</u>

65% of respondents value job candidates' environment and sustainability (E&S) knowledge, while 78% of respondents believe that the value of job candidates' E&S knowledge will increase in importance as a hiring factor within five years.

- Companies are not only anticipating that the value of E&S knowledge will increase, many are already providing some education to their employees about these topics.
- 75% of companies educate employees about corporate E&S goals and 56% of the respondents believe that their company has an advanced or very advanced E&S education program.
- The survey also indicated that many companies without an E&S education program are likely to adopt one soon.
- Nearly half (49%) of respondents whose companies have no program believe their company will begin educating employees in the next two years.
- The office responsible for E&S education varies among companies.
- Most companies cover a variety of environmental topics when communicating with employees.
- The most common topics include general E&S information and actions at work that can conserve or protect resources.
- According to survey respondents, the most important motivating factors for employees are concern for the environment and society, support or a mandate from the CEO, company reputation and job satisfaction.
- Despite the strong value placed on E&S education, companies indicated that they face several challenges when engaging employees, including lack of money, time, resources and executive support.
- The survey also indicates that companies were eager for tools to help them implement an E&S education program.

Source: Social Research Digest, May 2009 (Vol. 1, No. 5)

2.2.11 Sustainability Labour Market Trends Study

Author(s): Strandberg Consulting/University of British Columbia

This new study examines sustainability labour market trends from the perspective of employers, industry representatives and thought leaders across Canada. Twenty four in-depth interviews were conducted in

February 2009 with key informants who were themselves either employers, industry representatives or thought leaders.

Key findings

There was a common view among respondents that sustainability will be embedded into every discipline in future.

- Climate change and business sustainability were frequently mentioned trends impacting the labour market.
- Climate change and energy management related jobs also topped the list of sustainability jobs named as being important in the transition to a sustainable future. These were followed by community development related jobs.
- These trends are perceived to be global, for the most part, at least with respect to developed countries.
- There was no clear view on whether or not a 'generalist sustainability professional' would exist in the future labour market, although a slight majority (two thirds, including all the thought leaders) thought there would be demand for such a position.
- Most respondents agreed that general education in sustainability concepts and issues was important for incoming employees, though there was less consensus on the top sustainability attributes required of incoming employees.
- Responses were diverse, with life cycle and systems thinking and community-based developments out-ranking other responses, both of which share a holistic, integrative orientation.
- Some respondents felt that the future professional employee will be trained to move between the economy, social sciences and natural sciences so they can understand how sustainable development functions in the world. These employees will be generalists with competency across a wide range of issues, rather than a single deep expertise.

Source: Social Research Digest, Oct. 2009 (Vol. 1, No. 10)

2.2.12 Sustainability Dynamics Drive Professional Growth
Summary Report

Author(s): ISSP/Sustainable Plant

This survey report aims to uncover what types of organizations conduct sustainability-related work, what the educational and professional backgrounds of individuals who work in sustainability-related activities, and what are the important skills for a successful professional working on sustainability-related activity. The sustainability survey report is conducted in collaboration with the International Society of Sustainability Professionals (ISSP), receiving input from more than 700 professionals working in the field.

Key findings

The survey reveals that the most common educational backgrounds of sustainability professionals don't match the skills considered most successful in the field and nearly more than 80% of sustainability workers pursue more training.

- Sustainability professionals have extensive backgrounds from several disciplines.
- 77% are from health and safety; 67% from quality control, 66% from risk management and 62% from compliance jobs.
- 69% of respondents have less than 10 years experience in the sustainability profession.
- Communication was named as the most important skill in the profession.
- Other high-ranking skills influencing change management, technology and expertise, problem solving and financial analysis.
- Today's sustainability personnel are seeking additional education and training

Source: Social Research Digest, Mar. 2013 (Vol. 4, No. 3)

2.2.13 CSO Back Story: How Chief Sustainability Officers Reached the C-Suite

Author(s): Weinreb Group

Weinreb's report CSO Back Story is the first to chart the evolution of the position by surveying every exec with that title among the country's publicly traded companies. The group found 29 such execs, after searching SEC filings, LinkedIn and other sources.

Key findings

Nine out of ten CSOs are one or two steps removed from the CEO.

- Linda Fisher was the first CSO, appointed in 2004 at DuPont.
- Next to follow was Ed Fox at APS Pinnacle West in 2006.
- Kellogg's CSO Diane Holdorf is the first CSO to succeed another CSO, Celeste Clarke, who is set to retire later this year.
- Other companies with CSOs include UPS, EMC, AT&T, SAP, PG&E and Coca-Cola.
- Ten out of the 29 CSOs (35%) report directly to the CEO and 16 (55%) are no more than two degrees removed, reporting to another Clevel executive such as the COO or CMO.
- Of those surveyed, 12 sit on an executive committee responsible for all corporate strategic decisions, not just sustainability.
- With an average of 4.2 direct reports, these CSOs have few resources but often enjoy a growing team.
- They all have their own budget but not necessarily their own P&L.
- The emerging role is powerful in scope, strategic oversight, and overall management, with CSOs helping to lead their organizations through economic upheaval, internal discord, and environmental ruin.
- These professionals are good at leading new initiatives and cross-functional teams, and understand how to translate external factors into internal opportunities.
- CSOs have been at their companies for an average of 16 years before gaining their title, and 25 out of the 29 were selected internally.
- Most chief sustainability officers do not have an environmental background.

Source: CSR Research Digest, Oct. 2011 (Vol. 3, No. 10)

2.3   Recruitment and Application Practices

2.3.1   An Analysis of US Multinationals' Recruitment Practices in Mexico

Author(s): E. Daspro

In this study, the frequency of discriminatory language in job advertisements placed by U.S. multinational corporations operating in Mexico was compared with that of Mexican companies using content analysis. A sample of 300 advertisements placed by companies from each culture was analyzed and coded to calculate the frequency of discriminatory language in job advertisements with respect to age, gender, physical appearance and marital status.

Key findings

91.2% of Mexican citizens polled in the survey believe discrimination still exists on a broad range of variables including: ethnicity, sex, and socioeconomic class in all aspects of economic life.

- Thus, an apparent gap exists between inclusive labour laws on the one hand and exclusionary practices on the other.
- Empirical evidence suggests that the legal environment in which a company operates may also influence a company's propensity to discriminate in job advertisements.
- 18.7% of US advertisements discriminated based on age in comparison to 70% of Mexican adverts.
- Similarly, US adverts discriminated along gender lines in 10.7% of the cases, in comparison to 30% of the Mexican adverts.
- With respect to appearance, US adverts discriminated 5.7% of the time in comparison to 17.7% of the time in Mexican adverts.
- Moreover, only 1% of the US companies discriminated based on marital status in comparison to 8.3% of the Mexican adverts.
- Previous studies suggest that Mexicans may be more tolerant of social inequalities than Americans, an attitude that again may lead to the use of discriminatory employment recruitment practices.
- In the lax regulatory environment of Singapore, where no law governing equal employment opportunity exists, MNCs from the US, UK

and Japan did place discriminatory job advertisements. However, the extent to which they did so was a function of the home country's legal environment with regards to employment discrimination legislation and enforcement.

- In the case under study, Mexico possesses a regulatory framework that clearly prohibits discrimination in job recruitment, suggesting that the influence of the country of origin's legal framework may prove to be influential in their recruitment decisions.

- The culture of the company's country of origin many also play a role in influencing its decision whether or not to discriminate in the recruitment process.

- For example, if an MNC's country of origin is characterized by stronger enforcement of nondiscrimination in employment practices and the presence of a cultural context that supports the principles of equality of opportunity in employment in the US it may be less likely to occur and is less likely to be tolerated by the general population.

- In risk-averse countries such as Mexico, employers may feel resistance for adopting new policies or programs that in some way represent a change from long-held practices of discrimination.

Source: Social Research Digest, Aug. 2009 (Vol. 1, No. 8)

2.3.2   Talent Report: What Workers Want in 2012

Author(s): Net Impact

The study by Net Impact and Rutgers University provides a revealing picture of what students and professionals most value in a job, and demonstrates how opportunities to make a positive impact at work are linked to job satisfaction. The survey looked at a statistically-significant national sample of 1,726 individuals: currently enrolled university students about to enter the workforce, and currently-employed college graduates spanning three generations (Millennials, Generation X, and Baby Boomers).

<u>Key findings</u>

Employees who say they have the opportunity to make a direct social and environmental impact through their job report higher satisfaction levels than those who don't, by a 2:1 ratio.

- 65% of university students expect to make an impact on causes and issues they care about in their future job.
- The survey identified the five top job attributes, of 16 presented to rank, that workers want from their worklife: a good work/life balance, a positive work environment, good compensation, having interesting work to do and job security.
- Despite current employment outlooks and a lack of real-world experience, graduating students still maintain a desire to work for and with purpose, even if means a smaller paycheck:
  o Over half (58%) would take a 15% pay cut to 'work for an organization whose values are like my own.'
  o Almost half (45%) would take a 15% pay cut to 'have a job that makes a social or environmental impact on the world.'
  o Over a third (35%) would take a 15% pay cut to 'work for a company committed to corporate and environmental sustainability.'
- Around 15% of workers say they will definitely have a social or environmental impact through their job over the next few years, with another 31% saying they probably will.
- A strong majority of students (72%) have a life goal to have a job that they can make an impact on causes and issues important to them.
- Female students were more likely to select government, small business, or nonprofit jobs as their first choice, with male students more likely to select corporate jobs.
- Female students are more likely to say that a company that prioritizes corporate responsibility is more important to their ideal job over male students by 60% v. 40%.
- Having a positive work environment / positive culture ranks as the top quality students seek in an upcoming job (91%), followed by job security (90%) with financials (compensation/benefits) in third place at 87%.

Source: Social Research Digest, Oct. 2012 (Vol. 3, No. 10)

2.3.3 A Twenty-First Century Assessment of Values Across the Global Workforce

Author(s): D. A. Ralston, C. P. Egri, E. Reynaud, N. Srinivasan, O. Furrer, D. Brock, R. Alas, F. Wangenheim, F. L. Darder and C. Kuo, et al.

The article provides current Schwartz Values Survey (SVS) data from samples of business managers and professionals across 50 societies that are culturally and socio-economically diverse. The study reports the society scores for SVS values dimensions for both individual and societal-level analyses.

Key findings

The contributions of authors' evaluation of the SVS values dimensions are two-fold.

- First, authors identify the SVS dimensions that have cross-culturally internally reliable structures and within-society agreement for business professionals.
- Second, they report the society cultural values scores developed from the twenty-first century data that can be used as macro-level predictors in multilevel and single-level international business research.

Source: Social Research Digest, Nov. 2011 (Vol. 2, No. 7)

2.4 Ethics and Labour Standards

2.4.1 Ethics and Workplace Survey

Author(s): Deloitte

Deloitte LLP has released the results of its third annual Ethics and Workplace Survey. The survey sample included 2,008 employed men and women in the US, and 500 US business executives. Participants were surveyed in April 2009.

Key findings

60% of business executives believe they have a right to know how employees portray themselves and their organizations in online social networks.

- However, employees disagree, as more than half (53%) say their social networking pages are not an employer's concern.
- This fact is especially true among younger workers, with 63% of 18–34 year old respondents stating employers have no business monitoring their online activity.
- That said, employees appear to have a clear understanding of the risks involved in using online social networks, as 74% of respondents believe they make it easier to damage a company's reputation.
- A mere 17% of executives surveyed say they have programs in place to monitor and mitigate the possible reputational risks related to the use of social networks.
- Only 15% of executives surveyed are addressing these risks in the board room, though 58% agree it is important enough to do so.
- 30% of business executives state that their companies are already informally monitoring use of social networking sites.
- While less than a quarter have formal policies on the medium's use among their people, nearly half (49%) of employees indicate defined guidelines will not change their behavior online.
- One-third of employees surveyed never consider what their boss or customers might think before posting material online.
- 15% of respondents said that they would comment online of company actions that they personally disagreed with.
- 56% of business executive respondents feel that allowing employees access to social networking sites improves work-life balance. Only 31% of employees agree.

Source: Governance Research Digest, Jun. 2009 (Vol. 1, No. 6)

2.4.2   Labour Standards Report

Author(s): Maplecroft

Maplecroft has released a series of labour standards reports to provide in-depth analysis of the key labour issues. The reports help companies operating in, or sourcing from the key emerging economies of the Philippines and Vietnam and for those with manufacturing bases or supply partners in the USA.

<u>Key findings</u>

Maplecroft's labour standards reports analyse and compare the major labour issues affecting countries at both national and provincial levels.

- Philippines
  - The weak legal enforcement of labour laws poses high risks to investors of complicity in labour rights violations.
  - Since in the Philippines non-adherence to internationally recognised labour rights remains widespread, both in law and practice, and violations are frequently not effectively addressed by labour authorities, companies without mitigation strategies risk reputational and operational damage if found to be complicit in such practices.
  - Accordingly, responsible companies need to ensure their supply chain business partners and contractors respect all domestic labour laws and regulations, as well as strive to meet international labour standards, if they are to avoid alleged implication in what stakeholders could regard as labour exploitation.
  - In the Philippines, these risks are especially acute with respect to substandard working conditions, including widespread violations of minimum wage laws, and limitations on the right of workers to organise in unions.
  - Moreover, since respect for labour rights is reported to be particularly weak in the country's economic zones, multinational companies need to be aware that business partners operating in these zones pose heightened risks of association with violations of international labour standards.
- USA
  - The US's legal framework for the protection of labour rights falls short of international standards in several respects.
  - This is reflected by the fact that the US has only ratified two of the eight core labour rights conventions of the International Labour Organisation (ILO).
  - Key discrepancies between domestic federal law and international standards exist regarding freedom of association and collective bargaining in particular.

- o As a result, companies are at risk of perceived complicity in labour rights violations by their American business partners and suppliers.
- o Forced labour remains a concern in sectors such as manufacturing and warehousing, disproportionately affecting migrant workers.
- o Although child labour is mostly a concern in the agricultural sector, it can pose long term risks to businesses by damaging children's education and subsequently reducing the future skilled workforce.
- o In addition, recent calls for more flexible laws allowing children to do more work create a concern that certain restrictions on the use of child labour in other sectors may be removed.
- Viet Nam
  - o Despite gradual improvements, the labour rights situation in Viet Nam remains exceptionally poor.
  - o Viet Nam is ranked as an 'extreme risk' country on Maplecroft's Labour Rights & Protection Index 2012, 21st out of 197 countries.
  - o The level of risk is comparable to Cambodia and Indonesia, with only China presenting higher risks in East and South East Asia.
  - o The country's low score suggests that investors face a severe risk of labour rights violations within their own operations or those of their business partners.
  - o Key risks include substandard working conditions, including excessive working hours, breaches of minimum wage laws and hazardous workplaces.
  - o Moreover, trade union rights are effectively denied in practice, and child labour and forced labour remain serious concerns, especially in rural areas where labour law enforcement is generally weaker.
  - o Further, labour rights risks are likely to be higher in the country's numerous special economic zones where, in the absence of labour law enforcement and trade unions, in many cases workers are effectively unprotected.
  - o The situation is exacerbated by the vast informal economy that is believed to account from some 75% of employment.
  - o Most informal workers are employed without labour contracts, meaning that they effectively fall outside the remit of labour market institutions and lack access to social security protections.

Source: Social Research Digest, Feb. 2012 (Vol. 3, No. 2)

2.4.3 The Internal Significance of Codes of Conduct in Retail Companies

Author(s): M. Frostenson, S. Helin and J. Sandstrom

This paper focuses on the significance of codes of conduct (CoCs) in the internal work context of two retail companies. First, the paper identifies in what way employees use and refer to CoCs internally; second, the function and relevance of CoCs inside the two companies are identified; third, the paper explains why CoCs tend to function in the identified ways.

<u>Key findings</u>

In both cases, the CoCs are clearly decoupled in the sense that they do not concern the immediate work context of the employees.

- Counter-intuitively, this facilitates the process of establishing the CoCs.
- Even though the CoCs are not directly relevant for the employees, they are accepted and embraced with regard to contents, focus and function.
- Above all, the CoCs seem to confirm and even strengthen employee identity.
- On the basis of these observations, it is suggested that CoCs should not only be valued in light of their direct organisational consequences or lack of such consequences.
- The issue is not just whether CoCs are decoupled or not.
- Rather, it is argued that researchers should consider more closely a two-level analysis that takes into account not only the concrete application of CoCs but also their function and meaning.
- An implication of this is that what might appear as a decoupled code cannot be dismissed as irrelevant to the 'core' business processes of the organisation.

Source: Governance Research Digest, Sep. 2012 (Vol. 3, No. 9)

2.4.4 Time Affluence as a Path Towards Personal Happiness and Ethical Business Practice

Author(s): T. Kasser, K. M. Sheldon

This study proposes that businesses consider the possibility of "time affluence" as an alternative model for improving employee wellbeing and ethical business practice. The paper presents findings from four empirical studies which use a combination of archival and survey data.

Key findings

Time affluence (TA) is positively associated with subjective well-being (SWB), even after controlling for the effects of income.

- Analyses indicated that income related positively to both job and family satisfaction.
- Feelings of time affluence also related positively to both job and family satisfaction.
- The findings lend weight to previous studies which have found that at low levels of income, increases in income improved well-being, but at higher levels of income, equivalent increases in income did not improve well-being as much.
- Subjective reports of material affluence (MA) were correlated positively with income but unrelated to hours worked, whereas subjective reports of TA were negatively correlated with hours worked but not significantly related to income.
- Individuals who experience more time affluence apparently report higher subjective well-being in part because they experience more mindfulness and greater satisfaction of their psychological needs.
- The benefits of time affluence did not depend on personality characteristics such as being high in need for achievement or sensation seeking or reporting that one wants to "keep busy" because it is fun, challenging, or personally valued.
- While the studies sought to determine whether the benefits of TA were limited to certain situations or types of people, no consistent effects were evident from the empirical data.
- On the basis of the findings of these studies, the authors suggest that ethical businesses might institute policies to improve the time affluence of their employees.

Source: Social Research Digest, Mar. 2009 (Vol. 1, No. 3)

2.4.5   Ethical Issues Relating To The Health Effects of Long Working Hours

Author(s): A.E. Dembe

This article reviews the ethical implications of long and unconventional working hours, particularly from the points of view of employee health and wellbeing, and the risk of errors arising from fatigue. The paper uses the context of proposed changes to US legislation as a framework for the discussion.

<u>Key findings</u>

There is now abundant evidence that working in jobs requiring especially long hours or nonstandard shifts raises workers' risks for injury and disease.

- Working overtime increases the likelihood for on-the-job injuries by 61%, evening shifts carry a 38% greater chance of job injury and night shifts a 31% increased risk of job injury compared with working in a conventional day shift.
- Other studies have confirmed that long working hours and shift work raises the odds for workers to be injured, to be fatigued, stressed, and to suffer from a range of serious medical ailments.
- Health problems created by excessive working hours can have spillover effects for employees such as diminished performance, mistakes in judgment, and errors in performing work activities.
- These spillover effects are perhaps most worrisome when the affected worker is employed in a position that is critical to public safety and welfare, such as health care, law enforcement, air traffic control, nuclear power generation, firefighting, and other emergency services.
- The perils associated with schedules that endanger workers might also end up jeopardizing others in the society.
- The ethical considerations inherent in demanding work schedules are further complicated by the distinctive employment context in which the risks arise. In most employment contexts, employees are only partially in control of their work activities and their working environment.
- A number of areas of special ethical concern are raised in the paper. These include:

- o Mandatory overtime and the possibility of coercion - In the US It has been estimated that 27.7% of full-time workers are in jobs that potentially require mandatory overtime, and that over 76% of those (21.1% of full-time workers) end up actually working mandatory overtime schedules in any particular month.
- o Possible deception in overtime arrangements - A related concern arises from the potential to devise schedules designed specifically to circumvent overtime pay requirements or mandatory overtime regulations.
- o Limits to voluntary assumptions of risk – To the extent it exists, hazard pay generally does not adequately compensate for the additional risks incurred by the affected workers.
- o Effects on the welfare of others - A number of professions, including health care and public safety, involve working patterns which, when the cause of illness or fatigue, can have severe consequences for others. This has included catastrophic accidents such as oil spills and major transportation accidents.
- o Inequitable distribution of employment opportunities - Generally speaking, it is cheaper for an organisation to hire fewer workers to work longer hours. This has significant implications for gender and age balance in the workplace, as well as employee wellbeing.

Source: Social Research Digest, Apr. 2009 (Vol. 1, No. 4)

2.4.6 The Role of Personal-Related Factors on Corporate Travel Policy Compliance

Author(s): A. Douglas, B.A. Lubbe.

This article presents the results of the empirical testing of the corporate travel policy compliance model published in the Journal of Business Ethics in 2009. The authors focus on the influence of personal factors on policy compliance. The personal-related factors considered include: personal ethics, individual morality, self-interest, levels of job- and life satisfaction, and the conditions of travel. 193 corporate travellers from a range of South African organisations completed questionnaires which form the basis of the findings.

Key findings

83% of respondents reported experiencing Implementation problems in varying degrees in complying with their company's travel policies.

- 16% of respondents were classified as low compliance, 41% as medium compliance and 43% as high compliance.
- More than a fifth of respondents agreed that they had to compromise their beliefs so as to perform their jobs in the way their organisations wanted them to.
- 15% of travellers said they had to break company policy to perform their job.
- Many travellers felt that it was important to fly business class, even if this was not permitted, in order to present a degree of status to business colleagues.
- 92% of the low compliance group agreed with this, compared with 53% of the high compliance group.
- The most important consideration for travellers in this study was personal safety, reflecting the challenging environments in which they are expected to travel.
- 20% of respondents believed that anything not explicitly stipulated in a travel policy was therefore implicitly permitted.
- 15% believe that they do not harm their company when they miss a flight a simply take a later flight.
- 65% stated that there were consequences for non-compliance within their organisations.
- 38% of travellers stated that their companies had made an example of a non-compliant traveller colleague. For those organisations that did not, the authors suggest that an absence of disciplinary action may decrease the morale of honest employees.
- In order to encourage travellers to operate within company guidelines, companies could, for example, offer schemes where employees keep frequent flyer miles, or share in the cost benefit achieved when accepting inconvenience.

Source: Governance Research Digest, Oct. 2009 (Vol. 1, No. 10)

2.4.7 Investigating the Relationship Between Protestant Work Ethic and Confucian Dynamism: An Empirical Test in Mainland China

Author(s): S. Zhang, W. Liu and X. Liu

This study examined the relationship between the Protestant Work Ethic (PWE) and Confucian Dynamism in a sample of 1,757 respondents from several provinces in mainland China. Mirels and Garrett's PWE Scale and Robertson's Confucian Dynamism Scale were used to measure the work ethics.

Key findings

All the dimensions of PWE were positively related to Confucian Dynamism, but negatively to guanxi orientation.

- The 16 items of the PWE Scale and eight items of the Confucian Dynamism Scale were initially subjected to a principal components analysis.
- Factor analysis produced four factors of the PWE, which were labeled as follows: hard work, internal motive, admiration of work itself, and negative attitude to leisure.
- And three factors of the Confucian Dynamism, which were labeled: long-term orientation, short-term orientation, and guanxi orientation.
- The results also indicated that three PWE dimensions ("hard work," "internal motive," and "admiration of work itself") were positively and significantly related to long-term orientation, but two of them were related negatively and significantly to the short-term orientation of Confucian Dynamism.
- In addition, the results showed that the dimension—admiration of work itself—of PWE was significantly and negatively associated with the guanxi orientation, but significantly and positively to the short-term orientation.

Source: Social Research Digest, Mar. 2012 (Vol. 3, No. 3)

2.4.8 Toward a Better Understanding of the Link between Ethical Climate and Job Satisfaction

Source: Social Research Digest, Feb. 2012 (Vol. 3, No. 2)

Author(s): Y.-D. Wand and H.-H. Hsieh

The study is simultaneously investigating both the effects of individual-level and organization-level ethical climates on employees' job satisfaction. On the basis of a multilevel analysis, the present study used a sample of 472 full-time employees from 31 organizations in Taiwan to examine the above two effects.

Key findings

Results from the analyses showed that within the organizations, individual employees' instrumental climate perceptions were negatively related to job satisfaction, whereas their caring climate perceptions and rules climate perceptions were positively related to job satisfaction.

- Also, the results indicated that between organizations, organizational instrumental climate was negatively related to job satisfaction, whereas organizational caring, independence, and rules climates were positively related to job satisfaction.
- Implications for research and managerial practices were derived from these findings.

2.5 Conditions of Work: Sectoral and Case Studies

2.5.1 An Overview of Working Conditions in Sportswear Factories

Author(s): International Textile Garment and Leather Workers' Federation

The Global Union representing workers in the garment industry, the ITGLWF have released a report on working conditions in Asian sportswear supply chains. Through worker interviews and surveys the report uncovers a litany of workers' rights abuses in Indonesia, Sri Lanka and Philippines.

Key findings

Factories in three countries – the Philippines, Indonesia and Sri Lanka – were surveyed, and not one of them paid a living wage to their combined 100,000-strong workforce.

- Many of them didn't even pay the legal minimum wage.
- The report also makes clear is that this is a gender issue: 76% of the surveyed workforce are women.
- Globalised supply chains exploit predominantly female labour.
- Employment is becoming more precarious as more workers are put on to temporary contracts, day labour, on call rather than with permanent jobs.
- That enables employers to dodge holiday pay, sick pay and written contracts.
- Employers also imposed compulsory overtime, lower wages and higher production targets on workers on these short-term contracts.
- Such precarious employment makes it harder for trade unions to organise and recruit, because contracts are not renewed if the worker has been involved in trade union activity.
- On average, 25% of workers in Indonesia were short-term or temporary, while in the Philippines it rose to 85% in one factory, 50% at another.
- In Sri Lanka, wages were paid on productivity targets – despite such a practice being illegal.
- Excessive overtime was the "norm" in sportswear and leisurewear factories in Indonesia; workers in all the factories surveyed were doing between 10 and 40 hours of overtime a week.
- In Sri Lanka, workers were forced to work up to 130 hours per month in overtime, and anyone asking to leave would be verbally harassed.
- In the Philippines, 24% of workers said that they did not receive additional pay for their overtime.
- In many cases, the employers' behaviour was illegal, but the report – which picked factories at random – points out that what makes laws effective is a well resourced inspection regime.
- Without inspection, legislation is meaningless.

Source: Social Research Digest, May 2011 (Vol. 2, No. 1)

2.5.2 Summary of Research on the Labour Situation in the Beijing Development Area

Author(s): BSR

BSR conducted a research in the Beijing Development Area (BDA) to understand China's rapidly transforming labor market and its impact on manufacturing businesses in Beijing. The research focuses on migrant workers, which represent the greatest labor challenge, and specifically on the situation of companies in the Xingwang Park area of the BDA.

<u>Key findings</u>

Companies face significant challenges hiring and retaining staff, particularly at the operator level.

- This causes increased hiring and training costs, difficulty in planning production schedules, and additional labor costs arising from overtime.
- The main challenges facing companies in the Xingwang Park area of the BDA:
  o excessive and inappropriate overtime;
  o difficulties in recruitment;
  o high turnover;
  o challenges with line management quality.
- The main challenges facing companies in the Xingwang:
  o low salaries and high cost of living;
  o demand for more overtime;
  o need for better living conditions;
  o discriminatory treatment of ETLs;
  o lack of training and opportunities for promotion;
  o inadequate support for youth workers.
- The research found that few companies in the BDA have collaborated effectively with other companies or with the government beyond one-off events or through participation in the Admin-HR Working Group.
- However, companies recognize that these issues cannot be solved alone and may be solved more cost-efficiently if tackled together.

Source: Social Research Digest, May 2011 (Vol. 2, No. 1)

2.5.3 For Workers' Benefit: Solving Overtime Problems in Chinese Factories

Author(s): Verite

In this paper Verité outlines the sources and reasons for the problem of overtime in China. The report explains the Chinese Comprehensive System and illustrates how a systems-based approach can provide sustainable solutions.

Key findings

Some examples of work hours violations are extreme — workers not having a day off for 20 days and working upwards of 80 hours overtime per month.

- Workers' hours at factories with the Comprehensive System are still excessive, and
- Consistently in violation of companies' own Codes of Conduct.
- Involving staff from different functions within your company will provide insight into root causes and help you make operational changes.
- We work directly with companies and their suppliers to put the business controls in place to effectively control work hours while meeting production demands.

Source: Social Research Digest, Feb. 2012 (Vol. 3, No. 2)

2.5.4 Toying with Workers' Rights: A Report on Producing Merchandise for the London 2012 Olympic Games

Author(s): Play Fair

'Toying with Workers' Rights' investigates the true life accounts of workers in China producing Olympic branded goods for the London Olympic games. It looks into working conditions in two factories in China producing the Olympic mascots, Wenlock and Manderville, and London 2012 pin-badges.

Key findings

The struggle for rights for workers producing goods and merchandise for the Olympic brand continues.

- Poverty pay, in some cases below the legal minimum, where workers were not paid enough to cover their most basic needs, and benefit payments for pensions and medical insurance were not paid in accordance with Chinese law.
- For example, a worker making an Olympic mascot could be paid as little as £26 a week, while a mascot can retail for around £20.
- Excessive overtime, sometimes up to 100 hours a month, nearly three times the legal limit in China.
- Some workers were doing 24-hour shifts, while others were working seven days a week.
- Child labour was used in the factory producing pin badges.
- Workers were locked into a five-year contract and had to pay a fine if they tried to leave beforehand.
- At one factory, workers were not given a contract of employment, and in the other factory, workers did not receive pay-slips.
- In both factories, workers did not fully understand how their wages and over-time were calculated.
- Workers did not receive health and safety training in both factories, and would tend to forgo wearing protective equipment, when provided, so they could work faster and earn more – to top up their poverty pay.
- Workers were prevented from joining unions in both factories, and it was made clear to them that anyone engaging in trade union activities would be dismissed.
- Evidence of audit fraud – with workers coached on how to answer auditor's questions, and in some cases bribed to give the correct answers.

Source: Social Research Digest, Mar. 2012 (Vol. 3, No. 3)

2.5.5 Work Equity in Food and Agriculture: Practices at the 100 Largest and Most Influential U.S. Companies

Author(s): *Tellus Institute and Sustainalytics*

A joint report by the Tellus Institute and Sustainalytics sheds light on the often ignored issue of worker welfare in the food industry by highlighting practices and policies of some of the largest and most influential food companies in the U.S. Major challenges are identified across the industry and the authors propose avenues of influence for companies and investors going forward.

Key findings

The organic, local, natural food movement has a glaring blind spot: worker welfare.

- Despite popular assumptions, foods that are sustainable, organic, or locally grown are often produced under highly inequitable working conditions.
- In fact, workers that produce and deliver food to consumers face some of the lowest paying jobs, the highest levels of food insecurity, and some of the most dangerous working conditions in the U.S.
- Fewer than one in five companies shows evidence of having a high-level committee tasked specifically with oversight of worker equity issues.
- Managing supply chain risks at overseas operations tends to take precedence over local oversight of employees and contractors.
- Compared to other frontline workers in the U.S., food industry workers earn about onethird less – only $18,900 per year.
- Many food workers lack the rudimentary protections of wage and hour laws.
- Some of the most dangerous jobs in the U.S. are found in the food industry.
- While the fatality rate for all industries is 3.5 per 100,000 workers, in agriculture the rate is over 25, and for warehousing and transportation jobs it is 15.
- The prevalent cost-cutting model across the industry increases risks to workers and to food safety; preliminary findings suggest a direct correlation between worker equity and food safety.

Source: Social Research Digest, Nov. 2012 (Vol. 3, No. 11)

2.5.6 Killer Jeans: A Report on Sandblasting Denim

Author(s): Labour Behind the Label

In this study, the Clean Clothes Campaign and Labour Behind the Label have investigated the way in which UK and international brands and retailers are tackling the dangers presented by sandblasting within their own supply chains. Since October 2010 over 80 European and international brands have been contacted by the different national Clean Clothes Campaigns in order to highlight the serious impact of the process on the health of workers.

Key findings

At the time that this report was published, approximately 50 people in Turkey had dies as a direct result of exposure to silica dust whilst sandblasting denim.

- Whilst the use of sandblasting to achieve a wornout look on denim is a relatively new phenomenon within the clothing industry, the method itself has been widely used within the mining and building industries for many decades.
- Manual sandblasting with silica was banned in the European Economic Community in 1966 due to the severe risks associated with the inhalation of silica dust.
- Given the imposition of strict regulations on sandblasting in many European countries, the clothing industry has largely out-sourced production to as yet unregulated regions.
- Since 2000 sandblasting has mainly been located in countries such as Turkey, Syria, Bangladesh, Mexico, India and Indonesia.
- According to an estimate from the Turkish Solidarity Committee of Sandblasting Labourers about 5000 people working in the clothing industry in Turkey may have developed silicosis.
- Since the ban was introduced in Turkey the sandblasting industry has moved to other countries such as China, India, Bangladesh, Pakistan, Argentina and parts of Northern Africa.

Source: Social Research Digest, Jul. 2011 (Vol. 2, No. 3)

2.5.7 Fashion Industry Labour Report

Author(s): Labour Behind The Label

A new report, 'Let's Clean Up Fashion' by UK sweatshop campaigning group Labour Behind The Label accuses a number of leading UK high street brands of exploiting Asian factory workers. The report authors wrote to all the major high street retailers and all members of the Ethical Trading

Initiative (ETI). Using the information gathered, companies were placed into one of five groups based on how well they are performing.

<u>Key findings</u>

Only two companies, Gap and Next, made it into the category 'Pulling Ahead'. From their responses and case studies, they demonstrate more serious engagement with labour issues but still have some way to go.

- Those companies in the category 'Non-Responders' make no information available to consumers on their websites, and did not respond to enquiries in any meaningful way. The authors believe this lack of transparency indicates a lack of engagement.
- Non-Responders include: BhS, Diesel, House of Fraser, Kookai, Mothercare, Marshalis, Monsoon Accessorize, Moss Bros, Peacocks/Bon Marche, River Island, Ted Baker.
- Responses from companies 'Dragging Their Feet' indicate scant effort to tackle workers' rights issues. They have not participated in collaborative efforts to develop best practice, including the ETI.
- Companies 'Dragging Their Feet' include: Arcadia (Topshop. Dorothy Perkins, Miss Selfridge etc.), French Connection, Jigsaw/Kew, Laura Ashley, Matalan, Mosaic Group (Oasis, Karen Millen etc.), Primark, Principles.
- A third group of companies are deemed to be 'Resting on their Laurels'. While these companies have previously taken some steps to address working conditions, including joining the ETI, their responses suggest they are more interested in ticking the right boxes to stave off criticism than they are in achieving results for their workers.
- Companies 'Resting on their Laurels' include: Asda, Debenhams, Madison Hosiery, Pentland, Sainsbury's.
- Some companies provided mixed responses, which indicated some consideration and action in some areas, but didn't deal substantively with others. These companies 'Could Do Better'.
- Companies that 'Could Do Better' include: John Lewis, H&M, Levi Strauss & Co., M&S, New Look, Tesco, TK Maxx, Zara.

Source: Social Research Digest, Oct. 2009 (Vol. 1, No. 10)

2.5.8 Aiding and Abetting: How Unaccountable Fair Trade Certifiers Are Destroying Workers' Rights

Author(s): International Labor Rights Forum

The International Labor Rights Forum released a report that describes how certification bodies, paid directly by brands, can harm efforts by workers to unionize rather than help them. The "Aiding and Abetting" Report focuses on the illustrative case study of Theo Chocolate, where despite making public commitment to ensure workers' rights they actively campaigned against worker organizing efforts suing professional union avoidance consultants, intimidation, and dicriminatory treatment of workers.

Key findings

This case demonstrates the various structural failures of the IMO's Fair for Life certification model and proposes new approaches to improve the certification process.

- Focus of the report is the Institute for Market Ecology (IMO), an organization that audits companies in order to provide fair trade certification and labels to their products.
- IMO branded Theo Chocolate as fair trade, despite Theo workers claiming that the company hired an anti-union consultant and was violating U.S and international labor standards during union organizing campaign.
- When workers wanted to form a union, management responded with hostility, intimidation and retaliation.
- Despite pleads by worker to convince IMO to conduct an audit post-certification, it upheld Theo's fair trade certification and was not transparent with the audit results.
- Fair trade community must establish greater accountability among the certifying organizations they support.
- Recommendations include, and are not limited to:
  o Urge the global fair trade community to partner with the labor movement to create the "International Fair Trade of Appeal" to assess and remedy instances of fair trade mishandlings

- o Demand IMO to change its procedures and accountability to allow its audits to be reviewed by the International Fair Trade Board of Appeal
- o IMO must make audit findings transparent

Source: Social Research Digest, Apr. 2013 (Vol. 4, No. 4)

2.6 Employee Engagement

2.6.1 Corporate Social Responsibility and the Benefits of Employee Trust

Author(s): S. D. Hansen, B. B. Dunford, A. D. Boss, R. W. Boss and I. Angermeier

The two studies presented in this article draw on theory from both corporate marketing and organizational behavior disciplines to test the general proposition that employee trust partially mediates the relationship between CSR and employee attitudinal and behavioral outcomes. The study is driven by the evidence that research on corporate social responsibility (CSR) has tended to focus on external stakeholders and outcomes, revealing little about internal effects that might also help explain CSR-firm performance linkages and the impact that corporate marketing strategies can have on internal stakeholders such as employees.

Key findings

Both studies provide evidence in support of these general relationships.

- Theoretical and practical implications of these findings are discussed in the context of CSR and corporate marketing research.

Source: Social Research Digest, Sep. 2011 (Vol. 2, No. 5)

2.6.2 Toward Engagement 2.0: Creating a More Sustainable Company through Employee Engagement

Author(s): National Environmental Education Foundation / GreenBiz

This report, the third produced by NEEF's Business & Environment Program, examines how leading companies are moving toward a more strategic approach to employee engagement in corporate sustainability activities by creating a culture of sustainability throughout their firms. In this report, the reader will find company case studies and examples in practice, as well as practitioner-focused "how to" boxes about assessing corporate culture, making the business case and delivering value through employee engagement.

Key findings

Environmental and sustainability (E&S) knowledge remains both valued by companies and is expected to increase in importance as a hiring factor.

- A majority, or 58%, of respondents in companies that currently lack an E&S education program are planning on educating employees within the next two years.
- The report also shows how companies such as Procter & Gamble, Johnson & Johnson, PwC, Cisco Systems, eBay and BT Group plc, are creating innovative tools for employee engagement.
- These include green teams, engaging employees through social media like Twitter, and awards and incentives.
- Companies are encouraging their employees to take action on sustainability at work, as well as at home and in their communities.
- Through a five-step process companies are able to establish a culture of sustainability:
  - permit: granting employees permission to become involved in sustainability initiatives;
  - educate & engage: providing employees educational materials and engaging them in sustainability activities;
  - act: empowering employees to take action at work, as well as at home and in their community;
  - embed: making sustainability a regular part of their organizations, including their human resource processes, operations, product or service innovation & development, and beyond;
  - evaluate: measuring and evaluating employee engagement efforts to gauge impact, support continued integration into company culture and inform future employee engagement efforts.
- Highlights from the case studies include:

- o Baxter's World Environment Week grants employees direct permission to take sustainability action;
- o Stonyfield Farm and Walmart empower employees to take action at work, as well as at home and in their communities, resulting in reductions in company energy use (per ton of product) of more than 22% and 500,000 associates engaged in voluntary sustainability efforts;
- o at J.C. Penney, corporate social responsibility and human resources managers collaborate to embed sustainability into the corporate culture through resource teams, new employee orientation and training, alignment in communication related to corporate sustainability goals and an annual survey;
- o Pacific Gas & Electric (PG&E) evaluates employee engagement through an annual survey and tracks a number of indicators that measure employee engagement, such as employee volunteer hours and participation in employee-led groups that help foster diversity and inclusion, such as a growing grassroots green network.

Source: Social Research Digest, Oct. 2011 (Vol. 2, No. 6)

2.6.3 Employee Participation in Cause- Related Marketing Strategies

Author(s): G. Liu, C. Liston-Heyes, W-W. Ko.

This study focuses on the extent to which a firm's internal stakeholders (employees) are involved in the selection of social campaigns for cause-related marketing (CRM). Information was gathered through 43 semi-structured telephone interviews with corporate managers of UK firms operating in the financial services (11) and retail (13) industries, with managers of non-profit organisations (NPOs) (16) in social alliances with these firms and with a handful of relevant corporate consultants (3).

Key findings

Comments made by both corporate and NPO managers suggest that awareness of the benefits of internal cause-related marketing is on the rise. All respondents stated that they are exploiting, or have attempted to exploit, these strategically.

- By enhancing a firm's internal legitimacy, as CRM strategy can also boost productivity, provided that it meets employees' expectations about the social responsibilities of the company.
- To do this, a firm can organise its CRM strategy to reflect employee concerns, manage employees' expectations in line with company strategy, or do a bit of both. Both require involving employees in the CRM decision process.
- Employee involvement in CRM activities, when it exists, can occur at different levels and intensities, and differs considerably across firms.
- The interviews suggest that participation through employee representatives may have a greater potential to enhance internal legitimacy than a system that allows employees to nominate charities of their choice. This is because the former allows for deeper engagement.
- Individual participation appears to exert a less concentrated impact on corporate legitimacy but is used as a means of catering to diverse pAuthor(s)s that may not be accounted for by the general CRM strategy.
- The study data suggests that employee participation decreased with the size of the CRM commitment.
- Larger-scale CRM programmes are used to enhance external corporate legitimacy and are carefully selected to fit the image and persona the company is trying to project.
- These decisions are strategic and treated as major investments. As such, internal legitimacy objectives are not at the heart of such decisions.
- Interview respondents stated that 'important' corporate social engagements are carefully selected and assessed in terms of their contribution to the firm's business objectives.
- Financial services firms tended to be less 'ad hoc' with their CRM, requiring that any major decisions regarding social donations be scrutinised by the centre.
- Retail services came across as more flexible and generally happy to devolve CRM decisions to regional centres and, in some cases, local ones. Such decentralization of CRM issues typically gives more say to employees.
- Financial services firms will typically select larger-scale and longer-term projects with a national or even international reach, while retail

services firms will opt for more regional causes with campaigns of shorter durations.

Source: Social Research Digest, Dec. 2009 (Vol. 1, No. 12)

2.6.4 Organizational Commitment in Manufacturing Employees: Relationships with Corporate Social Performance

Author(s): J. P. Stites, J. H. Michael

The study examines the relationship between employee perceptions of Corporate Social Performance (CSP) and organizational commitment in a manufacturing industry setting. Survey data were collected from 136 production employees at three kitchen cabinet manufacturers in the United States.

Key findings

Both community-related and environmentally-related CSP are positively related to organizational commitment.

- The results imply that companies should communicate their CSP to all employees because it has the potential to increase their employees' organizational commitment, which may result in positive organizational outcomes.
- The study contributes to extant literature by highlighting the importance of employees as a relevant stakeholder for CSP research, as well as employing comprehensive perceptual
  o measures of both community-related and
  o environmentally-related CSP, in a
  o manufacturing context.

Source: Social Research Digest, May 2011 (Vol. 2, No. 1)

2.6.5 Employees Matter: Maximizing Company Value through Workforce Engagement

Author(s): SJF Institute

SJF Institute's new report, "Employees Matter: Maximizing Company Value through Workforce Engagement," profiles two dozen fast growing entrepreneurial firms that utilize employee ownership and engagement strategies which their executives say are closely linked with improved business performance. The report uses these company profiles to frame and illustrate ten best practices for engaging employees at all levels for increased business success.

Key findings

When team members understand their company's core values, they can be empowered to act quickly and make good decisions.

- And when employees think and act like owners, they provide better customer service and find every possible way to build company value.
- Top 10 employee engagement strategies:
  1. involvement hiring – carefully choosing employees that not only have the right skills but also are a long term fit with the company's culture;
  2. strong employee benefits – providing comprehensive benefits and a flexible work environment;
  3. extensive training and promotion from within – investing in employees to build their skills and enabling them to take on increased responsibility over time;
  4. culture of mutual respect and trust – consistently treating all employees with respect yields long term loyalty and may be valued over rewards;
  5. celebrating success – engaged teams work hard and spend time celebrating together when milestones large and small are achieved;
  6. communicating the company's core values clearly and consistently – maintaining the company culture by ensuring the core values are frequently heard and understood by all;
  7. sharing key success metrics – sharing the metrics that are critical to the company's financial success broadly with employees and articulating those that employees affect daily;
  8. employee Participation – making sure all employees have a say over how work is done and have some degree of autonomy;
  9. performance-based rewards and compensation – tying rewards such as bonuses to achieving company metrics or to increased efficiencies;

10. sharing ownership broadly via stock options, restricted stock, ESOPs, or co-ops.

Source: Social Research Digest, Jul. 2011 (Vol. 2, No. 3)

2.6.6 How Leadership and Commitment Influence Bank Employees' Adoption of their Bank's Values

Author(s): E. Wallace, L. Chernatony and I. Buil

The article explores how values are adopted by employees within a bank, specifically, the authors test the relationship between leadership style, employee commitment, and the adoption of values. Data was collected from a survey of 438 branch employees in a leading Irish retail bank.

Key findings

A structured and directive leadership style was effective at encouraging the adoption of the bank's values.

- Moreover, when employees are committed to the organisation, this has a significant impact on their adoption of values.
- Thus, this study supports the literature which suggests that leadership and commitment are prerequisites for values adoption.

Source: Social Research Digest, Aug. 2011 (Vol. 2, No. 4)

2.6.7 Green the Team

Author(s): BBMG

The report leverages brand consulting firm BBMG's recent experience helping Walmart create a global engagement platform. Walmart's My Sustainability Plan is retailer's platform for engaging its 2.2 million staff in sustainability programs across five continents.

Key findings

Programs to involve staff in sustainability programs break down into three key stages.

- The first stage in creating an employee engagement program. This involves:

- o Writing a vision statement to help employees understand the program's goals and what resources are available to them; involving employees, even at this early stage, will improve chances for longterm success.
- o Connecting the vision to specific calls to action, preferably in bite-sized chunks.
- o Framing complex issues in personal terms: emissions calculators such as the the EPA's personal GHG Calculator or Conservation International's Eco-Footprint Calculator can help.
- o Creating a flexible framework, so different business units in different geographic regions can adopt messages to suit local cultures and knowledge levels.
- o Identifying key metrics of success from the outset, measure results and report regularly; metrics to consider include retention, job satisfaction, volunteer hours, number of employees engaged in the program, and greenhouse gas emissions reduced.
- The next stage is to "build the buzz." Key steps include:
  - o Make the program voluntary; mandatory participation poses a risk of alienating employees.
  - o Reward employee efforts and achievements, through formal and informal recognition from their peers, managers and senior leadership; competitions can help to motivate staff.
  - o Keep up the internal communications: build the buzz in stages and using all the communications tools you have available – not just intranet and emails, but more creative ideas such as sleeves, Post-Its, screensavers and hangtags on breakroom refrigerators.
- Next comes celebrating success:
  - o Create opportunities for staff to share their activities, both in person and virtually; try using a Facebook page or a site on your intranet to facilitate dialogue.
  - o Keep the communication positive: don't scare your workforce into recycling; create guidelines to ensure communications stays upbeat.
  - o Close the loop: take success stories and re-apply them; make time during your annual strategy meetings to update the sustainability program.

Source: Social Research Digest, Dec. 2011 (Vol. 2, No. 8)

2.6.8   Corporate Social Responsibility Influence on Employees

Author(s): International Centre for Corporate Social Responsibility

The paper by ICCSR analyzes Corporate Social Responsibility's (CSR) influence on employees. In the study authors integrate social identity theory and social exchange theory in a new framework.

Key findings

This framework explains how employees' perceptions of CSR trigger attitudes and behavior in the workplace which affect organizational, social and environmental performance.

- This model bridges micro and macro researches on socially responsible behavior, articulates social identification and social exchange processes, and explains how CSR contributes to corporate performance by influencing employees' behavior.
- This paper shows that CSR can influence social exchange dynamics as well as social identification processes within the corporation.
- It integrates these two mechanisms in a new framework explaining how CSR perceptions stimulate the adoption of workplace attitudes and behaviors that may ultimately foster corporate performance.
- This model provides a roadmap for studying how corporations, in doing well by doing good, can push their employees to engage in both efficient and socially responsible behaviors.

Source: Social Research Digest, Jun. 2012 (Vol. 3, No. 6)

2.6.9   Do Employees Care About CSR Programs? A Typology of Employees According to Their Attitudes

Author(s): P. Rodrigo, D. Arenas

This paper examines employees' reactions to CSR programs at the attitudinal level. The analysis shows that the implementation of CSR programs generates two types of attitudes in employees: attitudes toward the organization and attitudes toward society. The results presented are drawn from an in-depth study of two Chilean construction firms that have well-established CSR programs.

Key findings

Important differences were discovered amongst employees in their reaction to the implementation of CSR initiatives. These differences were not dependent on the type of CSR activity, but instead reflected a range of commonly held values.

- Broadly speaking, the employers interviewed spoke about their organization from a citizen's perspective and about their society from an employee's perspective.
- While the results demonstrated that there are indeed workers with a positive attitude following CSR programme implementation, and others who have an indifferent or contrary attitude, the data did not provide evidence of a cautious type with a possible good general perception about CSR initiatives but who were keen to wait to see long-term social and corporate results.
- With the introduction of CSR programmes, employees developed different behaviors, emotions and cognitions about the new role that the company assumes as a satisfier of social needs beyond the delivery of highquality products or services, or handing over a salary at the end of the month.
- Due to the introduction of CSR programs, employees questioned whether the social context of their work was changing and whether companies need to reorient their priorities.
- Many employees did not previously show great concern for social issues (or were not aware of them) or took it for granted that it was the State that should concern itself with such issues.
- With the introduction of CSR programs in their companies, some employees acknowledged that in a globalized world the private company has a responsibility beyond its immediate and traditional business sphere and must concern itself with the social and environmental repercussions of its actions.
- Various degrees of employee acceptance are recorded, ranging from some employees who are immediately convinced of the new organizational role, subscribing to it wholeheartedly, to others who simply do not accept it.
- The perception that the organization has assumed a new role together with a favorable reaction to it leads many employees, who formerly felt

that the organization was simply a place of work, to view it as an institution that shares their own social views. As a result, employees also develop an attitude of identification with the organization.

- If employees feel that the organization is being a good citizen, they feel proud to be a part of it. This is partly related to the employee's perception of the results or effects of the CSR programs implemented by the organization: the individual feels that his or her contribution to society has a smaller impact compared with the social contribution that the organization can make, and so the employee's wish to make a social contribution is satisfied through the organization.
- If employees are dissatisfied with their specific job and the atmosphere around them, they are less likely to identify with the organization in spite of the implementation of CSR programs.
- The majority of employees at lower levels of the organizational structure who were interviewed expressed a low degree of satisfaction and said that they identified somewhat less with the organization as a result.
- Although appropriate CSR programs may be applied both internally and externally, the data showed that routine at work is a key negative factor with respect to the social importance attached to one's work.
- It was found that although many employees could reach the point of feeling that their work might be important, the recollection of the tediousness of an activity diminished or destroyed this incipient feeling.
- The more that employees feel that their work within the organization is important and has a social meaning, the more their sense of social justice is satisfied.

Source: Social Research Digest, Feb. 2009 (Vol. 1, No. 2)

2.6.10 Sustainability Leadership Survey

Author(s): Buck Consultants

A new survey of HR executives, conducted by human resource firm Buck Consultants, finds that employee involvement in green programs dramatically increases when organizations appoint an individual to lead the efforts. Almost 100 US HR professionals took part in the survey in 2008.

Key findings

Companies that put a single person in charge of sustainability programs are much more likely to inspire employees to support the effort.

- Over half of the companies surveyed have incorporated environmental management into business operations and have a formal green program in place or plan to implement one in the next 12 months.
- More than 60% of companies surveyed have made environmental responsibility a part of their organization's mission statement and view the promotion of social responsibility as the most critical objective of their green programs.
- In nearly 50% of companies, only five percent or less of their employees are actively involved in green programs.
- For companies with at least three-quarters of their employees actively involved in green programs, 71% have appointed individual leaders whereas only 29% have not.
- Incentives programs help too, the survey finds. Among companies that provide rewards to encourage green behaviors, 77% provide special employee recognition, 36% give prize incentives, and 14% offer a monetary reward.
- Four out of five companies use web- or videoconferencing to reduce business travel - making remote conferencing the top sustainability strategy cited by survey respondents.
- Other popular strategies include setting policies to conserve paper (76%) and implementing employee wellness programs (68%).
- The departments generally given responsibility for the implementation of green programmes are operations (47%) and HR (38%).
- The primary business objective for green initiatives was most frequently cited as the promotion of social responsibility (cited by 42% as very important and a further 33% as important).
- An important secondary objective was the attraction and retention of top talent, cited by a total of 47% of respondents as either important or very important.

Source: Social Research Digest, Apr. 2009 (Vol. 1, No. 4)

2.6.11 Transformational Leadership and Leader's Mode of Care Reasoning

Author(s): S. Simola, J. Barling and N. Turner

Previous research on the moral foundations of transformational leadership has focused primarily on stage of justice reasoning; this study focuses on developmental mode of care reasoning. Multilevel regression analyses were conducted on data coded from interviews with a sample of Canadian public sector managers (N = 58) and survey responses from their subordinates (N = 119).

Key findings

Managers' developmental mode of care reasoning significantly and positively predicted subordinates' reports of transformational (but not transactional) leadership, with significant differences in follower reports of transformational leadership between those using more versus less advanced modes of care reasoning.

- Conceptual implications for understanding transformational leadership and the ethics of leadership, directions for future research, and suggestions for leadership interventions are discussed.

Source: Governance Research Digest, Jun. 2012 (Vol. 3, No. 6)

2.6.12 Defining Respectful Leadership: What It Is, How It Can Be Measured, and Another Glimpse At What It Is Related To

Author(s): N. van Quaquebeke, T. Eckloff

This research explores the sort of leadership behaviours that are considered by employees to reflect respectful leadership. 426 German mid-career professionals took part in the survey which examined their experiences of respectful leadership throughout their careers.

Key findings

A total of 19 categories of respectful leadership were identified from the data. Each of these categories contains several specific examples of how that trait might be displayed in practice.

- According to these 19 categories, a respectful leader should, amongst other things:

- o demonstrate trust in employees;
- o grant employees autonomy;
- o confer responsibility;
- o consider employees needs;
- o acknowledge equality;
- o appreciate effort;
- o promote development;
- o be open to advice;
- o accept criticism;
- o show loyalty;
- o take interest in employees on a personal level.

- The more subordinates feel respected by their leaders, the more they will return that respect and be open to their leader's influence.
- In addition, respectful leadership also entails a message about the subordinates' autonomy, competence, and relatedness.
- These are important prerequisites for subordinates' independent and proactive reaction to changing organizational circumstances.
- Perceived respectful leadership was also related to participants' job satisfaction.

Source: CSR Research Digest, May 2010 (Vol. 2, No. 5)

2.6.13 Empirical Examination on Contextual Influences on Follower Perceptions and Reactions to Aversive Leadership

Author(s): Christian N. Thoroughgood, Samuel T. Hunter and Katina B. Sawyer

The study sought to determine the effects of an organization's climate and financial performance, as well as the leader's gender, on subordinate perceptions of and reactions (i.e., whistle-blowing intentions) to aversive leadership, a form of destructive leadership based on coercive power. 302 undergraduate participants read through a series of vignettes describing a fictional organization, its employees, and an aversive leader in charge of the company's sales department.

Key findings

Research on destructive leadership has largely focused on leader characteristics thought to be responsible for harmful organizational outcomes.

- Recent findings, however, demonstrate the need to examine important contextual factors underlying such processes.
- Consistent with Padilla and colleagues' (2007) toxic triangle theory, results suggest that both perceptions and reactions to aversive leadership depend on the three aforementioned factors.
- Specifically, aversive leaders were perceived more aversively and elicited greater whistleblowing intentions in financially unstable organizations possessing climates intolerant of negative leader behavior.
- Moreover, female aversive leaders were perceived more aversively than their male counterparts under such conditions.

Source: Governance Research Digest, Jun. 2011 (Vol. 2, No. 2)

2.6.14 The Relationship Between Being Perceived as Trustworthy by Coworkers and Individual Performance

Author(s): K.T. Dirks & D.P. Skarlicki.

In this article, the relationship between being perceived as trustworthy by one's coworkers and individual performance is examined. In the first part of the study, participants were drawn from the financial services department of a bank in Western Canada. 104 respondents comprised the final sample size. 72% of participants were women. In the second part of the study, 134 Canadian MBA students acted as participants. 66% of these were male.

Key findings

Being perceived as trustworthy by coworkers is associated with higher performance.

- Study One
  - Perceptions of a focal individual's capability and integrity interact to predict the trustee's performance. The positive relationship

between capability and performance is more pronounced when integrity is high than when it is low.

- o A similar relationship was not found between an individual's capability and their benevolence.
- o Being viewed by others as capable and benevolent can incur performance costs. It is possible that when it comes to one's own performance, the costs of benevolence can outweigh the benefits.
- Study Two
  - o Perceptions of a coworker's capability and integrity interact to predict individuals' willingness to provide resources to the coworker. The effect of the coworker's capability on the willingness to provide resources is stronger when the coworker's integrity is high versus low.
  - o Trust mediates the effect of the capability and integrity interaction on the willingness to share performance-related resources with a coworker.
  - o Being seen as trustworthy in terms of capability increased participants' willingness to share resources only when the target was also deemed high in integrity.
  - o When engaging in exchange relationships, individuals also consider whether the target person can be counted on to follow important norms, such as reciprocating benefits received (i.e., integrity).
- The results suggest that trust mediates the effect of the trustworthiness factors (capability and integrity) on individuals' willingness to provide resources to a coworker, demonstrating that trust is an underlying mechanism in this relationship.

Source: Governance Research Digest, Mar. 2009 (Vol. 1, No. 3)

2.6.15 Positive Group Context, Work Attitudes, and Organisational Misbehaviour: The Case of Withholding Job Effort

Author(s): R.E. Kidwell, S.R. Valentine

This study examines the relationships among variables such as cohesiveness, helping behaviour and peer leadership, employee job attitudes, and the likelihood of individuals' withholding on-the-job effort, a form of organizational misbehavior. 290 individuals working in various roles within the military and based in the north-east US took part in the study. 85% of participants were male.

Key findings

The more positive an individual's experience of the group context(s) in which they work, the more likely they are to experience job satisfaction, and the more effort they expect to put into their performance.

- Those with less positive experiences of work group contexts are more likely to withhold effort in the workplace.
- Those with lower satisfaction are also more likely to withhold effort.
- Individual effort-performance expectancy is negatively related to withholding effort.
- Managers who wish to impact employee job effort would do well to improve conditions that lead to positive group context and employee job satisfaction.
- For example, managers might encourage establishment of self-managed teams that would enhance positive group context through empowerment of team members and might include the establishment of peer mentoring within the team.
- Increased discussion and counseling on the linkages between job effort and job performance might be a beneficial strategy within the work group.
- Further, employees who are attempting to effectively manage their own performance should be aware that group influences, individual attitudes and their own perceptions about the relationship between effort and performance can have an impact on their actual effort levels and related job performance in current and future occupations.

Source: Social Research Digest, May 2009 (Vol. 1, No. 5)

2.6.16 The Joint Relationship of Communication Behaviours and Task Interdependence on Trust Building and Change in Virtual Project Teams

Author(s): R. Rico, C-M. Alcover, M. Sánchez-Manzanares and F. Gil.

This study examines how specific communication behaviours among team members interacted with task interdependence in relation to the building and changing of trust within 53 virtual project teams (VPTs). The findings develop extant trust theory in virtual teams, suggesting some useful guidelines to better understand and manage trust processes.

Key findings

Trust before the project mid-point is associated with task-oriented communications and, contrary to expectations, with enthusiastic communications but only when task interdependence is low.

- Trust from mid-point to project end is positively associated with predictable communication and with substantive communications when task interdependence is high.
- It is likely that organizational settings place a premium on task-oriented communication, enabling teams to perform quickly.
- In addition, task-oriented communication is a rich source of information regarding teammates' abilities.
- This information can be the main driver of initial trust formation in a team.
- The observation that task-oriented communication early on is positively related to trust later on calls attention to the importance of task-oriented communication for project teams, and the role that competence-based trust updated around competent work performance plays in trust levels over time.
- Task interdependence has not only direct but also moderating effects on the relationship between enthusiastic and substantive communications and trust at different times.
- The lack of relationship between task interdependence and trust early on can be explained by the role played by trustworthiness before the project mid-point transition.
- Further, the moderating role that task interdependence exerts over enthusiastic communication and substantive responses provides a more contingent view of the impact of task characteristics on trust in virtual project teams (VPTs).
- Overall, the findings suggest that managers should choose good specialists when forming VPTs, not only because trust is built on

taskoriented communication at the early stages but also because it is imported, and positive perceptions of others' abilities can increase trustworthiness and trust among team members.

- The findings may also be useful when training employees to work in VPTs. Just as it has been verified that an increase in ease of communication and availability of routines in the virtual context improve team performance, the importance of establishing a predictable communication pattern among team members in maintaining trust over time has been demonstrated.

Source: Social Research Digest, Aug. 2009 (Vol. 1, No. 8)

2.6.17   Transforming Work Experience into Work Inspiration

Author(s): Business in the Community

The report provides evidence of the business benefits of work experience, shares good practice and shows how different employers have overcome the challenges in offering work experience. The research is based on literature review, a survey of 192 employers and interviews of eight different organizations.

Key findings

The available literature showed how, to date, much of the research has focused on the benefits to young people.

- Far less has been done to ascertain how businesses use work experience programmes as part of their own business planning.
- This research identifies four key impact areas:
    o employee development and engagement: companies reported that their employees often benefit directly in terms of the skills they develop from managing and supporting young people on work experience;
    o diversity and talent: employers have used work Inspiration as a way of opening doors and encouraging young people from a range of different backgrounds to consider careers in their sector, for example attracting more women into engineering;

- o business development: particularly when it comes to winning public contracts, business engagement in local communities is viewed favourably by potential clients;
- o community engagement: work experience can help achieve profile – and not just with those they hope to employ in the future.

Source: Social Research Digest, Sep. 2011 (Vol. 2, No. 5)

2.7 Grievance Resolution

2.7.1 Seyfarth's Workplace Class Action Litigation Report

Author(s): Seyfarth

Seyfarth released its tenth annual edition of the Workplace Class Action Litigation Report examines the theoretical and strategic uncertainties stemming from the Supreme Court's employment law and class action rulings in 2013, and the challenges they pose for companies and their defense counsel. The 2014 Workplace Class Action Report analyzes 1,122 class action rulings on a circuit-by-circuit and state-by-state basis.

<u>Key findings</u>

The array of bet-the-company litigation issues that businesses face are evolving on a landscape that is continuing to undergo significant change.

- At the same time, governmental enforcement litigation remains "white hot" and regulatory oversight of workplace issues continues to be a priority, thereby challenging businesses to integrate their litigation and risk mitigation strategies to navigate these exposures.
- By almost any measure, 2013 was a year of evolving changes for workplace class action litigation. The U.S. Supreme Court issued several class action rulings in 2013 – in Comcast Corp. v. Behrend, 133 S. Ct. 1426 (2013), American Express Co. v. Italian Restaurant, 133 S. Ct. 2304 (2013), and Standard Fire Insurance Co. v. Knowles, 133 S. Ct. 1345 (2013) – that impacted all varieties of complex litigation in a profound manner this past year.
- More than any other development in 2013, the decision in Wal-Mart Stores, Inc. v. Dukes, 131 S. Ct. 2541 (2011), continued to have a wide-

ranging impact on virtually all types of class actions pending in both federal and state courts throughout the country.

- In many respects, Wal-Mart was the "800 pound gorilla" in courtrooms in 2013 as litigants argued and judges analyzed class certification issues. Rule 23 decisions in 2013 in large part pivoted off of Wal-Mart, and leverage points in class action litigation increased or decreased depending on the manner in which judges interpreted and applied Wal-Mart. Furthermore, Comcast Corp. fueled defense arguments by undermining attacks on class certification in a wide range of contexts, which were met with mixed success for employers.

- This year's ruling in Comcast Corp. also added a new weapon to employers' arsenals in challenging class certification. The Supreme Court interpreted Rule 23(b)(3) – which requires "questions of law or fact common to class members predominate over any questions affecting only individual members" – to mandate that a class' proposed damages model show damages on a class-wide basis. This decision provides companies with a significant and rational defense to class certification in class actions. Much like Wal-Mart, the decision in Comcast Corp. reverberated throughout the lower federal and state courts, and was cited a total of 178 times by the close of the year, a rather remarkable figure for a decision rendered in March of 2013.

- Against this backdrop, the plaintiffs' class action employment bar filed and prosecuted significant class action and collective action lawsuits against employers in 2013. In turn, employers litigated an increasing number of novel defenses to these class action theories, fueled, in part, by the new standards enunciated in Wal-Mart and Comcast Corp.

Source: Governance Research Digest, Jun. 2014 (Vol. 5, No. 6)

III. CONSUMER-ORIENTED CSR COMMUNICATION

3.1 CSR Advertising

3.1.1 The Advertising Effects of Corporate Social Responsibility on Corporate Reputation and Brand Equity: Evidence from the Life Insurance Industry in Taiwan

Author(s): K-T. Hsu

This study investigates the persuasive advertising and informative advertising effects of CSR initiatives on corporate reputation and brand equity. It is based on the evidence from the life insurance industry in Taiwan.

Key findings

Policyholders' perceptions concerning the CSR initiatives of life insurance companies have positive effects on customer satisfaction, corporate reputation, and brand equity.

- The advertising effects of the CSR initiatives on corporate reputation are only informative.
- The impacts of CSR initiatives on brand equity include informative advertising and persuasive advertising effects.
- This study contributes the literature by explicit defining the advertising effects of CSR initiatives.
- Following the first step made by McWilliams et al. (Journal of Management Studies 43(1):1–18, 2006), the hypotheses of this study crystallize their conceptual framework.
- The obtained results in this research first identify the informative advertising effects and persuasive advertising effects of CSR initiatives.

Source: CSR Research Digest, Sep. 2012 (Vol. 4, No. 9)

3.1.2 Profitable Growth Strategies for the Global Emerging Middle: Learning from the 'Next 4 Billion' Markets

Author(s): PwC

A new PwC study outlines the emerging class of citizens and consumers defining a critical growth horizon for companies over the coming decade. The report focuses on strategies adopted by leaders who have tried to grow profitably in this global emerging market.

<u>Key findings</u>

Globally, businesses are looking at the "Next 4 Billion" for growth, especially now, given the slowdown in mature economics.

- Businesses functioning in this group (which includes India, China, Indonesia parts of Africa and Latin America where over 4 billion of the world's 7 billion reside) have traditionally focused on the middle and upper middle income tiers.
- That the next big wave of business opportunity will come from the Global Emerging Middle (GEM), which lies just below the middle income segment and above the low income segment.
- GEM will represent a combined annual market, globally, in excess of USD 6 trillion by 2021.
- In India alone, this market is expected to cross the USD 1 trillion threshold by 2021.
- For companies seeking to succeed in this challenging environment, their strategy should consider three important vectors.
  - o Value proposition. Aspiration trade-offs: Understand the very different aspirations, influencers, and tradeoffs of this segment.
  - o Beyond low cost: Position product and services beyond cost, pricing beyond functional considerations.
  - o Platform Customisation: Design product and services with a few key features, but tailoring it for diversity
- Innovative business models
  - o Ecosystem Collaboration: Extract value by creating an ecosystem, collaborate with the unorganised sector.
  - o Modular scale: Have a modular design, aggregate local demand and think scale from the beginning.

- o Smart reach: Cluster marketing and distribution, create local financing mechanism, enable through technology and offline.
- Shift in mindset
  - o Trusted endorsements: Build the brand with aspiration in mind, but using word of mouth to drive awareness.
  - o Disruptive thinking: Seek Disruptive change in addressing this market often with leapfrog solutions.
  - o Values and metrics: Drive this business with broader values and incubate it with different metrics.

Source: Social Research Digest, Mar. 2012 (Vol. 3, No. 3)

3.1.3   The Marketing Mix

Author(s): G. Hastings

This paper questions the role of corporate marketing in society and suggests ways of combating it. The problems outlined in the article are urgent and the style is polemical.

Key findings

Social marketers have to take heed of and address marketing's failures if our discipline is to be taken seriously in debates about health, welfare and sustainability.

- In the hands of the corporate sector, marketing is turning us into spoilt, consumption-obsessed children who are simultaneously wrecking our bodies, psyches and planet.
- The fiduciary duty of the corporation, which demands a single-minded focus on shareholder value, turns concepts like consumer sovereignty, customer service and relationship marketing into corrosive myths that seduce us into quiescence, whilst furnishing big business with unprecedented power.
- CSR, meanwhile, is just a means of currying favour with our political leaders and further extending corporate power.
- Critical analysis is vital: if we do not want to become the apologists for corporate capitalism we have to research, write and teach about its failings as well as social marketing's potential to do good.

- As individuals we have enormous internal strength; collectively we have, and can again, change the world.
- Indeed marketing itself is a function of humankind's capacity to cooperate to overcome difficulties and long predates its cooption by corporations.
- In the hands of social marketers this potential force for good is being codified and deployed.
- If these talents and strengths can be combined with serious moves to contain the corporate sector, it is possible to rethink our economic and social priorities

Source: Social Research Digest, Aug. 2012 (Vol. 3, No. 8)

3.1.4 Consumer-Oriented CSR Communication: Focusing on Ability or Morality

Author(s): L. Schmeltz

The article aims to investigate young people's opinions and attitudes towards companies' engagement and communication about corporate social responsibility (CSR). The findings are based on responses from 82 Danish students, ages 18 to 30.

Key findings

The majority of respondents think it is important that companies engage in CSR, but they are not aware that companies actually do so.

- They want more CSR information than they are currently getting, but are not willing to actively seek it out.
- Respondents attach more importance to what is closest to them either physically or personally (environment, employees and local community vs. natural disasters and people from other countries).
- For companies to engage with consumers through CSR communication, they should clearly illustrate why particular CSR efforts are of importance to the consumers, and communicate this through multiple channels.
- Respondents primarily notice CSR communication on packaging, on television, and on websites.

- When asked why companies engage in CSR, 70% of consumers believe that companies do so to gain profits; 91% think it is to improve corporate image, 76% believe it is done to increase competitive advantage, 55% think companies do so for moral reasons.
- Rather than being skeptical about explicit communications, respondents say that CSR increases corporate credibility, and that the longer companies have been engaging in CSR, the more credible they are.
- Even when consumers think that companies are engaging in CSR for selfish reasons, the overall evaluation of such activities is positive.
- Rather than associating CSR with morals and ethics, young consumers may see it as a matter of corporate competence.
- A concern with morality thus seems to be exceeded by a concern with ability.

Source: Social Research Digest, Nov. 2012 (Vol. 3, No. 11)

3.1.5   Putting Purpose into Marketing

Author(s): *World Federation of Advertisers (WFA)*

This research identifies the extent to which marketers believe that consumer decisionmaking is driven by a brand's corporate responsibility efforts, as well as gaps and business opportunities. This research was presented as part of the Global Marketer Conference in Brussels and relies on survey responses from 149 senior marketers representing 58 companies.

Key findings

Marketers underestimate consumer interest in CSR and that there is clearly a dissonance between consumers and marketers when it comes to their perceptions of "purpose" and how it acts as a driver of purchase decisions.

- Consumers and marketers agree that "purpose" is defined as "protecting and improving the environment," "positively impacting local communities" and "having ethical business practices."
- However, marketers underestimate emerging consumers concern and failed to identify the markets where consumers are most driven by brand purpose.

- There is consensus among marketers the increasing significance of purpose: 88% agreed or strongly agreed it would be "increasingly important to building brands."
- Edelman's consumer data reveals that marketers seem to underestimate the extent support good causes (46% of marketers said consumers support good causes v. 60% consumers).
- Importantly, the biggest polarization in responses was marketer's perceptions of which region's consumers are most motivated by purpose.
- The continent with the greatest proportion of consumers who say they make purchase decisions based on good causes, 58% of marketers chose Europe, 36%.
- Edelman's research reveals the consumers in China, India, Indonesia, Malaysia, UAE and Brazil as being the most purpose-driven.
- The results demonstrate that consumers' passion and action on the part of a company's
- CSR efforts in these emerging markets is much stronger than in developed markets
- When asked to pick a purpose leader out of the Ad Age top 20 global marketers, 23% of respondents chose Unilever, Coca-Cola and P&G received 16% each, and McDonald's came in fourth with 11%.

Source: Social Research Digest, Mar. 2013 (Vol. 4, No. 3)

3.1.6   The Social Brands 100 – The FCMG Ranking

Author(s): Headstream

Headstream issued its leading benchmark for performance in social spaces, identifying the dominant FMCG brands and providing a snapshot of social media's evolution each year. The report aims to: 1) identify which of the top grossing FMCG brands are creating relevant content that engages their consumers; 2) look at how these brands are using social media to create deeper relationships with their fans and followers; and 3) compare which brands are performing well in this sector, looking at the strengths and weaknesses of the top and lowest performing brands.

Key findings

When comparing each of the brands positions within the two rankings, only one brand – Pepsi MAX, consistently appeared in the top ten for both.

- Exploring further we can see that there is in fact little correlation between a brand's ranking in the best-sellers list with their ranking in terms of engagement, and often the two seem quite estranged from one another. This can be seen through half of the brands in the top ten in Social Brands 100 rank within the bottom 25% of the best-sellers list.
- IRN-BRU have come out top of the ranking with the highest combined engagement score, whereas global powerhouse brands such as Coca-Cola and Red Bull have fared less well. There is a lesson to be learnt here in the fact that although a brand may have a massive community size (Coca-Cola and Red Bull boasting 85 and 44 million respectively), this just means they need to proportionally work harder to engage larger volumes.
- Facebook.
  - Notably 53% of the brand Facebook pages, and six of the top ten brands included in the ranking have less than 250k followers.
  - The average page engagement rates tend to decrease as the community size (total page likes) increases. However there is an exception to this as the 1M – 2M bracket has the third highest engagement rate. The brands in this bracket are Pepsi MAX, Maltesers, Evian, Heinz Ketchup and Capri Sun.
  - The ranking shows the average engagement rate on Facebook to be 0.169%. Despite this being an average, it is notable to mention that the majority of brands (66%) scored an engagement rate of below 0.1%, meaning the brands at the top of the ranking were creating well-received content.
  - Interestingly, the top two spots on Facebook were snapped up by pet food brands, and more specifically cat food with the likes of Whiskas (the brand ranked the highest on Facebook) and Felix. Behind them followed IRN-BRU, Clover and Surf.
- Twitter
  - Engagement rates were found to be lower on Twitter than Facebook.
  - Community sizes were smaller too, with only 4% exceeding 200k

followers and the majority of all brands (73%) having feeds with less than 20k followers.

- o The data suggests that engagement rates on Twitter do not tend to decrease as the total number of followers increases; as they do on Facebook.
- o Once a community surpasses 5k followers, engagement rates drop considerably suggesting this is the optimal size community for Twitter. The noticeable exception to this trend is the 50k – 100k bracket which has the second highest engagement rate.
- o The top performing brands on this platform were Fanta, followed by Snickers, Capri Sun, Heinz and HARIBO.

Source: Governance Research Digest, Oct. 2014 (Vol. 5, No. 10)

3.2 Cause-Related Marketing

3.2.1 A Strategy to Communicate CSR: Cause Related Marketing and its Dark Side

Author(s): I. Baghi, E. Rubaltelli, M. Tedeschi.

This study investigates the effect of vivid communications messages on cause related marketing (CRM) strategy. 730 students participated in the two experiments that form the empirical findings of this study.

Key findings

Corporate social responsibility may be promoted through cause related marketing activities that describe the extent to which the brand and the products of a company are consistent with the values and expectations of the public.

- If a charitable cause is described in vivid terms, then:
  - o it should induce people to choose products associated with it rather than products associated with pallid descriptions of the same charitable cause;
  - o it should induce people to pay more for products associated with it rather than products associated with pallid descriptions of the same charitable cause;

- o   it should induce participants to judge products associated with it as widely preferred among other people.
- If a marketing message is described using more details than a second message, then participants rate it as more vivid and specific.
- In addition, if people perceive the vivid message as more specific and concrete then they gain a clearer mental image of the charitable cause than people presented with a pallid message.
- If vivid and more detailed information helps people to create a better mental image of the event then their emotional involvement with the charitable project should be higher than that of people presented with the pallid message.
- If a product is associated with a charitable cause perceived as more vivid, then participants are more confident about the effective use of the money collected by selling this product rather than the 'pallid' one.
- Participants were willing to pay significantly higher prices for 'vivid products' than for 'pallid products'.
- Vividness could increase the money raised in favour of a socially responsible activity and enlarge, at the same time, the product market shares.
- Such evidence is consistent with more and more global enterprises associating their products with some sort of charitable cause.
- The study also showed a 'dark side' of CRM, since people seemed to trust more the use of money raised by selling 'vivid products' compared with 'pallid' ones, even if no information about the concrete use of the donations was provided.
- Such ease of influencing people's perception of the effective use of a donation raises several ethical concerns.
- In their striving for more and more profits many companies might not respect consumers' rights and try to take advantage of their willingness to support important socially responsible projects.

Source: CSR Research Digest, Apr. 2009 (Vol. 1, No. 4)

3.2.2   New Media is Revolutionizing Cause: Are You Ready?

Author(s): Cone

Cone offers insights how the new media is changing the way we do cause marketing today. Organizations are successfully using new technologies to promote their products and services, but the opportunity is equally as ripe to market the cause.

Key findings

Experimenting with everything from geolocation technology to QR codes, organizations are using then to raise funds, drive engagement and spur action.

- Most organizations, including REI and Southwest Airlines, have been experimenting with geolocation as a way to raise funds for nonprofit organizations.
- For each user check-in at a designated location, these companies are making a small donation to the nonprofits they support.
- Progressive organizations are also using geolocation to drive activism and action, including Marc Ecko's "Unlimited Justice" foursquare campaign to end corporal punishment in America's schools and MTV's partnership with foursquare to create the first cause related check-in badge, which encourages teens to get tested for STDs.
- Social media platforms bring you into the lives of your consumers and supporters, fostering conversation and advocacy around your cause.
- The ease and immediacy of social media mean you can easily adapt and evolve your communications and activities to align with changing consumer interests and current events.
- The 2010 earthquake in Haiti is testament to the power of mobile giving, but since then, some organizations have employed mobile giving on a smaller scale with great success.
- The "I Am Here" campaign raised enough to purchase a home for a homeless man in Austin, Texas after putting the man himself on a billboard, encouraging passing cars to text a donation.
- Functional, free and flexible, QR (quick response) codes are giving new meaning to "look behind the label."
- They can enhance transparency, such as a Boston nonprofit linking a QR code to question-and-answer site Quora, or tell stories, such as the tales of items donated to an Oxfam store in the U.K.

Source: Social Research Digest, Jul. 2011 (Vol. 2, No. 3)

3.2.3 Top Provider Rankings – PR, Communications and Advertising

Author(s): Corporate Responsibility Magazine

Corporate Responsibility Magazine has launched the ranking of top providers of cause marketing solutions. The list evaluates firms against their peers based on customer feedback and rates their ability to provide a diverse range of high quality counsel.

Key findings

CR Magazine surveyed more than 10 firms but only eight made the final list.

- The top listing:
    - Singer Associates
    - Cause Consulting
    - Green Impact
    - MSL Group
    - For Momentum
    - Cone
    - Ogilvy PR
    - Edelman

Source: CSR Research Digest, Apr. 2012 (Vol. 4, No. 4)

3.3 Green PR

3.3.1 Green Quadrant Sustainable Communications US 2010

Author(s): Verdantix

The Verdantix report, "Green Quadrant Sustainable Communications US 2010," studies the market of sustainability communications agencies. The study compares 18 U.S. agencies offering sustainability communications advice on 41 criteria.

Key findings

The four-month study shows a gap between the needs of Fortune 500 firms to communicate sustainability performance to business and consumer audiences and the lack of ideas, strategies and frameworks offered by most of the agencies in the study.

- Cone and OgilvyEarth lead the sustainability communications market due to a clear sustainability vision supported by processes and methodologies specifically designed to address sustainability communications challenges.
- They go beyond promoting current initiatives and create brand platforms that are catalysts for change.
- The study also indicates that investment could drive four agencies — Cohn & Wolfe, Context America, Edelman and Ketchum — ahead in 2011.
- The study shows that these agencies demonstrate a strong sustainable business perspective and investment in their sustainability practice.
- However, the Green Quadrant scores for these four agencies' capabilities are significantly below Cone and OgilvyEarth in a variety of different criteria.
- Edelman scores lower on the sustainability readiness assessment and in communicating sustainability to investors.
- Ketchum has lower scores in communicating sustainability to employees and in defining the sustainability- brand connection.
- The study suggests that all agencies should demonstrate they can "walk the walk" as well as "talk the talk" on sustainability by implementing innovative, transparent and authentic sustainability communications strategies that connect with their brands.
- The research analysts also recommend that chief sustainability officers and brand directors must select their agencies based on their expertise, and not on their brand presence or global scale.
- They should also develop "rigorous" selection criteria for choosing their marketing agencies.

Source: CSR Research Digest, Oct. 2010 (Vol. 2, No. 10)

3.3.2 Green Marketing Study

Author(s): EnviroMedia

A study by EnviroMedia highlights American consumers' preferences for a single comprehensive seal for green products over the hundreds now that are causing confusion. EnviroMedia commissioned Opinion Research Corporation (ORC) to conduct a national survey of 1,022 Americans.

<u>Key findings</u>

Hundreds of green seals of approval are confusing customers, according to a survey.

- 65% said having just one environmental label would give them more confidence that they were buying green.
- Four out of ten said a third-party program, such as the Good Housekeeping Seal, should enforce green product claims.
- Another 26% thought this should be the job of the Federal Trade Commission (FTC), while only 16% thought the advertising industry should police itself.
- The survey also showed confusion about energy sources.
- A quarter of those surveyed thought coal was a renewable energy source, and another 15% said they don't know.
- EnviroMedia said it's increasingly hard to determine if a product is really environmentally friendly.
- There are more than 350 labels or seals of approval that offer to help consumers know whether a product is green or healthy, which is classic information overload for the consumer's brain.
- Having one comprehensive national seal to identify the best green products would limit consumer confusion and also hold advertisers accountable to one set of standards.

Source: CSR Research Digest, Jan. 2011 (Vol. 3, No. 1)

3.3.3 Corporate Social Responsibility and Green PR Guidebook

Author(s): PR News

PR News' Guidebook is an invaluable resource for communications, PR and marketing professionals in any organisation – offering advice on CSR communications to diverse stakeholders and across different digital and off-line channels. It is packed with insights, case studies and tactics from the top CSR experts in the PR arena.

Key findings

Building, maintaining and communicating a reputation of good corporate citizenship is not just good business—it's a key to survival as the world economy grinds its way back to stability.

- Demonstrating good corporate citizenship is increasingly an integral part of building, maintaining and communicating a company's reputation.
- At the same time, the current economic climate illustrates how quickly a company's reputation can be damaged.
- The Guidebook describes how to link CSR and sustainability programmes to business goals, corporate strategies and brand messages.
- The book also provides advice on preparing communications to internal and external stakeholders as well as CSR reports and case studies.

Source: CSR Research Digest, Jul. 2012 (Vol. 4, No. 7)

3.3.4 Rethinking Sustainability: Brand Risks and Opportunities

Author(s): Verdantix

Verdantix conducted an analysis of how 80 firms link sustainability with corporate branding. The "Rethinking Sustainability: Brand Risks and Opportunities" report helps executives responsible for sustainability communications, and their colleagues across communications, marketing and sustainability teams to understand the different strategic approaches, the risks and opportunities, and the business case for enhancing communications to support the corporate brand.

Key findings

Failure to integrate sustainability in corporate brands prevents companies from driving revenue growth or reaping any business benefits from their efforts.

- The report identifies five strategies: Purists, Explorers, Advocates, Reactionists and Nothingists.
  1. For Purists Sustainability Is Synonymous With The Corporate Brand

2. For Explorers Sustainability Is Integrated Into The Corporate Brand
3. For Advocates Sustainability Communications Are Managed In A Silo
4. For Reactionists Sustainability Communications Are A Crisis Management Activity
5. For Nothingists Sustainability Is Off The Communications Agenda

- The majority of firms are categorized as advocates, a strategy where companies actively communicate on sustainability issues, but keep these separate from the corporate brand and push them out to a limited audience.
- Despite pressure to do more, spending for sustainability communications is typically flat.
- Companies are often stuck on using traditional CSR communication strategies focused on reports, ratings and not-for-profits.
- Chief marketing officers can add strategic value by integrating the company's sustainability ethic and messages into the corporate brand, an approach that will lead to revenue growth.
- CMOs need to take charge of sustainability communications in order to reap brand benefits. Once CMOs assess their current sustainability communications strategy and determine what their company spends in this area, they should benchmark their approach versus industry leaders.
- CMOs should collaborate closely with management responsible for sustainability within the company to devise a strategic approach and then craft future-looking messaging to avoid greenwash accusations.

Source: CSR Research Digest, May 2013 (Vol. 5, No. 5)

3.3.5 The Myth of the Sleeping Giant: Why Latinos are the Fastest Growing Segment the Sustainability Industry has (N)ever Seen

Author(s): Saatchi & Saatchi

A report by the advertising firm Saatchi & Saatchi sheds some light in the untapped opportunities of sustainability marketing for the Latino community. The report aims to spark dialogue within companies and inspire them to develop effective strategies and communications to engage Latinos in their corporate sustainability efforts.

<u>Key findings</u>

Latinos are the fastest-growing demographic in the nation, yet few companies are reaching out to this group in their sustainability initiatives.

- "The vast majority" of US companies – even those who are spending serious dollars to connect with Latinos – are not messaging to this audience about environmental sustainability.
- A series of myths exist in the sustainability community as to why this "sleeping giant" should not be targeted.
- The first myth is that Latinos are not environmentalists.
- In reality, "deep-rooted cultural connections and health reasons" give rise to an innate support of environmental conservation and stewardship among Latinos.
- Other myths include thinking that Latinos don't want to buy green – but, in fact, that demographic tends to be more loyal to brands that contribute positively to their communities and the environment.
- However, despite these misconceptions, there are a number of companies that have successfully targeted the Latino community with sustainability initiatives.
- NBCUniversal's Green is Universal campaign is a good example, which, for one week each year, invites viewers to learn about green issues by integrating such themes into its programming, runs across most of the company's channels including Spanishlanguage
- Telemundo and mun2, the bilingual cable network that targets young Latinos.
- General Mills' Qué Rica Vida campaign, which promotes healthy eating and living to Latinos by embracing culinary affinities and providing recipes, health tips and deals on General Mills products, is another good example of a welltargeted and successful campaign.

Source: Social Research Digest, Dec. 2012 (Vol. 3, No. 12)

3.4 Fair Trade

3.4.1 Fair Trade Rooibos Tea: Connecting South African Producers and American Consumer Markets

Author(s): L.T. Raynolds, S. Unathi Ngcwangu

This article analyses the recent growth and configuration of Fair Trade networks connecting South African Rooibos tea producers with American consumer markets. Fair Trade's growth in the Rooibos tea sector engages key national policy concerns related to black empowerment, land reform and sustainable development. This study identifies the key variations in Fair Trade buyers and their purchasing arrangements which shape the opportunities for small-scale black South African tea producers.

<u>Key findings</u>

In support of previous research, the findings demonstrate that buyers driver supplier relations but do so in different ways, depending on their structure and how they work with NGOs and government agencies.

- Resources accessed through Fair Trade networks may be used to increase small farmers' control over value-added activities, in this example, through co-operative owned post-harvest processing facilities and a packaging plant.
- As such, upgrading production techniques may represent a critical avenue for farmers to better their conditions.
- In addition to the economic returns from upgrading, the authors argue that extending producer control from field to shelf-ready product represents a key form of empowerment, strengthening producer capacity and bargaining power in international markets.
- Small-scale Rooibos producer gains are being threatened by rising competition in Fair Trade markets from large estates with questionable social justice credentials.
- There is mounting evidence to suggest that some of the share-equity schemes used by these competitors are not significantly improving black worker ownership or control of rural enterprises.
- Rooibos co-operatives are able to actively represent themselves via websites, in media forums and through a new Trust Organic Small

Farmers Alliance (TOSFA) seal, thus helping them to retain some control over symbolic as well as material production.

- At the same time, market-driven Rooibos distributors pursue conventional sourcing strategies, purchasing bulk tea through export brokers that is produced mostly on large South African estates.

- In these cases, Fair Trade networks do not fundamentally transform international relations, but largely reproduce traditional inequalities which concentrate control and profits in the hands of American buyers and allied South African exporters.

- While the findings of this study echo concerns raised in previous studies that Fair Trade mainstreaming is working to undermine the movements' transformative potential, the case of small-scale Fair Trade Rooibos networks suggests that more radical Fair Trade ventures animated by strong social and place-based commitments are being devised.

- For Fair Trade to maintain its transformative potential these more radical initiatives must open up opportunities for producers to integrate up the commodity circuit, shortening the distance between producers and consumers.

Source: CSR Research Digest, Feb. 2010 (Vol. 2, No. 2)

3.4.2 The Rise and Stall of a Fair Trade Pioneer: The Cafédirect Story

Author(s): I.A. Davies, B. Doherty, S. Knox.

This case study investigates the rise of Cafédirect as a Fair Trade pioneer. The authors develop strategic insights into how the company has used its ethical positioning to attain a prominent position in the mainstream coffee industry in the UK. The authors also acknowledge the slowdown in the company's growth and ask whether it can regain its former momentum with its current marketing strategy. The data that informs this paper is based on two longitudinal studies conducted between 1999-2004 and 1999 2009.

Key findings

Through the use of networks and the ways in which the company leverages its fair trade status, Cafédirect demonstrates creativity and ingenuity which can be generally characterised as an aggressive, market-orientated approach.

- At the same time, the company also presents a microcosm of the issues surrounding ethical brand management.
- Early on, Cafédirect could only rely on core product ethics (being fairtrade) and ethical messages to deliver a very limited market share.
- Product quality and corporate identity, combined with strong distribution and consumer awareness, have proved more important in achieving a greater market share and sales growth. Cafédirect has had to adapt its business model and core messaging to re ect this.
- Cafédirect's structures and processes for selling its products are similar to any other mainstream consumer business. Nevertheless, its ownership and engagement with supply chain development issues suggest that its claim to be the authentic voice for subsistence growers remains strong.
- The company is now competing against other organisations within the fair trade movement. If the coffee market follows that for chocolate, where brand leaders (such as Cadbury's) convert their mainstream brands to fair trade, this may force Cafédirect to adopt a defensive strategy to help protect its brand and revenues.
- Cafédirect does not directly license its products to other organisations for own-label production. It does, however, provide the opportunity for organisations in its network partnership to gain reputational bene ts whilst contributing very little to the movement.
- Ultimately, Cafédirect is one of the companies that set the standards for what fair trade has become. This case demonstrates that if the movement wishes to have a large market presence, it has to embrace a mainstream approach.
- Fair trade has gravitated towards being heavily brand-orientated in competitive market segments which effectively negate the notion of being a united movement.
- Within these segments, brands must fight for market position which means there may well be limits to size. As soon as the market segment becomes big and pro table enough, large commercial brands can quickly enter and draw a larger share of that market.

- The nal challenge raised in this case is whether consumers can variously differentiate between not only competing ethical claims (i.e. the new ethical labels) but also the number of claims that they can willingly process. A show of unity in fair trade messaging would help to ensure its survival as a distinct product offering.

Source: Governance Research Digest, Sep. 2009 (Vol. 1, No. 9)

3.4.3 Organizational Leadership, Ethics and the Challenges of Marketing Fair and Ethical Trade

Author(s): W. Low, E. Davenport

This article critically evaluates current developments in marketing fair trade-labelled products and "no sweat" manufactured goods. Specifically, the authors look at the concept of mission-driven organizations pursuing leadership roles in developing affinity relationships to promote fair and ethical trade and developing ethical spaces.

Key findings

The authors argue that both the fair trade and ethical trade movements increasingly rely on strategies for bottom-up change, converting consumers "one cup at a time".

- In response to the question, "What sort of organization do we want to be?" a range of organizations are responding to this question by restructuring their operations so that their mission is reflected in ethical practices throughout their operations, including product sourcing and product sales.
- Values-driven Businesses may willingly engage in selling the product and the message of fair trade, mainstream businesses are much more likely to be worried about their own market share than they are about promoting the transformative message about international trade reform".
- With respect to the fair trade movement, that an "Alternative High Street" is needed to counter corporate appropriation of the convenient elements of the movement and the
- "Clean-washing" of its transformational message in order to create a valuable market niche.

- A variation on the idea of "affinity marketing" is proposed as the means to grow ethical consumption. Affinity marketing refers to "a unique exchange process, in which value-expressive products and services are marketed to Author(s) groups with cohesiveness, common interests, and/or values, usually in return for the group's endorsement, as marketing leverage to its individual members of constituency."

- Thus, affinity marketing involves "customers who already have sympathy to one brand (be it commercial, not-for-profit or another membership organization) being sold another service, by another organization, with the endorsement of the affinity organization and using its channels of communication."

- The critical feature of affinity marketing is that "products or services are targeted at an identifiable group of consumers who have an emotional or psychological bond with a particular cause or organization"

- The authors suggest that the fair trade and ethical trade movements can use this strategy to build business-to-business (B2B) affinity relationships that take us out of the realm of individualized shopping for a better world and into a sphere of mission-led policy and practice.

- The scale of public sector spending means that public organizations offer many prospects for developing affinity marketing relationships with fair and ethical trade organizations.

- A major challenge facing efforts to expand on ethical spaces through affinity relationships in public and non-profit sectors is an ingrained culture of financial management that adheres to a narrow concept of "value-for-money".

Source: Social Research Digest, Jun. 2009 (Vol. 1, No. 6)

3.4.4 Britain's Bruising Banana Wars: Why cheap bananas threaten farmers' futures

Author(s): Fair Trade Foundation (DTTL)

The Fairtrade Foundation published a report that exposes the real impact British supermarket price wars are having on banana farmers and workers and their families. The report, Britain's Bruising Banana Wars seeks to analyse the functioning of UK banana supply chain and "assess how far a falling retail price translates in problems for producers".

Key findings

In the UK, seven large retailers control over 80% of all banana sales. Some retailers maintain that there is no direct relationship between the costs they incur in procuring bananas and the price they charge consumers. However, the Fairtrade Foundation asserts that there is "a clear long-term correlation between retail prices and prices paid in banana producing countries". This is based on an assessment of the average import prices of bananas, taking into account inflation.

- The Fairtrade Foundation research in the report shows that "the declining value of the export price combined with increases in living costs has made it hard for workers to achieve progress in earnings." In addition, the research shows that "small farmers are under pressure to match the prices paid to large plantations". It states that "average prices in countries that supply Britain's banana market are failing to keep pace with the costs of sustainable production," and that "the pressure on price has driven a trend towards... the marginalisation of smallholder producers."

- The report maintains that the Fairtrade minimum price (i.e. the price below which prices should never fall) is commonly taken as a market Author(s) price rather than the absolute minimum price that it was intended to be. According to the Fairtrade Foundation, "the pressure to reduce prices... means that no one in the supply chain – retailers, banana companies or growers – [is] able to adequately reinvest profits in improving the sustainability of the banana industry."

- As a result of these findings, the Fairtrade Foundation calls on retailers to:
  o "take their ethical responsibilities seriously", resist pressure to "drive down prices at all costs" and make a commitment to pay a fair price for bananas that covers the costs of sustainable production;
  o adopt policies to ensure a place for smallholder farmers' production on UK banana markets.

Source: Social Research Digest, Aug. 2014 (Vol. 5, No. 8)

3.5 Labelling

3.5.1 Cereal Crimes: How "Natural" Claims Deceive Consumers and Undermine the Organic Label

Author(s): Cornucopia Institute

The non-profit Cornucopia Institute addressed the issue of abusive marketing where companies label cereals as natural even though the foods contain "toxic agrichemicals" and genetically modified organisms. The non-profit also published a scorecard of breakfast cereals and granola brands, which it said would help consumers make informed grocery purchases.

Key findings

Kellogg's, PepsiCo and Whole Foods were accused by Cornucopia Institute to label cereals as natural.

- No government agency or certification group has defined what foods companies may label as "natural".
- In contrast, to display the USDA's "certified organic" label, foods must be produced without the use of petrochemical-based fertilizers, sewage sludge, synthetic toxic pesticides and genetically modified crops.
- The report charges that agribusinesses are trying to create the "illusion of equivalence" between the natural and organic labels, to intentionally mislead customers.
- This marketing move takes advantage of customer confusion, because many consumers do not understand the difference between the two terms.
- Some companies built customer loyalty as organic brands, but later switched to nonorganic ingredients and called themselves "natural".
- Cornucopia says "natural" products commonly use organophosphate pesticides, which it says have been proven harmful to humans.
- And it says that "natural" cereals from brands including Kashi (Kellogg's), Mother's (PepsiCo), Nutritious Living, Barbara's Bakery (Weetabix), and 365 (Whole Foods Market) contain at least 28% genetically-modified ingredients.
- Many of these companies present their products as "non-GMO".

Source: Environmental Research Digest, Nov. 2011 (Vol. 2, No. 7)

3.5.2   Eco-Labels Study

Author(s): International Institute for Management Development and Ecole Polytechnique de Lausanne

Joint research by IMD, the International Institute for Management Development, and EPFL, the Ecole Polytechnique de Lausanne, addresses the overwhelming ecolabels issue. Researchers surveyed more than 1,000 executives around the globe about their attitudes towards ecolabels.

<u>Key findings</u>

The practice of eco-labelling may be on the brink of saturation point and is becoming as confusing for companies as it is for consumers.

- Process has become so fragmented that the current industry perception is dominated by wide-ranging reappraisal.
- The trend towards fragmentation, which is made worse by a lack of consensus over qualifying criteria, is clearly causing ever more opposition and frustration.
- Major international companies such as Hewlett-Packard, Nestlé, Canon, Sara Lee and E.ON took part in the study, which first sought to investigate why firms adopt eco-labels.
- Respondents listed brand-strengthening, addressing consumers' sustainability demands and protecting against pressure-group attacks as key benefits of the practice.
- But they also expressed what the study called "substantial scepticism" over eco-labels' enduring credibility and the rigour of the criteria and certification procedures.
- The research found continuing fragmentation, consumer confusion and lack of consensus on qualifying criteria are viewed as the greatest challenges to hopes of eco-labelling continuing in its current form.
- The findings highlight a desire for improved consolidation and standardization as industry adoption of eco-labelling moves towards "saturation."
- Integration across whole supply chains would help the necessary shift enormously.

- Of course, as with new technologies, it would take time for a smaller number of more focused eco-labels to earn pre-eminence and secure large-scale adoption.
- But the bottom line – and the prevailing perception – is that right now there are just too many.
- In addition, there is plainly a nagging suspicion among firms that a worrying number of ecolabel providers launch with honourable intent but soon morph into organisations whose overriding desire is to survive rather than serve.
- This raises serious concerns about eco-labels' effectiveness in delivering real outcomes and their potential to help achieve genuine market transformation.

Source: Environmental Research Digest, Aug. 2012 (Vol. 3, No. 8)

3.5.3   GM Labelling Report

Author(s): Food Standards Agency

UK Food Standards Agency conducted a study that examines UK public views towards the labelling of GM on foods and the options for labelling food as GM-Free. The 'GM Labelling: Exploring public responses to the labelling of GM food and the use of GM-free labelling' report contains both quantitative and qualitative findings which are intended to demonstrate and describe the range of existent views on the topic and the linkages between these, rather than to measure their extent across the population at large.

<u>Key findings</u>

Although there was low or no awareness of current GM labeling requirements, there was a strong assumption that products containing GM would be regulated and labeled.

- This assumption tended to extend to only GM ingredients, as there was typically no awareness of the use of GM animal feed or GMOs used in food production.
- For those with less established opinions, or those lacking understanding, providing information about potential benefits and

drawbacks of GM often lessened initial negativity and assumptions regarding GM foods.

- Although a range of knowledge existed, GM technology still tends to feel new and unknown, with attitudes towards it being fairly undeveloped and knowledge levels quite low overall.
- Opinions towards GM tend to be based on more general attitudes towards „food technology" rather than based on specific knowledge of GM foods.
- This raised negative assumptions or concerns about the use of GM food – for example, that it is of lower quality or could impact on health.
- Without prompting GM information is not a strong need.
- However, when the topic of GM is raised, for example when discussed in the research sessions, GM information is seen as important in order to give consumers the right to choose.

Source: Environmental Research Digest, Jul. 2013 (Vol. 4, No. 7)

3.5.4   US Food Date Labeling Report

Author(s): The Natural Resources Defence Council (NRDC) and the Harvard Food Law & Policy Clinic

The Natural Resources Defence Council (NRDC) and the Harvard Food Law & Policy Clinic released a report that examines the historical incentive for placing dates on foodindicating product's freshness- and the ways in which the system has failed to meet this goal. "The Dating Game: How Confusing Food Labels Lead to Food waste in America" provides a legal analysis of the federal and the state laws related to date labels across all 50 states and gives recommendations for a new system for food date labelling.

Key findings

The misinterpretation of the date labels on foods is a key factor leading to food waste.

- Wasted foods cost consumers and industry money; squanders natural resources that are used to grow, process, distribute, and store America's good supply and represents missed opportunity to feed the millions of food insecure households that are struggling to access health, affordable food.

- For average family of four, this could translate to several hundred dollars' worth of food being thrown away every year.
- Various and inconsistent date labeling practices have resulted from the lack of binding federal standards.
- The date labeling system has lead consumers to believe, that date labels are the signals of a food's microbial safety and has consequently downplayed the importance of pertinent food safety indicators.
- The labeling confusion leads to considerable amounts of avoidable food waste as the mistaken belief that past-date foods are categorically unsuitable for consumption causes consumers to discard food prematurely.
- Inconsistent date labeling policies and practices harm the interests of manufacturers and retailers by creating increased compliance burdens and food waste at the manufacturer/retail level.
- To better communicate with consumers, it is recommended to:
  1. Make "sell by" dates invisible to the consumer. "Sell by" dates generate confusion and offer consumers no useful guidance once they have brought purchase home.
  2. Establish a reliable, coherent, and uniform consumer-facing dating system.
- In order to standardize and clarify date labels and to help implement a more effective system of consuming-facing dates that consumers can understand and trust, it is necessary to:
  1. Establish standard, clear language for both quality-based and safety-based date labels.
  2. Include "freeze by" dates and freezing information where applicable.
  3. Remove or replace quality-based dates on non-perishable, shelf-stable products.
  4. Ensure date labels are clearly and predictably located on packages.
  5. Employ more transparent methods for selecting dates.

Source: Environmental Research Digest, Sep. 2013 (Vol. 4, No. 9)

3.5.5 'Ethical' Labelling Report

Author(s): Overseas Development Institute

This report states that ethical consumer labels help too few producers in poor countries. The Overseas Development Institute has released a report (A Review of Ethical Standards and Labels: Is there a gap in the market for a 'good for development' label?) which recommends the development of a broader ethical labelling standard.

Key findings

Poor farmers would benefit from a simpler "good for development" label as well as existing standards like the Fairtrade mark.

- In the UK, Fairtrade-labelled produce made up less than 0.5% of food and non-alcoholic drinks sales in 2007.
- Existing schemes have a range of different objectives, from providing a better deal to producers (e.g. Fair Trade), to improving environmental and labour standards (e.g. Rainforest Alliance), to encouraging the use of good agricultural practices and improved farm management techniques (e.g. GlobalGAP).
- Some retailers and importers are already making an effort to strengthen their development impact, by engaging in a more supportive way with developing country producers.
- However, these efforts may go unrecognised and unrewarded if consumers are unaware of them.
- The broader ethical labelling standard proposed by the report would indicate to consumers the positive development impacts associated with purchasing most conventional developing country produce, not just products that qualify for existing ethical labelling schemes.
- Information on the pro-development contributions made by a particular product purchase could be presented in the form of a bronze, silver or gold 'Good for Development' label, which would enable consumers to compare at a glance the development contribution made by competing suppliers and products at the point of purchase.
- This may contribute to increased sales for those companies making the greatest efforts to improve their development contribution, boosting profitability as well as reputation.

Source: Governance Research Digest, Jan. 2009 (Vol. 1, No. 1)

3.5.6 Consumers and Carbon Labelling Study

Author(s): Carbon Trust

The Carbon Trust has released the findings of a recent study into consumer perceptions of carbon labelling. The research questioned more than 1,000 consumers across the UK to better understand their attitudes towards carbon reduction and the labelling of individual products.

<u>Key findings</u>

Almost two thirds of consumers (63%) are more likely to buy a product if they know action is being taken to reduce its carbon footprint.

- At the same time, 70% of consumers want businesses to do more to help them make more informed environmental choices about the products they buy.
- Committing to reduce a product's carbon footprint has a positive impact on the brand's reputation, as 58% of consumers say they value companies that are taking action to reduce their carbon emissions.
- Environmentally responsible brands must shout louder – only 12% of consumers think that companies are doing enough to cut carbon emissions and tackle climate change.
- This is linked to their call for help on making better choices, and a demand from just under half (47%) for information on how to reduce the footprint of a product when using it.
- 60% of consumers understood that a product such as a chocolate bar or loaf of bread has a carbon footprint.
- More than two thirds of the UK's carbon footprint comes from products and services, so acknowledging that these need to be reduced, as well as a company's or individual's carbon footprint, is vital.
- The Carbon Reduction Label has been developed to help brands demonstrate their commitment to carbon reduction and help consumers understand more about taking action on climate change.

Source: Social Research Digest, Aug. 2009 (Vol. 1, No. 8)

3.6   Greenwashing and Whitewashing

3.6.1   2011 Tomorrow's Value Rating

Author(s): Two Tomorrows

A new report, the 2011 Tomorrow's Value Rating, from international corporate sustainability agency, Two Tomorrows Group, addresses the issue of green-wash. The report uncovers the extent to which the companies widely recognised as sustainability leaders deserve their place within the leading sustainability rankings.

Key findings

There is a danger that leading companies are taking existing practices and passing them under the sustainability lens to give a compelling green picture of the company.

- Whilst these practices may have positive environmental impacts, they are fundamentally profit driven.
- The report warns that this can turn to greenwash when the sticky issues are ignored or given little consideration.
- The 2011 Tomorrow's Value Rating Aaa-rated companies are:
  o Campbell's
  o Danone
  o General Electric
  o Glaxosmithkline
  o HP
  o Intel
  o Nestlé
  o Nike
  o Panasonic
  o Siemens
  o Unilever
- Game-changing innovation to integrate environmental and socio-economic benefits into the heart of business strategy is a must for any company wishing to become truly sustainable.
- Sustainability leaders are widening their focus from their own operations to the entire value chain.

- They are placing pressure on suppliers to follow suit.
- While it is difficult to prove that a company is ethical, there are means to demonstrate to external observers that, when push comes to shove, sustainability issues will be considered alongside the financial implications of any business decision.
- What stakeholders want to know is that ethics will not be conveniently ignored when the opportunity for profit is present.
- Rapid change is a must for the sustainable company, but there are indications among the rated companies that this change is largely without direction.
- One of the most telling signs is the surprising lack of meaningful targets.
- This leaves stakeholders unable to judge whether a company has been successful with its sustainability commitments.

Source: Governance Research Digest, Oct. 2011 (Vol. 2, No. 6)

3.6.2   Preventing Greenwash Report

Author(s): Business For Social Responsibility/ Futerra Sustainability Communications

A new report from Business for Social Responsibility and Futerra Sustainability Communications aims to help businesses avoid what they call the 'seven sins of greenwashing'. The report lays out a "greenwash matrix" of the different types of poor communication about corporate environmental activities, and explores the ways firms can move toward messages that more clearly explain their green works.

Key findings

To avoid greenwash, a company's sustainability practices or products must be based on real, significant environmental impact. If a company is spending more on communications about their green projects than the green project itself, it's a likely sign of greenwashing.

- To properly align a green project, companies need to make sure there is significant internal and external support for the practice.
- The report authors recommend working with a credible third party to impartially evaluate the impact of any green activity.

- When communicating their successes, companies should focus on clarity and transparency, making sure that customers understand what the company has achieved and that the company can back their claims up with hard data.
- The report also includes a list of the top 10 "signs of greenwash" to help companies avoid making any unintentional mistakes. Those signs are:
  o Fluffy language. Words or terms with no clear meaning (e.g. "eco-friendly").
  o Green product vs. dirty company. Such as efficient lightbulbs made in a factory that pollutes rivers.
  o Suggestive pictures. Green images that indicate a (unjustified) green impact (e.g. flowers blooming from exhaust pipes).
  o Irrelevant claims. Emphasizing one tiny green attribute when everything else is not green.
  o Best in class. Declaring you are slightly greener than the rest, even if the rest are pretty terrible.
  o Just not credible. "Eco friendly" cigarettes, anyone? "Greening" a dangerous product doesn't make it safe.
  o Jargon. Information that only a scientist could check or understand.
  o Imaginary friends. A "label" that looks like third party endorsement - except that it's made up.
  o No proof. It could be right, but where's the evidence?
  o Out-right lying. Totally fabricated claims or data.

Source: Social Research Digest, Sep. 2009 (Vol. 1, No. 9)

3.6.3   You are the Target – Anti-Tobacco Campaign Report

Author(s): Corporate Accountability International, Campaign for Tobacco-Free Kids, Alliance for the Control of Tobacco Use, Tobacco Control Alliance, Framework Convention Alliance, InterAmerican Heart Foundation and Southeast Asia Tobacco Control Alliance

Corporate Accountability International, Campaign for Tobacco-Free Kids, Alliance for the Control of Tobacco Use, Tobacco Control Alliance, Framework Convention Alliance, InterAmerican Heart Foundation and Southeast Asia Tobacco Control Alliance released a report exposing an aggressive worldwide marketing campaign by the world's largest publicly-traded tobacco corporation, Philip Morris International (PMI). The report, titled "You're the Target," calls on PMI to immediately end the "Be Marlboro" campaign and it also calls on governments to enact comprehensive bans on all forms of tobacco advertising, promotion and sponsorship in accordance with the global tobacco treaty, known formally as the World Health Organization Framework Convention on Tobacco Control (FCTC).

Key findings

Tobacco kills nearly 6 million people worldwide every year. To maintain profits, tobacco companies must replace customers who quit or die from tobacco-related diseases with new smokers. Replacement smokers are often youth who are attracted to tobacco products through expensive marketing campaigns that use images that are highly appealing to young people around the globe.

- In spite of the German court's finding that "Be Marlboro" advertisements target young teenagers and are in conflict with PMI's own seemingly ineffective code of conduct, PMI continues to aggressively rollout the "Be Marlboro" campaign internationally, including in low- and middleincome countries struggling with the enormous tobacco epidemic. These countries include:
  o Brazil, where PMI is placing "Be Marlboro" posters at the point of sale (POS), taking advantage of the lack of regulation and inspection to enforce the existing POS advertising ban.
  o Indonesia, where tobacco advertising laws are weak and where PMI posts massive "Be Marlboro" billboards on the street.
  o Philippines, where tobacco companies continually attempt to thwart strong tobacco control policies through the courts.
- This report calls on PMI to immediately end all "Be Marlboro" marketing activities worldwide and publish a detailed accounting of "Be Marlboro" activities by country on its corporate website so that governments and public health organisations can assess the damage caused by the campaign.
- This report documents the global scope of Marlboro's multimillion dollar rebranding campaign and how it threatens the health of millions of youth around the world. It also documents how "Be Marlboro" appeals to teens without regard for advertising restrictions aimed at protecting youth in countries including Brazil, Colombia, Germany and

Switzerland.

- The report further emphasizes the ineffectiveness of voluntary marketing codes and partial tobacco advertising, promotion and sponsorship bans at curbing the tobacco industry's ability to market to youth.

Source: Social Research Digest, Apr. 2014 (Vol. 5, No. 4)

3.6.4 Sugar-Coating Science: How the Food Industry Misleads Consumers on Sugar

Author(s): Center for Science and Democracy at the Union of Concerned Scientists (UCS)

The Center for Science and Democracy at the Union of Concerned Scientists (UCS) a new report that documents how food companies use misleading marketing and front group campaigns to obscure the health consequences of added sugar in their products. The report, Sugar-Coating Science: How the Food Industry Misleads Consumers on Sugar reveals that the food industry obscures added sugar in products by marketing them as healthy.

Key findings

- Marketing sugary foods with a feel-good health claim. Whether it was Coca-Cola advertising its high-sugar Vitaminwater brand by using buzzwords like "defense," "energy," or "enhanced" or General Mills advertising Fruit RollUps as being "made with real fruit" when they in fact contain none, companies will do whatever it takes to make sugary foods look healthy.
- Using misleading language like "natural" and "naturally sweetened." Food companies may be taking heavily processed sweeteners like high-fructose corn syrup out of their foods—but those foods aren't any healthier if that corn syrup is being replaced with an equivalent amount of table sugar.
- Using an established brand with a healthy reputation to launch sugary "upgrades" lends a de facto health halo to those unhealthy products.
- Paying front groups. The Sugar Association and the Corn Refiners Association paid the Center for Consumer Freedom—through the public-relations firm that launched it, so as to cover up their monetary paper trail. Their goal: to promote the message that sugar is natural and

it's an individual's choice whether to consume added sugars or not. Targeting women and minorities with their ads. Minorities and low-income populations are disproportionately exposed to marketing and advertising of sugary foods and beverages relative to other demographic groups. Women are targeted with ads that prey on their vulnerabilities of wanting to lose weight and their insecurities as parents.

- Using "cause marketing" to sell sugary foods. According to the website for Yoplait (a brand owned by General Mills), the "Save Lids to Save Lives" campaign has donated more than $34 million to various breast-cancer causes. Yet a single cup of the brand's yogurts averages 26 grams of sugar.
  1. Sugar interests should be held accountable by experts, investors, decision makers, the media, and the public for their current efforts to obscure the science on sugar and its detrimental health effects.
  2. Congress should restore the Federal Trade Commission and Federal Communications Commission to their full capacity to regulate marketing to children so that the agencies can regulate youth-targeted marketing.
  3. The Food and Drug Administration should implement a strong rule requiring the labeling of added sugar in nutrition labels as the agency announced they intend to do.
  4. Federal, state, and local health agencies should develop aggressive public information campaigns to emphasize the scientific evidence demonstrating sugar's health impacts and counter the misinformation from sugar interests

Source: Social Research Digest, May 2014 (Vol. 5, No. 5)

3.7 Factual and Unbiased Information

3.7.1 Green Retail Information Report

Author(s): Miller Zell

A new report from retail strategists Miller Zell examines the extent to which consumers' need for information is being met. "The Green Scene", part of a larger suite of reports examining effective in-store triggers, presents the results of an online survey in which 999 US consumers took part.

Key findings

Around 40% of shoppers are left wanting when it comes to green information at retail store level.

- Overall, retailers scored a 'D-' for the quality of information they provide at store level.
- Members of the Generation Y and Millennial age groups tended to want more information.
- Shoppers want to know how 'green' is defined by different manufacturers and retailers.
- 62% of respondents indicated that green product options can influence unplanned product purchases.
- Across all age groups there is a willingness to pay extra for green everyday household items.
- However, willingness to pay a premium dipped significantly once the premium reached 28% of the base price of the product.
- Lower income shoppers are more willing to pay a ten cent premium, compared with middle and higher income shoppers.
- This may be heavily influenced by the large number of Millennials who are currently lower earners due to their recent entry into the workforce.
- Shoppers were most likely to select green products when grocery shopping. 79% of respondents said they would be happy to pay a green premium in grocery stores.
- However, consumer enthusiasm for shopping in department, electronics and speciality stores suggests that these retailers have an opportunity to sell more green products highlighting green offerings in-store.

Source: Social Research Digest, Sep. 2009 (Vol. 1, No. 9)

3.7.2 Companies Fail to Educate Consumers on Energy Management Systems

Author(s): Consumer Electronics Association

A survey by Consumer Electronics Association sought to better understand consumer awareness and attitudes regarding energy management and how energy efficiency gains in consumer electronics products have changed purchasing habits. The survey was conducted in April with a total respodents number of 1250 adults in US.

Key findings

Consumers are concerned about the cost of their energy use, yet lack awareness of emerging energy management systems.

- While many consumers turn lights off, shop for energy efficient devices and practice other ecofriendly practices, just 10.2 million of 119 million U.S. households are estimated to have enrolled in electricity management programs.
- Utility companies, the study found, are in the best position to raise awareness of these programs to boost consumers' understanding of energy consumption.
- Research shows consumers are interested in how electricity management programs could reduce their monthly electric bills.
- However, the survey found there is little difference in the bills of those enrolled in electricity management programs and those who are not; which indicates further development by industry, utilities and government is needed to realize the vision of a smart grid that could bring about more meaningful cost savings to consumers.
- More than half (55%) of consumers expressed interest in an electricity management program sponsored by a utility or electric company.
- Consumers also indicated whether they would prefer to use a device in the home (41%), an online portal (41%) or a mobile device (32%) to monitor energy use.
- Looking forward, 46% of respondents aware of electricity management programs available in their area expressed an interest in enrolling in the coming years.

Source: Social Research Digest, Jun. 2011 (Vol. 2, No. 2)

3.7.3 Consumer Communications Glossary: Defining Terms Used in Environmental Sustainability

Author(s): The Consumer Goods Forum

The purpose of this Glossary by the Consumer Goods Forum is to begin to harmonize and clearly define the terms that businesses use to describe their environmental sustainability efforts. The members of the Glossary Project were drawn from both manufacturing and retail, including the Kroger company, l'oréal, nestlé, Pepsico, Procter and Gamble, Sara Lee, Tesco, Unilever, and Walmart.

Key findings

Consumers are more likely to consider environmental impact in their purchasing decisions, and businesses are increasingly marketing themselves and their products based on their sustainability credentials.

- However, the absence of a common, welldefined lexicon of environmental sustainability terms makes it difficult for consumers to make informed choices.
- The variety of terms, usages, and claims that are being applied in the consumer goods industry can rob those terms of meaning, making it difficult for businesses that are genuinely leading in this area to differentiate themselves.

Source: Social Research Digest, Feb. 2012 (Vol. 3, No. 2)

3.7.4 Buying into It – Making the Consumer Case for Low-Carbon

Author(s): CBI

The CBI concluded in a recent report, 'Buying into it', that business is using the wrong language to persuade customers to make greener choices. This report focuses on a crucial piece of the puzzle in the creation of a low-carbon economy - consumers.

Key findings

Only when business and government properly connect with consumers on this agenda can we create the conditions for a mass market in lowcarbon goods and reap the longer-term economic benefits.

- The report said that two conversations are taking place.
- Policy makers and business leaders are fluent in the language of carbon impact and footprints, but the general public is not familiar with these terms.
- The research showed that nearly half of those surveyed could see the link between low carbon and climate change, but less than a third could identify a link between climate change and energy efficiency.
- With consumers accounting directly and indirectly for almost three quarters of UK carbon emissions, the CBI says a joint business-government taskforce should focus on the following areas to help build a mass market for low-carbon goods:
  - o working together to exploit upcoming campaigns, including the roll-out of smart meters and the Green Deal, to build consumer awareness about wider lowcarbon choices;
  - o delivering better standards and consistent labelling to provide consumers with simple, clear and comparable information to make informed choices on a wider range of products, including DVD players, games consoles and cookers;
  - o businesses also need to build trust in their green credentials through the use of common language and symbols;
  - o manufacturers and retailers working together to ensure that shop floor staff have the training necessary to help customers make greener choices.

Source: Social Research Digest, May 2011 (Vol. 2, No. 1)

IV. CONSUMER SOCIAL AND ENVIRONMENTAL RESPONSIBILITY

4.1 Consumer Attitudes and Expectations

4.1.1 Consumer Attitudes to Corporate Responsibility Report

Author(s): Business in the Community Ireland

A new report by Business and the Community Ireland suggests that companies which are socially and environmentally responsible can claim a major competitive advantage - but they need to communicate their activities to consumers. The 2009 Survey of Consumer Attitudes in Ireland towards Corporate Responsibility is the third such survey in the past decade, with previous versions taking place in 2003 and 2006.

Key findings

- When forming a decision to buy a product or service, 8 out of 10 people in Ireland say that an organisation's commitment to social and environmental responsibility is important.
- However, almost eighty percent (80%) of consumers could not name one company which treat staff well, give good customer service and are mindful of its impact on the environment.
- Whilst ninety-two percent (92%) of consumers are taking individual actions to limit their own environment impacts, three out of four people (75%) could not name a company doing the same.
- 72% of respondents named supermarkets as their most favoured industry. While maintaining its lead position since 2006, it has dropped by ten percentage points overall.
- The least favoured sectors are banks and building societies (43%), railway and bus companies (42%) and the construction industry (31%).
- When making a judgement about an organisation, the factors considered most important to the public are customer service (81%), being honest & open (69%) and product quality (66%).

- Environmental practices and impact were only considered important by 33% of respondents, although this was an increase of 3% from 2006.
- The most frequently-cited reason for actively choosing not to purchase from a particular company was poor customer service.

Source: CSR Research Digest, May 2009 (Vol. 1, No. 5)

4.1.2   2010 Cone Cause Evolution Study

Author(s): Cone

The 2010 Cone Cause Evolution Study explores consumer attitudes and expectations of company support for social and environmental issues. The study presents the findings of an online survey conducted in July 2010 among a demographically representative U.S. sample of 1,057 adults comprising 512 men and 545 women 18 years of age and older.

Key findings

A full 83% of consumers want more of the products, services and retailers they use to benefit causes.

- 41% of Americans say they have purchased a product in the past year because it was associated with a social or environmental cause, a two-fold increase since Cone first began measuring in 1993 (20%).
- 81% said companies should financially support causes at the same level or higher during an economic downturn.
- It appears business rose to this challenge - nearly two-thirds (64%) of consumers believe companies responded well to social and environmental issues during the recession.
- Americans' enthusiasm for cause marketing also emerged from the turmoil fully intact and continues to strongly influence their purchase decisions:
- 88% say it is acceptable for companies to involve a cause or issue in their marketing
- 85% have a more positive image of a product or company when it supports a cause they care about 80% are likely to switch brands, similar in price and quality, to one that supports a cause.
- Not only are consumers willing to switch among similar brands, they are also willing to step outside their comfort zones. When it supports a

cause:

- 61% of Americans say they would be willing to try a new brand or one unfamiliar to them
- 46% would try a generic or private-label brand
- Nearly one-in-five consumers (19%) would be willing to purchase a more expensive brand.

Source: CSR Research Digest, Oct. 2010 (Vol. 2, No. 10)

4.1.3   Brand Sustainable Futures

Author(s): *Havas Media*

Havas Media's global analysis and framework, „Brand Sustainable Futures", explores the challenges brands are facing in the new economic landscape. The survey encompasses worlwide consumers of over 30,000 people spanning 4 continents and 9 markets.

Key findings

2010 results reveal a strong correlation between a brand's "meaningfulness" and its perceived sustainable performance, suggesting that the more sustainable the brand is perceived, the more meaningful it becomes to consumers.

- Only one-third of brands are considered meaningful to consumers.
- While sustainability is a key issue for consumers worldwide few brands live up to increasing expectations.
- The vast majority of mainstream consumers wouldn't care if two thirds of today's global brands disappeared in the future.
- More than half of the consumers surveyed say confusion, a lack of clarity and perceived higher prices prevent responsible purchasing.
- Social issues and sustainability still rank as major concerns among consumers worldwide with 80% of consumers expecting business to act responsibly.
- In addition, an increasing majority (76% vs. 70% in 2009) place the responsibility for environmental and social issues on business rather than governments.
- Only 29% of respondents believe that brands are working hard to resolve sustainability issues and 68% (64% in 2009) believe companies

only act responsibly in order to improve their image.

- Opportunities for brands who adopt clear and engaging communications, offer greater product incentives (such as price) and availability, which were all cited as key barriers to responsible consumption.

- These barriers varied by country, with price the main issue in western economies (France, UK, US and Germany) and lack of information the most important in Spain and fast growing markets such as China, Brazil, Mexico and India.

- The brands with the most defined sustainability profiles last year included food and consumer product brands and retailers such as Danone, Nestlé and Unilever, say researchers.

- This year a more diverse selection of brands from other industries are making a difference versus their competitors by raising their sustainability brand profile including BMW, Volkswagen and Philips.

Source: CSR Research Digest, Nov. 2010 (Vol. 2, No. 11)

4.1.4 2011 Cone/Echo Global CR Opportunity Study

Author(s): Cone Communications / Echo Research

The global consumer movement surfaces in the 2011 Cone/Echo Global CR Opportunity Study, a 10-country survey released today by Cone Communications and Echo Research. The survey was fielded in countries comprising approximately half the world's population, including the United States, Canada, Brazil, the United Kingdom, Germany, France, Russia, China, India and Japan.

Key findings

Ten thousand consumers in major countries around the globe are demanding a higher level of responsibility by companies in dealing with societal issues, and consumers report they are already using their own spending and loyalty to press these demands.

- 81% of consumers say companies have a responsibility to address key social and environmental issues beyond their local communities.

- 93% of consumers say companies must go beyond legal compliance to operate responsibly.

- 94% of consumers say companies must analyze and evolve their business practices to make their impact as positive as possible.
- 94% would buy a product that has an environmental benefit; 76% have already purchased an environmental product in the past 12 months.
- 93% would buy a product associated with a cause; 65% have already purchased a cause-related product in the past 12 months.
- Consumers may be so apt to engage with corporate responsibility and cause-related efforts because they are seeing the impact.
- Ninety-three percent believe companies have made at least some positive impact on the world; a quarter say the impact has been significant.
- Nearly three-in-five consumers (59%) credit companies with helping to educate them on important issues, and a similar number (56%) say they have been inspired to support a new issue.
- Today's engaged consumers are willing to reward, but just as willing to investigate and punish.
- More than a third (36%) have researched a company's business practices or support of issues, and 32% have given their feedback about a company's responsibility efforts directly to the company.
- Most telling is the consumer willingness to boycott.
- Ninety-three percent would boycott a company for irresponsibility, and more than half say they already have (56%).
- Consumers believe it is important for companies to address a full range of social and environmental issues, including:
  - economic development – 96%;
  - environment – 96%
  - water – 95%;
  - human rights – 94%;
  - education – 90%;
  - health and disease – 90%;
  - poverty and hunger – 87%.
- Yet, if they must choose just one, the clear leader is economic development.
- Thirty-four percent of the consumers surveyed say this is the most important issue for companies to address.
- Combined with the environment (21%), these issues represent the

attention of more than half of the 10,000 respondents.

- Human rights comes in a more distant third (12%).
- Citizens globally may agree on what companies should address, but they are much more divided when it comes to where.
- Thirty-six percent of consumers believe companies should prioritize support of issues that affect the quality of life locally in their communities, 33% say nationally and 30% say globally.
- There is division as well among countries.
- Consumers in some of the larger countries want companies to focus locally, including Russia (51%), China (49%) and the U.S. (47%).
- By comparison, countries on the front line of globalization want companies to take a more global view, including Brazil (46%) and India (41%).

Source: CSR Research Digest, Oct. 2011 (Vol. 3, No. 10)

4.1.5   The Role of Personal Values in Fair Trade Consumption

Author(s): C.J. Doran

This study sought to determine which values are salient to American fair trade consumption, on which there has, to date, been little research. Empirical data were gathered via an online survey tool from online shoppers who purchased products from a range of internet-based Fair Trade retailers.

Key findings

Universalism values were ranked as the most important values by loyal fair trade consumers.

- Some of these values are focused on nature and the environment – unity with nature, a world of beauty, and protecting the environment.
- Both universalism and benevolence values are focused on supporting others; however, the focus of universalism values is on all people and nature, whereas benevolence values focus on the in-group.
- This is an important distinction in this study, as consumers who are loyal to the concept of fair trade ranked benevolence values lower than consumers who consume fair trade intermittently.

- Loyal fair traders ranked self-direction values higher than both non-consumers and intermittent consumers.
- This form of consumerism promotes breaking from convention and paying higher prices for products that are often hard to find; it might be described as a manifestation of the
- Independent and Freedom values.
- All respondents ranked power values as the least important of all values, as power values promote dominance over others and the preservation of a dominant position in society.
- From this study it is evident that it is no longer the case that younger consumers are more ethical than older individuals.
- This may be due in part to the fact that ethical products are no longer confined to the domain of the niche markets of the activist youthful consumer, but instead are widely available in mainstream distribution channels.
- Since products such as tea, coffee, bananas, sugar, and cocoa are now sold under the fair trade logo, fair trade is likely more appealing to males than was previously the case.
- Education was also expected to be influential in the decision to consume fair trade products in this study, but this did not turn out to be the case.

Source: Social Research Digest, Apr. 2009 (Vol. 1, No. 4)

4.1.6 Generational Differences in Young Adults' Life Goals, Concern for Others, and Civic Orientation

Author(s): J. M. Twenge, W. K. Campbell and E. C. Elise

A study of US young adults examines generational differences in environmental attitudes. The findings are based on two national surveys of high school seniors and college freshmen that have been taken for more than 40 years.

<u>Key findings</u>

Academic analysis of the surveys shows the socalled Millennial Generation (born after 1982) actually is less interested in the environment and conservation than baby boomers and Gen Xers (born 1962–1981) were at the same age.

- Fifteen percent of Millennials said they have made no effort to help the environment, compared to 8% of Gen Xers and 5% of baby boomers.
- Percentage who said it was important to become personally involved in programs to clean up the environment:
  o Baby boomers – 33%
  o Gen Xers – 25%
  o Millennials – 21%
- Percentage who said they'd made an effort to conserve electricity and fuel used to heat their homes:
  o Baby boomers – 78%
  o Gen Xers – 71%
  o Millennials – 56%
- The lack of environmental interest isn't exclusive to the younger generation, but rather, they are simply reflecting an overall change in culture.

Source: Environmental Research Digest, May 2012 (Vol. 3, No. 5)

4.1.7   2009 Cone Consumer New Media Study

Author(s): Cone

The 2009 Cone Consumer New Media Study is a three-part survey which explored new media users' interactions with brands, their support of social and environmental issues and their engagement with corporate responsibility practices. Data was gathered via an online survey which was conducted in September 2009. 1,048 US adults who are users of 'new media' took part.

Key findings

Two thirds of American new media users feel they can influence business practices by voicing their opinions online.

- About a quarter of respondents have contributed their point-of-view on an issue (24%) or contacted a company directly (23%).
- 74% expect companies to join conversations about their corporate responsibility practices happening on new media.

- New media users are more likely than their fellow consumers to bypass dialogue and go straight for action.
- 30% of respondents have made a purchase based on positive information learned about a product, company or brand.
- 23% have switched brands or boycotted a company based on negative information learned about a product, company or brand.
- Consumers are most interested in information that will inform their purchasing decisions.
- Respondents said they want companies to tell them what is in products and how they are made (85%) and provide additional details about information, labels and claims shared offline (e.g., in the store, on the package, in an advertisement) (83%).
- Overall, consumers show strong signs of empowerment, comfort and trust with corporate responsibility communications in new media. Three-quarters of new media users say it is an effective way to learn about CR efforts.
- 65% believe they know where to look for such information and 47% think companies are transparent and honest when talking about CR efforts through new media channels.
- Consumers are relying largely on Web 1.0 channels such as Web sites (27%) and email (22%) to explore CR, indicating channels that foster a dialogue and deeper engagement - such as social networks (15%) and blogs (11%) - are being underutilized.

Source: Social Research Digest, Nov. 2009 (Vol. 1, No. 11)

4.1.8   2012 Cone Communications Corporate Social Return Trend Tracker

Author(s): Cone Communications

In response to the importance of CSR reporting in communications, Cone has launched Corporate Social Return. It is an approach to CSR-focused public relations that centers on the conviction that CSR must deliver measurable business, brand and social impacts that yield benefits for vested stakeholders.

Key findings

When it comes to corporate social responsibility, consumers want more than aspirational mission statements.

- 84% of Americans hold companies accountable for producing and communicating the results of CSR commitments by going beyond the mission to robustly communicate progress against well-defined purpose.
- Some 40% go as far as to say that they will not purchase a company's products or services if CSR results are not communicated.
- Companies that proactively share the details and results of their CSR efforts, rather than just their aspirations, will be rewarded with increased consumer trust and purchasing.
- Some 86% of consumers are more likely to trust a company that reports its CSR results, and 82% say they are more likely to purchase a product that clearly demonstrates the results of the company's CSR initiatives than one that does not.
- Despite this strong belief in CSR commitments and results, 63% of consumers admit to not knowing where to find such information and 55% say that they don't understand the impact they are having when buying a product from a company that says it is socially responsible.
- But consumers do not expect a business to abandon profits in pursuit of CSR.
- Some 84% recognize that for a company to make societal impact, it must also realize a business return, such as increased revenue or reduced costs.

Source: Social Research Digest, Nov. 2012 (Vol. 3, No. 11)

4.1.9 Cultural Crossvergence and Social Desirability Bias: Ethical Evaluations by Chinese and Canadian Business Students

Author(s): P. Dunn, A. Shome

This study aimed to determine whether there are crosscultural differences between Chinese and Canadian business students with respect to their assessment of the ethicality of various business behaviours. 147 business school students took part: 72 Chinese and 75 Canadian. All were current students at an English-speaking Canadian university. Participants were surveyed for their responses to eight different ethical business scenario vignettes.

Key findings

Chinese and Canadian students exhibit different ethical attitudes toward questionable business practices at the individual level but not at the corporate level.

- The Canadians rated the micro-level actions (e.g. padding expense reports) as more unethical than the Chinese.
- Macro-level circumstances such as organisational infrastructure encourage convergence, while individual-level circumstances such as cultural and ethnic background encourage divergence.
- Crossvergence occurs when an individual incorporates both influences from national culture and ideology synergistically to form a unique value system that is different from the value set supported by either national culture or economic ideology.
- A social desirability bias (a tendency to deny socially unacceptable actions and to admit to socially desirable ones) is also found to be a cross-cultural phenomenon, with the Canadians demonstrating a greater bias than the Chinese.
- This is consistent with cultural expectations: a low social desirability bias would be consistent with a more collectivist Chinese culture, and a high social desirability would be consistent with a more individualistic Canadian culture.
- Similar studies from 2003 and 2007 found a social desirability bias among accountants from Malaysia, India, and Australia, but that the magnitude of the bias does not differ significantly among the respondents when grouped by nationality.
- This bias causes respondents to increase their assessment of the un-ethicality of questionable business activities.
- The cultural differences between Canadians and Chinese are highlighted: first, the Chinese tend to have a more long-term orientation than Canadians; second, they are more collectivist than

Canadians; and third, they are more accepting of established power structures within society than Canadians.

- The authors note that the research population for this study is comprised of students and that more education, employment, or work experience is positively related to ethical decision-making.
- The results also indicate that corporate ethics policies may be effective in establishing an international standard for employees, while still allowing for modifications given the local context and values.
- Macro-level decisions would be based on the firm's global policies concerning acceptable business behaviour regardless of the local country's values, while locally employees would follow the home country's cultural expectations of ethical business behaviour.

Source: Governance Research Digest, May 2009 (Vol. 1, No. 5)

4.1.10 Consumer Activism Study

Author(s): J.D. Power and Associates

Online commentary gathered from blogs and discussion board posts indicates that consumer conversations are shifting from simple discussion and debate on sustainability topics to indications of personal action to create change. The new study by J.D. Power and Associates of online conversations regarding sustainability topics monitored a range of online discussions in 2007 and 2008.

Key findings

During the second half of 2007, just 9% of all sustainability conversations mentioned a brand by name. By June 2008, this figure grew to 11%.

- Conversations about sustainability topics have more than doubled in number from the first quarter of 2007 to the fourth quarter of 2008.
- There was a marked rise in conversations in mid-2008 as gas prices peaked, with almost 160,000 conversations noted in June 2008.
- In early 2007, discussions about sustainability were dominated by people who were confused by conflicting evidence surrounding climate change and uncertain of their stance on the subject as well as by "negators" – those who denied the existence of climate change and

other environmental concerns and actively attempted to sway opinions of others.

- By December 2008, more than 7 out of 10 online posters who mentioned sustainability topics indicated they were concerned about the environment, and nearly half of posters reported that they were actively doing something about it, such as cutting back on electricity usage, reducing driving, recycling and buying more "green" products.

- Online commentary among consumers who are considered "rejecters" – those who are skeptical or ambivalent about environmental concerns and do not make purchase decisions based on environmental factors – declined from a high of 22% in early 2007 to only 3% by the end of 2008.

- The proportion of bloggers who consider themselves "activists" – those who actively encourage others to modify behaviour – increased considerably during the last six months of 2008, growing from 8% during the first half of 2008 to 18% of the total discussion set.

Source: Social Research Digest, Mar. 2009 (Vol. 1, No. 3)

4.1.11 Edelman Goodpurpose 2012

Author(s): Edelman

The goodpurpose study is Edelman's annual global research that explores consumer attitudes around social purpose, including their commitment to specific societal issues and their expectations of brands and corporations. The survey was conducted in 16 countries among 8,000 adults.

Key findings

Five Years of Data Reveals Purpose to Be a Driving Force Behind the Reengineering of Brand Marketing Around the World.

- Consumers in the U.S. are scaling back their participation in societal issues more than their peers throughout the world.

- With 82% of U.S. consumers affected by the economic downturn, the percentage of consumers involved in a cause dropped from 60% to 53% between 2010 and 2012, the only decline among the 16 countries surveyed.

- Yet, for the first time ever, the U.S. was the only country to believe the responsibility of tackling society's issues falls most heavily on the shoulders of "people like me" (35%) and not government (22%).
- Despite the declining involvement in the U.S., Purpose remains a deeply held belief around the globe that is driving consumer behavior and pAuthor(s).
- When quality and price of a product are deemed equal, social purpose has consistently been the leading purchase trigger for global consumers since 2008, muscling design and innovation and brand loyalty aside.
- Over those years, the relevance of Purpose as a purchase factor has risen 26% globally.
- Growth has been even more prominent over the last 18 months in markets such as Japan (+100%), China (+79%), Netherlands (+43%), India (+43%), and Germany (+36%).
- Brands aligning themselves with causes are not only securing more consumer consideration, but are also earning their dollars and support.
- Nearly half (47%) of consumers have bought a brand at least monthly that supports a cause, representing a 47% increase from 2010.
- Over the years, consumers have taken increased action on behalf of brands with
- Purpose:
  - 39% increase in "would recommend" cause-related brands;
  - 34% increase in "would promote" cause-related brands;
  - 9% increase in "would switch" brands if a similar brand supported a good cause.
- The study found that consumers are calling for business leaders to genuinely embed Purpose into their everyday operations:
  - 56% believe CEOs need to create innovative products that are socially responsible;
  - 55% believe CEOs need to make a long term commitment to address societal issues;
  - 55% believe CEOs need to publically support societal issues;
  - 52% believe CEOs need to motivate employees to take part in societal issues.
- goodpurpose 2012 also reveals that Purposeful organizations who treat employees well, listen to customers and work to protect the

environment drive not only future trust, but also future purchase intent.

Source: Social Research Digest, May 2012 (Vol. 3, No. 5)

4.1.12 Global Consumers Poll

Author(s): The Regeneration Project and National Geographic

The survey, conducted in collaboration with National Geographic, is part of a series of initiatives by The Regeneration Project in the lead up to Rio+20, a crosssectoral collaboration that aims to accelerate progress in the transition to sustainable development. It polled approx 1,000 adult consumers per country in 17 countries between March 2012 and May 2012.

Key findings

55% of people worldwide want their government to "play a leadership role in making ambitious international commitments to reduce global poverty in ways that improve the environment".

- A further 40% want their government to support moderate international commitments to the same end.
- The findings put pressure on summit negotiators to deliver an outcome that will satisfy constituents at home.
- Consumers in Latin America are particularly demanding of their governments at the conference, with strong majorities in Mexico (80%), Brazil (74%)—the summit's host—and Argentina (67%) calling for ambitious leadership positions at the conference.
- Indians (63%) are the next most likely to want their delegates to take ambitious action at the Rio+20 Summit followed by Canadians (58%).
- Half of American and Chinese consumers (51% each) call for their governments to provide ambitious leadership at the conference.
- Germans are the least likely of those in the 17 countries surveyed to support a leadership position by their government at the conference (43%).
- Perhaps the most compelling finding of the survey is that so few people—only 5% globally--want their countries to avoid committing to any international agreements at the summit.

- Americans are the most inclined to prefer that their government makes no international commitment, at 11%.
- The poll is a strong endorsement of the view that international agreements are needed to resolve international sustainable development challenges.

Source: Social Research Digest, Jun. 2012 (Vol. 3, No. 6)

4.1.13 2014 Aspirational Consumer Index

Author(s): BBMG and GlobeScan

BBMG and GlobeScan released a list of the world's most responsible companies based on an in-depth survey of consumer attitudes, motivations and behaviors relating to sustainable consumption among participants across 21 international markets. The 2014 Aspirational Consumer Index explores the intersection of consumer values, motivations and shopping behaviors and deepens understanding of four consumer segments along the sustainability spectrum, including highly committed Advocates (21%); style and social status-seeking Aspirationals (38%); price and performance-minded Practicals (25%) and less engaged Indifferents (16%).

Key findings

Coca-Cola, Microsoft, Samsung, Tata, Unilever and Nestlé top the list of the world's most responsible companies.

- On the Rise: In 2014, Aspirational consumers represent 38% of the global population, compared with 36% in 2013;
- Empowered Shoppers: Nine in 10 Aspirational consumers say "shopping for new things excites me" (93%), compared to 46% of all consumers;
- Trust in Brands: Half of Aspirational consumers globally say they "trust global companies to act in the best interest of society" (50%), compared with 43% of all consumers;
- Positive Influencers: Nine in 10 Aspirational consumers also say "I encourage others to buy from socially and environmentally responsible companies" (90%), compared to 59% of all consumers;
- Responsible Consumers: Similarly, nine in 10 Aspirational consumers

say "I believe we need to consume less to preserve the environment for future generations" (95%), compared to 69% of all consumers, and that they are "willing to pay more for products produced in a socially and environmentally responsible way" (90%) compared to 62% of all consumers;

- Young and Female: Demographically, Aspirational consumers are most likely to represent the GenX (35%) and Millennial (33%) generations, compared to 34% and 31% of the general population, respectively, and they are more likely to be female (53%) than male (47%); and

- Strength in Emerging Markets: Countries with the largest populations of Aspirational consumers include India (58%), South Korea (53%), China (51%), Turkey (48%), Russia (47%), Indonesia (46%), Nigeria (43%), Peru (42%), Canada (41%), the United Kingdom (41%), Australia (40%), Pakistan (38%), Kenya (35%), the United States (34%) and Brazil (33%).

- Along with the study, BBMG and GlobeScan launched the website TheAspirationals.com. The website aims to track the habits of so-called Aspirational consumers. Aspirationals make up about 38% of the survey's respondents, and are as conscious of shopping and style as they are of corporate responsibility. They are driven by shopping for new things, and believe in sustainability and preserving the environment.

Source: CSR Research Digest, Jul. 2014 (Vol. 6, No. 7)

4.1.14 2014 ACSI Travel Index

Author(s): University of Michigan's Ross School of Business

The University of Michigan's Ross School of Business issued the ACSI Travel Report 2014 which examines the implications of new customer satisfaction benchmarks for major companies in the travel sector, including commercial airlines, hotel chains, and online travel agencies that serve the U.S. consumer market. The 2014 ACSI Travel Index report on airlines, hotels, and Internet travel sites is based on interviews with 7,445 customers of these three industries, chosen at random and contacted via telephone and email between October 21, 2013 and March 11, 2014.

Key findings

Not a single hotel chain improves in guest satisfaction and Best Western tumbles 6%.

- Among airlines, JetBlue, Southwest, and United fall, but Delta, American, and US Air improve.

- The Internet travel agency business is up a fraction and continues to get good ACSI scores, but travelers find booking flights and hotel rooms through airline and hotel websites preferable to booking via travel agent sites.

- Passenger satisfaction is unchanged this year at an ACSI score of 69. Even though air travel has improved some over the years, only subscription TV, Internet service and social media sites have lower levels of customer satisfaction in ACSI. Uncomfortable seating and poor in-flight service contribute most to the low scores.

- Among the legacy airlines, Delta emerges as the best in the group, with a gain of 4% to an ACSI score of 71, inching ahead of the aggregate of smaller airlines (including Alaska Air, Frontier, and Spirit). This is a 27% improvement in customer satisfaction since 2011, when Delta plunged to an all-time low of 56 in the wake of its Northwest acquisition. Not coincidental perhaps, Delta's stock price is up 250% over the same period.

- After three years of record levels, guest satisfaction with hotels dips 2.6% to an ACSI score of 75. Both during and for a period subsequent to the 2008 – 2009 recession, hotel chains kept rates down while adding incentives and discounts. As the economy improved and the travel business rebounded, rates have gone up. To some extent, this is now reflected in lower ACSI scores.

- Marriott again leads with an ACSI score of 81, followed by several hotels slightly above the industry average. Hilton, Hyatt and InterContinental tie at 78, with Starwood down 3% to 76. Marriott, Hilton and Hyatt benefit from more properties of the upscale and luxury variety, with better service quality and more amenities.

- Customer satisfaction with travel websites for booking flights, hotels, and car rentals gains 1.3% to an ACSI score of 77. The aggregate of smaller travel websites leads at 78, with Orbitz trailing at 77, followed closely by Expedia. There is not much differentiation in this business, as evidenced by the fact that Priceline and Travelocity aren't far behind.

Source: CSR Research Digest, Jul. 2014 (Vol. 6, No. 7)

4.2 Consumers' Perceptions and Trust

4.2.1 Sustainability Leadership Report: Measuring Perception vs. Reality

Author(s): Brandlogic / CRD Analytics

The report summarizes a study that compared perceived and actual reported corporate performance on environmental, social and governance (ESG) factors for 100 leading companies across most industries. The global study measured perceptions in six countries among three key audiences: investment professionals, purchasing professionals and graduating university students soon entering the workforce.

<u>Key findings</u>

Out of 100 leading global brands across nine major industries it was found that 66 had perceived ESG performance that exceeded their actual performance.

*   Such brands included Visa, AT&T, Starbucks, Yahoo! and Toyota.
*   But a number of brands outperformed their reputations. These included BP, Deutsche Bank, UPS, Roche and BHP Billiton.
*   Meanwhile, companies successfully publicizing their achievements include Intel, Abbott Labs, Cisco, Johnson & Johnson and GlaxoSmithKline.
*   Regression analysis revealed social factors were, on average across the sample, twice as significant as either environmental or governance factors in determining survey respondents' perception of good corporate citizenship in 2011.
*   When asked about the importance of good corporate citizenship in respondents' decision making, we learned that an overwhelming majority–88%–state that it is "important."
*   Nearly half–45%–view it as "extremely important."

- From an industry sector standpoint, Pharmaceuticals stands out, with almost all surveyed companies leading in both actual and perceived performance.
- Several IT companies also displayed leadership in both measures.

Source: Governance Research Digest, Jun. 2011 (Vol. 2, No. 2)

4.2.2 British Public's Attitudes to Business

Author(s): IBE

Each year the IBE asks Ipsos MORI to survey the British public as to their attitudes to business and whether they believe business behaves ethically. A nationally representative quota sample of 1,001 British adults aged 16+ were interviewed throughout Great Britain using the Ipsos MORI Capibus across 156 sampling points.

Key findings

Six in ten (58%) people believe business behaves ethically, a third do not.

- But there is a disconnect between how they believe business behaves and trust in business leaders.
- In 2011, 58% of the public said they believe business behaves ethically; this is an 11%age point increase from when the survey was first run in 2003 (47%).
- However, the public were also asked which issues they think need to be addressed by business; the most common answer was that executive pay should be addressed (36%).
- In contrast, a survey conducted by IBE of FTSE250 companies revealed different issues emerging as priorities, albeit from a somewhat different list of options.
- "Executive pay" was not measured specifically, but business remuneration policies were only the 11th most important issue, far below issues such as bribery and corruption, discrimination and whistle-blowing (all of which were around 80%).

Source: Governance Research Digest, Dec. 2011 (Vol. 2, No. 8)

4.2.3 Business Strategy and Social Issues Poll

Author(s): Waggener Edstrom/RT Strategies

A recent poll of consumers and global marketing professionals has examined consumer attitudes to corporate social commitments. 511 consumers and 320 marketing professionals participated in the study, conducted by Waggener Edstrom Worldwide and RT Strategies in May 2009.

Key findings

86% of consumers believe that profitable businesses can address social issues.

- Nearly half of the consumers surveyed and over half of the marketing professionals surveyed rank the economy as their No. 1 concern.
- Despite growing concerns about corporate corruption, economic recession and global instability, consumers and marketing professionals believe companies can make a positive change in society through the products and services they sell.
- The poll showed that consumers are worried about the economy and are skeptical of business today, and want companies to focus first on running a successful business.
- Consumers' top expectations for business are that companies provide quality goods and services, provide good, stable working conditions for their employees, and operate profitably as well as responsibly.
- Consumers note that upon first impression, they are typically sceptical of business efforts to address social issues, with 31% feeling the efforts are a marketing ploy, and 16% feeling it takes a company away from its primary mission.
- 86% of consumers and 92% of marketing and communications professionals believe that for profit companies can successfully organize to address social issues.
- More than 70% of consumers and marketing professionals believe there are companies that are making a positive change in society through the products and services they sell today.
- When asked which key attributes for businesses and nongovernmental organizations (NGOs) consumers indicated businesses rank high in innovation, nimbleness and a focus on results, while NGOs rank highest on fairness and low cost.

- Consumers said they view business as bringing the needed resources to make a difference in society, not nonprofits or government. If they wanted to start over and make a difference in the world, 56% of consumers say they would want to be a business leader.
- Overwhelmingly, 60% of consumers believe that businesses are in the best position to effect positive results on social issues, as opposed to governments (14%).
- In addition, the study found that 53% of consumers were more likely to purchase goods and services from companies that clearly demonstrated their commitments to social responsibility.

Source: Social Research Digest, Jul. 2009 (Vol. 1, No. 7)

4.2.4   Chinese Consumers' Perceptions of Corporate Social Responsibility

Author(s): B. Ramasamay, M. Yeung.

This study aims to show that Chinese consumers are more supportive of CSR than their US or European peers. Survey data from 247 participants was collected in Shanghai and Hong Kong and compared with similar data for American and European consumers.

Key findings

Chinese consumers are more supportive of CSR than European or American consumers.

- The collective orientation of Chinese culture seems to be consistent with the support for CSR.
- The argument that consumer support for CSR is dependent on levels of economic development is not supported by this study's results. Shanghai, with the lower GDP per capita has the higher consumer support scores.
- This may in part be due to the fact that mass media in China and Hong Kong have been highlighting CSR issues such as the environment and working conditions more regularly over the last decade.
- The involvement of the government and the socialist past of China may explain the high consumer support for CSR in Shanghai compared to Hong Kong.

- In addition, rapid economic growth as a direct result of reform policies has resulted in a larger middle class population with increasing purchasing power.
- The growth in the purchasing budget has potential to result in a more socially responsible consumption as consumers are able to make choices from various sellers.
- In the Chinese cultural context, the traditional saying, 'one knows honour after getting rich' provides some justification as to why there is an increasing demand for CSR among consumers in China.
- The study results confirm that Chinese consumers are able to differentiate among the economic, legal, ethical and philanthropic responsibilities of businesses.
- However, the nature of differentiation among these responsibilities seems more varied than Western consumers.
- First, although the support for the four responsibilities is above the neutral point, consumers in Shanghai do not consider economic responsibilities as a social responsibility of businesses. In this sense, Shanghai's results are consistent with those found in studies of Western consumers.
- In Hong Kong there seems to be a general perception that all four components make up social responsibility. Thus, Hong Kong consumers may relate efforts at maximizing profits and decreasing costs to job protection and/or increased income among employees.
- However, in Shanghai, there may be an "us and them" attitude where economic performance is seen to benefit only employers.
- This may be the result of China's transition to a market economy which has resulted in large income inequalities.
- The emergence of an elitist entrepreneurial group who are owners of businesses may have created an environment where economic objectives are perceived to benefit only a minority and not the general consuming population.
- Economic responsibilities are considered to be the most important responsibility of the firm from a consumer perspective. In this regard, Chinese consumers are consistent in their evaluation and more similar to their American counterparts.

Source: Social Research Digest, Jul. 2009 (Vol. 1, No. 7)

4.2.5   Bahrain Responsible Business Survey

Author(s): 3BL Associates

3BL Associates has produced the first Bahrain Responsible Business Survey. A total of 109 respondents completed the survey, the greatest segment of whom were Bahraini males aged between 25-54 years old.

<u>Key findings</u>

Most respondents believed they understood CSR and sustainability, with 84% and 80% respectively saying they could explain either concept.

- Those able to explain the concept of a 'triple bottom line' formed the smallest percentage of respondents at only 27%.
- The most popular understanding of CSR— chosen by 87% of respondents—was community engagement.
- Yet despite the understanding of CSR and sustainability, a gap remains in practice and implementation.
- In fact, the percentage of respondents who believed that any given activity was part of social responsibility was higher in every instance, than the actual practice of that same CSR activity in respondents' organizations.
- One of the largest gaps between CSR understanding and implementation is a 45% gap between the recognition that environmental protection is part of CSR, and the actual practice of environmental protection CSR initiatives.
- This is somewhat disconcerting given that Bahrain is one of the highest carbon emitters per capita and is at risk from the associated threats of climate change.
- According to the 1st Bahrain communication report on Climate Change in Bahrain nearly 10% of Bahrain's area will be submerged in 2100 if sea level rise is only 1 metre.
- The most prevalent CSR activities—practiced by at least one third of respondents' organizations—are:
  - community engagement;
  - employee wellness;
  - transparency;
  - corporate governance;

- o   health and safety;
- o   and gender equality and diversity.
- Survey respondents largely want to work for ethical organizations with 83% saying they wanted to work for or own a company that is ethical and shared their values.
- The least important consideration, however, was the environment: only 55% cared whether the company they worked for or owned is environmentally responsible—despite the fact that almost 70% of respondents considered the environment a component of CSR.

Source: CSR Research Digest, Feb. 2013 (Vol. 5, No. 2)

4.2.6   CSR Perceptions Study

Author(s): Cone Communications and Echo Research

Cone Communications and Echo Research conducted a follow up to their 2011 global survey of consumer attitudes, perception and behaviors around CSR. The 2013 Cone Communications/Eco Global CSR Study includes the opinions of more than 10,000 people living in 10 of the largest countries in the world by GDP and is complemented with insights from country-specific CSR experts.

Key findings

Nine in 10 consumers surveyed want companies to go beyond the minimum standards required by law to operate responsibly and address social and environmental issues.

- 81% say they consider CSR when deciding where to work.
- 31% believe businesses should change the way they operate to align with greater social and environmental needs.
- 62% of surveyed global consumers say they use social media to address or engage with companies around CSR.
- In China, India and Brazil approximately 90% report using social channels to engage with companies around their CSR efforts.

Source: CSR Research Digest, Jun. 2013 (Vol. 5, No. 6)

4.2.7   Meaningful Brands Index

Author(s): Havas Media Group

Havas Media Group released an analytical framework that aims to measure the benefits brands bring to people's lives. The Meaningful Brand Index covers 700 brands, more than 134,000 consumers across 23 countries and measures the impact of the brand's benefits alongside its affect on 12 different different areas of well-being, such as health, happiness, financial, relationships and community.

Key findings

Most people worldwide would not care if more than 73% of brands disappeared tomorrow.

- There is a wide difference in brand attachment among markets with a strong polarization between developed and emerging markets. For example, in Europe and the US, people wouldn't care if 92% of brands disappeared. In Latin America, that figure drops to 58% and in Asia 49% wouldn't care if brands disappeared.
- Only 20% of brands worldwide make a significant, positive effect on people's wellbeing.
- There is a huge gap between people's expectations and what brands actually deliver.
- As a result, there is dramatic growth of consumer cynicism and distrust towards brands — especially in advanced economies, and increasingly in developing countries.
- Making a meaningful difference in consumers lives pays off for companies. Companies considered so-called Meaningful Brands outperformed the stock market by 120%, according to the 2013 analysis.
- The brands that top the index systematically improve personal and collective well-being of consumers and are rewarded by stronger brand equity and attachment.
- Google, Samsung, Microsoft, Nestle and Sony are the five most meaningful brands of 2013.

Source: CSR Research Digest, Jul. 2013 (Vol. 5, No. 7)

4.2.8   2013 Best Global Green Brands

Author(s): Interbrand

Interbrand produced their 2013 Best Global Green Brands report that examines the gap that exists between a corporation's environmental practices and consumers' perceptions of those practices. When identifying the top 50 Best Global Green Brands, Interbrand starts with the 100 brands that make up its annual Best Global Brands report and then conducts extensive consumer research to capture public perception of the brand's sustainable or green practices and compares that to environmental sustainability performance data provided by Deloitte—data that is based upon publicly available information.

Key findings

Automotive brands account for four of the top five spots in this year's ranking with innovation driving their success.

- After first-placed Toyota, Ford came in second, Honda third and Nissan fifth. Volkswagen ranked seventh.
- Although most automotive brands have invested in meeting sustainability goals and complying with regulations, those brands that have invested in creating innovative products as evidence of their commitment to sustainability — for example the Toyota Prius, Ford EcoBoost or Nissan LEAF — are receiving more recognition from consumers.
- At No. 4, Panasonic is the lone non-auto brand in the top five and also the top-ranked electronics manufacturer. The company earned its position as the tech category leader by continuing to offer innovative, eco and smart solutions to its global consumer base.
- Despite automakers accounting for most of the top spots, technology brands dominate the overall report.

Source: CSR Research Digest, Jul. 2013 (Vol. 5, No. 7)

4.2.9   2010 Gibbs & Soell Sense & Sustainability

Author(s): Gibbs & Soell

A new sustainability survey "2010 Gibbs & Soell Sense & Sustainability" finds U.S. consumers and executives skeptical about corporate sustainability commitment. The study surveyed both U.S. consumers and Fortune 1000 executives on their views of corporate efforts to improve the health of the environment through sustainable practices, products, or services.

<u>Key findings</u>

Only 16% of U.S. consumers and 29% of Fortune 1000 executives believe that a majority of businesses are committed to sustainability.

- 54% of executives and 48% of consumers believe only "some" businesses are committed to "going green".
- Financial inefficiency, market reluctance and unclear measurement are impeding the path to corporate sustainability.
- Executives cite insufficient return on investment (78%), consumers' unwillingness to pay a premium for green products or services (71%), and difficulty in evaluating sustainability across a product life cycle (45%) as the top barriers to more businesses going green.
- Businesses are taking more conservative approaches to resource management by asking "green" stewards to share duties.
- While more than two-thirds of executives (69%) indicate their companies have people responsible for sustainability or "going green" initiatives, most have added responsibilities for green efforts to the primary duties of a team of individuals (35%), or a C-suite or another senior level position (15%).
- Only about one in 10 say they have a C-suite or other senior level title/position dedicated solely to sustainability (12%), while 31% said there is no one at their organization who is primarily or partially responsible for green initiatives.

Source: CSR Research Digest, Sep. 2010 (Vol. 2, No. 9)

4.2.10 2013 Gibbs & Soell Sense & Sustainability® Study

Author(s): Gibbs & Soell

Gibbs & Soell, a global business communications firm with expertise in sustainability consulting and employee engagement, polled US employed adults about corporate commitment to environmental and social responsibility. The 2013 Gibbs & Soell Sense & Sustainability® Study focused on five primary areas: Perceptions of businesses' commitment to sustainability; Responsibility for sustainability initiatives; Interest in learning about companies "going green" and social responsibility initiatives; Strong link between sustainable choices made at work and at home; and, Media coverage about companies "going green" and social responsibility initiatives.

Key findings

Nearly three-quarters (73%) of employed U.S. adults who take part in environmental and social responsibility efforts at work are more likely to make sustainable choices at home as a result.

- Sustainability-engaged employees express a mutual relationship between sustainable activities at work and the choices they make at home. They also want to see their company and others more actively involved in sustainability initiatives.
- 80% of sustainability-engaged employees report encouraging others to make sustainable choices – meaning "going green" or engaging in social responsibility initiatives.
- Many employed adults reveal a gap in or express uncertainty about their own company's practices. Two-thirds (67%) of employees are not sure whether there is anyone at their company who is responsible for sustainability, or they say no one is responsible for sustainability at work.
- Nearly one-fifth (19%) of employees say their company does not promote sustainability at all.
- Among employed adults, there is a strong link between knowledge gained about a company's sustainability efforts and intent to purchase from that company.
- Three-quarters (75%) of employed adults say they would be more likely to buy a company's products or services if they learned it was making a great effort to adopt environmentally-conscious practices.
- The general public continues to doubt corporate America's commitment to sustainability.
- Only 21% of U.S. adults believe that a majority of businesses ("most," "almost all," or "all") are committed to "going green" – defined as "improving the health of the environment by implementing more sustainable business practices and/or offering environmentally friendly products or services."

- Most Americans (72%) and employed adults (74%) express interest in learning what companies are doing in terms of sustainability and "going green."

Source: CSR Research Digest, Sep. 2013 (Vol. 5, No. 9)

4.2.11 The Missing Link Between CSR and Consumer Trust: The Case of Fair Trade Products

Author(s): S. Castaldo, F. Perrini, N. Misani, A. Tencati.

This paper investigates the link between the consumer perception that a company is socially oriented and the consumer intention to buy products marketed by that company. The empirical study was conducted by interviewing 400 retail chain customers in two Italian cities (Milan and Florence).

Key findings

Trust can account for the success (or the failure) of a socially responsible company in the marketplace.

- In particular, socially oriented companies can achieve competitive advantage in those areas where trust is crucial in determining consumer choices, provided that the companies have the social reputation expected to accompany it (in this case, a reputation for respecting consumers' rights and for satisfying their needs).
- Trust in the Fair Trade concept correlates positively with trust in Fair Trade products.
- Consumer perceptions that a retailer is sensitive to consumer rights and needs correlates positively with trust in the Fair Trade products marketed by that retailer.
- Consumer trust in the Fair Trade products marketed by a retailer correlates positively with loyalty to and continued purchase of those products.
- Consumer trust in the Fair Trade products marketed by a retailer also correlates positively with a willingness to pay a premium price for these products.
- The study suggests that each particular category of stakeholder will be sensitive to different aspects of the CSR policies of the same company. A

reputation for environmental concern does not always imply a reputation for being responsive to consumers.

- Investment in social reputation (of any kind) must be complemented by investments in product lines where a company's specific kind of social reputation is relevant and appreciated by the particular stakeholders involved.

- The findings support the hypothesis that retailers could leverage their social reputation, based on greater attention to consumer needs, when they sell Fair Trade products or other trust-intensive products.

- Other socially labelled products such as organic food could be subjected to the same strategy.

- The role of retailers as a driving force in the CSR field warrants special mention, according to the authors, in that their intermediate positions between manufacturing companies and consumers frequently enable them to influence the decisions of both parties.

Source: CSR Research Digest, Apr. 2009 (Vol. 1, No. 4)

4.2.12 Consumer Perceptions of the Antecedents and Consequences of Corporate Social Responsibility

Author(s): A. J. S. Stanaland, M. O. Lwin and P. E. Murphy

The research examines CSR from the consumer's perspective, focusing on antecedents and consequences of perceived CSR. Perceptions of a firm's stance on corporate social responsibility (CSR) are influenced by its corporate marketing efforts including branding, reputation building, and communications.

<u>Key findings</u>

The findings strongly support the fact that particular cues, namely perceived financial performance and perceived quality of ethics statements, influence perceived CSR which in turn impacts perceptions of corporate reputation, consumer trust, and loyalty.

- Both consumer trust and loyalty were also found to reduce the perceived risk that consumers experience in buying and using products.

- From these significant findings, authors draw several conclusions and implications, including the importance of enhancing firm focus toward its ethical commitment and long-term reputation.

Source: CSR Research Digest, Sep. 2011 (Vol. 3, No. 9)

4.2.13 Globe Scan Radar 2012

Author(s): *Globe Scan*

Globe Scan Radar addresses the controversial issue of social citizenship as perceived by the general public. Globe Scan polled citizens' attitudes in 23 countries towards compelling companies to become socially and environmentally responsible.

Key findings

Nearly nine in ten citizens (88%) across 23 countries are in favour of laws and regulations to compel corporate good behavior.

- Among the populations who feel most strongly that governments should apply further pressure to force corporate responsibility are many with large, often controversial commodities sectors, such as Russia (95%), Nigeria (93%), Peru (92%), and Indonesia (91%).
- Other countries where over 90% of those surveyed feel further governmental action is required are crisis-hit Spain (97%) and Greece (91%), as well as France (94%), which recently elected a socialist government committed to higher levels of taxation for both businesses and the rich.
- There are some surprises—India, location of the Bhopal disaster, one of the most infamous incidents of corporate negligence in history, has the lowest proportion of respondents who support government-mandated corporate responsibility in the survey—but even in India three out of four citizens support a firm government hand in this area.
- While these results cast further light on the anti-business narrative GlobeScan has previously highlighted in the West, the breadth of this consensus—particularly in the developing world—demonstrates that business as a whole urgently needs to improve its approach to social citizenship.
- Continued failure in this regard risks a general upswing of anti-corporate feeling around the world, as well as specific impacts, driven by reputational damage, to the share prices of unresponsive

corporations.

Source: CSR Research Digest, Oct. 2012 (Vol. 4, No. 10)

4.2.14 The Product Mindset

Author(s): Underwriters Laboratories

UL's 2012 annual global study examines manufacturer and consumer perceptions about how products are made, sold, bought and consumed. For the study, researchers interviewed 1,201 consumers and 1,202 manufacturers in China, Germany, India and the US about topics related to safety, performance, innovation and sustainability.

Key findings

More than 80% of manufacturers say sustainability is essential to the success of their business.

- Eight-one percent of manufacturers agree sustainability products affect their ability to compete in the marketplace, and 89% say the same thing about operational sustainability.
- This represents an increase from 2011, when 76% and 85% said sustainable products and operations were important, respectively.
- But the overall percentage of manufacturers that say environmentally friendly products can be profitable has declined by 5% compared with 2011.
- Sixty percent still agree that the environment can be profitable.
- Two-thirds (67%) of manufacturers say they "strongly agree" the environment is becoming more important to consumers, while 53% say consumers are demanding more eco-friendly products that cost the same as their traditional counterparts.
- And while consumers say being environmentally friendly is important, it's not the top purchase driver.
- Quality and safety are the top issues consumers consider when making a purchase; nine percent cite environmental friendliness as the main reason they buy a product.
- However, consumers also say manufacturers don't put sufficient emphasis on being environmentally friendly.

Source: CSR Research Digest, Feb. 2013 (Vol. 5, No. 2)

4.2.15 Consumer Perceptions of Ethical Behaviour in Former Eastern Block Countries

Author(s): J. Tsalikis, B. Seaton

This paper presents the findings of a research project which aimed to initiate the measurement of consumer sentiments towards business ethical behaviour in Bulgaria, Poland, Romania and Russia. 3650 respondents from eight federal regions participated in Russia. 1003 respondents were from Poland, 1250 from Romania and 1019 from Bulgaria. National market research companies assisted with carrying out the face-to-face interviews. The findings are presented in the context of the Business Ethics Index (BEI).

Key findings

Russia was found to have the highest BEI of 135.8. Romania was placed second, followed by Poland with Bulgaria placed fourth.

- It is noteworthy that all four countries' scores were higher than the 2006 US BEI of 102.6. A BEI over 100 represents positive consumer sentiments, while a BEI under 100 represents negative consumer sentiments.
- Bulgarian respondents reported that, both based on personal experience and based on media coverage and comments from others, they felt that businesses behaved either somewhat or very unethically.
- Respondents from all four countries exhibit an optimism that business will behave more ethically in the future. Romanians appear to be the most optimistic.
- Interestingly, Russians perceived the past ethical behaviour of Russian companies to be largely positive. This could be explained by the fact that bribery was viewed as a positive practice under communism and by the fact that a number of fraudulent activities are still legal. However, the authors believe "fear" to be a plausible explanation.
- When asked specifically about personal experiences of ethical business behaviour, most Russian and Romanian comments related to the "quality of the product" while the Poles and Bulgarians mentioned particularly "good service".

- However, experiences of unethical behaviours were far more widely cited. For Russians, the most frequent complaint was with "defective products". Romanians and Bulgarians were concerned with "overcharging" and Poles with both "overcharging" and "rudeness".

- Both Poles and Romanians expressed concern about "poor treatment of employees" as an example of unethical business behaviour they had learned of through others or via the media.

- The paper recommends that Western companies make an effort to understand the ethical challenges they may face in postcommunist countries.

Source: Governance Research Digest, Jan. 2009 (Vol. 1, No. 1)

4.2.16 Corporate Reality of Consumer Perceptions Report

Author(s): Greenbiz

A new green paper from Greenbiz provides research findings from the Earthsense Eco-Insights Survey on how consumers perceive corporate environmental responsibility. Findings are based on Earthsense Business Indicator (EBI) metrics that identify companies which consumers see as sustainability leaders. They also identify the businesses consumers support based on eco-friendly products, and they track changes in perceptions over time.

Key findings

Companies are reluctant to communicate with consumers due to fears of greenwashing complaints and, as a result, take a 'don't tell, don't ask' stance, keeping their sustainability initiatives behind closed doors.

- Others are skeptical that consumers would be interested, aware or even comprehend their sustainability plans.

- Some companies are interested in a consumer point of view but have no access to the kinds of metrics they need to measure and track consumers' perceptions.

- The following 35 companies scored highest on the Earthsense Business Indicator, which assesses companies based on consumer views of their Sustainability, Product Impact, Investment Attractiveness, and Advocacy.

Amazon	H.E. Butt	Stonyfield Farm
Apple	Hess	Target
Benjamin Moore	Kashi	Tesla
Burt's Bees	Kraft	Tom's of Maine
Discovery	Lowe's	Trader Joe's
Earthbound Farm	Method	United Natural Foods
E & J Gallo	Microsoft	Wal-Mart
Fresh & Easy	MOM's	Walt Disney
General Electric	Odwalla	Wegmans
Google	Peet's	Whole Foods
Green Mountain Coffee	Publix	Yahoo
Hain Celestial Group	Sinclair Oil	

Source: Social Research Digest, Mar. 2009 (Vol. 1, No. 3)

4.2.17 Measuring Consumer Perceptions of Business Ethical Behaviour in two Muslim Countries

Author(s): J. Tsalikis, W. Lassar.

Measurements of consumers' perceptions of businesses ethical practices have, to date, largely overlooked Muslim countries. This study examines consumer perceptions of company behaviours in Turkey and Egypt. 2000 Turkish nationals and 1100 Egyption nationals, representing both urban and rural areas of each country, took part in the survey.

<u>Key findings</u>

Consumers in both Turkey and Egypt over- whelmingly perceive business as largely unethical.

- Egyptians perceive unethical business behaviours happening around them constantly, but do not feel that these affect them personally.
- Egyptians also seem less pessimistic about the future ethical behaviour of businesses.
- No significant effect of gender was found for either country.
- Businesses were perceived as behaving ethically when they were polite and courteous to the consumer personally.

- The acceptance of returned items was considered the highest determinant of ethical business behaviour.
- Defective products and overcharging were the most widely-cited personal experiences of perceived unethical business behaviour. Rudeness also received a high number of complaints.
- While there is increasing awareness of business ethics in Turkey, Turkish businesses are only at the beginning of embracing this process. Many companies are still involved in deceptive business practices.
- It should also be remembered that the concept of ethics as understood in the West, is not widely understood in other countries and cultures.

Source: Social Research Digest, Oct. 2009 (Vol. 1, No. 10)

4.2.18 Does Having an Ethical Brand Matter? The Influence of Consumer Perceived Ethicality on Trust, Affect and Loyalty

Author(s): J. J. Singh, O. Iglesias, J. M. Batista-Foguet

This study analyzes the nexus between perceived ethicality at a corporate level, and brand trust, brand affect and brand loyalty at a product level. It uses a theoretical framework with hypothesized relationships is developed and tested through structural equations modeling and specifically looks at 4,027 Spanish consumers. The results show a positive relationship between perceived ethicality and both brand trust and brand effect.

- There has been a recent rise in ethical consumerism in tandem with increasing number of corporate brands projecting a socially responsible and ethical image.
- The main research question is whether having a corporate brand that is perceived to be ethical have any influence on outcome variables of interest for its product brands?
- Results from the study demonstrate that:
  - There a positive relationship between perceived ethicality of a brand and both brand trust and effect.
  - Brand trust and brand affect both show a positive relation with brand loyalty.

Source: Social Research Digest, Feb. 2013 (Vol. 4, No. 2)

4.2.19 Shared Responsibility Study

Author(s): Cone

The findings of the 2010 Cone Shared Responsibility Survey have been released. The study asked more than 1,000 Americans about how they feel companies are performing on social and environmental issues.

<u>Key findings</u>

Although most businesses see their customers as central to their success, frequently customers feel their voices go unheard.

- 47% of respondents in the Cone survey gave companies a 'C' grade for how they are engaging with their customers on CSR issues.
- 9% gave companies an 'F' grade, while only 7% have the private sector an 'A'.
- The most common forms of engagement presented by respondents were a willingness to participate in company-led research or surveys (70%), buying or boycotting a company's products (44%), and emailing or calling a company to express concerns or support (32%).
- In addition to a willingness to engage companies on these issues, 92% of respondents also said they want to hear how companies are working on their products' environmental and social impacts.
- The two main obstacles to effective engagement are widespread scepticism about corporate communications - 87% believe companies only share positive information, and hide or withhold negative information - and confusion about what companies are actually saying about their work.
- The study also found that most individuals hold high expectations for corporate behaviour, including:
  - Ensuring product quality and safety (e.g., removing lead) (92%);
  - Ensuring worker health and safety (92%);
  - Ensuring proper product disposal/recycling (89%);
  - Ensuring human rights (e.g., eliminating child labour) (87%);
  - Reducing energy use and emissions to combat climate change (84%);
  - Preserving natural resources (e.g., forests) (84%);
  - Ensuring availability and access to safe water (83%);

- o Promoting diversity (81%);
- o Protecting threatened and endangered species (75%);
- o Minimizing disease (72%);
- o Improving nutrition and combating obesity (69%);
- o Alleviating poverty (62%).

Source: CSR Research Digest, Jun. 2010 (Vol. 2, No. 6)

4.2.20 Corporate Social Responsibility: The Wealthy Consumer's Viewpoint

Author(s): Luxury Institute

The Luxury Institute has published a new report mapping out consumer behavior by those with higher incomes, starting from $150,000 per year. The report compared data with a previous, similar survey carried out in 2007.

Key findings

Most (82%) wealthy Americans define social responsibility by a company behaving ethically with employees, customers and suppliers.

- 58% of respondents name Environmental behavior and philanthropic actions as an essential component of CSR (58%).
- 45% of wealthy consumers say they seek out brands with high ethical standards, but only 39% of these shoppers would be willing to pay a premium.
- This represents a sharp decrease from 2007, when 56% of respondents said they would pay a premium.
- Social networks have become important tools to find out more about a company's CSR stance.
- 27% of wealthy consumers said they learn about companies' socially responsible behavior via Facebook or Twitter.
- That's up from eight per cent who received their information from social media in 2007.
- Reading news articles remains the most popular method (52%), but it has decreased from 64% compared with five years ago.

- Amongst the companies most often cited for their ethical behavior are Apple, BMW, Coach, Lexus, Mercedes-Benz, Nordstrom, Starbucks and Whole Foods.

Source: Social Research Digest, Aug. 2012 (Vol. 3, No. 8)

4.2.21 Consumer Ethics in Japan: An Economic Reconstruction of Moral Agency of Japanese Firms – Qualitative Insights from Grocery/ Retail Markets

Author(s): Sigmund Wagner-Tsukamoto

This article reconstructs, in economic terms, managerial business ethics perceptions in the Japanese consumer market for fast-moving daily consumption products. Twenty interviews were conducted between October 2005 and January 2006. Twenty different retail or grocery companies were represented.

Key findings

Several managers argued that a reasonable level of product safety or high product quality were sufficient for characterizing 'the ethical product' and corporate business ethics.

- Managerial comments on the production of safe products, of high quality products and/or products that were priced competitively reflect on unintentional moral agency (the unintended generation of ethical outcomes through selfinterested economic exchange) in firmcustomer interactions.
- A second group of respondents spoke of 'customer orientation' or 'customer satisfaction' thus linking corporate moral agency with conventional marketing.
- Some managers related further, idealistic issues to the actual selling of their products and thus qualified – idealistically – the conception that customer orientation or customer satisfaction, as previously interpreted, were already sufficient to justify the selling and marketing of products.
- A self-confessed idealistic string of managers viewed a reasonable level of product quality and product safety or competitive pricing as

insufficient when it came to corporate marketing and firm-customer interactions.

- They argued that the ethical product should be distinguished from conventional products by factors such as life-cycle assessment for a product's production process or sourcing process.

- The majority of interviewees expressed concern that current laws pertaining to product safety, product liability, sanitation and recycling were open to (mis-)interpretation, that 'laws could be played with', or that laws did not cover all issues that required regulation, and that unregulated grey areas existed. A related problem raised in this connection was one of legal complexity.

- The majority of those managers who raised the issue of legal grey areas went on to say that internal rules had been implemented that ensured rule-following behaviour that considerably exceeded what was seemingly suggested by law.

- When asked about active moral agency, the features most widely reported were: the implementation of ISO standards, organic production methods, and universal product design aimed at being easy to use for the elderly and disabled.

- While such examples of active moral agency are themselves noteworthy, it should be acknowledged that the main bulk of respondents' discussion of business ethics related to unintentional and passive intentional agency.

Source: Governance Research Digest, Mar. 2009 (Vol. 1, No. 3)

4.2.22 The Aesthetics of Trust

Author(s): Mitch Baranowski, BBMG

A recent blog article from branding and marketing company BBMG outlines the findings of an investigation into the effectiveness of 'trustmarks' - seals on consumer products which denote a form of certification. 13 trustmarks were shown to 2,000 US consumers in order to gauge which characteristics make a trustworthy trustmark.

Key findings

The top three symbols — Energy Star, Recyclable and USDA Organic — are all federally sponsored and have benefited greatly from prominence and exposure, two factors that seem to go a long way toward cultivating trust, regardless of aesthetics or even the actual standards behind the mark.

- The article offers a number of recommendations for creating an effective trustmark:
  - Claim ownership. If you're going to go through the time and trouble of establishing and promoting certification standards, you deserve credit. Acronyms need help. The LEED trustmark is clearly from the US Green Building Council.
  - Design for the long haul. Reducing a complex idea to its visual essence takes time and expertise. But it's done every day. Give designers clear direction (and space) to create symbols that are durable, functional and beautiful. Most people will only know the certifications through the symbol; it's important.
  - Go for one clear idea. It's amazing how many trustmarks say... nothing at all... or way too much. Make sure your mark sends a clear message.
  - Break the box on colour. How many green logos can there be? Or blue, for that matter? Blue is often considered the safest colour. Energy Star earns points for breaking out with a brighter blue.
  - Get metaphoric. How might we move beyond the obvious — checkmarks, light bulbs, the scales of justice — without compromising legibility? Whatever metaphor you land on, make sure it has a clear connection to the standards at hand. Does that leaping bunny connote cruelty-free on its own? Does the Vitruvian-esque figure in the Fair Trade label capture empowering farmers and farm workers?
  - Think avatar. Long before Second Life, avatars have advanced logo design: Elsie the Cow, Elmer the Bull, the Energizer Bunny. The Rainforest Alliance frog is often brought to life to support awareness-raising campaigns. How might your trustmark feature a character that can give the program real personality?
  - Connect the dots for us. At the end of the day, make sure the mark on the front of the package is clearly connected to a communications platform on the back-end: how easy is it to find out what's behind the mark, how the standards were created, how they

are upheld and how it makes a difference in our lives today? Consumers care more than you think.

Source: Governance Research Digest, Nov. 2009 (Vol. 1, No. 11)

4.2.23 CEO, Social Media and Leadership Survey

Author(s): BRANDfog

The purpose of the survey is to better understand the connection between C-Suite engagement on social media, and the attitudes of customers and employees toward the brand. It surveyed several hundred employees of diverse companies, spanning in size from startups to Fortune 500 companies, and working at all levels of their respective organizations.

Key findings

Executive engagement on social media channels raises the brand profile, instills confidence in a company's leadership team, and builds greater trust, brand loyalty and purchase intent for its customers.

- Survey findings overwhelmingly confirmed that C-Suite executives who engage in social media are viewed as better equipped to lead a company, communicate values and shape a company's reputation in today's changing world.
- Specifically, the survey found that more than 80% of respondents believe that CEOs who engage on social media are better equipped than their peers to lead companies in a Web 2.0 world.
- What's more, 93% of respondents believe that CEO engagement on social media helps communicate company values, and grow and evolve corporate leadership in times of crisis.
- 82% of survey respondents said they were more likely to trust a company whose CEO and leadership team engage in social media.

Source: Social Research Digest, Mar. 2012 (Vol. 3, No. 3)

4.2.24 Sustainability Brand Map Study

Author(s): Climate Counts/Angus Reid Public Opinion

A new consumer study conducted by Climate Counts and Angus Reid examines the relationship between real and perceived sustainability action by a range of top brands. 97 companies represent ten industry sectors in the study. 2,032 American adults took part in the online survey. The first report covers the food and beverage, apparel, household products and internet/software/media sectors. Subsequent reports will cover electronics, airlines, hotels, banks, consumer shipping and food services.

Key findings

Sector	Brand	Perceived	Actual
Food & Beverages	General Mills	82	49
	Kellogg	81	42
	Kraft Foods	79	58
	Nestle	71	63
	The Coca-Cola Co.	64	66
	Sara Lee	59	33
	PepsiCo	55	62
	Stonyfield Farm	44	81
	Anheuser-Busch InBev	37	54
	ConAgra Foods	36	31
	Group Danone	33	64
	Unilever	32	79
	Molson Coors Brewing	24	44
	SABMiller	14	44
Apparel	Levi Strauss	86	58
	Nike	73	83
	Gap Inc.	62	52
	Liz Claiborne	42	7
	Limited Brands	24	35
	Jones Apparel Group	22	20
	VF Corporation	14	6
Household	Procter & Gamble	70	63

- In some sectors, brands with high perception scores actually had average actual scores. This suggests that the overall positive perception of these popular brands has a positive 'halo' effect on their perceived sustainability.
- In some cases, this could be linked to the trend of large master brands

buying smaller brands known for their emphasis on sustainability. The smaller brands imbue the larger master brand with a halo of sustainability.

- On the other hand, brands with the highest actual scores sometimes had relatively low perception scores. This suggests that the corporation's sustainability activity might not be consumer-facing, or that the activity might be focused in areas outside of the products/services being produced.

- This represents an opportunity to improve perception through increased consumer-facing sustainable product innovations and improved communications.

- On the flip side, brands already benefiting from a positive consumer perception have an opportunity to strengthen this position through increased sustainability efforts and continuing to innovate new, consumer-facing sustainable products.

Source: CSR Research Digest, Feb. 2010 (Vol. 2, No. 2)

4.2.25 The 2013 Cone Communications Social Impact Study

Author(s): Cone Communications

Cone Communications published a pioneering analysis of Americans' attitudes, perceptions and behaviors around corporate support of social and environmental issues. The 2013 Cone Communications Social Impact Study presents the findings of an online survey conducted February 7-28, 2013 by Ebiquity (formerly Echo Research) among a demographically representative sample of 1,270 U.S. adults, comprising 623 men and 647 women 18 years of age and older.

Key findings

The majority of Americans are uncertain of the extent to which corporate and individual efforts result in meaningful change.

- Despite a plethora of cause initiatives, fewer than one-in-five consumers (16%) believes companies have made significant positive impact on social or environmental issues, and just 25% believes their own purchases substantially influence those issues.

- 54% bought a product associated with a cause over the last 12 months, increasing 170% since 1993

- 89% of Americans are likely to switch brands to one associated with a cause, given comparable price and quality, jumping nearly 35% since 1993
- 91% wants even more of the products and services they use to support cause
- 88% wants to hear how companies are supporting social and environmental issues
- 79% says they would donate if given the opportunity, and 65% has actually done so in the past year
- 76% says they would volunteer, but only 42% has reported doing just that in the past 12 months
- 84% indicates they would tell friends and family about corporate cause efforts, but just 38% actually has
- 88% would boycott, but fewer than half (42%) reports doing so in the past year.

Source: Social Research Digest, Feb. 2014 (Vol. 5, No. 2)

4.2.26 Best Global Brands 2014

Author(s): Interbrand

Interbrand issued it annual top 100 most valuable brands, examining three key aspects that contribute to a brand's value: the financial performance of the branded product and service, the role the brand plays in influencing customer choice and the strength the brand has to command a premium price or secure earnings for the company. In addition to identifying the top 100 most valuable brands, this year's Best Global Brands report also examines three pivotal ages in brand history that have reshaped business for the better: the Age of Identity, the Age of Value, and the Age of Experience.

Key findings

For the second year in a row, Apple and Google claim the top positions on Interbrand's Best Global Brands ranking. Valued at USD $118.9 billion, Apple (#1) increased its brand value by 21%. Google (#2), valued at $107.43 billion, increased its brand value by 15%.

- For the first time in Best Global Brands two global brands – not just one – have each earned a brand value that exceeds USD $100 billion.
- Huawei (#94), the Chinese telecommunications and network equipment provider, also makes Best Global Brands history as the first Chinese company to appear on Interbrand's ranking. With 65% of its revenue coming from outside of China and with its earnings continuing to climb both domestically and across Europe, the Middle East, and Africa, Huawei is quickly becoming one of the largest telecommunications equipment makers in the world. The company is currently the third largest smartphone manufacturer in the world – just behind Samsung and Apple. The Chinese brand is one of five new entrants to enter the Best Global Brands ranking – the others being DHL (#81), Land Rover (#91), FedEx (#92), and Hugo Boss (#97).
- Interbrand contends that a new, emerging era is upon the global business world: the Age of You.
- 2014 TOP RISERS: Facebook (#29, +86%), Audi (#45, +27%), Amazon (#15, +25%), Volkswagen (#31, +23%), and Nissan (#56, +23%)
  - Facebook (#29, +86%): The world's largest social network, Facebook continues to exceed expectations. Reported on its Q2 earnings call, income from its operations was a staggering USD $1.4 billion. One year prior it was USD $562 million. Facebook's ad business on mobile phones has been particularly strong. For the first time in its history, the company reported that revenue from advertising on mobile phones exceeded half (53%) of all its advertising for the quarter.
  - Audi (#45, +27%): Audi is the top-rising automotive brand in this year's Best Global Brands report. It was a record-breaking year for the brand, having sold the greatest amount of cars in its history, and having achieved an operating profit of more than USD $6 billion.
  - Amazon (#15, +25%): It was another banner year for Amazon, "Earth's most customer-centric company." Amazon's commitment to responsiveness has become part of the brand's mythos. It continues to grow its core business through services such as Amazon Prime, which, at one point, garnered more than a million subscribers in a single week.

Source: CSR Research Digest, Nov. 2014 (Vol. 6, No. 11)

4.2.27 Global Best Retail Brands Report

Author(s): Interbrand

Interbrand has released its 4th annual global report dedicated to the retail sector. The global Best Retail Brands report ranks the top 50 North American retail brands, the top 50 European retail brands, the top 30 Asia-Pacific retail brands and the top 20 Latin American retail brands—all by brand value.

Key findings

Major retailers are looking beyond their core business models to gain competitive advantage.

- They are doing this by using online innovation to bridge the divide between in-store and online shopping and by developing a strategic understanding of sales data so that they can meet customer needs and desires better and faster than ever before.
- Walmart is the most valuable retail brand in North America and across all four regions, with a brand value of USD $131.877 billion. Looking beyond North America, the following brands ranked as the top retailer in their respective regions: H&M – USD $18.168 billion (Europe), Woolworths – USD $4.948 billion (Asia-Pacific), Natura – USD $3.156 billion (Latin America)
- The remarkable success of apparel brands can be attributed to their sheer scale in addition to their unique brand attributes and strategies. Beyond real estate dominance, leading brands ably manage to stay on top of trends while feeding shoppers' social media appetites. Online-only players are increasingly creating real world interaction with customers, such as pop-up shops, showrooms, and kiosks in enhancing the overall customer journey.
- Most consumer electronics brands dropped in brand value this year. Retailers around the globe face a fiercely competitive environment. Ongoing challenges include waning customer loyalty and shrinking profit margins. Aiming to break down all the barriers between its stores and its internet and mobile sites, leading brands are focusing their efforts on their omnichannel strategies.
- Although the biggest retailers still have name recognition, the

traditional department store format is largely fading away. Celebrated brands saw little growth in their stores throughout North America and Europe. Other parts of the world where department store growth is generally flat include Japan, Australia, and Korea. Such stagnant growth indicates the need for fresh brand appeal to new consumer segments.

- Two critical market trends continue to impact the growth of the drugstore category. First, is the world's aging population, which is accompanied by rising levels of heath consciousness. Second, there's a rising demand for affordable and accessible healthcare worldwide. While the traditional drugstore format continues to carry health and beauty products, the pharmacy is moving away from simple prescription dispensing to an active healthcare service function.

- Grocery retailers are reinventing themselves according to how consumers want to shop. Trends driving change include mobile technology, home delivery, consumer income disparity, and the strategic necessity of e-commerce.

- To remain relevant in an increasingly competitive sector, top brands are creating meaningful experiences for their customers and communities. Shoppers are encouraged, inspired, and supported with service and instruction. Internationally, companies continue to experiment with the best way to expand.

Source: CSR Research Digest, Jul. 2014 (Vol. 6, No. 7)

4.3 Purchasing Decisions and Motivations

4.3.1 Willingness to Pay for Socially Responsible Products: Case of Cotton Apparel

Author(s): Jung E. Ha-Brookshire, Pamela S. Norum

This study seeks to investigate significant factors influencing consumers' willingness to pay a premium for three different socially responsible products – organic cotton, sustainable cotton, and US-grown cotton shirts. Through random-digit-dialing, the study data were collected from 500 respondents nationally via telephone surveys.

Key findings

More than half of the respondents indicated that they were willing to pay a premium for organic, sustainable, and US-grown cotton shirts ($5.00 or more for these cotton shirts at the $30.00 retail value).

- Consumer attitudes toward socially responsible apparel, attitudes toward environment, age, and gender were found to be significant factors for consumers' willingness to pay a premium.
- Four apparel product evaluative criteria, brand name, laundering requirements, color, and fit, were also found to be important for consumers' willingness to pay a premium.

Source: CSR Research Digest, Aug. 2011 (Vol. 3, No. 8)

4.3.2   Consumer Purchasing Motivations Study

Author(s): Yahoo

Search engine company Yahoo has conducted a study into the extent to which consumers purchasing decisions reflect their intentions to be conscious of their health and the environment. This study surveyed 1,500 people between the ages of 18-54 around the US.

Key findings

While 77% of consumers describe themselves as "green" - actively living their lives conscious of their health and environment – these green consumers have different purchasing motives.

- The study divides its respondents into four main consumer groups:
  - Deeply Committed (23% of market), who are mostly female adults in their mid-30s, more educated, live in metropolitan areas and respond most to the "positively impact the environment" message.
  - Trendy (24% of market), who are ethnically diverse consumers aged between 18 to 34. They respond to message about "everybody else is doing it" and newest technology.
  - Practical (13% of market), who are generally over 45 years-old consumers with children and live in rural areas.
  - Passive (17% of market), who are generally younger women aged 25 to 34 with children. They respond to messages about providing a better life for their family.

- The remaining 23% of the market says they don't care about the environment, or they say they care, but don't take any action.
- The study found that the "deeply committed" and "trendy" consumers present the biggest opportunity for advertisers.
- 80% of the "deeply committed" and 69% of the "trendy" consumers say they have made a green purchase in the past six months.
- Around 70% of the "deeply committed" and "trendy" say they have recently convinced a family or friend to buy the same green alternative product as them.

Source: Social Research Digest, Jan. 2009 (Vol. 1, No. 1)

4.3.3 Consumer Purchasing Decisions Study

Author(s): Grocery Manufacturers Association/ Deloitte

A new study, "Finding the Green in Today's Shoppers: Sustainability Trends and New Shopper Insights", has been released by Deloitte and the Grocery Manufacturers Association. The report examines the extent to which consumers are considering the sustainability attributes of products when they grocery shop. More than 6,400 consumers in 11 major retailers took part in the study.

<u>Key findings</u>

54% of shoppers demonstrated that they actively consider environmental sustainability characteristics in their buying decisions

- Most shoppers surveyed, 95%, are open to considering green products, 67% of shoppers looked for green products, but only 47% actually found them.
- Despite the fact that shoppers are often thinking green, they actually bought green products on just 22% of their shopping trips.
- This highlights the need for better shopper marketing programs to close the gap.
- The rate of green purchasing in stores was very sensitive to the use of in-store communications and information.
- A significant minority of committed and proactive green shoppers will pay a premium for sustainable products.

- However, the larger potential population of shoppers that lean toward green want price and performance parity for sustainable products because it is not their dominant purchase driver.
- Demographically, green shoppers are diversely spread along all income ranges, age brackets, education levels and various household sizes.
- On average, green shoppers tend to be older, have higher income and are more educated, but they can be found across the consumer population.
- Green shoppers represent a high value segment who buy more products on each trip and visit the store more regularly.
- Green shoppers are less price sensitive than the average shopper and they are generally not bargain hunters.

Source: Social Research Digest, Jun. 2009 (Vol. 1, No. 6)

4.3.4   Socially Conscious Consumerism Report

Author(s): Network for Business Sustainability

This systematic review, conducted by the Network for Business Sustainability, synthesizes thirty years of research on whether consumers are willing to reward firms for their positive sustainability actions either by changing their behaviour or by paying a price premium. The authors summarise findings from over 90 academic and practitioner articles to summarise current knowledge in this area.

Key findings

The typical average premium that consumers indicate they would be willing to pay is around 10%.

- Some evidence suggests that consumers will demand a discount for 'unsustainability' and that this is greater than a premium for sustainability.
- Consumer willingness to change their behaviour (towards the socially conscious choice) is more common than willingness to pay a premium.
- Consumers often appear to expect the socially better choice to be of the same quality and price – it does not appear that they will trade-off functionality.

- There is currently no coherent view of who a socially conscious consumer is. All the usual descriptors used in consumer research, such as demographics and psychographics, have provided conflicting results thus far.
- There is some evidence that factors other than sustainability attributes are more important in driving consumer behaviour, such as prompting consumers, making their purchasing decisions visible, and making them feel like their purchases will make a difference.
- Companies should not chase the conscious consumer, as if there is only one kind. Instead, they should figure out which elements are important to different groups of customers.
- Managers should communicate how one consumer's purchase actually contributes to the broader social goal.
- Negative company behaviours (acting unethically or irresponsibly) have more impact than positive firm behaviours, often because consumers do not know the positive information.
- Managers need to strike the balance between legitimately informing consumers of their positive sustainability actions, whilst not being perceived as over-emphasising modest claims.

Source: Social Research Digest, Nov. 2009 (Vol. 1, No. 11)

4.3.5 Through Thick and Thin: How Fair Trade Consumers Have Reacted to the Global Economic Recession

Author(s): T. Bondy and V. Talwar

The study examines the effects of recessionary economic conditions on fair trade consumers' purchasing behaviour. An online survey was administered to 306 fair trade consumers from Canada, the United Kingdom and the United States of America.

Key findings

The results reveal a discrepancy among fair trade consumers as only consumers that purchase fair trade on an occasional basis adhered to established consumer behaviour norms, i.e. decreasing their purchases of fair trade products and becoming significantly more price aware.

- Respondents who actively consume fair trade generally remained loyal to their purchase.
- While some active consumers altered their purchasing behaviour, this phenomenon was not common amongst this group as no statistically significant changes were observed.
- Differences were also noted among the three countries as the Canadian and US fair trade consumers significantly decreased their consumption of fair trade as a result of the recession, whereas the UK consumers did not.

Source: Social Research Digest, Aug. 2011 (Vol. 2, No. 4)

4.3.6   Do Consumers Care about Ethical-Luxury?

Author(s): I. A. Davies, Z. Lee and I. Ahonkhai

This article explores the extent to which consumers consider ethics in luxury goods consumption. In particular, it explores whether there is a significant difference between consumers' propensity to consider ethics in luxury versus commodity purchase and whether consumers are ready to purchase ethical-luxury.

Key findings

Prior research in ethical consumption focuses on low value, commoditized product categories such as food, cosmetics and high street apparel.

- It is debatable if consumers follow similar ethical consumption patterns in luxury purchases.
- Findings indicate that consumers' propensity to consider ethics is significantly lower in luxury purchases when compared to commoditized purchases and explores some of the potential reasons for this reduced propensity to identify or act upon ethical issues in luxury consumption.

Source: Social Research Digest, Feb. 2012 (Vol. 3, No. 2)

4.3.7   UK Grocery Retailing: Back to the Future?

Author(s): City Food Lecture

Sainsbury's chief executive, Justin King, discusses of how UK consumers have not neglected their beliefs in the pursuit of value for money. The discussion took place at City Food Lecture which is an annual fixture in the City of London and food industry calendars.

<u>Key findings</u>

UK consumers have not neglected their beliefs in the pursuit of value for money.

- Despite the current strain on household incomes, consumers still want products that are sourced sustainably and as such, businesses need to embed corporate responsibility into their operations.
- Consumers want to buy products that are value for money and give them quality and the high ethical standards they have come to expect.
- In the UK, sales of Fairtrade food products alone rose 36%, from £749 million in 2009, to over £1billion in 2010.
- And sustainable fish sales grew 16.3%, from £178 million in 2009 to £207 million in 2010.
- Today, consumers enjoy greater transparency and access to information than ever before.
- Increasingly this is through the use of technology and social media where consumers can compare information and talk to each other about products.
- CR today has to be embedded in your business and be part of 'the way we do things'.
- And consumers expect us to demonstrate our CR values every day and to communicate with them directly about them.

Source: Social Research Digest, Mar. 2012 (Vol. 3, No. 3)

4.3.8   The Return on Investment Lifestyle

Author(s): Natural Marketing Institute

Natural Marketing Institute examines the underlying consumer trends and its implications to businesses. The research is based on the NMI's Health and Wellness database as well as NMI's LOHAS Consumer Trends database.

Key findings

Almost a third of consumers indicate that when given the choice to buy a product or service, they make their decisions with an understanding of the effect they will have on the health and sustainability of the world, its environment, and people.

- In essence, corporate social responsibility (CSR) is gradually taking a foothold in how consumers view a company and its products and will increasingly impact consumers' purchase decisions.
- Increased corporate responsibility measures are not only viewed by consumers as the "right thing to do", they are impacting consumers' willingness to pay for that added value.
- One out of five consumers indicate they are willing to pay 20% more for products which are made in an environmentally-friendly and sustainable way and one out of four feel products that are environmentally-friendly have a higher quality quotient.
- Planetary health will continue to be a consumer-required foundational aspect of products across all categories and across all stages of production, as environmental responsibility will be a "must-have" dimension impacting future purchase decisions.
- Food also has value differentials such as disease prevention, anti-aging and quality of life issues.
- In fact, the majority of consumers feel that eating healthy helps them to be in control of their life and can also improve the quality of their life.
- Even further, the majority of consumers are more likely to purchase a food or beverage product if it provided the additional value of heart health benefits, boosted their immunity, lowered cholesterol, helped prevent cancer, or enhanced their energy levels.
- Company supported causes can also have significant impact on purchase decisions.
- Two-thirds of consumers agree that if they knew that a company supported a specific cause or charity, such as childhood hunger or cancer research, it would positively impact their decision to do business with that company.
- In addition, fair trade continues to emerge as a differentiating factor, having grown 35% in importance since 2004.

- Consumers are recalculating their ROI based on a new set of measures and beliefs.
- While monetary cost will always be a factor in an unstable economy, consumers are increasingly evaluating the real value of products as they continue to seek more emotional return on their investment.
- Corporate social responsibility, sustainability, functionality beyond traditional function, fair trade practices, and fortification are just a few of the differentiating factors which help create increased ROI to the consumer.

Source: Social Research Digest, Jun. 2012 (Vol. 3, No. 6)

4.3.9   Ethical Consumer Market Report

Author(s): The Co-operative Group

A report by Cooperative Group examines the UK markets for ethical goods and services in 2011. The report has been produced since 1999 and acts as a barometer of ethical spending in the UK.

Key findings

The request for ethical consumer goods and services continued to grow despite the economic recession, with the total market edging up to £47.2bn.

- Although ethical consumers are vitally important agents of change, the recent expansion of the market has been driven by an increase in the number firms switching to key products into ethical categories.
- In order for sustainable solutions to endure, it requires a government committed to long-term interventions.
- The market has increased more than three times since 1999. Accordingly, the increase means that average household spends £989 a year on ethical goods and services.
- Businesses beginning to respond to the challenge to provide ` with more sustainable products and services.
- This is evidenced and supported by figures illustrating that the sales of ethical food and drink rose 7.8% in 2011 to £7.5bn with fairtrade, Rainforest Alliance and Organic certified products.
- Sales of green home products rose 10.6% to £8.4bn.

- Sales of eco-travel and transport rose 11.8% to £3.1bn with sales of the most efficient cars up 29% to just over £1bn.
- The report confirmed that despite the economic downturn, the sustainability and ethical sector—which was predicted by experts to suffer—is healthy and growing.
- In order for the efforts of responsible business and ethical consumers to endure, sustainable solutions require a government committed to long-term intervention.

Source: Social Research Digest, Jan. 2013 (Vol. 4, No. 1)

4.3.10   The Better Consumer: Trend Report

Author(s): texSture

texSture produced a report that demonstrates that there may be demand for more responsible products in EU countries and if retailers overlook consumer requirements they may miss out on important market opportunities. "The Better Consumer: Trend" Report is based on available secondary data included in business reports, publications, and academic articles; it incorporates insights on consumer attitudes and combines all available data about the increasingly popular consumer behavior towards better products in France, Germany, Italy, Scandinavia, France, United Kingdom, and the Netherlands.

<u>Key findings</u>

Though price is a preeminent factor in consumer choice, increasingly buyers are willing to choose sustainable products, given a comparable price/quality ratio.

- Consumers believe that sufficient information about products is not readily accessible in order to help them rationalize their purchasing decisions.
- Convenience is important to consumers; however, if chain retailers and department stores offered more sustainable products, the market would be favourable.
- The price/quality ratio is fundamental for consumers, particularly if a sustainable product is on par as its conventional counterpart and on a similar price point.

- Consumers are skeptical of large brands and corporations and view them to be nontransparent thus untrustworthy and therefore are more inclined to purchase from local sellers.
- Because sustainability vernacular varies from country to country, it affects consumer-based communications and the products that are the most popular are most likely to be found in their ranges.

Source: Social Research Digest, Apr. 2013 (Vol. 4, No. 4)

4.3.11 Warm Glow or Cold, Hard Cash? Social Identity Effects on Consumer Choice for Donation versus Discount Promotion

Author(s): K. P. Winterich and M. J. Barone

Across five studies, the authors investigate how social identification influences consumer pAuthor(s) for discountbased promotions (i.e., cents-off deals) versus donation-based promotions (in which purchase results in a donation to a charitable cause). In doing so, they demonstrate the interplay between self-construal and a specific social identity (i.e., that associated with the particular charity featured in a donation-based promotion) on consumers' pAuthor(s)s for these two types of promotions.

Key findings

In general, consumers possessing interdependent self--construals prefer donations to a greater extent than those with independent self-contruals.

- However, the findings further indicate that these effects of self-construal are attenuated if
  - the donation-based promotion does not involve a charity that is identity congruent or
  - a cause-congruent identity is more salient than self-construal at the time of decision making.
- The authors also identify boundary conditions of charity efficiency and product type for these self-construal effects.
- In addition to demonstrating how multiple identities interact to influence consumer promotion, the authors discuss important managerial implications on discount vs. donation-based promotions.

Source: Social Research Digest, Oct. 2011 (Vol. 2, No. 6)

4.3.12   Doing Well By Doing Good

Author(s): The Nielsen Company

The Nielsen Company, a global information and measurement company issued a report that investigates the willingness of customers to put their money on companies committed to social responsibilities when it comes to spending in goods and services. The report, Doing Well by Doing Good is based on responses from more than 30,000 consumers from Asia-Pacific, Europe, Latin America, the Middle East, Africa and North America.

Key findings

Increasingly consumers expect companies to have a positive environmental and/or social impact, indeed and interests is translated even in choice of workplace, with 66% of the participants stating a pAuthor(s) for responsible companies.

- 55% of the participants of the study stated to be willing to pay an extra for products or services delivered from responsible companies, marking a 10% increase in interest from 2011 and a % from 2012. On the other hand, most consumers are however not willing to make any trade-offs in quality of the product/service as they go green.
- Willingness to pay an extra is lower in North America and Europe, whereas respondents from Asia-Pacific, Latin America and Middle East exceeded the global average. Similar responses were reported for stated past purchases of sustainable products though 52% of the participants stated to have made a purchase from a responsible company in the last 6 months (as of time of publication of the report).
- Family and friends, in the Middle East, Africa and Asia Pacific regions, are deeply influential regarding to ethical purchases and eco-friendly attributes of brands.
- Sustainable products, promoted and advertised on the packaging as such, sell better than non-sustainable brands, with an increase between 2%- 5% of annual sales. Interestingly, 52% of the respondents' check product packaging to ensure sustainable impact.
- When reaching the right consumers and undertaking precision marketing techniques, age matters. Of the 2/3 of the respondents belonging to the "sustainable mainstream community", half are

Millennials.

- Half of the respondents (49%) stated that they actively engaged in volunteer work and or/donated monetarily to social and environmental programs. The top causes of extreme concern they survey found consumers most passionate about include: access to clean water, access to sanitation, poverty and hunger, non-communicable diseases, child mortality and environmental sustainability.

- The most successful "go green" campaigns have been those that appealed to a heterogeneous group of buyers that have also kept a focus on the most profitable consumer segments.

Source: CSR Research Digest, Aug. 2014 (Vol. 6, No. 8)

4.3.13 From Marketing to Mattering

Author(s): Accenture and Havas Media RE:PURPOSE

Accenture and Havas Media RE:PURPOSE issued a study which reveals the reasons for the disconnect between business and consumer expectations of sustainable products and services. From Marketing to Mattering, based on a survey of 30,000 consumers in 20 countries, was commissioned in response and as a companion to the 2013 UN Global Compact-Accenture CEO Study on Sustainability.

Key findings

Only a third of consumers regularly consider sustainability in their purchasing decisions.

- To engage more effectively with consumers, companies must:
  - Promote a commitment to honesty and transparency throughout their organization's operations in order to realize their full value. Trust is critical: Corruption is seen as the leading challenge for countries to address, ahead of job creation and economic growth, and a top-five challenge for businesses. Companies must be able to hold themselves accountable to consumers now armed with greater access to information that helps them expose disingenuous corporate behavior.
  - Meet expectations for responsible business practices while delivering tangible improvements to consumers' lives. This is

particularly so in mature markets, where consumers increasingly consider corporate engagement in sustainability as a given.

o Shift their communication with consumers from a focus on their sustainable credentials and performance to a clearer demonstration of their purpose and relevance to society and the environment. This is especially relevant in emerging markets where companies are seen as playing a major role in improving health, education and other fundamental quality of life factors.

- There are dramatic differences in sentiment and purchasing behavior between consumers in developing and developed markets:

o 85% of Indian respondents and 66% of Chinese believe their quality of life will improve in the next five years; 73% of Indians and 79% of Chinese say they actively buy responsible brands.

o By comparison, 37% of Western Europeans and 51% of Americans believe their lives will improve over the same period. And only 49% and 44%, respectively, say they actively buy responsible brands.

Source: CSR Research Digest, Sep. 2014 (Vol. 6, No. 9)

4.4   Sustainable Consumption and Green Spending

4.4.1   Sustainable Consumption: Green Consumer Behaviour When Purchasing Products

Author(s): W. Young, K. Hwang, S. McDonald, C.J. Oates.

This paper examines the extent to which UK consumers make 'green' consumption choices when purchasing technology products. Data were collected from 81 self declared green consumers via indepth interviews on the subject of recent purchases of technology products.

Key findings

The most widely-cited criteria mentioned by respondents when deciding which electronics products to purchase were: product environmental performance (energy efficiency and rating, durability, water consumption, fuel consumption, etc.); product manufacturing (recycled material content, chemical content, repairability); and second hand availability.

- Moving house was the most common situational context in which respondents made decisions to purchase new electrical items.
- Lack of time influenced interviewees to exclude criteria that can be time consuming to research, such as the details of a company's CSR record.
- Lack of time for research, decision-making and the purchase itself was the first of five main barriers for interviewees considering making green purchases.
- The second barrier was the price of a product, as those with higher energy ratings, for example, were often found to be more expensive.
- The third major barrier was the lack of available information on the environmental and social performance of products and manufacturers. Respondents found such information difficult to find and, when it was located, it was described as vague.
- This lack of information was most prevalent for computers, televisions, DVD players and hi-fis.
- In some cases, the lack of information prompted respondents to discard green criteria when making their selection of product.
- Fourth, the respondents in this study found that the cognitive effort in researching, decision-making and searching for the products was significant.
- The final barrier for interviewees was the prioritizing of non-green criteria.
- The inclusion of non-green criteria, habits and
- desires in their decision making included: specification, brand, size, price (including discount), information source (Which magazine, previous experience), reliability, type (e.g. sports car), model, appearance, design, colour, age, sales technique, service history, retailer choice and free and timely delivery.
- Interviewees knew the environmental impacts of the products they were purchasing but a few found that the eco-efficiency consumer approach was not far reaching enough.
- These individuals tried to avoid purchasing electronics products because the environmental and social problems were so great.
- Many were also anti-multinational brands and companies and tried to buy from local or small retailers and companies.

- Three factors were found to facilitate the consideration of green criteria in product purchasing decisions.
- The first method interviewees used to reduce cognitive effort, especially under time pressure, was to trust certain information sources, labels or organizations providing a shortcut to choosing a greener product.
- The second facilitation factor is the availability of green products, usually via mainstream retailers. This may be a particular factor for technology products, which are one-off expensive purchases with which the consumer does not want to take high levels of risk.
- The third facilitating factor was feelings of guilt. Respondents reported feeling guilty for, amongst other things, having other (nongreen) priorities, not prioritizing green criteria, not being able to purchase the greenest product, and not knowing about certain issues at the time of purchase that they discovered afterwards.
- The authors highlight six key factors that they feel will help consumers to purchase a more ethical technology product. These are:
  o the consumer's green value is strong;
  o the consumer has purchase experience;
  o the consumer has plenty of time for research and decision-making;
  o the consumer has good knowledge of the relevant environmental issues;
  o green products are reasonably available and
  o the consumer can afford and is prepared for the financial costs.
- The authors suggest that if any one of these criteria is a weak or negative influence, then this may water down the influence of the green criteria on the final purchase.

Source: CSR Research Digest, May 2010 (Vol. 2, No. 5)

4.4.2   Sustainable Consumption Report

Author(s): BSR

BSR's latest report examines the newest frontier of sustainability, outlining the opportunities for companies to deliver value to customers, society, and the planet by promoting sustainable consumption – an economic and social system that allows all individuals to meet their basic needs without disrupting the planet's healthy ecosystems. The report identifies opportunities for companies to deal with sustainable consumption through three key parts of the business value cycle — product design, consumer engagement and use, and end-of-use.

Key findings

In a world where our consumption patterns outpace the planet's ability to regenerate resources by 30%, businesses that figure out how to deliver enhanced value by radically reducing material inputs and engaging consumers on product use will be well positioned for success.

- Design choices about things like material weight and packaging have direct impacts on transportation costs and fuel use, while choices about energy efficiency directly impact energy consumption in a product's use phase.
- In some cases, a focus on sustainable consumption may result in the radical redesign of familiar products, and in other cases, there may be an opportunity to deliver the same value through services (such as car-sharing) rather than products (such as car sales).
- Consumers may be in the driver's seat when it comes to choices about products and use, but companies can give consumers the keys to more sustainable behavior by embedding sustainable options into products and giving consumers simple, accessible information about how to use their products in a more sustainable manner.
- Companies are setting targets to eliminate all waste from products' end-of-life. This focus allows business to incorporate waste prevention into the design phase of products.
- Some companies are drawing inspiration from nature by implementing "closed-loop systems" that mirror the natural life cycles of living plant cells.

Source: CSR Research Digest, Aug. 2010 (Vol. 2, No. 8)

4.4.3   Sustainable Consumer Study

Author(s): BBMG

Brand innovation firm BBMG has recently releases a comprehensive study, Unleashed: How New Consumers Will Revolutionize Brands and Scale Sustainability. New multimedia study examines the marketplace's most powerful segment; illustrates how they will revolutionize branding and drive green innovation.

Key findings

More than 70 million adults across the United States are considered New Consumers, defined less by demographics than by shared values.

- Early adopters and "box turners" increasingly concerned with products' impact on the planet and its people, these savvy shoppers are twice as likely to try new things, share their opinions online and reward (or punish) brands based on corporate practices.
- Even during the recession, 25% are willing to pay more for sustainable products.
- At the same time, they're re-evaluating purchasing priorities, often opting for DIY projects and choosing to enjoy experiences instead of new commodities.
- This increasingly important group – currently 30% of the U.S. population – is poised to help sustainable brands enter the mainstream, while forcing large brands to accelerate their pathways to sustainability.
- Their influence will be so great that BBMG identifies 2011 as the dawn of a new economy with unlimited opportunities for innovative, values-driven, authentic brands.

Source: CSR Research Digest, Apr. 2011 (Vol. 3, No. 4)

4.4.4   Product Environmental Impact Study

Author(s): Eurobarometer

Findings from a recent study of European consumers suggest that they are increasingly likely to consider the environmental impacts of the products they buy. The findings were released by the EU through the recent Eurobarometer survey on consumer attitudes to sustainable consumption and production.

Key findings

Four out of five Europeans say that they consider the environmental impact of the products they buy.

- Environmental consideration was highest in Greece where more than 9 in 10 of those surveyed said the impact of a product on the environment plays an important role in their purchasing decisions.
- Czechs were the least likely to consider the environment (62%).
- Nearly half of the total respondents thought that a combination of increased taxes on environmentally-damaging products and decreased taxes on environmentally-friendly products would best promote eco-friendly products.
- There was also strong support for retailers to play a role in promoting environmentally-friendly products and for mandatory carbon labelling.
- Respondents were evenly divided about claims by producers about the environmental performance of their products with 49% trusting the claims and 48% not trusting such claims.
- The Dutch were more likely to trust these claims (78%) while Bulgarians were the least likely (26%).
- Some 46% of EU citizens also thought that the best way to promote environmentally-friendly products would be to increase taxes on environmentally-damaging products and decrease taxes on environmentally-friendly products.
- Britons were most in favour of such a double taxation system, while the Maltese much less so (28%) preferring instead reducing taxes on environmentally-friendly products only.
- Those surveyed were strongly in favour of retailers promoting environmentally-friendly products. Approximately half of EU citizens (49%) thought that they should increase the visibility of such products on their shelves or have a dedicated green corner in their store.
- A third (31%) of Europeans said that the best way for retailers to promote green products is for them to provide better information to consumers.
- Despite just under half of Europeans saying that ecolabels play an important role in their purchasing decisions and only 1 in 10 saying the total amount of greenhouse gas emissions created by a product should feature on environmental labels, some 72% of EU citizens thought that a label indicating a product's carbon footprint should be mandatory in the future.
- Attitudes on the subject varied widely between Member States with the

Czechs the least in favour of such labelling (47%) and Greeks wholeheartedly behind the idea with 90% in favour.

Source: Environmental Research Digest, Aug. 2009 (Vol. 1, No. 8)

4.4.5 Mainstream Green: Moving Sustainability from Niche to Normal

Author(s): Ogilvy & Mather

In the 2011 study Mainstream Green: Moving sustainability from niche to normal, OgilvyEarth presents fresh insight into the factors behind the Green Gap and identifies a host of innovative ways we can begin to close it. The research approach, being mindful that the very premise for this study is the discrepancy between people's stated intentions and actions, went at it from every angle in order to triangulate to the truth.

Key findings

82% of Americans have good green intentions but only 16% are dedicated to fulfilling these intentions, putting 66% in what we're call the Middle Green.

- Considering green behavior on a continuum, most of the dialogue and marketing to date has focused on Super Greens on the one hand and Green Rejecters on the other.
- There has been limited success in motivating the masses or the Middle Green, for a number of reasons.
- Half of study respondents think the green and environmentally friendly product category is for "Crunchy Granola Hippies" or "Rich Elitist Snobs" rather than "Everyday Americans."
- The number-one barrier Americans claimed was holding them back from more sustainable behaviors was money.
- The price premium many eco-friendly products carry over "regular" products is not just a financial barrier; it also says to the regular consumer, "this is for someone sophisticated, someone rich...not you."
- The valiant minority that venture into the green space do so with a relatively high social and emotional cost.
- Upper Middle and Super Greens told us they feel ostracized from their neighbors, families, and friends; the mainstream said they fear

attracting the negative judgment of their peers if they go out on a limb to purchase green products.

- Nearly half of Americans claim to feel guiltier "the more they know" about how to live a sustainable lifestyle.
- Super Greens feel twice the guilt as the average American.
- The barrier is even higher for men.
- Fully 82% of our respondents said going green is "more feminine than masculine."
- Eighty-two percent of Americans from our survey don't have a clue on how to calculate their carbon footprint.
- The study shows that it is time to forge a new era of sustainability marketing.
- It's time to acknowledge human nature; selfinterest will always trump altruism.
- It's time to focus on changing behavior, not attitudes.
- And it's time we all agree that "normal" is neither a dirty word nor a boring strategy.
- Normal is mainstream; normal is popular; and above all, normal is the key to sustainability.

Source: Environmental Research Digest, Jul. 2011 (Vol. 2, No. 3)

4.4.6   2011 ImagePower Global Green Brands Study

Author(s): Cohn & Wolfe / Esty Environmental Partners / Landor Associates / Penn Schoen Berland

The 2011 ImagePower Green Brands Survey by branding consultants Cohn & Wolfe, environmental strategists Esty Environmental Partners, branding design firm Landor Associates and research agency Penn Schoen Berland identifies emerging trends in consumer perceptions and purchasing behaviors related to products marketed with environmentally positive attributes. Researchers interviewed over 9,000 respondents in eight countries in the spring of 2011.

Key findings

Majority of consumers believe Seventh Generation to be the country's leading corporate environmental performer.

- The top brands offer clear price value through co-benefits: a great innovative product that meets my functional needs plus green attributes that meet my values needs.
- These companies also tend to have robust lifecycle insight and complete sustainability strategies across their value chains, which enable them to draw from rich experience and data for their consumer communications.
- Consumer appetite for green products — in the past focused on personal care, food and household products — has expanded to include big-ticket purchases.
- Consumers worldwide intend to purchase more environmental products in the auto, energy and technology sectors compared to last year.
- Consumers still buy the most green products in the grocery, household and personal-care categories, with roughly half of respondents making purchases in these categories, consistent with last year's survey.
- But they are looking more closely at making green purchasing decisions on more expensive items.
- 22% of U.S. consumers said that they intend to purchase green tech products in the next year, up from 14% in 2010.
- In the automotive sector, 12% of U.S. respondents said that they intend to go green, while 6% said that they purchased green vehicles last year.
- In energy, 27% of U.S. respondents intend to purchase green power, up from 24% in 2010.
- 73% said it is important to buy from green companies, but price perception remains a challenge — 62% see cost as the biggest barrier to buying green products.
- When evaluating what makes a brand a green leader, respondents mentioned their awareness of a brand's corporate actions, values, recycling and packaging efforts, sustainability and supply chain decisions.
- Overall, the report found that 54% of U.S. consumers think the environment is on the wrong track, up from previous polls: 47% of Americans thought so in 2010, while only 41% had this concern in 2009.

- Meanwhile, around the globe, the poll found that only 43% of U.K. consumers feel the environment is off-track, down from 53% in 2009.
- In China, 39% reported environmental concerns, up from 29% last year. Germany, India and Brazil all had about 60% of respondents in 2011 indicating that they think the environment is on the wrong track.

Source: Environmental Research Digest, Jul. 2011 (Vol. 2, No. 3)

4.4.7 Sustainable Consumption Facts and Trends: From a Business Perspective

Author(s): WBCSD

A new report from the World Business Council for Sustainable Development (WBCSD) calls on business to work in partnership with its customers and stakeholders to define sustainable products and sustainable lifestyles. The report, entitled "Sustainable Consumption Facts and Trends: From a Business Perspective", observes that global consumption levels are increasing due to such factors as rapid population growth, a rise in global affluence, and a culture of consumerism among higher-income groups.

Key findings

Consumers are willing to embrace sustainable lifestyle, but need access to products and services to do so effectively.

- As a result of global consumption patterns, 60% of the Earth's ecosystem services have been degraded or used unsustainably in the past 50 years.
- Consumption of natural resources has increased to 125% of global carrying capacity and could rise to 170% by 2040.
- Consumers are increasingly concerned about environmental, social and economic issues, but because of a variety of factors such concerns do not always translate into sustainable consumer behavior.
- The report calls on business to encourage sustainable consumption by:
  o developing products and services that maximize social value and minimizing environmental cost;
  o marketing campaigns that enable consumers to choose and use products more sustainably;

- o removing unsustainable products and services from the marketplace.
- The report concludes that consumers need the support of business and government in order to lead sustainable lifestyles based on informed purchasing decisions and changes in behavior.
- By acting on their capacity to mainstream sustainable consumption, leading global companies can provide the products and support that consumers need.
- By effective regulatory action, government can ensure that consumers receive the most sustainable products and services available.

Source: Social Research Digest, Feb. 2009 (Vol. 1, No. 2)

4.4.8 ˙ Sustainability: The Rise of Consumer Responsibility

Author(s): The Hartman Group

The Hartman Group has released a new report, "Sustainability: The Rise of Consumer Responsibility." The group conducted its online survey about consumer spending with 1,856 US adults in September 2008.

Key findings

Although current economic conditions have meant that consumer spending has reduced, when people do spend these days more than 75% consider environmental and social aspects in deciding what to buy and about a third are willing to pay more for those benefits.

- More than 88% of consumers surveyed said they engage in what the researchers described as sustainable behavior.
- Consumer desires for "responsibility" and "doing the right thing" prevailed even though those being surveyed weren't always entirely sure about how to define sustainability.
- Only 56% of those surveyed said they are familiar with the term, only slightly more than the 54% who said in 2007 that they are familiar with the word.
- Almost three-quarters (71%) of consumers say they don't know or were uncertain which companies support sustainable values. Fewer than 25% of those surveyed in 2008 could name a sustainable product when asked, according to the study.

- Many of the sustainability related attitudes, practices and behaviours voiced by consumers in this study serve to underscore the depth and breadth of attitudes that, while commonly grouped under the aegis of "green" or "environmental," now include at the consumer level much broader expectations and knowledge of topics relating to individual as well as corporate responsibility.

- In circumstances such as the current economic climate, when consumers are forced to make tradeoffs, cutbacks are more likely to be made in product categories that consumers view as less essential.

- Some of the categories researched in this study, such as food, personal care, and household cleaners, typically remain consistently purchased as consumers perceive them to be most important to their quality of life.

- The findings suggest that consumers are seeking out those products, services and retail outlets that they feel represent forwardthinking, higher domain experiences within which sustainability has important connections at personal, social and global levels.

Source: Social Research Digest, Feb. 2009 (Vol. 1, No. 2)

4.4.9   Young Consumers and Green Products Survey

Author(s): *Generate Insight*

A new survey from Generate Insight looks at the extent to which young consumers are employing their knowledge of the environment when choosing products. The survey of 13-29 year olds, which was designed to gauge how members of the Millennial generation perceive the green movement and brands' attempts to be green, revealed an extremely high level of education about green issues overall.

Key findings

Despite being the most environmentally educated, younger members of this generation are not taking action on what they know because they are often confused about green products and feel powerless to help

- Millennials report they do not always put their knowledge to use because of the high cost of environmentally friendly products, as well as the seeming enormity and insurmountability of environmental problems and doubts about whether they can really make a difference.

- While 76% of Millennials ages 13-29 feel it's very important or important for brands to get involved in the green movement, 71% of teens (ages 13-17) surveyed say if they had to choose between a less expensive product or one that "gave back" to the environment, they would choose the less expensive product.

- In contrast, the majority of older Millennials would choose the more expensive brand that gave back in a green way.

- The majority of Millennials surveyed found it confusing as to why products that are better for the environment are more expensive.

- The study also found several other deterrents to Millennials living greener lives.

- These include products that require too much effort, are too time consuming and are not convenient; products that are confusing and difficult to understand, and families that are not involved in, supportive of or knowledgeable about the green movement.

- 87% of Millennials recycle; 84% turn off lights when not in use; 80% reduce water use; and 73% use energy-efficient light bulbs.

- 76% of Millennials feel it's very important or important for brands to get involved in the green movement.

Source: Social Research Digest, Jun. 2009 (Vol. 1, No. 6)

4.4.10 Greenest Consumers Survey

Author(s): National Geographic/Globescan

The results of the 2009 Greendex Survey have been released by National Geographic and international polling firm, Globescan. The second annual Greendex survey canvassed 17,000 adults online in 17 countries this year to gauge consumer attitudes and their behaviour.

Key findings

For a second year in a row, consumers in India, Brazil and China scored the highest - and those in the U.S., the lowest - for green behaviour.

Greendex Overall Scores			
1	India	=10	Germany
2	Brazil	=10	Sweden
3	China	12	Australia
=4	Argentina	=13	France
=4	South Korea	=13	UK
6	Mexico	15	Japan
7	Hungary	16	Canada
8	Russia	17	US
9	Spain		

- Only consumers in Brazil reported slight drop in green behaviour, which moved the country to the No. 2 spot on the list.

- Not surprisingly, respondents in most countries named the economy as their No. 1 national issue, much more so than in 2008. However, the results indicate that economic troubles may have worked to the environment's advantage in a number of instances.

- Among those who reported that they reduced energy consumption at home over the past year, some 80% say that cost was one of the top two reasons they did so.

- Of those who say they reduced their consumption of fuel for motorized vehicles in the past year, nearly three-quarters cite cost as one of their top two reasons.

- Majorities in four countries — Argentineans, Mexicans, South Koreans and Chinese — said that high fuel prices motivated them to change their transportation habits permanently due to fuel prices.

- While, overall, consumers felt the economy was the most important issue facing their countries, consumers in many countries registered strong concern about the environment.

- Many said this concern was one of the top two reasons for recent behavior changes.

- Fifty-five percent of consumers across the 17 countries agreed they are "very concerned about environmental problems"; only 14% disagreed.

- Chinese, South Korean and Brazilian consumers were the most likely to register concern about the environment.

- Air pollution, climate change/global warming and water pollution ranked fourth through sixth on a list of 12 global concerns, just behind the economy, fuel costs and poverty.
- Roughly two-thirds of consumers said they were concerned about each of these environmental issues.
- Six in 10 consumers across the 17 surveyed countries agree that people need to consume less in order to improve the environment for future generations (only 12% disagreed), showing that consumers recognize the connection between their actions and the environment.

Source: Social Research Digest, Jun. 2009 (Vol. 1, No. 6)

4.4.11 Sustainable Packaging Report

Author(s): Datamonitor

A new report identifies sustainable packaging as a growing consumer issue, driven by issues such as ethics, economics and environmentalism, according to market research company Datamonitor. Consumers in 15 countries were surveyed by Datamonitor in the second half of 2008.

Key findings

Of the 15 countries surveyed, the UK had the greatest proportion of survey respondents showing high levels of concern about the packaging of products in the household goods market, followed by China at 56% and India at 53%.

- The US fell at the lower end of concern at 34%. Only Germany, Brazil and Russia scored lower than the US.
- The results also showed that in the US 49% of consumers felt that packaging design has a medium or high level of influence over their choice of food and drink products.
- However, of this proportion, only 6% felt that it exerted a high level of influence on their purchases.
- It seems that few consumers will admit to the influence that packaging has on their decisionmaking process, however, increasing consumer concern about ecological matters means that packaging is an issue that is rising to prominence.

- One of the most obvious methods that consumers can use to bring about change is to boycott products that do not meet their requirements or expectations.
- According to the survey, consumers are starting to make their buying decisions based on concerns about excessive packaging.
- In 2008, 40% of UK respondents agreed that they seek alternative products if they believe their first choice is packaged excessively.
- This is a slightly higher proportion than in the US at 35% but lags behind other European countries such as France, Spain and Sweden. In the Netherlands, consumers are less likely to boycott products than in the UK.
- Updating packaging can also be a more credible way to achieve cost savings rather than using methods such as "package shrink" or "portion shrink," where a smaller amount of the product is sold at the same price.
- Product packagers are getting the message. Sustainable packaging is projected to grow to 32% of the total global packaging market by 2014, up from just 21% in 2009.

Source: Social Research Digest, Aug. 2009 (Vol. 1, No. 8)

4.4.12 Consumer Green Spending Survey

Author(s): ORC Guideline

A new survey has investigated the extent to which consumers are still willing to buy green during the recession. ORC Guideline surveyed over 1,000 US consumers in May 2009.

Key findings

Consumers are willing to put their money where their hearts are, even in this economic environment.

- Nearly two thirds (64%) of employed respondents said they would be willing to put their salary on the line and forego pay raises to support green initiatives at work.
- A company's environmental policies affected people's workplace decisions at every stage, from choosing an employer to their desire to see their current employers actively pursue green initiatives.

- Over half of the respondents (54%) said that a company's environmental policy was important in their decision to join a company.
- In addition, over three quarters (76%) of respondents indicated that it was important or very important that a company take action to reduce its environmental impact.
- The commitment to "going green" also seems to extend beyond the workplace, with 77% of respondents indicating the "energy footprint" of a product, such as a low energy-certified appliance or locally grown food, affects their purchasing decisions as consumers.
- Even the prospect of paying a higher price does not change people's opinions, with 76% saying they would pay more for an environmentally friendly product.

Source: Social Research Digest, Jul. 2009 (Vol. 1, No. 7)

4.4.13 Green Consumer Communications Report

Author(s): Grail Research

A new report, The Green Revolution, released recently by Grail Research aims to helps companies with their communications strategies and effectively influence the shopping behaviours of green consumers. The study is based on a survey of 520 US green consumers conducted in June 2009. Target individuals were between the ages of 18-65 years old, aware of green products and had purchased green products in the past.

Key findings

85% of US consumers have bought green products and nearly all of them will not revert their course. However, only 8% (termed 'dark green' consumers) choose to buy green products for the majority of their purchases.

- Of the few respondents who had never purchased green products, 67% have considered making the shift.
- Price is the main reason consumers choose not to buy green products.
- 'Dark green' consumers are more committed and proactive when buying green, have a better understanding of what green means and are more driven by environmental and health concerns.

- For 'light green' consumers, the decision to first buy green is driven mostly be curiosity.
- While both 'light' and 'dark green' consumers tend to be married women with no children, 'dark green' consumers are more likely to be older, more educated and more affluent than their 'light green' counterparts.
- When shopping, 41% of green consumers compare green and conventional products along dimensions such as safety (72%), health (70%), and quality (66%).
- 90% of respondents feel that a company being green is important to their purchase decision. However, most are not aware or cannot recollect the green initiatives of companies that are leading the green revolution.
- Important sustainability initiatives, such as reducing water usage, are not perceived as green practices by most consumers.
- The report highlights six important insights that will help companies succeed in 'the green revolution'. These are:
  o Green is here to stay: If you are not playing in the green space, you are competing against it. Either fold it into your strategy or have a clear competitive advantage over green competition.
  o All green consumers are not created equal: Know your customer. Different 'shades' of green consumers mean different demographics, behaviours, and segment- ation plans.
  o Being green doesn't equal success. Being green is not enough. Consumers expect companies to have green products that are superior or at least on a par with conventional products.
  o Different product categories = different green attributes: There is no 'one size fits all' green product strategy. Companies need to align green attributes to the product category.
  o Green consumers are listening, but are not being heard: companies' green initiatives do influence consumer purchasing behaviour – but only when communicated through the right channels.
  o Recessions affect green, but don't trump it: Less money doesn't necessarily mean less green. Consumers continue to buy (and switch to) green, even in a recession.

Source: Social Research Digest, Dec. 2009 (Vol. 1, No. 12)

4.4.14 Consumer Futures 2020

Author(s): Sainsbury's, Unilever and Forum for the Future

The report outlines the scenarios for what the sustainable consumer will look like in 2020 and how companies can respond. It contains four different but entirely plausible scenarios which explore how patterns of consumption and consumer behaviour may have changed by 2020.

Key findings

Companies must drive sustainability, rather than waiting for consumers to demand more sustainable products and services.

- Companies should create consumer demand through marketing, communications and innovation; this tactic will make money for the most savvy brands.
- Possible future trends identified by the report include:
  - increased local sourcing of energy and food;
  - a greater number of vertical farms – producing more food per unit of land;
  - and retailers and brands leasing a lifetime's supply of key goods to consumers.
- The outlined scenarios can be used in three main ways:
  - firstly for strategy (testing existing strategy or developing new strategies fit for the challenges of the 21st century);
  - secondly, for innovation (innovating new sustainable products and services);
  - and thirdly, for collaboration (e.g. bringing retailers and manufacturers together in exciting new ways).
- Sainsbury's and Unilever are already using this work to explore new ways of collaborating on initiatives that will deliver sustainability and commercial benefit to both organisations.

Source: Social Research Digest, Nov. 2011 (Vol. 2, No. 7)

4.4.15 More with Less: Scaling Sustainable Consumption and Resource Efficiency

Author(s): World Economic Forum

The report focuses on how consumption can be made more sustainable through decoupling growth from environmental impact at the scale and speed required. It builds on four years of engagement by the World Economic Forum with leading businesses around the issue of sustainable consumption.

Key findings

Through this engagement with chief executive officers, business leaders and experts, the report aims to answer six key questions.

- The key questions are as follows:
  o What are the key trends in sustainable consumption?
  o What is the size of the opportunity for countries, companies and consumers?
  o What are the barriers to scaling existing models of sustainable consumption?
  o What does getting to scale look like?
  o What new solutions are needed to get to scale in sustainable consumption?
  o How can we achieve scale by working collectively and creating action on new fronts?
- A systems view of sustainable consumption has been taken throughout the report.
- Rather than focusing just on the demand side, the discussions that informed this work have taken the lens of consumer engagement (demand), value chains and upstream action (supply) and the policies and enabling environment to accelerate change (rules of the game).
- However, in this report the narrative always begins with demand as the consumer and customer are at the heart of sustainable consumption.

Source: Social Research Digest, Jan. 2012 (Vol. 3, No. 1)

4.4.16 Green Gauge Global

Author(s): GfK

The study provides global marketers an in-depth look into green consumer trends, attitudes and behaviours. Now in its third year, the study includes interview with more than 35,000 consumers in 25 key markets.

Key findings

Consumers in emerging markets China and Brazil are buying more green products, despite a widespread and growing perception that environmentally friendly alternatives are too expensive.

- The proportion of consumers who factor environmental protection into their purchase decisions grew 6%age points in China and 5 points in Brazil from last year.

- Mexico and South Africa also recorded significant increases in the past year.

- Globally, six in 10 consumers surveyed feel environmentally friendly product alternatives are too expensive, roughly the same results found in 2011.

- That sentiment is on the rise in the same nations where green buying increased, such as China and South Africa.

- Knowing this, green-friendly companies entering new markets should be attuned to price concerns from the start and price products competitively to win loyal customers.

Source: Social Research Digest, Aug. 2012 (Vol. 3, No. 8)

4.4.17 Regeneration Consumer Study

Author(s): BBMG, GlobeScan and Sustainability

The study is an indepth online survey of consumer attitudes, motivations and behaviors relating to sustainable consumption. It was conducted among 6,224 respondents across six major international markets (Brazil, China, Germany, India, the United Kingdom and the United States).

Key findings

Consumers are buying less and buying better, while price, performance and credibility remain barriers to further growing sustainable consumption.

- Two-thirds of consumers in six countries say that "as a society, we need to consume a lot less to improve the environment for future generations" (66%), and that they feel "a sense of responsibility to purchase products that are good for the environment and society" (65%).

- The affinity toward sustainable consumption is being led by consumers in developing markets (Brazil, China, India), who are more than twice as likely as their counterparts in developed markets (Germany, UK, US) to report purchasing products because of environmental and social benefits (51% to 22%, respectively), being willing to pay more for sustainable products (60% to 26%) and encouraging others to buy from companies that are socially and environmentally responsible (70% to 34%).

- However, significant barriers to sustainable purchasing remain for consumers across all markets, including perceptions of product performance, high prices, skepticism about product claims and a lack of knowledge about what makes a product socially or environmentally responsible.

- Two-thirds of consumers globally (67%) are "interested in sharing their ideas, opinions and experiences with companies to help them develop better products or create new solutions," while seven in ten consumers (72%) globally "believe in voting and advocating for issues important to me."

Source: Social Research Digest, Dec. 2012 (Vol. 3, No. 12)

4.4.18 Americans' Actions to Limit Global Warming

Author(s): The Yale Project on Climate Change Communication and the George Mason University Center on Climate Change Communication

The Yale Project on Climate Change Communication and the George Mason University Center on Climate Change Communication produced a report that investigated four types of climate and energy-related behavior: consumer, civic, household and transportation, and communication. The "Americans' actions to limit global warming" report is based on findings from a national survey of 1,045 adults.

Key findings

Consumer purchases are somewhat influenced by environmental practices.

- Half of all Americans consider the environmental impact of products and services when deciding whether or not to make a purchase.

- Nearly half of environmentally-conscious consumers say it is "essential" or "very important" to them that the products they buy are recyclable.
- Three in 10 Americans have rewarded companies in the past 12 months for taking steps to reduce global warming by buying their products.
- Alternatively, one in five Americans surveyed say they have punished companies for opposing steps to reduce climate change by not purchasing their products.
- Eight in 10 American surveyed said they intend to buy locally grown or produced food and six in 10 intend to buy organic food in the next 12 months.
- About half of Americans surveyed deliberately bought an energy efficient kitchen appliance.

Source: Environmental Research Digest, Jul. 2013 (Vol. 4, No. 7)

4.4.19 Green Gauge US Report

Author(s): GfK Roper Consulting

The GfK Green Gauge US Report has been examining environmental attitudes and behaviors of global consumers since 1992. A sample of 2012 adults 18 years of age or over in the United States was interviewed for this study using the GfK Online Consumer Panel.

<u>Key findings</u>

Amid a climate of economic uncertainty, Americans now place a higher value on their own financial stability over environmental responsibility.

o However, they are still looking to make sensible environmental choices.
o 41% of Americans say "first comes economic security then we can worry about environmental problems".
o This dramatic 13%age point increase from the pre-recession levels of 2007, when just 28% would put economic considerations ahead of the environment, clearly reflects today's low levels of consumer confidence and increased personal worry about the nation's current economic malaise.
o In addition, while most think concern about the environment is at least somewhat serious, fewer are saying that concern about the

environment is "very serious and should be a priority for everyone" (33% in 2011 vs. 46% in 2007).

o At the same time Americans are refocusing their efforts when it comes to green activities, concentrating more on actions that are simple and practical.

- Compared to 2008, more consumers today are drinking tap water instead of bottled water (63%, up 5%age points) and are bringing their own re-usable bags to the supermarket (39%, up 11%age points).

- However, during that same period, fewer consumers are avoiding products that they feel are not environmentally responsible (24%, down 6%age points).

- The report also found an increased showing of goodwill to corporate environmental protection.

- Since 2007, the number of respondents saying business and industry are fulfilling their responsibility to the environment has increased eight percentage points to 37%.

- There is also evidence that Americans are increasingly comfortable with business' green claims.

- 39% say business' claims about the environment are not accurate, compared to 2008 when 48% said that business' claims were not accurate.

Source: Environmental Research Digest, Oct. 2011 (Vol. 2, No. 6)

4.4.20 The Harris Poll

Author(s): Harris Interactive

Since the summer of 2009, the Harris Poll has been tracking Americans' attitudes toward the environment as well as their engagement in various environmentally-friendly, or "green," behaviors. The poll surveyed 2,451 US adults ages 18 and older online between March 12 and March 19, 2012.

Key findings

Thirty-one percent of 18- to 24-year-olds say they take environmental issues into consideration when making purchases.

- This number that has risen from 24% in 2010 and 22% in 2009.

- While concern and awareness around environmental issues has slipped since 2009, this hasn't affected how consumers say environmental issues influence their purchasing behaviour.
- The exception is young adults, ages 18 to 24, who are actually more likely to consider the environment in their spending than before.
- In 2012, US adults are now less likely to do each of the following in their daily life: reuse things they have instead of throwing them away or buying new items (65% in 2009 vs. 61% in 2012);
  - make an effort to use less water (60% in 2009 vs. 57% in 2010 and 2012);
  - buy food in bulk (33% in 2009 vs. 30% in 2012);
  - purchase all-natural products (18% in 2009 vs. 16% in 2012);
  - purchase organic products (17% in 2009 vs. 15% in 2010 and 2012).
- A quarter of US adults (26%) say that environmental issues are either "extremely" or "very" important to them when deciding which products or services to purchase.
- Americans also show a pAuthor(s) for products and services that are "green," with 79% seeking out green products, slightly up from 78% in 2010 and 76% in 2009.
- Additionally, 31% of US adults say they are willing to pay extra for a "green product," up from 28% in 2010.
- Thirty-two percent said the same in 2009.
- Again, 18- to 24-year-olds show the biggest change: 35% say they are willing to pay extra for a green product, an increase from 27% in 2010 and 25% in 2009.

Source: Environmental Research Digest, Jun. 2012 (Vol. 3, No. 6)

4.4.21 Re:Thinking Consumption Consumers & the Future of Sustainability

Author(s): Regeneration Roadmap, BBMG, GlobeScan and SustainAbility

Regeneration Roadmap, BBMG, GlobeScan and SustainAbility produced an online survey of consumer attitudes, motivations and behaviors around sustainable consumption among 6,224 respondents in six major international markets (Brazil, China, Germany, India, United Kingdom and

United States). 'Re:Thinking Consumption Consumers & the Future of Sustainability' is a holistic exploration of sustainability market trends, priorities and engagement pathways, including information on sustainable consumption, trust, transparency, social issues, behavior change, consumer collaboration, participation and advocacy actions.

Key findings

Consuming Less, Consuming Better: While 66% of consumers across the six countries surveyed believe in consuming less, the pattern varies across markets, with 76% of consumers in developing markets and 57% in developed markets being inclined to believe that "as a society, we need to consume a lot less to improve the environment for future generations."

- Similarly, consumers in emerging markets are much more likely than consumers in developed markets to "feel a sense of responsibility to purchase products that are good for the environment and society" (82% to 49%, respectively).
- Shifting Perceptions: Views on Price, Performance and Credibility Most Frequently Undermine Sustainable Purchasing: A majority of consumers globally agree or strongly agree that they would "purchase more products that are environmentally and socially responsible" if they "performed as well as, or better than, products they usually buy" (75%), "it didn't cost more" (70%), "companies' health and environmental claims were more believable" (64%), they "had a better understanding of what makes products environmentally or socially responsible" (63%), or they "could see environmental or social benefits of the products right away" (63%).
- Price is the top barrier to green purchasing in developed markets (78%) while product performance (74%) is the top barrier in developing markets along with needing "a better understanding of what makes products socially and environmentally responsible" (72%).
- Collaboration and Participation – Being Part of the Solution: Two-thirds of consumers globally (67%) are "interested in sharing their ideas, opinions and experiences with companies to help them develop better products or create new solutions," while seven in ten consumers (72%) globally "believe in voting and advocating for issues important to me."

Source: Social Research Digest, Jan. 2014 (Vol. 5, No. 1)

4.5 Climate-, Resource- and Energy-Related Awareness

4.5.1 Climate Confidence Study

Author(s): HSBC

The fourth annual HSBC Climate Confidence Monitor provides valuable insight into consumer perceptions of the climate change issue. The study format was an online survey of a total of 15,000 consumers in fifteen countries whose populations make up over 50% of the global total.

Key findings

Climate change is one of the top three concerns globally, on par with economic stability and terrorism.

- On average 38% of survey respondents strongly agree that climate change is among their biggest concerns.
- This ranges from 57% in China to 16% in the UK.
- 18% of U.S. respondents say climate change is one of their biggest issues.
- 64% of respondents in China claim to be making a significant effort to help reduce climate change, compared to 23% in the UK, 20% in the U.S. and 11% in Japan.
- The report also reveals that one in three people in Vietnam, India and China believe climate change can be halted, compared to just one in twenty in France and the UK.
- Survey respondents in Hong Kong and Vietnam also rank climate change as their number one concern.
- In terms of creating jobs, more than half of respondents in Brazil, India and Malaysia strongly agreed their country would prosper and create new jobs by responding to climate change.
- In comparison, one-third of respondents in the UK and the U.S. think economic opportunities and new jobs can be created.
- Nearly 75% of respondents in France and 67% in Germany agreed that greater business investment is needed.

Source: CSR Research Digest, Nov. 2010 (Vol. 2, No. 11)

4.5.2   Climate Change Claims Study

Author(s): Carbon Trust

A study on claims for action on climate change has been commissioned by the Carbon Trust and supported by global brand analysis, from BrandZ. The study examined opinions from 1,000 adults across the UK during February and March 2011.

Key findings

Businesses risk facing a costly backlash due to consumer mistrust of firms' claims of action on climate change.

- 66% of the public question authenticity of company climate change claims.
- The research revealed that 90% of the public want firms to commit to the average 3% per year emissions cut required for the UK to meet 2050 climate change targets.
- Consumers cite the threat of climate change, which polled as the greatest issue facing the environment, as the root of the heightened public expectation for firms to prove their commitment.
- 70% of people want businesses to mandatorily disclose their carbon emissions.
- 56% are more concerned about business' actions to reduce their impacts on climate change than they were five years ago.
- The greatest concern around company claims is that firms simply make one-off improvements to win publicity, and then just return to business as usual (53%).
- 56% are more loyal to brands that can show, at a glance, evidence of action.
- 53% want to work for companies which can clearly demonstrate commitment to reducing their impacts.

Source: CSR Research Digest, Apr. 2011 (Vol. 3, No. 4)

4.5.3   Optimism about Climate Change Survey

Author(s): Accenture

Global research company Accenture has conducted a global survey to gauge the levels of optimism relating to climate change in developed and developing nations. The survey was conducted between September and October in respondents' native languages. Around 3,650 people were interviewed from the emerging economies of Argentina, Brazil, Chile, China, India, Russia and South Africa. The survey also included 1,732 interviews in North America, 4,244 interviews in Western Europe, and 1,100 interviews in Japan and Australia.

Key findings

The Chinese, Brazilians, South Africans, and citizens of a number of rapidly-developing nations, care more about climate change than Americans.

- The majority of those questioned from developing countries said they believe climate change will have an impact on their lives. Meanwhile, only 28% of those surveyed from developed economies - North America, Western Europe, Japan and Australia – said they feel the same way.
- 70% of those surveyed in emerging economies described themselves as optimistic that climate change can be solved, compared to 48% from developed nations who believed that.
- Over half (53%) of people in emerging markets said they would certainly switch to a new product if it was certified to minimize damage to the climate, versus a mere 24% in developed economies. 61% said they would certainly switch to an energy provider offering lower carbon products and services if this was an option, versus only 30% in developed economies.

Source: Environmental Research Digest, Feb. 2009 (Vol. 1, No. 2)

4.5.4 Global Opinion Survey on Japan's GHG Emissions Reductions

Author(s): Japan For Sustainability

Japan For Sustainability has conducted a survey gauging global responses to its GHG emissions reductions targets for 2020. 202 responses were received from participants in 59 countries between 1 and 16 May 2009.

Key findings

The largest number of respondents, exactly half the sample, advocated the largest proposed cut of 25% below 1990 levels.

- 26% of respondents advocated the setting of even stricter targets.
- 20% stated that they "hope Japan will show some leadership."
- 8% believed that Japanese advanced technology will contribute to GHG emissions/ climate change solutions.
- 4.6% believe that "Japan should fulfill its responsibility as original host country of the Kyoto Protocol."
- 4.1% also believe that "the cost of emission reduction measures per unit of GDP should be considered."
- Some respondents felt that Japan is already doing much in terms of GHG reductions and that to reduce further might have negative effects on the national economy.
- A respondent from the Philippines suggests that a form of report card might be developed in order to record the contributions of Japanese companies to environmental sustainability in those countries in which they operate.
- Both social awareness and technical capabilities are marked out as key enabling factors in Japan's aim to reduce GHG emissions.

Source: Environmental Research Digest, Jul. 2009 (Vol. 1, No. 7)

4.5.5 Consumer Attitudes to Renewables Study

Author(s): Natural Marketing Institute, Center for Resource Solutions

The Natural Marketing Institute and the Center for Resource Solutions have released the findings of a study looking at US consumers' attitudes towards the certification of renewable energy products. Over 4,000 American consumers were surveyed as part of the study, which was conducted in July 2008.

Key findings

The majority of Americans surveyed agreed that businesses should reduce greenhouse gas emissions.

- The majority also stated that they are more likely to purchase products bearing a seal that proves corporate sustainability commitments, like buying or using renewable energy.

- Four out of five US consumers support clean energy and 55% want companies to increase their use of renewable energy.
- The study also found that 60% of consumers want claims to be endorsed by a third party, and most prefer that the third party be a non-profit organization.
- More than three-quarters of consumers say that almost all companies are saying they are environmentally friendly and it is hard to know which companies are telling the truth.
- 80% of respondents would like to see trusted sources endorse the claims made by companies and, of these, 85% would like the endorser to be a nonprofit organization.
- Over 40% of all consumers are motivated to purchase a product by the presence of a seal or certification, a predisposition that grew 5% between 2007 and 2008.
- Over 40% of consumers perceived that environmental protection is the most important benefit of renewable power, while only 8% report that it is better for human health.
- This signals an opportunity to market the collective benefits of renewable electricity:
- environmental sustainability, personal health, energy independence, and economic development and job creation.

Source: Environmental Research Digest, Aug. 2009 (Vol. 1, No. 8)

4.5.6   How Much Do People Who Live Near Major Nuclear Facilities Worry About Those Facilities?

Author(s): M.R. Greenberg

This study examines the extent to which US citizens who live close to nuclear facilities have concerns related to the sites. A survey of 2101 residents living near 11 nuclear power plants and nuclear waste management sites and laboratories was carried out to determine residents concerns. 600 other participants who lived elsewhere formed a comparison group.

Key findings

Although nuclear site-related issues were of more concern to those living close to a nuclear facility than those living elsewhere, many respondents were more concerned about global warming, traffic congestion and loss of open spaces than nuclear technologies.

- Residents living close to the nuclear waste management sites were the most concerned.
- Least concerned were generally affluent and educated white males, recognized as a politically formidable group.
- Monitoring the environment and people were the actions deemed most likely to reduce public concern.
- Respondents also wanted specialized training and equipment provided for emergency responders, and support for individuals willing to gather and report information to the public about the site.
- Public trust of responsible parties was relatively high, although the relative lack of trust in private owners and facilities operators was deemed disconcerting.
- 82% of respondents agreed that independently appointed watchdog scientists were competent to assess risks and report information back to the community.
- There was also concern regarding the state government's capacity to competently oversee health and safety at the site and to communicate information to the community.
- The most significant ongoing challenge is faced by state and local environmental planners and managers, since they will bear the responsibility for adjusting local land use, transport and utilities as sites develop.
- Furthermore, these local experts will be required to explain their decisions to local elected officials as well as the public.

Source: Environmental Research Digest, Nov. 2009 (Vol. 1, No. 11)

4.5.7   Public Attitudes Towards Water Sustainability Survey

Author(s): Circle of Blue/GlobeScan

US news and science organization, Circle of Blue, and global polling organization, GlobeScan, have released the findings of a survey into public attitudes towards water sustainability and management. The survey questioned 1,000 respondents in each of fifteen countries. Respondents from seven of these countries (Canada, China, India, Mexico, Russia, the US, and the UK) participated in additional in-depth questions. The research was carried out in June, July and August 2009.

Key findings

People around the world view water pollution as the most important facet of the fresh water crisis, with shortages of fresh water are very close behind. Concern about both issues tended to be higher in developing countries than in developed nations.

- For both Mexico and the UK, lack of safe drinking water was of more concern than water pollution.
- People in Mexico and India, which are growing rapidly and rely heavily on agriculture for jobs and economic development, expressed the highest level of concern about water shortages in the farm sector.
- In all seven countries, respondents consistently said that governments were the most responsible for ensuring clean water.
- Respondents said that large companies were nearly as responsible as governments for ensuring clean water.
- Nearly eight of 10 respondents from the seven nations said that solving drinking water problems "will require significant help from companies." This sentiment was especially strong in China, with 94% of respondents agreeing with the statement.
- In an expression of the results of $1 trillion dollars invested in regulations and water delivery and treatment infrastructure in the last two decades, Americans said they were less worried about safe drinking water and pollution than people in most of the other countries, though more than half still expressed concerns.
- Except for India, where 60% of respondents said they were "very concerned," well under half of the respondents in the six other nations surveyed said they were not terribly worried about the "high cost" of water.

Source: Environmental Research Digest, Dec. 2009 (Vol. 1, No. 12)

4.5.8   American Climate Attitudes

Author(s): Resource Innovation Group's Social Capital Project

The new report from our Social Capital Project describes the trends in American's attitudes about climate change along with recommendations for how to account for those trends in when communicating with the public. The study is based on polling data, research and the authors' experience as climate and environmental communicators.

Key findings

Whether one has to acknowledge that global warming is real and happening to accept action on climate is a key question that demands further study.

- Practitioners may want to emphasize the multiple benefits of taking action, particularly actions that have appealing outcomes regardless of whether global warming is the motivating concern.
- Increasing the public's literacy with climate science is critical, particularly for younger Americans.
- However, given the fact that worldviews, ideologies, and political affiliations influence adult decision making as much as information, it is as important to consider non-sciencebased outreach as well.
- For example, emphasizing the moral responsibility we have to act as stewards in light of the needs of future generations may be as critical as improving science communication and education.
- Peer-to-peer networks and influence are essential tools to consider when delivering information and inspiration to those deliberating over what global warming is and what it means to them.
- Facts play an important role in informing people why they might want to act, yet the decision to act is ultimately an emotional one based on core values and is best supported through trusted relationships.
- Because national priorities shift over time, it is wise to determine how to weave global warming into a number of policy conversations while considering how those choices influence long-term global warming communication and outreach objectives.

- With jobs at the forefront of Americans' minds, constant effort needs to be directed at countering the notion that economic growth and environmental protection are at odds.
- The public's low sense of efficacy around global warming must be addressed – both in terms of our society's ability to address the issue, as well the role individuals can play.
- Clearly communicating the benefits of policy and behavior change solutions is also critical.

Source: Environmental Research Digest, Jun. 2011 (Vol. 2, No. 2)

4.5.9   Japan's Energy Policy Survey

Author(s): Japan for Sustainability

The aim of the survey is to see what people in other countries think about Japan's energy policy direction in order to provide input into debate in Japan. Using mainly its overseas network, Japan for Sustainability invited responses to an online survey conducted from July 26 through August 14, 2012 with a total of 322 responses being received from 53 countries.

Key findings

70% of the respondents supported the Zero Scenario, with the ratio of dependence on nuclear power dropping to zero as soon as possible before 2030.

- As for the reasons, of the respondents who chose the Zero Scenario, 53% pointed out risks of nuclear power generation and nuclear waste, saying "Nuclear power plants bring a huge risk of accidents" (36% of the Zero Scenario respondents), and "Human beings can never manage nuclear waste disposal" (17%).
- Meanwhile, others pointed out expectations for renewable energy and the need for review of energy consumption, saying "I hope Japan will take international initiatives" (10%), "The Zero Scenario is possible if renewable energy will have much more share" (8%), and "The Zero Scenario is possible by the efforts for energy saving and efficient energy use" (5%).
- Of the respondents who chose the 15% Scenario, 30% answered "Nuclear power plants should have adequate safety measures," and

another 30% answered "It is important to promote development and utilization of renewable energy."

- Of the respondents who chose the 20 - 25% Scenario, 44% stated the need to reduce carbon dioxide emissions as the reason.

Source: Governance Research Digest, Sep. 2012 (Vol. 3, No. 9)

4.5.10 Climate Change in the Indian Mind

Author(s): Yale University

The report is part of an ongoing effort to understand how Indians are thinking about and responding to climate change by the Project on Climate Change Communication at Yale University. It is based on a national survey conducted in November and December 2011 of 4,031 Indian adults, using an approximately 75% urban and 25% rural sample.

Key findings

Millions of Indians are observing changes in their local rainfall, temperatures, and weather, report more frequent droughts and floods, and a more unpredictable monsoon.

- A majority of respondents said their own household's drinking water and food supply, health, and income are vulnerable to a severe drought or flood and that it would take them months to years to recover.
- Only 7% of respondents said they know "a lot" about global warming, while 41% had never heard of it or said, "I don't know."
- However, after hearing a short definition of global warming, 72% said they believe global warming is happening, 56% said it is caused mostly by human activities, 50% said they have already personally experienced the effects, and 61% said they are worried about it.
- Scientists were the most trusted sources of information about global warming (73%), followed by the news media (69%), and environmental organizations (68%).
- Government and religious leaders were trusted by about half of respondents.
- 54% said that India should be making a large or moderate-scale effort to reduce global warming, even if it has large or moderate economic costs.

- Majorities favored a variety of policies to waste less fuel, water, and energy, even if this increased costs.
- 70% favored a national program to teach Indians about global warming.

Source: Social Research Digest, Oct. 2012 (Vol. 3, No. 10)

V. COMMUNITY INVOLVEMENT AND CONTRIBUTION

5.1 Activism and Social Change

5.1.1 Survey on Activism and Rio+20

Author(s): GlobeScan / SustainAbility

Latest poll from GlobeScan and SustainAbility addressed the activists' role on the sustainability agenda and experts' view on Rio+20 Summit. A survey panel of more than 500 sustainability experts from corporate, government, nongovernmental, academic/research, service/media, and other organizations.

Key findings

Experts and practitioners agree that activists continue to play a critical role on the sustainability agenda.

- 2011 welcomed the re-emergence of the campaigning NGO as civil society organizations reclaimed and reinvigorated their activist spirit.
- From relentless campaigning by 350.org against the Keystone XL Pipeline to the populist multi-channel campaign by Hugh's Fish Fight to end discards of by-catch in Europe to Greenpeace's string of victories from 'zero discharge to 'unfriend coal' NGOs have once again found their voice and are effectively playing an important role holding business and governments to account.
- Four in five respondents agreeing that society needs activists to achieve meaningful progress.
- Activist tactics that directly impact business value drivers (e.g., product boycotts on sales or shareholder activism on access to capital) are perceived as the most effective.
- Despite recent social protest movements, socially responsible investors and NGOs are the most important influencers on business and government.

- Nearly nine in ten experts expect public criticism through online social media to increase in importance over the next three to five years.
- Experts consider Rio+20 a critical opportunity to make progress on sustainability; the corporate sector is seen as a key determinant of the outcome.
- Business leaders must take a multi-faceted approach to ensure a successful Rio+20; focus on engaging with industry groups and setting priorities within an industry-specific context.

Source: CSR Research Digest, Jan. 2012 (Vol. 4, No. 1)

5.1.2 Future Role of Civil Society Report

Author(s): World Economic Forum in collaboration with KMPG International

World Economic Forum in collaboration with KPMG International issued a report that presents the main global trends impacting the relationships between sectors, highlights the value that civil society provides and explores how the role of civil society might change over the coming two decades as a result. "The Future Role of Civil Society" report is the outcome of an eight-month project, in collaboration with KPMG International and involving over 200 leaders and experts, looking at how trends are affecting the evolution of civil society and its implications for stakeholders.

<u>Key findings</u>

The power and influence of civil society are growing and should be harnessed to create trust and enable action across sectors.

- By being engaged with government, business and international organizations, civil society actors can and should provide the resilient dynamism the world urgently needs.
- The changes that civil society is undergoing strongly suggest that it should no longer be viewed as a "third sector";; rather, civil society should be the glue that binds public and private activity together in such a way as to strengthen the common good.
- In playing this role, civil society actors need to ensure they retain their core missions, integrity, purposefulness and high levels of trust.

Source: Governance Research Digest, Mar. 2013 (Vol. 4, No. 3)

5.1.3   Social Change Impact Report

Author(s): Walden University

The Social Change Impact Report provides a detailed picture of the state of social change engagement in America. The report was commissioned by Walden University and conducted online in March 2011 by Harris Interactive among 2,148 U.S. adults.

<u>Key findings</u>

More than nine in 10 (92%) Americans have taken action to engage in positive social change in the past year and that more than three-fourths (77%) say it is important to them personally to be involved in social change.

- Americans have a strong belief in their own power to effect change with nearly nine in 10 adults (85%) agreeing that they can make the world a better place by their actions.
- Fifty-two percent say they are most likely to personally get involved in social change in the future as individuals acting on their own or in informal groups.
- When it comes to social change issues, education is the most important issue on American's minds and will play a key role in the future of social change in more ways than one.
- Adults find education to be the most important social change issue (40%), followed by health issues (35%) and poverty issues (33%).
- Education will also remain at the forefront of social change issues in the future, with 63% of respondents stating it will be very important to address.
- Most adults believe that elementary, middle or high schools (80%) and colleges or universities (80%) will have the same or larger role in social change in the future.
- Results show that digital technology empowers individuals to get involved in positive social change issues faster and more frequently than ever before.
- Nine in 10 adults (88%) agree that digital technology can turn interest in a cause into a movement more quickly than anything else.

- Four in five adults (81%) agree that digital technology has created a fundamental shift in how social change occurs.
- A majority of adults (65%) do not believe that using social media to get involved is just a fad.
- Americans believe that digital technology enhances social change by making it easier to do many things, particularly following news and events related to social change (79%) and increasing awareness about social change issues or needs (77%).
- According to the report, most adults believe the world will become more globally connected in the future, with 83% agreeing that the world's economies, trade, competition and cultures will become more integrated.
- They also believe social change issues are both local and global, with 88% stating the best way to have an impact on the world is to make a change at the local level.
- While all generations of Americans are taking action on social change, the survey reveals that Baby Boomers (age 47–65) and Matures (age 66+) are the driving force of social change in America and are engaging at the highest levels.
- Members of the Mature and Baby Boomer Generations are more likely than those in Generation X (age 35–46) or Generation Y (age 18–34) to have participated in activities to engage in social change in the past 12 months (99% vs. 93% vs. 89% vs. 90%, respectively).

Source: Social Research Digest, Oct. 2011 (Vol. 2, No. 6)

5.1.4   Social Change Impact Report: Global Survey

Author(s): Walden University

The report describes the perceptions on the importance of social change, the top issues in various countries and the future of social change. A continuation from the American survey released in the fall, the Global Survey includes the perspectives of more than 12,000 adults in Brazil, Canada, China, France, Germany, Great Britain, India, Japan, Mexico, Spain and the United States.

Key findings

"Think globally, act locally" has become a worldwide mentality, with a majority of citizens around the world (73%, on average) agreeing that what happens in other parts of the world can impact their local community.

- The global survey also found high levels of engagement in social change, with three quarters of adults (75%, on average) involved during the past six months, which most commonly included donating money, goods or services (41%, on average).
- On average, eight in 10 adults (81%) around the world say involvement in positive social change is important to them personally; adults in Mexico (95%), Brazil (93%), China (91%) and India (91%) are most likely to say it is very or somewhat important to be involved.
- While levels of engagement and importance vary by country, four in five adults (81%, on average) agree they want to be more involved in positive social change in the future.
- This year brought heightened social change awareness with global challenges such as economic uncertainties, political uprisings, changing climate conditions, poverty, health issues and others at the forefront of societal concerns.
- Yet despite the various global challenges and issues, adults around the world on average said education (37%) is the most important issue for positive social change to address.
- Social change issues of greatest importance vary by country, and where people live impacts their beliefs on social change issues.
- According to the survey, education is the most important social change issue in Brazil (63%), India (56%) and the United States (40%) and health issues are the most important for adults in France (46%), China (46%), Canada (43%) and Great Britain (36%).
- Thinking about the future, half or more of adults in each of the countries (66%, on average) say that the environment and "green" issues in other parts of the world will have a major impact on life in their own country in the next few years, particularly those in Mexico (83%) and Brazil (77%).
- This view is particularly strong among young adults.
- In nearly all of the countries, young adults say the environment in other parts of the world is the top issue most likely to have a major impact on

life in their own country (65%, on average), most commonly in Mexico (80%) and France (79%).

- The sole exception is in the United States, where conflict, war and terrorism in other parts of the world is the issue that is most likely to have a major impact at home (71%).

Source: Social Research Digest, Dec. 2011 (Vol. 2, No. 8)

5.1.5   2012 Social Innovation Awards

Author(s): Justmeans

The Justmeans Social Innovation Awards exist to honor the global leaders from the business and nonprofit sectors that are tackling global issues through social innovation. Since the Social Innovation Awards launched in early 2009, they have recognized companies that have implemented groundbreaking strategies and programs that drive social and environmental responsibility and innovation.

Key findings

This year marked one of the most diverse years ever as applications came from over 17 countries on five continents and ranged in organizational size from the small startup nonprofit to the Fortune 100 company.

- 2012 Social Innovation Awards winners are:

Best Social Investment Strategy	Vestergaard Frandsen
Best Employee Engagement Strategy	Santander Brasil
Best Use of New Media	Stonyfield
Best Online Report	Nestlé Waters North America
Best Integrated Report	SAP
Best Stakeholder Engagement	SAP
Best Product Design	Be Green Packaging, LLC
Best Incorporation of Ethical Sourcing/ Certification	H.J. Heinz Company
Most Strategic Use of Philanthropic Funds	Hewlett-Packard
Best Sustainability Performance	Novo Nordisk

- Last year alone over 40% of the Fortune 100 participated in the awards program.
- Previous winners include Thomson Reuters Foundation, SAP, S. C. Johnson & Son, Inc., Nokia, Cisco Systems, Novo Nordisk, Herman Miller, Inc., Gap Inc., Better World Books, amongst other leading companies and organizations.

Source: Social Research Digest, May 2012 (Vol. 3, No. 5)

5.1.6   2012 Social Change Impact Report

Author(s): Walden University

The report by Walden University provides a diverse global perspective on why adults engage in social change and the roles individuals, nonprofit organizations, government, and the media play in facilitating it. The annual Social Change Impact Report desribes findings from a survey among more than 8,900 adults in eight countries.

Key findings

Global economic conditions impact the ways in which people become involved in social change and their motivations for doing so.

- Economic conditions cause behaviours to change.
- On average 65% of adults agree it is more important to be involved in social change when economic conditions are poor.
- Half of adults surveyed participate in social change by donating money; however 37% reduce their donations during difficult economic times.
- Instead, 29% are likely to increase participation in volunteer work.
- On average, 60% of adults become involved through institutions, companies or organisations and 48% through digital technology.
- In China this figure is 72%.
- Non-profit organisations rank among the top two participation methods in all countries except Jordan where adults act individually or through a religious organisation.
- However, 59% agree individuals are the most important agent of social change.
- An average 57% agree they can act to make the world a better place.

- Respondents in all countries agree the media is biased in its reporting of social issues – 57% on average and 71% in the US.
- More than eight in ten adults have participated in social change in the past six months.
- The primary motivator in the US and Canada is a desire to help others less fortunate whereas in Brazil and India participation makes them feel good.

Source: Social Research Digest, Jul. 2012 (Vol. 3, No. 7)

5.2   Cross-Sector Partnerships

5.2.1   Community – It's Our Business

Author(s): Deloitte

"Community - it's our business" documents Deloitte's pivotal decisions and key learnings on its journey to complete a $50 million pledge to Billion+ Change, a federal initiative to encourage American businesses to champion pro bono work. Deloitte's pro bono projects were completed by professionals from all four of the organization's business subsidiaries - Audit & Enterprise Risk Services, Consulting, Financial Advisory Services and Tax.

Key findings

Although nonprofits are not in business to make a profit, they often struggle with the same strategic, operational and financial issues as for-profit companies.

- Nonprofits that receive pro bono work to meet those challenges can reap significant benefits.
- However, to maximize the advantages, contributions require more planning and infrastructure - on the part of donors and recipients - than cash philanthropy.
- Over the past three years, Deloitte has completed more than 275 pro bono engagements helping numerous pro bono clients increase organizational efficiencies, allocate resources more effectively, manage risk and strengthen expansion plans, among many other outcomes.

- The key insights covered in the report:
    - a client is a client, whether we get paid or not;
    - the company makes the commitment, so the company is responsible for it;
    - "begin with the end in mind";;
    - pro bono is time. And time is money;
    - giving away $50 million in service poses different challenges that giving away $50 million in cash.

Source: Social Research Digest, Jul. 2011 (Vol. 2, No. 3)

5.2.2   Collaborating for a Sustainable Future

Author(s): GlobeScan and SustainAbility

A report by SustainAbility and GlobeScan aims to better understand the renewed hope, future prospects and potential pitfalls for collaboration on sustainable development challenges. The study surveyed 800 global experts in 74 countries representing business, government, NGO and academic perspectives.

Key findings

Despite pessimism of national governments' willingness and ability to make substantive progress on the sustainability agenda, experts overwhelmingly believe that progress requires companies collaborating with multiple actors, including governments.

- However, significant doubt remains about the approach companies will take in their engagement with the public sector.
- All forms of collaboration are expected to increase over the next five years, although experts believe the most effective forms will involve actors focused on addressing a single issue, rather than a broad set of topics.
- Public policy advocacy and consumer engagement on sustainability topics are seen as having the most upside when addressed through multi-actor collaboration.
- Perhaps more surprisingly, experts see a significant opportunity for collaboration to accelerate more sustainable business models.
- Nearly half of experts cite access to diverse perspectives and expertise

and pooling risk as keys to the business case for collaboration; cost reduction is not seen as a primary reason to collaborate.
- Whether partnering with an NGO or company, shared purpose and the transparent exchange of information are important pre-requisites for collaboration.

Source: CSR Research Digest, Jan. 2013 (Vol. 5, No. 1)

5.2.3   Lobbying For Good Report

Author(s): FSG Social Impact Advisors

Nonprofits are increasingly working with their corporate partners to leverage companies' political clout and governmental affairs departments in support of cause related lobbying efforts. This report offers a number of case studies as well as an analysis of what kinds of lobbying are best for companies and for society.

Key findings

The closer CSR lobbying initiatives are to a company's business, the better they are for both the company and society.

- Corporations are often better equipped to make the case for pressing social change than nonprofits.
- As such, some nonprofits are finding that the fastest path to the heart of legislation may be through corporate partners with political clout.
- In 2006 alone, U.S. companies spent a record US$2.6 billion on federal lobbying. Meanwhile, for the entire period from 1998 to 2004, nonprofit organizations spent only US$222 million on federal lobbying.
- In Europe, companies spend between €750 million and €1 billion (US$1.1 billion to US$1.4 billion) annually to lobby the European Union. 70% of these European lobbyists represent a business interest, whereas only 10% work for social issues.
- Not all corporations lobby for good in the same way. The report three different targets of lobbying for good:
  - generic social issues, which are critical to society but not immediately consequential to a company's business;
  - value chain social impacts, which are the footprints a company leaves behind through its normal operations;

- o social dimensions of competitive context, which are the external conditions (e.g., strong schools and good roads) that a company needs to succeed.
- Currently, leading CSR organizations rarely mention how companies can use their government affairs departments and outsourced lobbyists to advocate for social issues; nor do CSR executives tend to discuss lobbying for good at conferences on corporate citizenship. Europe leads what little discourse there is.
- The report suggests three reasons why companies have been slow to lobby for good:
  - o the outcomes are more difficult to value than financial contributions or reducing footprints;
  - o lobbying might invite skepticism as consumers worry about companies' hidden agendas;
  - o companies like quick results, although the gains from successful lobbying can dwarf those of conventional CSR approaches.
- Companies that are serious about aligning their lobbying and CSR agendas should first make sure that their government relations do not undermine their CSR initiatives.

Source: Social Research Digest, Feb. 2009 (Vol. 1, No. 2)

5.2.4 Business Partnerships with Non- Profits: Working to Solve Mutual Problems in New Zealand

Author(s): G. Eweje, N. Palakshappa

Collaboration between business and non-profit organizations is becoming increasingly essential as organizations grow in both size and influence, and public pressure intensifies for organizations to address pressing social issues and environmental concerns. Social partnerships between business and nonprofits are widely promoted as an important new strategy which will bring significant benefits to society. This paper examines how they might collaborate to achieve mutually beneficial objectives.

Key findings

All of the partnerships reported by this paper were formed to help create a meaningful change in society, i.e. they had a direct impact on the key issues and stakeholders.

- CEOs of both businesses and non-profits sought to find a 'strategic fit' between their organizations, to use the skills and resources available to them for the community projects initiated in the collaboration.
- Partners tend towards retaining organizational autonomy while joining forces to tackle a shared social problem.
- Firms facing a less coercive external environment and an internal context that supports relationships are more proactive in identifying opportunities to create new knowledge through collaborations.
- The case study organizations exhibit a significantly high level of knowledge of their joint projects and confirm that the skills jointly acquired through the collaborations are significant to the successful outcome of their projects and have been one of the key factors in moving their partnerships into an integrative stage.
- Business and nonprofit partners appear to be actively engaged in the partnerships and have dedicated personnel responsible for the partnerships.
- Business partners in New Zealand have rarely used their collaboration with nonprofits to enhance public perceptions which is in stark contrast with their counterparts in many developed countries.
- Factors such as enduring links, shared understanding, longevity of bridging members, alignment with the institutional environment, and structure have all contributed to successful outcome of collaborations in New Zealand.
- In New Zealand, for a social partnership to be successful, the strategic management of each organization must incorporate the goals of different partners, rather than focusing on selfinterests. In addition, rather than operating as individual organizations.
- What remains unclear is how companies in New Zealand can use the relationships as a competitive advantage due to the fact that businesses do not really make their relationship with nonprofits a public issue. Moreover, in a situation where little information is available in the public arena, companies do not make information about social alliances a public relations issue.
- The interview data suggests that this is because it is not 'the kiwi way' to 'shout' about such activities.

- This is in contrast to most EU countries and the United States, where companies are eager to showcase their collaboration and inform the public and their customers about the projects they have with nonprofits.

Source: Social Research Digest, May 2009 (Vol. 1, No. 5)

5.2.5 Corporate-NGO Partnerships Study

Author(s): C&E

The 2010 C&E Barometer of Corporate-NGO Partnerships pin-points current practice as well as the expectations, drivers, key trends and changing practices in cross-sector partnerships. The report is based mainly on an online survey of practitioners from 114 leading Companies and NGOs engaged in cross-sector partnership, as well as a series of depth interviews with a smaller number of organisations.

Key findings

Cross sector partnerships are important to businesses and NGOs and are set to become more important over the next three years.

- 86% of charities and 72% of businesses expect to increase their investment in partnerships over the next three years.
- The Barometer highlights the success of the voluntary sector in developing high-profile partnerships with high-street retailers and supermarkets.
- Over a third (37%) of the most admired charity-business partnerships were those involving retailers and supermarkets followed by banks at 17% and soft drinks manufacturers at 7%.
- Marks and Spencer's collaboration with Oxfam was the most admired corporate-charity partnership with 13% of practitioners choosing it as the best example of a partnership delivering on corporate mission for both the business and the charity.
- The partnership involves both organisations sharing knowledge and working together to create sustainable production and consumption.
- The collaboration famously includes the Clothes Exchange, where anyone donating an item of M&S clothing to Oxfam receives a money-off voucher for use in store.

- HSBC and WWF's partnership to combat climate change came in second place (8%) while Pampers' (Proctor & Gamble) work with UNICEF to provide tetanus shots in the developing world was the third most admired partnership (7%).
- While practitioners claim that the most successful partnerships innovate, deliver corporate mission, help to build brands and are based on mutual benefit, it is clear that many voluntary sector organisations still regard generating income as the main driver in working with the corporate sector.
- 87% of voluntary sector practitioners viewed generating resources as more important than delivering corporate mission (69%).
- This contrasts with the business sector with 95% of practitioners rating delivery of their corporate social responsibility (CSR) agenda as vital with delivery of their business agenda in second place (50%).
- The challenge to deliver partnerships which meet strategic goals across both sectors is reflected in the views of many practitioners:
- Six out of ten (61%) practitioners said that half of their partnerships were not strategic
- One in ten (10%) were not confident the relationships were delivering their objectives
- Four in ten (43%) believed the partnerships were skewed in favour of the business

Source: CSR Research Digest, Nov. 2010 (Vol. 2, No. 11)

5.2.6 Working Together: Critical Perspectives on Six Cross-Sector Partnerships in Southern Africa

Author(s): M. Rein, L. Stott

This paper examines six cross-sector partnerships in South Africa and Zambia that were part of a research study undertaken between 2003 and 2005. The case studies were selected because of their potential to contribute to poverty reduction in their respective countries. The paper examines the context in which the partnerships were established, their governance and accountability mechanisms and the engagement and participation of the partners and the intended beneficiaries in the partnerships.

Key findings

There is a need to move beyond the one-size-fitsall approach to partnerships.

- While a partnership approach which has proven successful in one context can be used as a valuable learning resource for another, a partnership's work cannot necessarily be transferred directly to another partnership without a thorough and locally informed analysis of the context in which it is implemented.
- Partnership replication should focus more strongly on the transfer of learning about partnership processes instead of simply copying partnership activities.
- It can be difficult to assess whether the good intentions behind partnerships are translated into real benefits for target groups as effective monitoring and evaluation procedures are often not in place.
- Similarly, the absence of regularised governance and accountability systems in partnerships can make it difficult to support partner and beneficiary participation and engagement.
- The development of stronger mechanisms for assessing and ensuring accountability towards both partners and intended beneficiaries is required if partnerships are to meet their intended objectives.
- A detailed and attentive consideration of context is likely to have constructive and beneficial effects both on partnership practice and on policy-making.
- The collaboration of institutions from different sectors enabled resources to be directed to key development concerns, such as the provision of education, health care and economic development.
- In some instances, such provision could be seen to be filling a gap created by government inaction or resource shortage whereas, in others, it served to establish innovative ways of meeting the needs of developing commercial markets.
- Exit strategies had not been agreed upon in any of the partnerships covered by the case studies.
- Further work needs to be done to support and improve the capacity of cross-sector partnerships to identify, monitor and evaluate their own objectives and impacts even if this is not a problem-free exercise in itself.

- While the development of stronger mechanisms for assessing and ensuring accountability towards both partners and intended beneficiaries is important if partnerships are to meet their intended objectives, the actual experience of ground-level implementation also points to the need for more rigorous investigation into the barriers that thwart such a process and how they might be overcome.

Source: Social Research Digest, Jul. 2009 (Vol. 1, No. 7)

5.2.7   Building Sustainable Communities through Multi-Party Collaboration

Author(s): ICCR

The ICCR's published Social Sustainability Resource Guide (SSRG) functions as a framework, learning tool and guide for integrating social sustainability into business operations and implementing social sustainable initiatives. The guide examines current approaches to measuring corporate impact and suggests ways to improve corporate impact through collaborative multi-party and multi-sector engagement.

Key findings

While a number of companies have implemented sustainability initiatives, few measure the social impacts of their operations and programs in communities.

- Social Sustainability Resource Guide is contributing to the development in four areas:
  - social sustainability needs greater participation from the corporate sector: many companies have programs addressing their environmental impacts; however, few focus the same resources on their social impacts;
  - measuring social impacts is still in its infancy: it is critical to know whether or not programs and initiatives designed to address specific social issues are meeting their goals and having an impact;
  - inclusive, collaborative frameworks have the potential to make substantial progress on measuring social impact and making change: the SSRG proposes a rigorous, collaborative, multi-party,

multi-sector approach to social sustainability that is rooted in on-the-ground realities that impact people's lives;

o   multi-stakeholder case studies advance our knowledge of how community groups, along with companies and other stakeholders have tackled tough issues and made progress: the eight case studies in this guide are indicators of a growing focus on social sustainability and the challenges that impact measurement poses.

Source: Social Research Digest, Aug. 2011 (Vol. 2, No. 4)

5.2.8   Corporations and NGOs: When Accountability Leads to "Cooptation"

Author(s): D. Baur and H. P. Schmitz

Interactions between corporations and nonprofits are on the rise, frequently driven by a corporate interest in establishing credentials for corporate social responsibility (CSR). In this article, authors show how increasing demands for accountability directed at both businesses and NGOs can have the unintended effect of compromising the autonomy of nonprofits and fostering their "co-optation".

<u>Key findings</u>

Greater scrutiny of NGO spending driven by selfappointed watchdogs of the nonprofit sector and a prevalence of strategic notions of CSR advanced by corporate actors weaken the ability of civil society actors to change the business practices of their partners in the commercial sector.

- To counter this trend, authors argue that corporations should embrace a political notion of CSR and should actively encourage NGOs to strengthen "downward accountability" mechanisms, even if this creates more tensions in corporate–NGO partnerships.
- Rather than seeing NGOs as tools in a competition for a comparative advantage in the market place, corporations should actively support NGO independence and critical capacity.

Source: Social Research Digest, Feb. 2012 (Vol. 3, No. 2)

5.2.9   A Strategy for the Commons: Business-driven Networks for Collective Action and Policy Dialogue

Author(s): Bertelsmann Stiftung and Global Compact

The study features the UN Global Compact as an exemplary platform for addressing global sustainability challenges. Examples from 23 Global Compact Local Networks around the world as well as 36 case studies of collective action and policy dialogue are featured.

<u>Key findings</u>

Study highlights collective action and policy dialogues as the right governance mechanisms for the safeguarding of common goods and presents five enablers for the successful initiation and implementation of such initiatives.

- The current challenges involved with ensuring global sustainability are daunting.
- Climate change is increasing the incidence of severe weather events, natural resources are undergoing rapid depletion, labor conditions in global supply chains are often inhumane and degrading, and corruption around the globe is undermining competition and destroying wealth.
- These and other global challenges pose serious problems not only to mankind in general, but also to the sustainability of companies. Indeed, companies rely on enabling environments, local and global alike, for long-term success.
- Collective action and policy dialogue are two governance mechanisms that enable companies to jointly address sustainability challenges, invest in the creation of common goods, and to do so in concert with governments and other stakeholders.
- Collective action entails a coordinated and sustained process of collaboration among different parties who invest resources to achieve a common objective.
- Policy dialogue entails addressing regulatory and community issues through the involvement of all relevant public and private sector stakeholders in a policy development and implementation process.

- Both mechanisms can bring together stakeholders from different sectors and different countries in structured processes targeting common objectives.
- If collective action and policy dialogue initiatives are to reach their fullest potential, five enablers should be implemented:
  (1) participants need to share common ground;
  (2) the initiative needs to be perceived as legitimate by other stakeholders and society as a whole;
  (3) a sufficient implementation capacity needs to be in place to coordinate activities;
  (4) basic resources are required to start a joint process;
  (5) initiatives need to reflect the global and local nature of the issues they address.

Source: Social Research Digest, Aug. 2012 (Vol. 3, No. 8)

5.2.10 Corporate Innovation and Sustainable Community Development in Developing Countries

Author(s): J. N. Muthuri, J. Moon and U. Idemudia

The role of multinational corporations (MNCs) in fostering or undermining development within poor communities in developing countries has been a subject of intensive debate within academic and practitioner circles. MNCs are not only considered an obstacle to development but also as sources of solutions to some of the pressing social and environmental problems facing these communities.

Key findings

This article reviews the way in which companies frame (a) sustainable community development, and (b) their engagements in the community.

- It then considers the implications of both for sustainable community development and poverty alleviation in developing countries.
- The article then proposes an agenda for future research centering on how corporations innovate in their governance roles and the conditions in which community development innovations are created, take shape, and are put into practice.

Source: Social Research Digest, Oct. 2012 (Vol. 3, No. 10)

5.2.11 Global Partnership for Development: The Challenges We Face Gap Task Report 2013

Author(s): The MDG Gap Task Force

The MDG Gap Task Force published a report to improve the monitoring the Millennium Development Goal 8 by leveraging inter-agency coordination. The "Global Partnership for Development" Report tracks delivery on the commitments listed under Millennium development Goal 8-the global partnership for development.

Key findings

The indicators show progress, but efforts towards United Nations target of allocating 0.7% of gross national income to development aid have been receding in the past two years.

- A policy package needs to address the most salient concerns today, including: strengthening international cooperation in tax matters; strengthening systemic financial regulation; and advancing negotiations to address climate change.
- Official development assistance (ODA) suffered a second consecutive year of contraction in 2012 for the first time since 1997, falling 4%, down to $125.9 billion, from $134 billion in 2011.
- Donor governments urgently need to reverse the two-year contraction of ODA and make greater efforts to reach the United Nations targets, especially in assistance to LDCs.
- The developing-country share of world trade rose to 44.4% in 2012, although shares for Africa and the LDCs remained at 3.5% and 1.1%, respectively.
- Total external and government debt in developing countries as proportions of GDP increased slightly in 2012, to 22.3% and 45.9% respectively.
- External debt service increased from 24.0% of exports in 2011 to 27.1% in 2012.
- Essential medicines were available in only 57% of public and 65% of private wealth facilities in 2012.

- Pharmaceutical companies should make essential medicines more, affordable and, through innovation, develop new medicines most needed by developing countries.
- The number of individuals using Internet in developing countries has burgeoned, growing at 12% in 2013 compared with 5% in developed countries.
- Governments of developing countries should continue to increase the use of information, communication technologies (ICT) applications to improve the provision of services especially those with a direct impact on MDGs.

Source: Social Research Digest, Sep. 2013 (Vol. 4, No. 9)

5.3   Corporate Volunteering

5.3.1   CSR as Support for Employee Volunteers: Impacts, Gender Puzzles and Policy Implications in Canada

Author(s): F. MacPhail, P.Bowles

This article examines an under-researched form of corporate social responsibility, namely, employer support for employee voluntary activity. The study examines the impacts of employer support on the total number of hours volunteered and on the voluntary activities which are undertaken. Second, we examine how employer support is distributed between male and female employees. Statistical data on employer support for volunteering from Statistics Canada is complemented by empirical findings from 123 large Canadian companies.

Key findings

Employer support is associated with a greater amount of volunteer activity by both men and women employees and in a wide range of voluntary activities.

- Over 50% of the 123 employers surveyed indicated that they actively encouraged volunteer activity among their employees.
- 85% of employers agreed or strongly agreed with the statement that employees' volunteer activities improved the organizations' reputation.

- Employers indicated that CSR and pressures from shareholders for "triple bottom line" reporting had led them to seek more ways of increasing and supporting voluntary activities by their employees.
- Women in all population groups have higher volunteer rates than men; for employed women, the volunteer rate is 31.2% compared to 25.7% for men.
- Although employed women are more likely to volunteer than employed men, they do provide fewer hours of volunteer work on an annual basis (122 and 156 hours annually for women and men respectively).
- Among employed people who volunteer, 50.8% of employed male volunteers and 47.1% of employed female volunteers receive support from their employers.
- Volunteers with employer support do provide a greater number of volunteer work hours on average. Male volunteers with employer support provide an additional 6.7 hours (or 4.3% more) per year of volunteer work, compared to male volunteers without employer support. The comparable increase in hours for women with employer support is 11.7 hours (or 9.6% more) per year.
- Employed volunteers 35 years and older have lower odds of receiving employer support compared to employed volunteers aged 25–34 years.
- Employed workers with at least a high school diploma have higher odds of receiving employer support compared to employed volunteers without a high school diploma.
- Married workers have lower odds of receiving employer support, compared to other marital status groups.
- Organisations provide support for voluntary activities in a range of forms of support, including:
  - donating financially to the organization (69%);
  - giving approval to take time off or to use work time for volunteer activities (67%);
  - giving approval for use of facilities or equipment (66%);
  - giving approval of change of work hours (63%);
  - donating prizes etc. (62%).
- Decisions relating to employee volunteering took place at a number of different levels within organizations:
  - Decisions made at the local level (50%),

- o Following company-wide policies but with considerable local discretion (22%),
  - o Referred to head office (20%);
  - o Following detailed company-wide policy manual (7%).
- Approximately one third of the respondents indicated that their company has a formal policy regarding staff volunteering.

Source: Social Research Digest, Mar. 2009 (Vol. 1, No. 3)

5.3.2 Corporate Volunteering Survey

Author(s): Deloitte

According to the 2009 Deloitte Volunteer IMPACT Survey, both nonprofits and corporations are overlooking a high-impact opportunity to leverage pro bono and skilled volunteer support to offset a decline in corporate giving dollars. Online interviews with 300 executives involved in their company's charitable donations and volunteering decision-making were conducted in February 2009.

Key findings

Despite the challenging economic backdrop, nearly 40% of nonprofit executives say they will spend between $50,000 and $250,000 or more of "hard-won" cash on outside contractors and consultants this year.

- Yet nearly one-quarter (24%) of nonprofit respondents have no plans to use skilled volunteers or pro bono support in any capacity in 2009.
- Corporate grant makers (77%) and nonprofits (75%) place a high value on employee skills.
- 95% of nonprofits agree they are in greater need of pro bono or skilled volunteer support.
- However, these statements are inconsistent with corporations' efforts to contribute skilled volunteers and nonprofits' efforts to seek them.
- Approximately one-third (35%) of nonprofits do not have the appropriate infrastructure needed to successfully deploy volunteers.
- Nearly one quarter (24%) of nonprofits surveyed have no one in charge of volunteer management or have someone in charge with less than three years of experience (23%).

- Similarly, more than one-in-four (26%) corporations have no one to oversee an employee volunteer program. 17% of corporations have no employee volunteer program at all.
- Nearly all nonprofits surveyed (97%) do not know who in a company to approach with pro bono requests. 95% do not know which companies to appeal to with these requests.
- This lack of familiarity with ways to secure pro bono services could also be driven by the fact that half (50%) of corporations nationwide do not offer skilled volunteer support, despite a belief in its value.

Source: Social Research Digest, May 2009 (Vol. 1, No. 5)

5.3.3   Deloitte Volunteer IMPACT Survey

Author(s): Deloitte

Deloitte's eight Volunteer IMPACT survey offers new insights into volunteerism and its links to employee engagement and perceptions of positive organizational culture. The survey is based on online interviews with 1,500 millennials (ages 21-35) who work at organizations with 1,000 or more employees that offer employee volunteer activities or programs.

Key findings

Millennials who frequently participate in workplace volunteer activities are far more likely to be proud, loyal and satisfied employees compared to those who rarely or never volunteer.

- Survey reveals that, compared to those who rarely or never volunteer, millennials who frequently participate in their company's employee volunteer activities are:
  o twice as likely to rate their corporate culture as very positive (56% versus 28%);
  o more likely to be very proud to work for their company (55% versus 36%);
  o more likely to feel very loyal toward their company (52% versus 33%);
  o nearly twice as likely to be very satisfied with the progression of their career (37% versus 21%);

- o more likely to be very satisfied with their employer (51% versus 32%); and;
  - o more likely to recommend their company to a friend (57% versus 46%).
- More than one-third (37%) of those who frequently volunteer are more likely to be very satisfied with the progression of their career.
- These and other findings from the survey suggest a link between volunteerism and the quality of employee engagement as well as favorable employee perceptions of organizational culture.
- Deloitte survey findings also suggest that the benefits of creating a culture of service extend well beyond active volunteers.
- As expected, millennials strongly favor (70%) companies committed to the community.
- However, even among those millennials surveyed who rarely or never volunteer, more than half (61%) say they are likely to factor a company's commitment to the community into their decision if choosing between two jobs with the same location, responsibilities and pay and benefits.
- Millennials, who are often characterized by their passion to change the world, are also motivated to volunteer by more than altruism; half (51%) of all millennials surveyed want to benefit professionally from their volunteerism.
- Skilled volunteers, who use their business acumen to help nonprofit organizations, are more likely to seek a professional return on investment for their volunteer efforts than "hands-on" volunteers:
  - o skilled volunteers are more likely than traditional volunteers to say it is important that their volunteer efforts benefit them professionally (72% versus 56%);
  - o skilled volunteers are also more likely than traditional volunteers to be motivated by career advancement (47% versus 34%).

Source: Social Research Digest, Jun. 2011 (Vol. 2, No. 2)

5.3.4 The New Paradigm: Volunteerism. Competence. Results.

Author(s): Forbes

To get a handle on how companies are approaching corporate social responsibility, why they do it, what they perceive the benefits are, and how they are allocating their resources, Forbes Insights surveyed top-level management at consumer, financial services, technology, energy, and healthcare companies. In addition, this report spotlights CSR programs at three companies—Hewlett-Packard, Eli Lilly, and MasterCard—to showcase the way three industry leaders are engaging this issue.

Key findings

Corporate philanthropy, social innovation, and corporate citizenship are no longer merely buzzwords for companies.

- Giving back to the community has now established itself within corporate DNA.
- Forty-five percent of companies address social services in their corporate social responsibility (CSR) efforts.
- At number two: environmental causes (44% of companies).
- Community development came in third with 40% support.
- These are followed by health services and economic development.

Source: Social Research Digest, Apr. 2012 (Vol. 3, No. 4)

5.3.5 UN Volunteers Report

Author(s): UN Volunteers

UN Volunteers launched a report that captures the essence of the contributions of UN Volunteers, UNV staff and partners to advancing peace and development in 2012. Each chapter of 'UNV Annual Report:Creating Lasting Impact' outlines the work of UNV and of its UN Volunteers, coupled with examples of projects and partnerships that are fostering sustainable peace and development.

Key findings

In 2012, UNV deployed 966 international and national volunteers in the age range defined by the new United Nations youth volunteer modality – that is between the ages of 18 to 29. Of these, around 60% were national volunteers, working within their own countries and communities, and 60% were women.

- These UN Volunteers worked primarily in the areas of administration, relief, justice and public information, and were hosted by six different United Nations entities.
- During the course of the year, UNV funded eleven youth projects in 15 countries: Bosnia and Herzegovina, Egypt, Ethiopia, Indonesia, Jordan, Lesotho, Morocco, Peru, Rwanda, Tanzania, Tunisia, Yemen, the Ukraine, Uzbekistan and Zambia.
- These projects built confidence, social responsibility, peer models and skills for future employment. They also had a ripple effect, mobilizing some 20,500 community volunteers.
- In addition, UNV supported governments in establishing national volunteer schemes with a youth focus in 11 countries, namely Benin, Burkina Faso, Cape Verde, Guinea, Liberia, Mali, Mauritius, Mozambique, Senegal, Sierra Leone and Viet Nam, which mobilized another 22,500 community volunteers.
- In 2005, the Economic Community of West African States (ECOWAS) signed a Memorandum of Understanding with UNV, requesting its expertise to create the ECOWAS Volunteers Programme, a cadre of youth volunteers to entrench peacebuilding and reconciliation as development tools in three pilot countries: Guinea, Liberia and Sierra Leone.
- Three UN Volunteers were recruited as programme Country Advisors and two UN Volunteers were assigned as Monitoring and Evaluation and Knowledge Management and Communication Specialists in the programme's regional office in Burkina Faso.
- In 2012, the number of UN Volunteers fielded under the programme increased to 24, with 19 stationed in Liberia and five in Guinea. The deployment of 40 additional volunteers in Sierra Leone and 35 in Guinea is expected in 2013.

Source: Social Research Digest, Oct. 2013 (Vol. 4, No. 10)

5.4   Corporate and Public Philanthropy

5.4.1   Philanthropic Giving in 2010

Author(s): Committee Encouraging Corporate Philanthropy

CECP releases first look at changes from pre-economic crisis levels in philanthropic giving. The survey on 2010 contributions included 184 companies, 63 among the top 100 companies of the FORTUNE 500 list, combining to report a total of more than $15 billion in cash and product giving.

Key findings

65% of companies gave more in 2010 than they did in 2009, with 40% of companies increasing giving by 10% or more.

- However, median total giving, indicative of the typical company's giving in the CECP sample, remained largely unchanged at $24.88 million.
- Aggregate total giving surpassed 2009 levels by almost 18%, driven by increases from a handful of companies.
- More than half of this increase can be attributed to pharmaceutical companies that made significant investments in their signature initiatives or donated more medicine through their Patient Assistance Programs (PAPs).
- In addition, upward shifts were also driven by the Consumer Staples, Financials, Industrials and Information Technology sectors, most of which gave 20% to 30% more in 2010 than the year before.
- By contrast, the Consumer Discretionary and Utility industries reported reduced aggregate giving.
- Setting these 2010 gains in context, CECP found that 53% of companies gave more in 2010 than in 2007, before the economic crisis set in.
- Companies frequently cited the impact of corporate financial performance on giving budgets as reasons for both increased and decreased giving in 2010.
- 70% reported increased profit, with 50% reporting increases of 10% or more.
- For some companies, this improved corporate performance contributed to expanded corporate giving levels, but for others, the enduring economic uncertainty resulted in reduced giving budgets.
- Among other reasons for increased contributions, giving professionals reported additional funding for disaster relief and recovery efforts for the major disasters of 2010 (including the earthquake in Haiti and the Pakistan floods), heightened contributions for signature philanthropic

programs and areas of strategic focus, and combined budgets that exceeded historical contributions resulting from mergers and acquisitions.

Source: CSR Research Digest, Jun. 2011 (Vol. 3, No. 6)

5.4.2 Moving Beyond Boundaries: The Rise of International Giving

Author(s): Global Impact

Using multiple sources across the giving industry, the report highlights today's trends in international philanthropy. This resource includes data on key donor segments, such as corporations, and explores driving factors behind corporate international giving.

<u>Key findings</u>

Giving to international causes is the fastest-growing area of interest for donors. U.S.-based corporations and donors are increasingly generous in their international contributions to help people in need, even in the midst of current economic climate.

- 6.2% increase in giving to international causes over the previous year.
- 10.4% average annual growth rate for giving to international causes since 1987.
- 22% of American households make donations to international charities.
- 37% of major U.S. companies plan to increase their funding focus on international issues and causes.
- The report also states that companies express greater interest in giving to international organizations that help the people in the regions where they have operations.
- The number of organizations that establish partnerships with Global Impact increases year over year.

Source: CSR Research Digest, Jun. 2011 (Vol. 3, No. 6)

5.4.3 India Philanthropy Report 2013

Author(s): Bain & Co.

Bain & Company published the fourth annual India Philanthropy Report which delved into how charitable organisations assess the impact of their work, and how they can better communicate that impact to donors. 180 high-net-worth individuals (HNWIs1) across four major cities as well as leaders at more than 40 nongovernment organisations (NGOs) were surveyed.

Key findings

Indian donors, foundations, NGOs and the government need to come together on the issue of impact definition.

- The gap in understanding about what creates philanthropic success is exacerbated by infrequent communication from NGOs to their donors about the results of their work.
- Donors will benefit from making efforts to understand specific-sector challenges and the various methods to tackle them at the beginning of projects.
- NGOs will benefit from clearly articulating their goals and the expected routes to achieve them.
- Frequent and more detailed communication from NGOs to donors can improve their credentials.
- Foundations could support NGOs in testing innovative approaches to difficult and underrepresented sectors with their longer range vision and ability to fund qualitative, impact-producing activities, such as advocacy, policy and research efforts.

Source: CSR Research Digest, May 2013 (Vol. 5, No. 5)

5.4.4 EuroCharity Yearbook 2010: The Future of Responsible Investing

Author(s): EuroCharity

Yearbook 2010: The Future of Responsible Investing informs key stakeholders on the latest trends, research, indices, best practices, case studies, intelligence and viewpoints related to this important theme. A total of 31 guest authors from the U.S.A., Canada, U.K., The Netherlands, France, Italy, Greece, Belgium, Denmark, Norway, Switzerland, South Africa,

Australia, Bangladesh and other countries participated in the 4th EuroCharity Yearbook.

Key findings

A total of 16 corporations have been profiled in the "EuroCharity Yearbook 2010: The Future of Responsible Investing".

- The sustainability-driven firms that have been showcased in the album are as follows:
  - AB Vassilopoulos (Delhaize Group) - "Nutritious, healthy, safe and affordable! We deliver the best for life!"
  - Athenian Brewery - "Athenian Brewery's three-year plan to become the Greenest Brewer in Greece"
  - Cosmote Mobile Telecommunications S.A. - "How can we operate without harming the environment"
  - Diversey - "The future of responsible cleaning"
  - Fiat- "Investing in the future of responsible mobility
  - Gefyra S.A. - "The Rio - Antirio Bridge: Investing in the citizens"
  - Genesis Pharma - "A pharmaceutical company with corporate social responsibility in its heart"
  - Halyps Cement (Italcementi Group) - "Sustainable development as a key driver of environmental and social value
  - Hellenic Petroleum - "Energy for life"
  - Hellenic Telecommunications Organization S.A. (OTE) - "For OTE, responsible business means building ties in the marketplace, in society, with employees and the environment"
  - Interamerican S.A. - "On the right track to sustainability"
  - JT International (JTI) - "Making a positive difference through effective partnerships"
  - Maersk Line - "Why it makes sense to highlight the issues"
  - Mytilineos Group - "Investing in sustainability"
  - TT Hellenic Postbank - "Little, everyday moves can make the big difference"

Source: Governance Research Digest, Jul. 2011 (Vol. 2, No. 3)

5.4.5   Exploring the Geography of Corporate Philanthropic Disaster Response: A Study of Fortune Global 500 Firms

Author(s): A. Muller, G. Whiteman

This article draws on comparative research on corporate social responsibility and corporate philanthropy to explore the geography of corporate philanthropic disaster response. The study analyzes donation announcements made by Fortune Global 500 firms from North America, Europe and Asia to look for regional patterns across three recent disasters: the South Asian Tsunami, Hurricane Katrina, and the Kashmiri earthquake.

Key findings

Firms from different regions demonstrated significant differences in the likelihood and cash value of corporate philanthropic disaster response (CPDR).

- Fortune Global 500 firms donated in excess of US$1.2 billion to the three disasters collectively. The Tsunami received the greatest overall donations at US$595 million, with
- US$545 million going to Katrina and just over US$70 million going to the Kashmiri earthquake.
- Corporate philanthropic disaster response was, broadly speaking, equally distributed globally. The companies from Russia, Mexico, Malaysia, Taiwan and Luxembourg are the only exceptions.
- Regional differences in donation likelihood depend on the disaster in question.
- The greatest likelihood of donating was for European firms to the Tsunami.
- North American firms were more than two times as likely to donate to the Tsunami as
- Asian firms were to donate to Kashmir, and more than four times as likely to donate in response to Hurricane Katrina.
- There were significant differences among North America, Europe, and Asia in the case of the Tsunami; between North America and Asia in the case of Katrina but not between Europe and Asia; and no significant differences among North America, Europe, and Asia in the case of the Kashmiri earthquake.

- Differences in donation value between regions are significantly greater than differences within regions, across multiple disasters.
- The main effects of 'Local Presence' are also significant, revealing that firms that referred to local activities, employees and/or business relations in the disaster zone in their donation announcements gave significantly more than firms that made no mention of such concerns.
- The relatively low cash value of donations by Asian firms could imply that Asian firms are subjected to specific factors that constrain how much they give.
- Given that shareholders are the most important stakeholders to Asian executives, Asian executives may perceive agency constraints when considering the degree to which they should engage in CPDR.
- If companies perceive CPDR to be a form of social responsibility, the leading role of North American and, to a lesser extent, European firms in this type of CSR is in accordance with previous research.
- The possibility exists of a local presence effect for vacationing nationals, since a large number of Europeans were affected in particular by the Asian tsunami.

Source: Social Research Digest, Mar. 2009 (Vol. 1, No. 3)

5.4.6 The Value of Corporate Philanthropy during Times of Crisis: The Sensegiving Effect of Employee Involvement

Author(s): A. Muller and R. Kräussl

The article extends the contingency perspective that philanthropy's value to the firm is largely mediated by contextual factors such as managers' assumed motives for charity. For the empirical investigation in this study, authors analyze abnormal returns to announcements by U.S. Fortune 500 firms documenting their donations to Hurricane Katrina disaster relief in 2005.

Key findings

Article used a "sensegiving" lens, by which external actors' interpretations of organizational actions may be influenced by the way in which the organization communicates about those actions.

- Authors consider how sensegiving features in philanthropy-related press releases affect whether investors value those donation decisions.
- It is expected that in general, donation decisions would be controversial given the uncertainty surrounding the hurricane's economic effects at the time.
- However, it is also proposes that announcements emphasizing employee involvement in the donation send investors positive signals about the firm's ability to bounce back from the disaster's adverse effects.
- Authors find empirical support for the proposed hypotheses, and discuss the implications for theory and practice.

Source: Social Research Digest, Oct. 2011 (Vol. 2, No. 6)

5.4.7   How to Help: 5 Steps to Effective Corporate Disaster Giving Campaigns

Author(s): Network for Good

Network for Good has released a new guide to help corporations mobilize relief efforts in response to humanitarian disasters. The report provides insights gleaned from ten years of powering disaster donations for nonprofits and corporate partners and includes recommendations to help companies expand their corporate social responsibility (CSR) programs to include timely and effective disaster giving campaigns for customers and employees.

Key findings

As events have shown time and again, American companies are extremely generous in the aftermath of a humanitarian disaster.

- Many companies are compelled to help in the wake of a tragic event.
- However, most lack a disaster plan that can be activated easily and have not laid a foundation to ensure that the right people, resources and messaging are deployed at the right time.
- This guide provides a framework to lay that groundwork.
- The 5-step disaster plan:
  o decide when to respond;
  o set the response scope;

- o choose your cause partner(s);
- o frame the call to action;
- o tell your story.
- The publication also highlights lessons learned from companies such as AOL, Campbell Soup Company, Capital One, Dell, Ryder and Yahoo! during recent disaster response campaigns.

Source: Social Research Digest, Nov. 2011 (Vol. 2, No. 7)

5.4.8 Changing Lives, Empowering Communities, One Philanthropist at a Time

Author(s): Turkish Philanthropy Funds

Turkish Philanthropy Funds (TPF), a diaspora community foundation channeling social investments of Turkish-Americans to social needs, released its annual report. The report describes TPF's unique approach to philanthropy, primary areas of focus, and stories of TPF donors and grantees.

Key findings

The report reaffirms the growing influence of Turkish diaspora in the United States.

- TPF's outreach and philanthropic giving in primary areas of focus – education opportunities; empowering women and girls; improving livelihoods and raising awareness through arts.
- Accomplishments with TPF grantee partners such as are Sabanci University, Mother Child Education Fund (ACEV), Community Volunteers Foundation of Turkey (TOG), Association for the Support of Contemporary Living (CYDD) and Aziz Nesin Foundation.

Source: Social Research Digest, Nov. 2011 (Vol. 2, No. 7)

5.4.9 Giving in Numbers: 2011 Edition

Author(s): Committee Encouraging Corporate Philanthropy

Giving in Numbers represents a comprehensive look at 2010 corporate giving trends. The report is drawing on data from 184 companies, including 63 of the top 100 companies in the Fortune 500.

Key findings

Median total giving in CECP's sample was $22.10 million in 2010.

- 94% of companies offered at least one matching gift program in 2010.
- 89% of companies had a formal domestic employee volunteer program.
- 81% of companies reported having a corporate foundation.
- Health, education, and community and economic development were top priorities for the typical company.
- Corporate Giving in an Economic Downturn
- Since the financial crisis affected the profits of different industries at different times, recovery has not been uniform.
- CECP identified strikingly divergent paths in corporate contributions since 2007: a quarter of companies increased giving by more than 25%, while 21% reduced contributions by more than 25%, demonstrating that while some companies have been able to surpass pre-crisis giving levels, others are still in a period of rebuilding.
- Grant Recipients
  - o Hardship in their communities prompted many companies to support basic health and social service programs in 2010.
  - o Education and community and economic development were also cited as program areas receiving considerable targeted funding.
- Employee and Stakeholder Engagement
  - o The competition to attract and retain talented employees has encouraged many companies to offer innovative and meaningful employeevolunteer opportunities.
  - o Dollars for Doers, employee recognition awards, flexible scheduling, and paid-release time were programs most frequently offered.
- Organization, Motivation, and Program Costs
  - o Companies are increasingly targeting one or two societal issues rather than spreading funding widely across multiple program areas.
- The median number of grants per full time contributions employee has declined by 27% since 2007, while the median grant size has increased by 12%.

Source: Social Research Digest, Dec. 2011 (Vol. 2, No. 8)

5.4.10 Chinese Foundation Development Handbook: A Practical Guide to the Establishment and Management of a Private Foundation

Author(s): BSR

BSR's new guidebook helps Chinese individuals and companies establish and run effective private foundations. The guide provides information on managing a foundation, developing a mission and strategy, implementing governance practices, and engaging volunteers.

Key findings

Over the past 30 years, China's foundation sector has grown from 140 foundations in the 1980s to more than 2,000 in 2011.

- The Chinese government's Foundation Registration and Management Regulations catalyzed this growth in 2004 by providing clear requirements for registering new private foundations; directives on governance, fundraising, donors, and beneficiary rights; and a framework for the structure and operations of foundations.
- The handbook will help individuals and companies with the following common challenges in establishing and running foundations:
  o registering foundations, due to an onerous, lengthy, and unpredictable registration process;
  o effectively balancing the role and wishes of the founder with the mission of the foundation;
  o attracting and retaining professional staff;
  o gaining expertise in accounting and financial management, program management, and impact measurement;
  o accessing practical, localized resources and case studies
  o supporting projects to address China's pressing social/environmental issues, either through funding or implementation
  o effectively using the diverse resources of their donors, who may be corporate executives or successful entrepreneurs
  o helping build a stronger nonprofit sector in China by supporting NGOs and community-based service providers.

Source: Social Research Digest, Dec. 2011 (Vol. 2, No. 8)

5.4.11   The Bottom Case for Product Philanthropy

Author(s): Indiana University

The study provides the first detailed examination of the return on investment for donating inventory as opposed to liquidating or destroying it. In addition to providing an economic justification for retailers, manufacturers and distributors to donate excess merchandise, the report gives managers a framework for analyzing the costs, benefits, risks, and opportunities of implementing a product philanthropy program.

Key findings

Businesses can do well by doing good through product philanthropy.

- Donating products to charities helps corporate bottom lines, reduces waste in landfills, and provides relief for people in need.
- Product giving presents a considerable financial advantage over cash donations because it can carry an enhanced tax deduction.
- Product donations can provide the same image enhancement benefits as marketing and advertising programs and at a lower cost.
- Companies that engage in product philanthropy avoid fees and negative branding implications associated with disposal of excess inventory.
- Product donation is superior to liquidation in most circumstances, and the report provides a rule of thumb for companies wishing to make quick cost comparisons.

Source: Social Research Digest, Jan. 2012 (Vol. 3, No. 1)

5.4.12   Essay: Philanthropy Works when the Giver Can Gain Too

Author(s): Ethical Corporation

Successful philanthropy brings about lasting social change while creating business value. The essay describes how companies can design philanthropy programmes for maximum business and social benefit.

Key findings

The best philanthropy programmes identify how a company's resources can be used for the greatest possible impact.

- The author proposes two criteria for successful corporate philanthropy programmes:
  o giving creates value for the company and
  o giving achieves more than shareholders can achieve individually.
- Enhancing the customer experience is a third consideration.
- To identify philanthropy programmes that create maximum value for business and society, companies should evaluate internal resources and assets against what needs doing in the world.
- The author argues that for a true measure of success, companies should look at the impact of philanthropy programmes, rather than how much is spent on them.
- To illustrate these points, the author compares the programmes of two banks and demonstrates the value Goldman Sachs created by using it's unique talent and resources to create real benefits for developing communities.
- Vaccinations enabled by Bonds issued by Goldman Sachs protect 500+ million children in over 70 of the world's poorest countries.

Source: Social Research Digest, Jul. 2012 (Vol. 3, No. 7)

5.4.13 Constructive Capitalism for Goodness Sake: Exploring the Relationship between Giving Attitudes, Intentions and Behaviours

Author(s): Adessy Associates

A survey was conducted by Adessy Associates to explore current trends in giving attitudes, intentions and behaviours. The research is based on an online survey, which included open and closed questions, conducted between March and June 2012.

Key findings

Over 85% of respondents give between 0.5% and 2% of their income, showing a strong sense of responsibility and willingness to contribute.

- About 20% of the participants receive a bonus, and of those, about one quarter has donated portions of their bonuses.
- When participants were asked to rank, in orderof pAuthor(s), their motivations for giving, the top three responses were:

- o solve specific global issues;
- o better society as a whole;
- o effect 'social change' and solve large scale problems.
- Of participants, 90% gave in their home country.
- Over 64% donate in less socio-economically developed regions.
- Most clearly favoured is giving to local issues over tackling wider issues.
- When participants were asked what would prompt them to start giving more, in order of pAuthor(s):
  - o 62% stated that understanding the positive impact of their giving was the single most important driver for giving more;
  - o 49% deemed effecting social change as very important;
  - o 35% indicated sensitivity to social inequalities.

Source: Social Research Digest, Nov. 2012 (Vol. 3, No. 11)

5.4.14 Corporate Philanthropy in China: A Practitioner's Guide for Foreign Donors

Author(s): The Conference Board

This research conducted by The Conference Board analyses the size and scale of China's non-profit sector, explains its idiosyncratic political and cultural characteristics, and produces a practical guidance for practitioners on effective engagement in the nonprofit sector in China. It aims to inform, educate, and provide practical guidance for effective decision making on corporate philanthropy in China.

Key findings

The overall lack of transparency, oversight and good governance in the Chinese nonprofit sector, and the number of of unregistered NPOs, limits the research's access to accurate sector data.

- China is an extremely difficult environment to navigate for corporate donors.
- First, changes in nonprofit sector are occurring quickly and unevenly across different provinces.
- Two, financial and operational date of charities is limited.

- Three, the structure and regulatory environment governing the nonprofit sector is fundamentally different from the West.
- Despite continuous regulatory and political obstacles, the number of legally registered nonprofit organizations (NPOs) has more than doubled.
- Private industries and individuals were not allowed to establish NPOs until late 1990s.
- Today, the government has the role of regulator, stakeholder and direct participant of civil society.
- A large share of China's nonprofit sector is called GONGOs (government-organized nongovernment organizations).
- Accordingly, the line between state and society is murky.
- Regulations limit the ability of the nonprofit sector to recruit and grow a qualified workforce to recruit qualified talent.
- Corruption and inconsistency fetter Chinese government's approach.
- Practitioners have to make decisions based on a pragmatic assessment of what is sensible and conducive in the current Chinese operation environment
- Successful engagement in China requires a panoptic understanding and acknowledgement of the realities and boundaries of China's current political and regulatory environment juxtaposed with NPOs and philanthropic work.

Source: Social Research Digest, Jan. 2013 (Vol. 4, No. 1)

5.4.15 Capital For The Future: Saving and Investment in an Interdependent World

Author(s): The World Bank

The World Bank released "Capital for the future" report, a research on the future world savings and investments. The publication highlights the main role developing economies will play and try to examine which countries will drive investment in a multipolar world, whether an aging world will run out of saving to fund investment and how savers and investors will be matched in the future.

Key findings

The developing economies will be major investors in the world economy, accounting for 60 cents of every investment dollar by 2030.

- While there will be demographic pressures, the world will not "run out" of saving in the future.
- Before 2020, total investment in the developing world is expected to overtake that in high income countries.
- The developing countries will become key players in the international arena and will become for the first time the main sources and destinations of global gross capital flows.
- Policy and international reforms are necessary in order to achieve positive results and preparing this change of the dynamics of future wealth and global capital.
- National governments, policy makers and international institutions will be affected by the future trends regarding saving, investment, spending and capital flow.

Source: Social Research Digest, Aug. 2013 (Vol. 4, No. 8)

5.4.16 US Nonprofit Fundraising Survey

Author(s): CompassPoint and Evelyn and Walter Haas, Jr. Fund

CompassPoint and Evelyn and Walter Haas, Jr. Fund surveyed more than 2,700 executive directors and development directors across the US so as to uncover potential solutions to the fundraising challenges nonprofits face. The 'UnderDeveloped: A National Study of Challenges Facing Nonprofit Fundraising' study includes a great diversity of organizations—a wide range of budget and staff sizes, a multitude of mission types, and diverse geographic representation.

Key findings

Many nonprofit organizations are stuck in a vicious cycle that threatens their ability to raise the resources they need to succeed.

- The report is organized around three main challenges and concludes with a set of recommendations to jumpstart a national conversation about how we can all help nonprofits take their fund development to the next level.

- *Revolving door* – Organizations are struggling with high turnover and long vacancies in the development director position.
- *Help wanted* – Organizations aren't finding enough qualified candidates for development director jobs. Executives also report performance problems and a lack of basic fundraising skills among key development staff.
- *It's about more than one person* – Beyond creating a development director position and hiring someone who is qualified for the job, organizations and their leaders need to build the capacity, the systems, and the culture to support fundraising success. The findings indicate that many nonprofits aren't doing this.
- *Breaking the cycle* – UnderDeveloped offers urgent calls to action for the nonprofit sector, citing key steps that nonprofit executives, funders, and sector leaders should consider as they set out to address the challenges detailed in the report.

Source: Social Research Digest, Sep. 2013 (Vol. 4, No. 9)

5.4.17 2013 Aid Transparency Index

Author(s): Publish What You Fund (The Global Campaign for Aid Transparency)

Publish What You Fund (The Global Campaign for Aid Transparency) released the 2013 version of the industry standard for assessing the state of aid transparency among the world's major donors. The 2013 Aid Transparency Index uses a revised methodology that reflects the changes in the aid transparency landscape and the resulting need to better assess the quality of published data and ranks 67 donor agencies – like USAID and DFID – based on the information they publish about their development projects, which is then scored on 39 indicators.

Key findings

The US Millennium Challenge Corporation (MCC) is the most transparent aid donor in the world.

- Global Alliance for Vaccines and Immunizations ranked #2 overall in the Index, and the Global Fund to Fight AIDS, Tuberculosis and Malaria ranked #6.

- MCC was one of six US agencies ranked in the index, but those US agencies do not score well.
- The Department of the Treasury and USAID are both in the Fair category, while the Department of Defense, Department of State, and the President's Emergency Plan for AIDS Relief (PEPFAR) score in the Poor and Very Poor categories.
- Both MCC and the Department of the Treasury have made large improvements since last year's assessment.
- The US did hit several aid transparency milestones in 2013. The US first published data to the IATI registry in January, and has followed up with more publications in subsequent months. However, the US government is unlikely to meet its own goal of publishing 70% of aid flows to IATI by the end of 2013 without publication by the State Department.
- In general, large donors perform better overall on the index.
- Very large donors – those with spending over $10 billion like the World Bank IDA and USAID – have an average score of 57%, while very small donors with spending under $100 million score an average of only 12%.
- Multilateral organizations like the World Bank and African Development Bank in general score well, but scores vary significantly.

Source: Social Research Digest, Oct. 2013 (Vol. 4, No. 10)

5.4.18 Crowdfunding's Potential for the Developing World

Author(s): Crowdfund Capital Advisors (CCA), infoDev, World Bank (WB)

The World Bank created a report in response to the rapid growth of crowdfunding as a form of financing for high-growth entrepreneurs and start-ups. The study, "Crowdfunding's Potential for the Developing World" investigates and discusses the opportunities, risks and relevance of crowdfunding for developing countries.

Key findings

Building a crowdfunding ecosystem depends on key enablers to build trust.

- The key factors that have facilitated crowdfunding in developed countries include:

1. A regulatory framework that leverages the transparency, speed, and scale that advances in technology and the Internet can deliver to early-stage funding marketplaces.
2. Strong social media market penetration and Internet usage, which is necessary to harness demographic and technology trends to drive collaboration and cultural shifts.
3. A regulated online marketplace that facilitates capital formation while providing prudent investor protections through education and training.
4. Collaboration with other entrepreneurial events and hubs including business plan competitions, incubators, accelerators, universities and co-working spaces to create a channel for opportunity and oversight.

- In order for crowdfunding to work, individuals must have access to reliable broadband

Internet or mobile data networks. Technology to facilitate ongoing communication between investors and entrepreneurs and enabling tools to systematize and streamline the business lifecycle must also be employed and allowed to operate freely.

Source: Social Research Digest, Dec. 2013 (Vol. 4, No. 12)

5.4.19 The Age of Engagement: New 2011 Social Good Survey

Author(s): Fenton / GlobeScan

The survey by Fenton and GlobeScan examines people's views of nonprofits/charities and planned giving for 2012. Online panels in the U.S. and U.K were used targeting respondents aged 18 years or older and who had made a minimum of $20.00/10.00 pounds Sterling in charitable donations in the past year.

Key findings

People in the United States and United Kingdom overwhelmingly trust nonprofits and charities ahead of governments and corporations to create social change, yet most say they will make charitable donations at the same or reduced levels as last year.

- Seventy-two percent of U.K. respondents and 65% of U.S. respondents say they expect their giving to remain the same in 2012.

- A notable minority say their giving will decrease (16% U.K. and 17% U.S.).
- Forty-one percent of U.K. respondents and 55% of U.S. respondents say they believe nonprofits and charities are highly effective at bringing about positive social change.
- People say an organization's commitment to a cause they feel strongly about (54% U.K.; 44% U.S.) is the most important factor for their decision to give.
- Respondents who report knowing more about how nonprofits are managed are also more positive about their support, but less than half say they believe nonprofits/charities do a good job spending funds and managing operations.
- The majority of responses underscore the value of social media to keep them up to date and provide opportunities for engagement.
- While social media may not be the most effective tool to reach new audiences, it is an effective for engaging existing supporters.
- News stories and television commercials rank higher than social media as persuasion tools to bring new people into an effort.

Source: Social Research Digest, Dec. 2011 (Vol. 2, No. 8)

5.4.20 Understanding Public Attitudes to Aid and Development

Author(s): Overseas Development Institute (ODI) and Institute for Public Policy Research (IPPR)

The report examines longterm aims and impacts of development. It summarises results of four workshops across the UK, explores public attitudes towards aid and development.

Key findings

While there is broad public support for UK development efforts, there is also increasing sceptism.

- Government and non-profit organisations must find a new approach to campaigns and communications to retain public support.
- While the public broadly supports UK development efforts, a growing number of people support a reduction in aid spending.

- Others believe that "charity should begin at home" and that government refocus efforts to local communities.
- There is also a call to focus on the quality of results rather than the amount of money spent.
- People who represent the middle ground of public opinion do not fully understand the complex realities in developing countries.
- However, individuals want to better understand impacts and how and why development works.
- Development is viewed more favorably than aid since it focuses on long-term change and incorporates local participation.
- Most people felt that governments, NGOs, international institutions and companies all have a role to play in development.
- Recommendations for the UK development community to maintain public support include:
  - communicate how change happens in developing countries in campaigns;
  - understand the impact of communications and campaigns on the wider public;
  - generate greater public involvement;
  - link debates about 'responsible capitalism' to challenges faced by developing countries.

Source: Social Research Digest, Jul. 2012 (Vol. 3, No. 7)

5.4.21 LBG Annual Review Report

Author(s): LBG

The latest annual review from LBG shows how its 130 corporate members work together to improve the measurement and impact of their community contributions. LBG is a robust, credible and international framework that enables LBG members across the globe to measure the totality of their contribution to the community, and then assess that in the light of the results achieved.

Key findings

At a time when overall donations to charities are said to be declining, leading international companies are increasing their contributions.

- LBG companies are more and more serious about the contributions they make and the results they achieve.
- By focusing on the long-term they invest more strategically, they build stronger relationships with their community partners, leading to more efficient programmes, greater impact and reliable reporting.
- Total corporate community contribution reported in LBG is £1.65 billion (US$ 2.65 bn, €1.90 bn).
- Over half (57%) of contributions were classified as 'community investments' i.e. longer-term strategic partnerships to address specific causes.
- On average, the main subject focus is health (34% of contributions), followed by education & young people (21%) and social welfare (12%).
- More than half of members now attempt to assess impacts across their programme and results continue to improve the understanding of the difference members are making.

Source: Social Research Digest, Dec. 2012 (Vol. 3, No. 12)

5.4.22 Philanthropy and the Social Economy: Blueprint 2014

Author(s): Oxford Economics in cooperation with AARP

Grant Craft issued the latest annual forecast of the philanthropy industry. Philanthropy and the Social Economy: Blueprint 2014 covers a wide range of topics, including European vs. American philanthropy, digital civil society, key buzzwords of 2013, and predictions for next year.

Key findings

The frame of the social economy more effectively "captures the full set of options for both donors and doers (entrepreneurs and organization execs)" than our traditional lens of nonprofits and philanthropy.

- A key part of this economy is the adoption of digital practices that "has the potential to change its root structures."
- "Privacy" was 2013's Top Social Economy Buzzword.
- Other top buzzwords of 2013 include "Peer-to-Peer Services", another word for the sharing economy, "Makers" or the newfound interest in old-fashioned handmade goods, and "Bitcoin" the virtual currency popular with financial speculators and some nonprofits.

- Some of the predictions and wildcards for 2014 are:
  o At least one major nonprofit/foundation infrastructure organization will close up.
  o We will experience a major scandal in the crowdfunding marketplace.
  o One winner of the Gates Foundation's Data Interoperability Grand Challenge will launch a widely used new product or service for social sector data by December 2014.
  o New mobile money tools will make informal networks of people even more visible, viable, and important.
  o Github will become a widely used, meaningful sharing platform for nonprofits.
  o Americans and Europeans will make greater use of "personal privacy" protection services on the Internet, allowing them to control/own their own data.
  o U.S. foundations will launch several new initiatives rooted in concerns about the polarized and paralyzed state of American democracy.
- Wildcards (or, "Predictable Unpredictables")
  o The American system will split social welfare organizations out of the nonprofit, 501(c) tax code.
  o Proposals for moving oversight of American nonprofits out of the IRS and creating a new charities regulatory authority will come to pass.
  o Benefit corporations and nonprofits will be on opposite sides of policy battles about tax privileges.
  o A major natural disaster will set new fundraising records, begging the question "as these disasters become more predictable, will philanthropic responses change?"

Source: Social Research Digest, Feb. 2014 (Vol. 5, No. 2)

5.4.23 Clowning Around with Charity: How McDonald's Exploits Philanthropy and Targets Children

Author(s): Michele Simon, president of Eat Drink Politics in partnership with Corporate Accountability International and the Small Planet Fund

Author Michele Simon, president of Eat Drink Politics in partnership with Corporate Accountability International and the Small Planet Fund produced a report, Clowning Around with Charity: How McDonald's Exploits Philanthropy and Targets Children, that exposes the burger giant's most sophisticated and subversive form of marketing—its exploitation of charity to market its brand and deflect criticism. The report pulls back the veil on McDonald's modest giving relative to the marketing boost and goodwill it receives in return for its branded charity and presence in schools.

Key findings

For its "charity of choice," the Ronald McDonald House Charities (RMHC), McDonald's reaps 100% of the branded benefit while giving the cause only a small fraction of its revenue.

- McDonald's philanthropic giving is 33% lower than leading corporations.
- The average American earning over $50,000 donates 4.7% of their discretionary income to charity, which is 14 times more than what McDonald's gives.
- McDonald's spent almost 25 times as much on advertising as it did on charitable donations in 2011.
- Based on available information, in 2012, on average, McDonald's donated about one-fifth of the revenues of Ronald McDonald House Charities, the corporation's "charity of choice"—yet McDonald's enjoys 100% of the branded benefit of this charity.
- Local Ronald McDonald Houses use common disclaimers on their websites to explain how little McDonald's contributes and to encourage community members to give.
- Local Ronald McDonald Houses (as distinguished from the global Ronald McDonald House Charities entity) report receiving only about 10% of their revenue from McDonald's, including from direct customer donations.
- Ronald McDonald Houses report that the Ronald McDonald name causes many people to assume that McDonald's provides 100% of the charity's funds – and that this "common misperception" is "absolutely confusing."
- Recommendations:

- o McDonald's should rename the Ronald McDonald House Charities organization it controls and stop licensing its brand to local chapters and houses to enable these entities to change their name.
- o McDonald's should retire Ronald McDonald and stop marketing to children.
- o McDonald's should conform to philanthropy best practices by being more transparent regarding its charitable giving practices.
- o McDonald's should abide by its voluntary pledge to not market in schools.
- o Organizations and schools should reject McDonald's "partnerships" and funding

Source: Social Research Digest, Apr. 2014 (Vol. 5, No. 4)

5.5   Shared Value and Social Innovation

5.5.1   Measuring Socio-Economic Impact: A Guide for Business

Author(s): WBCSD

A new guide by WBCSD aims at helping navigating the complex landscape of socioeconomic impact measurement. It intends to assist companies in selecting the impact measurement tools that work best for their business.

Key findings

A fundamental first step is to understand how business activities translate into socio-economic impacts.

- Measurement can happen anywhere along the results chain.
- In the development community, the gold standard is to reach that last link in the results chain; that last link is what is known as "impact".
- Measuring "impact" in the technical sense of the word is challenging to do.
- Prioritization and the judicious use of proxies can be key.
- The 10 tools profiled are:
  - o Base of the Pyramid Impact Assessment Framework
  - o GEMI Networks Navigator
  - o Impact Measurement Framework

- o Impact Reporting and Investment Standards
- o MDG Scan
- o Measuring Impact Framework
- o Poverty Footprint
- o Progress out of Poverty Index
- o Socio-Economic Assessment Toolbox
- o Input-Output Modeling

Source: CSR Research Digest, Mar. 2013 (Vol. 5, No. 3)

5.5.2 The Social and Economic Impact of Standard Chartered in Indonesia

Source: Social Research Digest, Jul. 2013 (Vol. 4, No. 7)

Author(s): World Business Council for Sustainable Development (WBCSD) & Standard Chartered

The World Business Council for Sustainable Development released a report that aims to analyse the Standard Chartered's role in stimulating economic and social development in Indonesia. "The Social and Economic Impact of Standard Chartered In Indonesia" report draws mainly on official government statistics and corporate data from Standard Chartered Indonesia and Permata Bank.

Key findings

The direct, indirect and induced impacts of Standard Chartered's Indonesian operations and onshore financing amounted to USD 4,504 million of value-added in 2009, or about 0.8% of Indonesia's GDP.

- In 2009, Standard Chartered Indonesia directly and indirectly supported approximately 1 million jobs throughout the Indonesian economy, while it generated millions of dollars in income for households and tax revenues for the government.
- Relative to Indonesia's workforce of 113 million, the bank's total impact of 1,029,000 jobs amounted to 0.9% in 2009.
- Therefore, the private sector can be a major contributor to economies when it is allowed to operate and to thrive.
- Given a reliable political and economic environment, with clear rules of the game and profit-making opportunities, the private sector will

respond through investments and innovation, all of which help promote sustainable growth

5.5.3   Community Involvement Index

Author(s): Boston College Center for Corporate Citizenship

The Boston College Center for Corporate Citizenship has released research findings which illustrate corporate community involvement during 2009. The 2009 Community Involvement Index, which is drawn from an online survey responded to by more than 300 companies, offers a snapshot of the community involvement field.

Key findings

In the context of the recent tough economic climate, while a significant percentage of companies cut their community involvement budgets, 62.1% maintained or increased budget levels.

- Although 37.8% of respondents' companies cut their community involvement budget, only 20.9% decreased staffing.
- The link between community involvement and business strategy, and its integration with other business functions, is the rule rather than an exception.
- Community involvement is linked both to broader corporate citizenship strategy in most companies (72.6%) and to business strategy (73.8%) with senior management involvement and support.
- Staff from media and public relations departments (90.9%), human resources (82%), and marketing staff (77%) were the most widely-cited internal stakeholders during assessments of planning and implementation of community involvement programmes.
- A majority of companies (54%) generate strategy and direction from the top but put implementation into local hands.
- Measurement of programmes remains a challenge for companies and the findings indicate the practice is inconsistent. More companies (41%) routinely evaluate strategy than routinely measure business benefits (27.3%) or social impacts (25.4%).
- Environmental issues are now emerging as a critical area. Though not yet approaching the level of education, the environment is the only other area that garners top billing or near top billing among critical

issues for more than 60% of respondents' companies.

- More than 80% of respondents believe their companies' various community involvement programmes are delivering value to both society and the business.
- Volunteering remains a core element of most companies' community involvement programmes. 56.7% of companies in the survey offer employees paid time off to volunteer in at least some of their locations.

Source: CSR Research Digest, Feb. 2010 (Vol. 2, No. 2)

5.5.4   Social Impact Study

Author(s): Weber Shandwick

The second annual Social Impact survey explores the following topics: Why are corporations motivated to invest in CSR? And, what are the key success factors and lessons learned from recent CSR efforts? The study is based on a survey of more than 200 corporate executives in large-sized companies with responsibility for philanthropic, social responsibility or community relations.

<u>Key findings</u>

Having an impact on critical issues is the number one reason why corporations invest in philanthropic or socially responsible activities (30%).

- Other motivators included:
    o   seeing an organization's values in action (25%);
    o   building customer loyalty (15%);
    o   differentiating the company from competitors (6%);
    o   and engaging employees (4%).
- The last finding suggests the need for companies to better understand the link between CSR and employee satisfaction.
- The news for nonprofits is very positive, with 8 in 10 executives saying they consider nonprofits valuable partners.
- Nonprofits are seen as ideal partners because they make their CSR investment more effective, provide a critical foundation and infrastructure, contribute expertise and help engage consumers.
- Additionally, nearly all executives agreed that strong and vocal support

from senior managers (94%), and well-defined objectives and outcomes (91%), are the most important ingredients in successful CSR programs.

Source: CSR Research Digest, Jan. 2011 (Vol. 3, No. 1)

5.5.5 Measuring Shared Value: How to Unlock Value by Linking Social and Business Results

Author(s): M. E. Porter, G. Hills, M. Pfitzer, S. Patscheke and E. Hawkins

The report by Michael E. Porter and FSG explains the specific purpose of shared value measurement. It offers a step-by-step process and pragmatic approaches to measurement with examples from leading companies.

Key findings

Measuring shared value allows companies to maximize opportunities for innovation, growth, and social impact at scale.

- Despite its complexities, the pathway to shared value measurement is clear.
- First, companies must anchor shared value measurement in shared value strategy.
- An iterative and integrated shared value process provides focus to measurement activities and yields data that validates and improves shared value strategies.
- Second, shared value measurement must establish a direct link between meeting social needs and improving the business; understanding this linkage is the key to unlocking additional value creation.
- Third, measurement must assess the extent of value creation—tracking social and business results relative to the costs—in order to ensure the efficiency of current and future efforts.
- Fourth, companies must clearly distinguish shared value measurement from other important forms of measurement, including compliance, sustainability, and impact assessments.
- Fifth, companies must adopt pragmatic approaches to navigate shared value measurement challenges.

Source: CSR Research Digest, Jan. 2013 (Vol. 5, No. 1)

5.5.6   Guide to Social Innovation

Author(s): European Commission

The European Commission released a Guide to Social Innovation how public authorities can support and enhance social innovation. The guide also provides assistance to implement Social Innovation and focuses on real examples funded by the Structural Funds: Social inclusion, Migration, Urban regeneration, the social economy, microfinance, health and ageing, incubation, workplace innovation and regional strategies.

Key findings

Social entrepreneurship is interconnected with social innovation, being the new hybrid model aiming to create social value in an entrepreneurial innovative and scalable way.

- The EU's strategy Europe 2020 has the objective to reach a smart, sustainable and inclusive economy where social innovation plays an important role and has identified specific targets in five main areas:
- Employment: 75% of the 20-64 year-olds to be employed
- R&D/innovation: 3% of the EU's GDP to be invested in R&D/innovation
- Climate change/energy: greenhouse gas emissions 20%(or even30%, if the conditions are right) lower than 1990; 20% of energy from renewables; 20% increase in energy efficiency
- Reducing school drop-out rates below 10%
- Poverty: at least 20 million fewer people in or at risk of poverty and social exclusion
- Public authorities have an important role in festering social innovation and in particular the European Union needs to develop a new capacity to influence the policy frameworks and to reinforce the current policies' role for a more efficient and affective outcome.
- The 1989 Structural Funds' Reform introduced four principles into the revised regulations (additionally, concentration, partnership and programming) and since then the Funds have supported innovative approaches and practices.
- The Structural Funds regulations for 2014-2020 offer several opportunities for social innovation and the guide describes practical

examples showing how cohesive policies have fostered social innovation in the past.

- Social Innovation represents a key element of the Cohesion policy framework, one of the main instruments of the EU for the implementation of the Europe 2020 strategy.

- The guide presents a model aiming to promote social innovation and helping regions to individuate existing problems, like youth unemployment, migrations, healthcare inequalities and poverty, and presents three main areas: (1) changing minds & creation of a smart specialisation strategy, (2) actions on accelerating implementation and (3) scaling-up regional exchange and systemic change.

- The framework provides 10 steps: learn about Social Innovation and put the pieces together; develop a smart specialisation strategy and plan; transition innovation platform; incubation trajectory specifically targeted at Social Innovation; Social Innovation cluster/park; special economy zone for Social Innovation; cross-regional and International trade and exchange of social innovation within the innovation Union framework.

Source: Social Research Digest, Aug. 2013 (Vol. 4, No. 8)

5.5.7   Business-Driven Social Change

Author(s): Ute Stephan, Malcolm Patterson and Ciara Kelly, Sheffield University, Network for Business Sustainability

Experts from the University of Sheffield's Management School formulated a handbook offering advice for businesses of every kind to help drive much needed social change the world over. The report, 'Business-driven Social Change' provides an overview of the 19 mechanisms companies can use to drive positive behaviour change and how change efforts should be managed.

Key findings

Businesses are most credible and successful when they pursue change projects that are aligned with their core competencies.

- Managing change projects is a realistic goal for business. While complex, such projects are not necessarily difficult.

- Still, more evidence is needed on the role of business as a driver of change as research to date has primarily studied change initiated by social enterprises and non-profits.
- Motivation-based mechanisms motivate actors to change
- Opportunity-based mechanisms create opportunities for actors to change
- Capability-based mechanisms enable actors to change.

Source: Social Research Digest, Dec. 2013 (Vol. 4, No. 12)

5.5.8 Inclusion Matters: The Foundation for Shared Prosperity (New Frontiers of Social Policy)

Author(s): World Bank

World Bank issued a report that tries to put boundaries around the abstraction that is 'social inclusion'. Inclusion Matters: The Foundation for Shared Prosperity (New Frontiers of Social Policy) is intended for policy makers, academics, activists and development partners – indeed anyone who is curious about how to address inclusion in a world that is witness to intense demographic, spatial, economic and technological transitions.

<u>Key findings</u>

1. Excluded groups exist in all countries.
2. Excluded groups are consistently denied opportunities.
3. Intense global transitions are leading to social transformations that create new opportunities for inclusion as well as exacerbating existing forms of exclusion.
4. People take part in society through markets, services, and spaces.
5. Social and economic transformations affect the attitudes and perceptions of people. As people act on the basis of how they feel, it is important to pay attention to their attitudes and perceptions.
6. Exclusion is not immutable. Abundant evidence demonstrates that social inclusion can be planned and achieved.
7. Moving ahead will require a broader and deeper knowledge of exclusion and its impacts as well as taking concerted action.

Source: Social Research Digest, May 2014 (Vol. 5, No. 5)

5.5.9   Shared Value in Chile

Author(s): The Shared Value Initiative and FSG

The Shared Value Initiative and FSG released a report that provides practical guidance for companies—not just on what shared value is, but on how to create it and highlights many of the major opportunities for shared value creation in Chile. The report, 'Shared Value in Chile - Increasing Private Sector Competitiveness by Solving Social Problems' is a call to action for Chilean private and public sector and civil society.

<u>Key findings</u>

A few Chilean companies have started developing shared value strategies.

- There are three major country challenges in Chile— increasing MSME competitiveness, bridging the skills gap that Chilean companies face, and promoting healthy lifestyles to reduce obesity.
- These three challenges are focal points for several reasons: (1) the problems themselves are serious and affect a large number of Chileans; (2) the link between the social problem and company competitiveness is evident and has particular relevance to vital Chilean industries; (3) they illustrate the potential to create shared value in three critical social realms—poverty, education, and health.
- Notwithstanding the importance and magnitude of these examples, there are many other shared value opportunities that companies can and should explore, such as lowering the cost and increasing the sustainability of the energy supply, fostering responsible financial inclusion, and lowering the cost and improving the quality of healthcare to name a few.
- The success of MSMEs is critical to Chile's competitiveness and social prosperity. As suppliers, contractors, and retailers, MSMEs play a critical role in the value systems of many companies.
- They affect cost, quality, and reliability in the value system, can facilitate access to new resources and markets, and may be important sources of innovation. They can be an important customer base as well.
- MSMEs have an inherent social value, generating the vast majority of employment in most economies. Given MSMEs' position at the nexus of social and business value creation, there is an opportunity to create

value simultaneously for MSMEs, large companies, and society.

- In Chile, a few leading companies, such as BHP Billiton, Codelco, and Bci, are starting to recognize this opportunity. They are moving beyond traditional transactional relationships with MSMEs to build collaborative partnerships.
- These companies are developing a deep understanding of the challenges MSMEs face. They are partnering to innovate, generate cost savings, and improve the quality and reliability in their value systems.
- Some are even building new markets by offering products and services tailored to unmet MSME needs. By increasing MSME competitiveness through shared value strategies, Chilean companies have an opportunity to improve the livelihoods of the up to 85% of Chilean workers employed by such enterprises.

Source: CSR Research Digest, Oct. 2014 (Vol. 6, No. 10)

5.6 Inclusive Business

5.6.1 Inclusive Business Report

Author(s): Business Action for Africa

Following world leaders' anti-poverty summit that called on the private sector to accelerate progress towards the Millennium Development Goals (MDGS), Business Action for Africa and eight other leading business organizations launched a report geared towards helping businesses join the fight against poverty. The report, 'Delivering Results: Moving Towards Scale', highlights the best practices, lessons learnt and challenges that companies face when developing inclusive business models.

Key findings

There is potential to accelerate progress towards the Millennium Development Goals (MDGs) by harnessing the power of business more creatively: by spreading the practice of 'inclusive business'.

- The report identifies eight main focus areas that will prove essential in advancing the future development of Inclusive Business, including:
  - o the need for experimentation and room to innovate;

- o the imperative for understanding low-income consumers;
- o the necessity for collaboration;
- o the importance of the right government policies and regulations to incentivize companies to further invest;
- o the need for practical tools and resources to support inclusive business development;
- o the importance of leadership;
- o the necessity for striking a balance between short and long-term business goals, and overcoming infrastructure challenges through innovative partnerships.
- The report also provides concrete examples of how businesses worldwide are a catalyst for social and economic progress including The Coca-Cola Company's efforts to enable jobs, entrepreneurship and opportunities for women through its innovative micro-distribution network across Africa while growing its business.
- Another example includes Diageo's commitment to promoting the development of local sorghum supply chains in Cameroon and securing its own access to a supply of quality grain by investing in farmers.

Source: CSR Research Digest, Nov. 2010 (Vol. 2, No. 11)

5.6.2 Inclusive Business: The Next Frontier for Corporate Responsibility

Author(s): Corporate Citizenship

In this report, Corporate Citizenship analyses a number of multinational companies' Inclusive Business models in emerging and developing markets. Corporate Citizenship looks at the motivations behind the business models, the role of partnerships, financing and profitability, as well as challenges.

Key findings

An increasing number of multinationals are enhancing social and economic benefits through their core businesses by the adoption of Inclusive Business models.

- The opportunities Inclusive Business present for global companies are significant.

- It can drive product and service innovation, provide access to new markets, help differentiation from competitors and strengthen brand reputation.
- On the sourcing and supply side, benefits include cost reductions, secured access to critical raw materials and visible supply chains.
- In addition, by contributing to local economic growth, the company strengthens its license to operate in the country and facilitates positive relations with key stakeholders such as the government and local authorities, ensuring a longterm presence in the market.
- Inclusive Business models have spread opportunities to poor and disadvantaged people through job creation, regular income generation, connection to markets, access to education and training, as well as access to finance.
- However, Inclusive Business success stories are still few and challenges remain significant.
- Companies have told us about the difficulties they face in understanding the markets, developing effective marketing channels, challenging distribution networks and regulatory hurdles.
- Businesses should take the following steps when exploring and building Inclusive Business models:
- Conduct a socio-economic impact assessment. As a starting point, explore the socio-economic impact of your company's activities and operations in a given market. Such assessment will further your understanding of the actual value your company spreads across the value chain.
- Assess opportunities across the value chain. Following the socio-economic impact assessment, take a value chain approach assessing the opportunities of your business. Where across the value chain could social and economic benefits be further enhanced?
- Focus on core competencies and strengths. What are the core skills of your business, and how can you apply them to address societal and development challenges through your business activities?
- Leverage the skills and expertise of your CSR department, to develop and test innovative ideas and business models.
- Get senior management on board. At the start of your Inclusive Business journey, ensure that senior management are involved from

the idea stage through to implementation. This is crucial for the long-term success of the business model.

- Decide on the commercialisation of the business model early on. The options to commercialise the business model should be integrated in the strategy from the beginning.

- Explore funding opportunities. Explore funding opportunities in the emerging social investment landscape, including development agencies, foundations and international organisations. Explore partnerships. Take a collaborative approach and explore partnerships with government agencies, NGOs and local grassroots organisations. Cooperate with local partners who have a deep understanding of market conditions, as well as insights on consumer needs and behaviour.

- Invest in understanding the local market context. A valuable approach can be to tap into local networks to gain market understanding and insights, both at an initial product development stage, but also throughout the process identifying marketing channels and distribution methods.

- Develop a robust performance measurement system. Incorporate social, environmental and economic Key Performance Indicators (KPIs) and targets with longer-term Return on Investment (ROI).

Source: Social Research Digest, Jun. 2012 (Vol. 3, No. 6)

5.6.3 The Business Environment for Inclusive Business Models: A Policy Note by the IFC

Author(s): *International Finance Corporation (IFC)*

The IFC released a policy note on inclusive business at the recent G20 Summit in Mexico. The IFC's policy note describes how public policy can support inclusive business models and recommends how governments and institutions can support companies.

<u>Key findings</u>

Despite promising inclusive business initiatives, companies require support of government, as well as greater governance, to extend the reach and impact of inclusive business models.

- The policy note describes how public policy can support inclusive business models, for instance implementing regulations that provide structure without stifling innovation.
- It also describes the institutional frameworks that define the environment in which businesses operate in a given country – for instance, legal systems, infrastructure and skilled resource.
- The document includes analysis of a survey among 167 applicants for the G20 challenge on inclusive business innovation.
- The survey identified specific regulatory hurdles companies face and recommendations for creating a business environment conducive to inclusive business.
- These recommendations include the suggested role of governments, donors and financial institutions to help companies effectively create and manage inclusive business models.

Source: Social Research Digest, Jul. 2012 (Vol. 3, No. 7)

5.6.4   Inclusive Business: Creating Value in Latin America

Author(s): Alliance for Inclusive Business

The Alliance for Inclusive Business between the World Business Council for Sustainable Development (WBCSD) and SNV Netherlands Development Organization has launched a report highlighting its joint work in Latin America over the past 4 years. The report features 11 case stories from a variety of sectors and captures key learnings and success factors of inclusive business in practice, based on the Alliance's experience on the ground.

Key findings

Inclusive business ventures are both profitable and expand social and economic opportunities for the low-income segment.

- The case studies demonstrate how low-income communities are engaged across companies' value chains – through direct employment; the development of suppliers, distributors and service providers; or through the innovative development and delivery of affordable goods and services that address unmet needs.
- The report also explains how, working through the local

representatives of both organizations, the WBCSD-SNV Alliance has focused on three areas of activity: raising awareness about inclusive business models; brokering of new business opportunities that benefit low-income communities in the target countries; and advocating for the improvement of framework conditions for this type of inclusive business.

Source: CSR Research Digest, Jul. 2011 (Vol. 3, No. 7)

5.6.5   Enhancing Value Through Inclusive Business Strategies

Author(s): Business Call to Action

The report highlights the Business Call to Action's hosted workshop in New York City on the topic of creating scalable inclusive business models. The event attracted over 80 senior executives from small, medium, and multinational enterprises as well as highlevel representatives from donor and international organizations and academia that were in town for the United Nations General Assembly.

Key findings

Inclusive business offers the potential for development impact along with commercial success by integrating the poor into corporate value chains as producers, suppliers, distributors, consumers, and employees.

- The following themes were discussed at the event:
  - o   understanding the needs of low-income communities;
  - o   understanding what works and what doesn't;
  - o   catalyzing new sources of finance;
  - o   and collective action.

Source: CSR Research Digest, Jan. 2012 (Vol. 4, No. 1)

5.6.6   Accelerating Inclusive Business Opportunities

Author(s): IFC

The International Finance Corporation (IFC), a member of the World Bank Group, has released its latest report on inclusive business. It identifies seven inclusive business models that expand access to goods, services, and livelihood opportunities for the world's poorest people while generating strong financial returns.

<u>Key findings</u>

The models are helping companies turn underserved populations into dynamic consumer markets and diverse new sources of supply.

- In the process, companies are developing product, service, and business model innovations with the potential to tip the scales of competitive advantage in more established markets as well.
- The report's findings are based on an analysis of IFC's portfolio, which found that mature investments in companies with inclusive business models show financial returns very similar to those of IFC's portfolio as a whole, while having a larger impact on development.
- The seven models identified in the report are:
  o micro distribution and retail, reaching base of the pyramid end consumers who tend to make small, frequent purchases through retailers who need small, frequent deliveries and the ability to buy on credit;
  o experience-based customer credit, lending to customers the company knows are credit-worthy through past experience;
  o last-mile grid utilities, extending infrastructure grid coverage to more distant and often lower-income neighborhoods;
  o smallholder procurement, turning geographically dispersed smallholder farmers into reliable sources of quality supply;
  o value-for-money degrees, making university education accessible to lowincome students;
  o value-for-money housing, making home ownership possible for low-income buyers through a combination of high-value-formoney housing and facilitated access to mortgage financing;
  o e-transaction platforms, enabling lowincome people to pay for goods and services electronically, at lower cost and risk than paying in cash.

Source: Social Research Digest, Oct. 2011 (Vol. 2, No. 6)

5.6.7   From Gap to Opportunity: Business Models for Scaling Up Energy Access

Author(s): IFC

A new report from IFC breaks new ground by estimating the market for energy services offered at the household level to low-income people. It profiles companies with innovative business models and explores in detail what it takes for them to succeed.

<u>Key findings</u>

There is a $37 billion opportunity for the private sector to improve energy services for people who live in relative poverty.

- With the right business models and conditions—the private sector can play a vital role in providing energy solutions that are better for people's health and better for the environment.
- Private enterprises have started to seize the opportunity.
- While this is still a nascent sector, many businesses are rapidly moving beyond being cottage industries and are successfully serving tens of thousands to hundreds of thousands of customers.
- Some companies are seeing profit margins of 10% to 30%, often with fairly small subsidies on capital costs or no subsidies at all.
- To scale up successful business models, the report offers a series of recommendations for key stakeholders—including companies, social and commercial investors, governments, policymakers, and donors.
- For instance, it suggests that governments resist give-away programs and unrealistic promises, remove discriminatory taxes on energy access products, and leverage public-private partnerships and smart subsidies for extending electricity grids.
- For investors seeking both social impact and financial returns, the report recommends that they keep investment mandates broad and beyond a single technology, develop a local presence, provide appropriate funding for each part of the business life cycle, support enterprise development and business model refinement, and fund the provision of public goods.

Source: Social Research Digest, Sep. 2012 (Vol. 3, No. 9)

5.6.8   Doing Business at the Base of the Pyramid: The Reality of Emerging Markets

Author(s): R. Abraham

This research paper highlights the possibility of serving goods and services profitably to the base of the economic pyramid (BOP). It examines a few commercially sustainable business models that have worked in these markets, and investigates a few sectors that commercial capital will find highly attractive and investable.

<u>Key findings</u>

Wealth creation is the best antidote to poverty, and any country that has made great strides in getting rid of absolute poverty has done so through rapid economic growth.

- Therefore, there is a very strong case to be made for business, especially private business, to assume a central role in the development process of poor countries.
- Not through the mechanism of social entrepreneurs or any such feel-good process, but through regular entrepreneurs following their risk/reward instincts.
- Given the right business climate, re-pricing of risk, and lowering of information asymmetries, we expect a large number of entrepreneurs to address the inefficiencies of what is called the social sector, but in fact represents huge investment opportunities.
- After all, the biggest entrepreneurial opportunities of all lie in building up a country, and opportunities the size of India and China come along maybe once every 200 years, if not less frequently.
- If entrepreneurs are successful at scale, they are bound to replicate in India, Africa and elsewhere, the remarkable run they've had in the 20th century in East Asia, most recently in China, including bringing down the levels of absolute poverty dramatically.

Source: Social Research Digest, Sep. 2012 (Vol. 3, No. 9)

5.6.9 Building an Inclusive Green Economy for All: Opportunities and Challenges for Overcoming Poverty and Inequality

Author(s): Poverty-Environment Partnership

This joint Poverty-Environment Partnership paper aims to stimulate a dialogue among developing country policymakers, development partners and other stakeholders on how best to support country-led efforts to build inclusive green economies. This publication has been prepared on behalf of the Poverty-Environment Partnership by a PEP Working Group including staff from ADB, Australia (AusAid), Finland (MoFA), Germany (GIZ), IIED, IUCN, OECD, UNDP, UNEP, The World Bank, WBCSD and WRI.

<u>Key findings</u>

Developing countries confront an array of economic, social and environmental challenges overcoming poverty and inequality that are unprecedented in their scale, complexity and to growing interconnectedness.

- Ecosystem degradation and climate change, in particular, pose major threats to livelihoods and economies.
- In the face of these global challenges, 'business as usual' strategies for economic growth and development are no longer economically, socially or environmentally sustainable—a new approach is needed to accelerate poverty reduction and to achieve more equitable and sustainable development.
- Transitioning to an 'inclusive green economy' is increasingly recognized as an alternative pathway that can deliver low-carbon and climate-resilient development, significantly improved resource efficiency, healthy and more resilient ecosystems, and greater economic opportunities and social justice for disadvantaged groups.
- Evidence suggests that investing in improved natural resource and environmental management in rural and urban areas—such as sustainable forestry and fisheries, reducing carbon emissions or better urban planning and infrastructure—makes strong economic sense and can have a high social rate of return.

- This is particularly true for the rural and urban poor in low and middle-income countries who depend strongly on the environment for their livelihoods, health and well-being, and who suffer the most from environmental degradation and the growing impacts from climate change.
- Transitioning to an inclusive green economy that can deliver equitable and sustainable development is possible, but will not be automatic.
- Supportive policy, institutional and governance reforms and targeted investments at local, national and global levels are needed to remove barriers and to enable poor and vulnerable groups to participate in, contribute to and benefit from the transition.
- While the transition to an inclusive green economy will be specific to the context of each country, five critical 'building blocks' are proposed that can provide a framework for a shared policy agenda between developing country governments, civil society, the private sector and international development partners:
  o National economic and social policies: Governments in low and middle-income countries will need to capture the higher economic returns that investments in sustainable use of ecosystems and in lowcarbon and climate resilient development can generate—and to ensure that these investments and revenues contribute to poverty reduction and inclusive growth.
  o Local rights and capacities: Poor women and men need rights and security of tenure over their natural resource wealth and the means and incentives to sustainably manage and benefit from these resources; this includes rights to information, participation and access to justice to ensure a voice in decisions affecting how these assets are managed and their benefits distributed.
  o Inclusive green markets: Innovative business models and an enabling policy and institutional environment are needed to build and expand the poor's access to markets and supply chains for green products and services—in ways that sustain and restore natural ecosystems, contribute to low-carbon and climateresilient development, and provide better and more secure livelihoods.
  o Harmonized international policies and support: Higher-income countries need to ensure the coherence of their development, trade, technology, environmental and other relevant policies that

influence the ability of low and middle-income countries to succeed in the transition to an inclusive green economy.

- o New metrics for measuring progress: The transition to an inclusive green economy will require new metrics that go beyond the prevailing narrow focus on income poverty and Gross Domestic Product (GDP) to a broader way of tracking economic, social and environmental progress and well-being.

Source: Social Research Digest, Sep. 2012 (Vol. 3, No. 9)

5.6.10 Inclusive Business Initiatives: Scaling Innovation for an Emerging Middle Class

Author(s): Accenture

This research report investigates inclusive business initiatives (IBIs) particularly why certain initiatives achieve scale, bringing both social benefits to benefit to low-income populations and profits to the company. The research report undertakes a comparative study on innovation, focusing on 18 initiatives in Brazil, China, Ghana, India and Nigeria.

Key findings

It was discovered that there are three key requirements for achieving the scale companies need to thrive (1) getting top leadership on board (2) collaborate with government in strategic partnerships (3) partnering with local NGOs and small entrepreneurs.

- When board members and senior leaders are committed, initiative sponsors and managers will have enough to develop the local connections necessary for achieving scale.
  - o For example: In India, Hindustan Unilever Limited's CEO initiated high-level of commitment to IBIs by building decisionmaking structure that enticed the board's entrepreneurial spirit.
- Government regulations can become platforms for launching business initiatives that create value for low-income communities, for companies and for governments.
  - o For example: the Brazilian sugarcane producers under the umbrella of UNICA and the cane cutter union with support from the sugarcane supply chain launched the "Renewal" program aimed at

provided specialized training. This is an example of business collaborating with government in strategic partnerships where everyone wins.

- In order to build strong network of NGO partners, inclusive business initiatives must be able to identify with authentically local NGOs.
  - For example: in 2005, Klabin, partnered with Apremavi, where the former built and maintained long-term relationships with local producers and thus able to convince them that sustainable forests would help secure their industry's long-term viability.
- By creating innovations for low-income markets, large companies help consumers enter the middle class and fuel profitable new growth for themselves.

Source: Social Research Digest, Mar. 2013 (Vol. 4, No. 3)

5.6.11 Access to Food and Improved Nutrition at the Base of the Pyramid

Author(s): BoP Innovation Centre

In this study five different business interventions for BoP ventures were identified that achieve social impact and financial sustainability. It is based on the analysis of 16 cases and expert interviews.

Key findings

The five business interventions are an entry point for companies and other stakeholders to develop products and services to improve access to food and better nutrition with and for the BoP.

- Deliberately choosing one of these strategies, implementing a suitable governance structure and leveraging existing elements in specific models not only enables companies to become more effective in the food value chain, but also to interact and partner with the BoP.
- Interventions focusing on smallholders to improve quality and volume of production.
- For example, DADTCO, a social enterprise, develops mobile small-scale cassava processing units in Nigeria allowing first processing close to farms.

- Commercial buyers to assure access to a supply of produce that meets specific volume.
- Interventions focusing on BoP intermediaries between (smallholder) producers and consumers.
- For example, Hariyali Kisaan Bazaar is a rural retailer selling agri-inputs and consumer goods through its chain of centres, which also serve as a common platform for providers of financial services or health services.
- Adaptation of existing products, services, processes to serve BoP consumers.
- Innovative strategies that seek to create new markets at the BoP, through the introduction of new (specialized) products.
- For example Danone has ventured with Grameen in Bangladesh to create a business Grameen Danone Food Ltd that produces an ultra low cost fortified yoghurt for small children distributed by entrepreneurial Bangladeshi ladies.
- The following building blocks of a BoP proposition have been identified to successfully achieve impact with BoP ventures:
  o Drivers: Motivations for the private sector to enter BoP markets with products and services that contribute to access to food and better nutrition.
  o Governance: Establish an adequate structure to develop the BoP venture.
  o Leveraging: Leverage your own business and partners to ultimately co-create value.
  o Finance: Develop and use innovative financial mechanisms for BoP venture development and for access to finance for the BoP.
  o "Resynchronization" in the food value chain: Identify the specific part of the value chain your business is in, and create links with other essential parts in order to create business opportunities and to drive innovation.

Source: Social Research Digest, Sep. 2012 (Vol. 3, No. 9)

5.6.12 All on Board: Making Inclusive Growth Happen

Author(s): OECD

OECD released a report that provides evidence of the consequences of inequality, sets out a framework for action and allows governments to assess how policies impact different social groups in different ways. The report, All on Board: Making Inclusive Growth Happen is part of an Organisation-wide effort to develop an inclusive agenda for growth and well-being, and is a natural offshoot of the OECD New Approaches to Economic Challenges (NAEC) project to reflect on the causes of the crisis and the lessons for policy.

Key findings

Economic and social policies should be designed to foster both equity and growth. Investing in skills and education, for example, can have far-reaching impact on these twin objectives.

- Local government has a key role to play, particularly by investing in quality housing, public transport and in providing training for disadvantaged groups.
- Sound structural policies are a precondition for sustained growth, employment and poverty alleviation, but that there are trade-offs. For instance, reducing regulatory barriers to domestic and foreign competition as well as stepping-up job search support and labour market activation programmes can lift the incomes of the lower middle class faster than the overall rise in GDP per capita through the positive effect on employment.
- However, a tightening of unemployment benefits for the long-term unemployed reduces disposable incomes at the bottom end of the distribution, an indication of the importance of combining reforms of unemployment income support with a strengthening of active labour market policies.
- Promoting inclusive growth can also help restore citizens' trust in governments. Today, fewer than one in two people in OECD countries have confidence in their nation's political leadership.

Source: CSR Research Digest, Aug. 2014 (Vol. 6, No. 8)

5.6.13   Realizing Africa's Wealth – Building Inclusive Businesses for Shared Prosperity

Author(s): United Nations Development Programme

The United Nations Development Programme released a report that takes a detailed look at the approaches and conditions required to bring economic growth closer to low-income communities in Africa, focusing on how businesses can include them as consumers and entrepreneurs. With 170 in-depth case studies and a database of 600 institutions, the new report, titled "Realizing Africa's Wealth – Building Inclusive Businesses for Shared Prosperity," paints a broad picture of the state of inclusive business in Africa, examining a wide spectrum of sectors from banking to agribusiness.

Key findings

Africa's wealth lies primarily in its people – a young and growing population in search of opportunity. By enabling these individuals to engage in business, the private sector unleashes people's potential.

- Inclusive businesses integrate low-income people into their value chains, thus creating opportunities for this group in a targeted way.
- There has been considerable innovation and entrepreneurial drive in creating inclusive business in Africa. Yet constraints in the business context mean these businesses often struggle to reach a larger scale.
- Supportive ecosystems that provide appropriate information, incentives, investment and implementation support can stimulate the development of more inclusive businesses with greater impact.
- Sub-Saharan Africa is growing, but not everyone is sharing the benefits. Sub-Saharan Africa is today among the fastest-growing regions in the world. Though market conditions remain challenging in many places, regulatory frameworks and capital availability are improving, fuelling significant economic growth. However, many people remain excluded from the benefits of this growth, without access to basic goods and services or opportunities for employment and regular income.
- Inclusive business creates profits and unleashes potential. Inclusive businesses integrate low-income individuals into value chains in various capacities, be it as consumers, producers, employees and entrepreneurs. Thus, they bring the benefits of growth directly to low-income communities. This is not charity. Inclusive businesses create a strong foundation for profit and long-term growth by bringing previously excluded people into the marketplace.

Source: CSR Research Digest, Sep. 2014 (Vol. 6, No. 9)

5.7 Social Protection and Financial Inclusion

5.7.1 The Social Protection Index: Assessing Results for Asia and the Pacific (2013)

Author(s): Asian Development Bank (ADB), Terry McKinley, Sri W. Handayani

The Asian Development Bank (ADB) issued a report that documents the role of social assistance in social protection systems across Asia and the Pacific. 'The Social Protection Index: Assessing Results for Asia and the Pacific (2013)' policy brief examines the six major subcomponents of social assistance and draws out policy lessons based on comprehensive data for 35 countries in the region.

Key findings

Social assistance accounts for only 36% of total expenditures on social protection in Asia and the Pacific but benefits 58% of total target beneficiaries.

- Social transfers and child welfare comprise two-thirds of social assistance spending.
- Although cash transfers are gaining popularity in Asia and the Pacific, they should not be considered the centerpiece of national social protection systems.
- While social assistance programs will remain relevant for the poorest and disadvantaged groups, they cannot address all problems associated with poverty and vulnerability.
- Disaster relief is another form of social assistance that has increased in importance due to rising vulnerabilities brought about by natural shocks, including those associated with climate change.

Source: Social Research Digest, Oct. 2013 (Vol. 4, No. 10)

5.7.2 Socially Responsible Distribution: Distribution Strategies for Reaching the Bottom of the Pyramid

Author(s): Sushil Vachani, N. Craig Smith.

This paper builds on the research into the economic potential at the "base of the pyramid" by suggesting specific strategies and business models for successful engagement. The focus is on distribution strategies for reaching the rural poor, who can be more challenging to reach than their urban counterparts. The examples in the report focus on rural India, and case studies of Indian private, government and civil society organizations are featured.

<u>Key findings</u>

The market access disadvantages suffered by the rural poor are rooted in many factors, including poor road, communication and electricity infrastructure; lack of adequate information on buying/selling options; lack of appropriate skills; and illiteracy.

- The report defines socially responsible distribution as initiatives that provide poor producers and consumers with market access for goods and services by helping neutralize the disadvantages they suffer from inadequate physical links to markets, information asymmetries, and weak bargaining power.
- Governments, civil society, and the private sector can all play a role in providing socially responsible distribution.
- As it would be difficult to justify significant government funding in rural regions, the report identifies three creative market-based alternatives:
  - Taking cost out. This approach increases access by lowering the costs of distribution.
  - Reinventing the distribution channel. This approach increases access through innovation, by identifying different routes for reaching rural consumers and for rural producers to get their products to market. New technologies provide one type of solution. Other solutions come in business process redesign.
  - Taking the long-term view and investing for the future. This approach entails increased private sector investment anticipating a longterm payback and/or as a social commitment.
- A number of specific strategies are suggested that can enable organizations to design and implement socially responsible distribution. These include:

- o Selective bridging of the infrastructure gap in ways that do not call for prohibitive levels of investment but that are appropriate to specific targeted objectives;
- o Aggressively control cost through differential, or layered, distribution, i.e. use lower-cost distribution methods to reach the remotest extremities of the network;
- o Leverage distribution – by creating bidirectional and shared networks;
- o Empowering those at the base of the pyramid through information and education;
- o Harness the advantages of technology appropriate to the area in which it could be deployed;
- o Collaborate across sectors;
- o Ensure scalability.
- The following procedures are recommended for setting up rural operations:
  - o Develop a scalable delivery system;
  - o Set up strong centralized service design, supervisory and control systems;
  - o Cluster retail locations;
  - o Develop benchmarks for retail locations;
  - o Derive higher volume by shared distribution;
  - o Engage the community to facilitate entry;
  - o Select trustworthy retail representatives;
  - o Carefully adjust price and perceived product features.
- The report suggests that there are worthwhile payoffs for the private sector, NGOs and government, as well as benefiting those at the bottom of the pyramid.
- Private companies, for example, can achieve sustainable competitive advantage and lower procurement costs.
- NGOs gain in scalability and lower costs of delivery, and Government keeps costs down while extending service reach to serve the countries poorest people.

Source: Social Research Digest, Jan. 2009 (Vol. 1, No. 1)

5.7.3 Two Generations, One Future: Moving Parents and Children Beyond Poverty Together

Author(s): The Aspen Institute

The paper outlines the emerging case for and shares a framework for two-generation approaches. Key economic and demographic trends are driving the need for these approaches.

Key findings

The United States in 2012 is at a crossroads about ways to ensure that all its people fuel progress in the 21st century.

- By creating partnerships across programs, policies, and systems that are now focused separately on children and parents, we can create an America in which a legacy of economic security and educational success passes from one generation to the next.
- This report offers a framework for the ways in which new two-generation strategies can help parents, especially women, and children achieve their dreams together.

Source: Social Research Digest, Apr. 2012 (Vol. 3, No. 4)

5.7.4 Measuring Financial Inclusion: The Global Findex Database

Author(s): World Bank

The paper provides the first analysis of the Global Financial Inclusion (Global Findex) Database, a new set of indicators that measure how adults in 148 economies save, borrow, make payments, and manage risk. It is part of a larger effort by the World Bank to provide open access to its research and make a contribution to development policy discussions around the world.

Key findings

The data show that 50% of adults worldwide have an account at a formal financial institution, though account penetration varies widely across regions, income groups and individual characteristics.

- In addition, 22% of adults report having saved at a formal financial institution in the past 12 months, and 9% report having taken out a new loan from a bank, credit union or microfinance institution in the past year.
- Although half of adults around the world remain unbanked, at least 35% of them report barriers to account use that might be addressed by public policy.
- Among the most commonly reported barriers are high cost, physical distance, and lack of proper documentation, though there are significant differences across regions and individual characteristics.

Source: Social Research Digest, Mar. 2012 (Vol. 3, No. 3)

5.7.5   Towards Sustainable Development For All In Africa

Author(s): UNDP

The UNDP in partnership with Tokyo International Conference on African Development (TICAD) released a brief report in partnership that highlights the partnership with Japan to accelerate sustainable development in Africa The "Towards Sustainable Development for All in Africa: Japan and UNDP At Work On Rising Continent" report that illustrates examples of programmes that Japan and UNDP have cooperatively implemented in Africa.

Key findings

The UNDP and Japan aim to work within three main issues for Africa: Robust and Sustainable Economy; Inclusive and Resilient Society; and Peace and Stability

- As a co-organizer of TICAD, UNDP has been helping to set its agenda and to formulate, implement and monitor programmes in support of TICAD priority areas
- Advancing peace and security: there have been major improvements in peace building and conflict resolution in Uganda where between 2009 and 2012, the program solved 2,288 community conflicts.
- Promoting inclusive and resilient societies: between 2010 and 2012 with USD 2.76 million from the Japan-financed Africa Adaptation Programme (AAP) partnered with Government of Ghana to bolster

disaster risk reduction and climate change adaption resulted in stronger institutions and funds in 20 African countries
- Building robust and sustainable economies: with support from Japan, North African countries respond effectively to popular aspiration for inclusive and political and economic development. For example in Algeria, 100 young people are being placed with Civil Society Organizations to strengthen access to a first professional experience

Source: Social Research Digest, Jun. 2013 (Vol. 4, No. 6)

5.7.6   The Women's World Banking: Annual 2012 Report

Author(s): The Women's World Banking

The Women's World Banking, the global nonprofit devoted to giving more low-income women access to the financial tools and resources they require to achieve security and prosperity, released it's annual 2012 report. The "The Women's World Banking: Annual 2012 Report" provides financial institutions with indepth market research, sustainable financial products and financial education tools to help meet women's needs.

Key findings

There is a clear link between becoming the provider of choice for women and the employer of choice for women.

- This research includes analysis of the ways gender shapes women's financial lives with respect to family responsibilities, cultural norms, and self-image.
- The United Nations estimates that as of 2010 roughly 30% of the combined population of Africa, Asia, Latin America and Caribbean, are under the age of 15.
- Market research conducted by Women's World Banking concludes that girls as young as 10 years old accumulate money actively manage it and want a save place to save it.
- Therefore, financial institutions need to reconsider their traditional orientation towards adults as costumers and need to consider youth as viable.
- A project was debuted to adapt credit products for rural women based on a comprehensive assessment of all household income with three

network members in Latin America: Interfisa Financiera (Paraguay) Fundación de la mujer (Colombia) and Caja Arequipa (Peru).

- Each of the aforementioned institutions was able to increase the percentage of women in the rural portfolio—the goal is to reach 24,200 clients by the end of 2014.
- Women's World Banking's Center for Microfinance Leadership was developed and it offers executive leadership programs with an explicit focus on (1) developing principled (2) diverse leaders committed to the double bottom line of financial returns and (3) social progress, and (4) a suite of services to support, (5) design and implement diversity strategies.

Source: Social Research Digest, Aug. 2013 (Vol. 4, No. 8)

5.7.7   Global State of the Poor

Author(s): World Bank

World Bank released a study on global poverty, analyzing its dynamics over the last 30 years. 'The State of the Poor' is the first effort to provide an indepth profile of the world's poorest people who pose the greatest challenge to reducing global poverty levels to nine percent by 2020, which would mean increasing incomes of an additional 510 million people to greater than USD 1.25 a day in real terms.

Key findings

721 million fewer people lived in extreme poverty in 2010 – defined as under $1.25 a day – compared to 1981.

- Children accounted for one in three of those living in extreme poverty around the world in 2010, compared with only one in five of those living above the poverty line.
- In low-income countries, the percentages were even worse, with half of all children living in extreme poverty.
- While the reduction in poverty moved significantly in middle-income countries such as China and India, low-income countries showed much slower progress.
- Although extreme poverty rates have declined in all regions, the world's 35 low-income countries – 26 of which are in Africa —

registered 100 million more extremely poor people today than three decades ago.

- In 2010, 33% of the extreme poor lived in low-income countries, compared to 13% in 1981.
- The poor in 2010 were as bad off as they were in 1981, with the exception of India and China.
- The "average" poor person in a low-income country lived on 78 cents a day in 2010, compared to 74 cents a day in 1981. But in India, the average income of the poor rose to 96 cents in 2010, compared to 84 cents in 1981, while China's average poor's income rose to 95 cents, compared to 67 cents.
- The report also calculated that the amount of money needed every year to lift more than a billion people out of extreme poverty would be $169 billion in 2005 dollars. This was less than half than in 1981

Source: Social Research Digest, Oct. 2013 (Vol. 4, No. 10)

5.7.8 Promise and Progress: Market-Based Solutions to Poverty in Africa

Author(s): Monitor Group

The Monitor Group has published a comprehensive analysis of financially sustainable enterprises that address challenges of poverty in Africa. The report is the outcome of a 16-month research project on the operations of 439 enterprises in nine sub-Saharan nations

<u>Key findings</u>

The report shows conclusively that MBSs make a significant difference in the fight against poverty by delivering social impact in a sustainable way, at scale.

- These "market-based solutions" (MBSs) engage poor people as customers, offering them socially beneficial products at prices they can afford, or as business associates— suppliers, agents, or distributors— providing them with improved incomes.
- Some examples:
  - o Aggregators collecting cash crops and staples from smallholder farmers to supply large, top-of-the-supply-chain buyers. To help

guarantee stable supply, many of these aggregators provide the farmers with services such as credit, storage, and transport, as well as with low-cost seeds and fertilizer to help improve their yields.

o The farmers participating in such arrangements benefit from income increases of as much as 40%.

o Companies organizing and upgrading informal retail operations and working with vendors to sell socially beneficial products such as health care goods and agricultural inputs. The vendors benefit from training and demand stimulation, while the goods improve the lives of consumers.

o Vocational colleges that provide high-quality, no-frills training to a range of individuals, including the very poor. These institutions also enhance employability by helping students obtain internships and work experience. Institutions in South Africa report graduates earn between 170-220% of their prior wages.

• Promise and Progress is addressed to the broad community of actors concerned with making real and enduring improvements in the lives of the poor.

• The report discusses implications and conclusions of the research for the founders and leaders of MBSs; large and multinational corporations that seek to engage low-income people as customers or suppliers; impact investors, donors and philanthropists; and governments.

Source: CSR Research Digest, Jun. 2011 (Vol. 3, No. 6)

5.7.9 Profiting from the Poor? Considerations for Investing at the Bottom of the Pyramid

Author(s): KPMG

KPMG has released a new report: "Profiting from the Poor? Considerations for Investing at the Bottom of the Pyramid". Building on a series of in-depth interviews with leading multinational companies, the report aims to help companies decide whether and how to approach low-income consumers in emerging economies. With a company's profit considerations serving as the starting point, KPMG proposes a number of steps for the scoping, implementation and impact measurement of 'base-of-the- pyramid' strategies.

Key findings

Companies are increasingly looking at investment opportunities in developing countries, rather than the large emerging economies of countries such as Brazil and China.

- Some of the benefits to companies which invest in developing countries include not only increased revenues and competitive advantage, but also the opportunity to become more deeply embedded in the countries in which they operate and contribute to sustainable development.
- Developing countries offer impressive rates of growth and access to many 'first-time' consumers who only recently have gained the spending power to put branded products in their reach.
- Companies considering such investment opportunities should reflect on three areas:
  - Scoping: this process should identify the opportunity; be clear about the specific ambition; identify company strengths; position the Base of the Pyramid (BoP) within the company overall.
  - Action: which should embed BoP in the corporate strategy; identify internal constraints; be locally responsive; work in partnership.
  - Impact: in which the key factors are profitability, development, environment and communication.

Source: Social Research Digest, Jan. 2009 (Vol. 1, No. 1)

5.7.10 Credit Accessibility and CSR in Financial Institutions: The Case of Microfinance

Author(s): F. Prior, A. Argandoña.

This paper considers the social responsibilities of financial institutions in developing countries, including helping to tackle to problem of poverty. The authors consider the performance of microfinance in Latin America and provide a series of recommendations that help to define financial institutions' social responsibility in such regions.

Key findings

The low levels of bank penetration in developing countries require solutions that solve the problems of the high prices of financial services, low branch density and risk methodologies that are not matched to the country's economic reality and inadequate legislation.

- Countering the low branch density and the high prices for financial services will require a strategy that generates new business models in the distributions of low-cost financial services, thereby increasing competition within the industry.

- ⟨OBJ⟩⟨OBJ⟩⟨OBJ⟩⟨OBJ⟩⟨OBJ⟩⟨OBJ⟩The low levels of bank penetration in developing countries require solutions that solve the problems of the high prices of financial services, low branch density and risk methodologies that are not matched to the country's economic reality and inadequate legislation.

- The reduced efficiency of the risk methodologies must be countered by creating systems that take into account the vast informal economy existing in developing countries.

- Recommendations:
  - The development of low-cost financial products: through the generalized use of electronic payment methods to improve institutions' efficiency, the use of low-cost distribution channels, and application of credit risk monitoring systems.

- Economies of scale may also be generated through the creation of networks linking different types of electronic banking products.
  - The creation of low-cost intermediary networks: use of alternative distribution networks to bank branches, generating economies of scope and decreasing transaction costs.

- Alternatives may include cash dispensers, remittance distribution networks or alliances with shopping centres.
  - The use of alternative risk analysis methodologies: i.e. alternatives to those used in developed nations. These are based on the analysis not only of economic variables also of socio-demographic variables.

- The model proposed in the paper uses credit risk monitoring systems, made possible by electronic payment systems. Such systems improve the level of customer monitoring and decrease the moral risk inherent in the financial asset transformation process.
  - Optimisation of the impact of emigrants' remittances: The growing importance of emigrant remittances in developing countries, particularly for the low-income segments of the population,

requires an efficient, low-cost services distribution model that includes mechanisms for optimizing remittance impact.

- Remittances offer major opportunities to lending institutions in emerging countries, as they provide funds and confer greater liquidity to the system.
- They also allow the exploitation of economies of scale, scope to decrease transaction costs, access to new populations groups and alliances to be formed with institutions in the developed countries, incorporating the latter's knowledge and techniques into their practice.
- The operational synergies generated by these economies are particularly important because they are based on elements that are common to both businesses' value chain, such as distribution networks and information processing capacity.
  - The development of a networked nodal structure: This will exploit economies of scale required to lower transaction costs. This scale, in the popular savings and lending sector, can be obtained through networked structures, with a coordinating node that provides central services.
- Government intervention may be vital to assure cost efficiency, since the increased competition arising from network compatibility will lead to diminished revenues. Government intervention may be aimed at creating a publicly owned node or creating incentives to encourage membership of a network.

Source: Social Research Digest, Nov. 2009 (Vol. 1, No. 11)

5.7.11 BoP Insights Inclusive Marketing Research: Three Pilots for Pro-Poor Innovation Consortium

Author(s): BoP Innovation Center

This research report covers the main challenges and aims to discover and understand new ways to research the BoP market. This report is based on insights gathered through the programme 'Three Pilots for Pro-Poor Innovations' and it is the second publication of a series of five. The series covers key challenges and solutions for any organization that wishes to have impact through inclusive innovation strategies in BoP markets.

Key findings

Understanding the local BoP system and individuals within this system—consumers, producers, and entrepreneurs—is fundamental to ensuring the successful development of 'inclusive innovations.'

- An increasing number of companies and NGOs have launched innovative products and services in the Base of the Pyramid (BoP).
- BoP represents the four billion people with an income of less than 4 USD a day of local purchasing power.
- Understanding the local BoP system and individuals is fundamental to ensuring the successful development of 'inclusive innovations.'
- The purpose of gaining BoP Insights is to identify, understand, assess and engage BoP actors in co-creating inclusive innovations that create impact in a socio-economic and ecologically sustainable manner.
- The population of the BoP predominantly lives in developing and emerging economies of Asia, Africa and Latin America.
- There are four phases of inclusive marketing research:
  - Search: The BoP market is not homogenous and segmentation such as rural v. urban, men versus women, stable v. unstable income etc., is useful to understanding potential future consumers.
  - Understand: Deep dialogue is vital when entering BoP market and helps collect large amount of information in short-term period.
  - Co-create: market consumer research is top-down and target audience should be involved in the market research right from the start.
  - Commercial Pilot: putting the product or service up for sale in a shop, stall and community. A commercial trail gives you direct response to your production proposition and tells you whether a market exists in the first place.
- Although, BoP markets vary in terms of cultural and geographical setting, available capabilities and needs, there are several challenges facing products and service development which most BoP markets have in common (known as the 4 A's of BoP Marketing):
  - Affordability: the extent to which BoP individuals are capable of investing their limited financial resources in a product, service or business proposition

o Acceptability: the extent to which BoP are willing to adopt a proposition and/or to participate in the value chain as a producer, entrepreneur, investor

o Availability: the degree to which BoP individuals have easy and regular access to a proposition

o Awareness: level of understanding and knowledge BoP individuals have of the product, service or business proposition

Source: Social Research Digest, Mar. 2013 (Vol. 4, No. 3)

5.7.12 Breaking Barriers to Financial Inclusion

Author(s): Banking on Change (a partnership between Plan UK, CARE International UK and Barclays)

Banking on Change has released a report which examines the barriers to financial inclusion in developing countries. The study, entitled 'Breaking Barriers to Financial Inclusion', also describes the potential boost to the global economy that large-scale financial inclusion represents.

Key findings

For any financial inclusion programme to be ultimately sustainable it must offer formal links with the banking sector, which requires much greater co-operation from local and global financial institutions.

- Members of the UN High-level Panel – including UK Prime Minister David Cameron – that are identifying a new international framework to replace the current Millennium Development Goals after 2015 should ensure financial inclusion is on the agenda
- National governments, donors and financial services providers should recognise and support the expansion of savings-led microfinance solutions as part of an overall strategy for tackling poverty
- Governments should invest in and extend access to financial education and entrepreneurship training, with a particular focus on women and young people
- Financial institutions and regulators should recognise community-based savings models and support the development of appropriate, transparent products.
- Around 2.7 billion adults have no access to financial services, yet if they

all participated in savings-led microfinance programmes like Banking on Change, up to US$157bn could be added to the global economy each year.

- Where these savings groups are then linked to the formal financial system, this could provide an influx in banking deposits, which could in turn be used to finance businesses and households.

Source: Social Research Digest, Jan. 2014 (Vol. 5, No. 1)

5.7.13 The Chronic Poverty Report 2014–2015: The Road to Zero Extreme Poverty

Author(s): The Chronic Poverty Advisory Network (CPAN), Andrew Shepherd, Lucy Scott, Chiara Mariotti, Flora Kessy, Raghav Gaiha, Lucia da Corta, Katharina Hanifnia, Nidhi Kaicker, Amanda Lenhardt, Charles Lwanga-Ntale, Binayak Sen, Bandita Sijapati, Tim Strawson, Ganesh Thapa, Helen Underhill, Leni Wild

The Chronic Poverty Advisory Network (CPAN) produced a the 3rd Chronic Poverty Report that shines a light on the millions of people worldwide who are thought to be living in chronic poverty – the grinding and long-term poverty that scars their lives, and often the lives of their children. The Chronic Poverty Report 2014–2015: The road to zero extreme poverty proposes a new framing for a post-2015 goal to eradicate extreme poverty, focused on improving poverty dynamics – tackling chronic poverty, stopping impoverishment and supporting sustained escapes from poverty.

<u>Key findings</u>

There is a tripartite challenge to the world: countries need to tackle chronic poverty, stop impoverishment and assist people escaping poverty to sustain those escapes. All three are needed if the eradication of extreme poverty is to be sustained, and all three require massive global investment.

- There are three policies that address all three legs of this tripod. All three are needed if the eradication of extreme poverty is to be sustained, and all three require massive global investment.
- Social assistance brings the poorest people closer to a decent standard of living, provides a safety net for them in tough times, and encourages them to make the investments and take the risks that could propel

them out of poverty, and keep them out of poverty. One prime example of social assistance that has been taken to scale is Ethiopia's Productive Safety Net Programme, which has enabled thousands of vulnerable households to withstand drought without having to cut back on education spending.

- Massive investment in education, which enables escapes from poverty and sustains the climb away from it, also has the advantage of being a 'portable asset' that is resilient to crises.

- Pro-poorest economic growth ensures that the benefits of increasing national prosperity reach the very poorest people – one example can be seen in South Africa's extension of the minimum wage to groups such as domestic workers.

- These three policies apply everywhere, and in every context.

- However, they do need to be part of policy packages that will, inevitably and quite rightly, vary from one context to the next. It is the context that defines the priorities, sequences and combinations of policies required.

- For example, in situations where the households sinking into poverty outnumber those escaping from it, policies should prioritise stopping impoverishment before it happens, as well as investing in poverty escapes.

Source: Social Research Digest, Aug. 2014 (Vol. 5, No. 8)

5.7.14 Living Standards, Poverty and Inequality in the UK: 2014

Author(s): Institute of Fiscal Studies

The Institute for Fiscal Studies published a report that analyses government statistics about the distribution of income in the UK (Households Below Average Incomes or HBAI). The report, Living standards, poverty and inequality in the UK: 2014 digs deeper to explore the driving forces behind key trends in living standards, inequality and poverty.

Key findings

Average incomes have just begun to stabilise after falling sharply in the aftermath of the Great Recession.

- Income inequality has fallen back to levels last seen one or two decades ago, depending on the measure.
- Whilst relative poverty has also been falling, this is only because the poverty line fell in line with average incomes.
- In absolute terms, the poor have become worse off in recent years – particularly when their housing costs are properly accounted for.
- Important new themes have emerged, including the falling-behind of young adults as they have struggled in the labour market and large differences in trends in the cost of housing across the population as mortgage interest rates have plummeted.

Source: Social Research Digest, Aug. 2014 (Vol. 5, No. 8)

5.7.15 World Social Protection Report 2014-15: Building Economic Recovery, Inclusive Development and Social Justice

Author(s): International Labour Organization (ILO)

The International Labour Organization (ILO) released a report that presents the latest social security trends and provides information on social protection systems, coverage, benefits and expenditures in more than 190 countries. The report, World Social Protection Report 2014-15: Building economic recovery, inclusive development and social justice follows a life-cycle approach, starting with social protection for children, followed by schemes for women and men in working age, and closing with pensions and other support for older persons and it also assesses progress towards universal coverage in health.

<u>Key findings</u>

Many older people lack financial resilience. The financial provision for people in later life is poor.

- Social protection policies are an essential element of realizing children's rights, ensuring their well-being, breaking the vicious cycle of poverty and vulnerability, and helping all children realize their full potential.
- Despite a large expansion of schemes, existing social protection policies do not sufficiently address the income security needs of children and

families, particularly in low- and middle-income countries with large child populations. About 18,000 children die every day, mainly from preventable causes: many of these deaths could be averted through adequate social protection.

- Social protection plays a key role for women and men of working age by stabilizing their incomes in the event of unemployment, employment injury, disability, sickness and maternity, and by ensuring that they have at least a basic level of income security. While the labour market serves as the primary source of income security during working life, social protection plays a major role in smoothing incomes and aggregate demand, thereby facilitating structural change within economies.

- Worldwide, 2.3% of GDP is allocated to social protection expenditure for women and men in ensuring income security during working age; regionally, levels vary widely, ranging from 0.5% in Africa to 5.9% in Western Europe.

- Where they exist, unemployment benefit schemes play a key role in providing income security to workers and their families in the event of temporary unemployment, contributing thereby to preventing poverty; supporting structural change in the economy; providing safeguards against informalization; and, in the event of a crisis, stabilizing aggregate demand, helping the economy to recover more quickly.

- However, only 28% of the labour force worldwide is potentially eligible for benefits (contributory or non-contributory) under existing legislation should they become unemployed. Within this overall figure, regional differences are considerable: 80% of the labour force is so covered in Europe, 38% in Latin America, 21% in the Middle East, 17% in the Asia and Pacific region, and 8% in Africa.

- Only 12% of unemployed workers worldwide actually receive unemployment benefits, and again regional differences are large, with effective coverage ranging from 64% of unemployed workers in Western Europe to just over 7% in the Asia and Pacific region, 5% in Latin America and the Caribbean, and less than 3% in the Middle East and Africa.

- A number of emerging economies have introduced unemployment benefit schemes, such as Bahrain or Viet Nam, as a means to ensure income security for unemployed workers and facilitate their search for jobs matching their skills in the formal economy.

Source: Social Research Digest, Sep. 2014 (Vol. 5, No. 9)

5.7.16 New York State of the Homelessness 2014

Author(s): The Coalition for the Homeless

The Coalition for the Homeless released its 2014 State of the Homeless report documenting new record levels of homelessness reached in Mayor Bloomberg's final year in office, with more than 53,000 New Yorkers and 22,000 children sleeping in shelters each night by the end of 2013. The report also outlines concrete, cost-effective steps the new Administration can take to begin moving families out of the shelter system and prevent New Yorkers from becoming homeless in the first place.

Key findings

Record homelessness: Over the past year, the number of homeless people sleeping each night in the New York City shelter system increased by 7% from 50,135 people in January 2013 to 53,615 people in January 2014, the highest level ever recorded.

- Child homelessness continues to surge: The number of homeless children increased by 8% over the past year, reaching an all-time-high 22,712 children sleeping in homeless shelters in January 2014.
- Length of stay rises, again: Average shelter stays for homeless families with children rose by a remarkable two months (60 days), or 16%, during the past year. The average shelter stay for homeless families with children is now 14.5 months, the longest ever recorded.
- Not just families: The number of homeless single adults sleeping each night in the New York City shelter system rose 5% to 11,342 women and men, another new all-time record.
- Record numbers all year long: During FY 2013 more than 111,000 different New Yorkers – including more than 40,000 different children – turned to the homeless shelter system, 5% more than the previous year
- Concrete Measures to Reduce Homelessness:

o Target long-term housing subsidies to help homeless families and children move from costly emergency shelter to stable, permanent housing – which will save taxpayer dollars squandered on stop-gap measures.

o Convert "cluster-site" shelter units back to permanent housing, significantly reducing family homelessness and phasing out this wasteful program.

o Invest in the creation of new permanent supportive housing for homeless people living with mental illness and other disabilities – another cost-effective measure that saves $10,000 per person annually.

o Improve access to emergency shelter to prevent harm to vulnerable homeless children, youth, and adults.

o Enhance homelessness prevention efforts through cost-saving homelessness prevention programs and better coordination of services

Source: Social Research Digest, Nov. 2014 (Vol. 5, No. 11)

5.7.17 Business Solutions to Enable Energy Access for All

Source: Environmental Research Digest, Jan. 2012 (Vol. 3, No. 1)

Author(s): WBCSD

The document highlights the critical role that business plays in enhancing access to energy and, more broadly, in the expansion and transformation of national energy systems to deliver clean, reliable and affordable energy for all. It was released to coincide with the launch of the International Year of Sustainable Energy for All by the United Nations' Secretary-General, HE Ban Ki-moon in January 2012.

Key findings

Business solutions to enable energy access for all demonstrates clearly how business is already expanding access to clean, reliable and affordable energy services for poor customers, featuring 19 member company case studies.

- These cases highlight concrete examples of how business model innovation helps provide more affordable and reliable products and services, overcomes market barriers or failures, and increases the profitability and scalability of sustainable engagement in lowincome energy markets.

- However, mobilizing the required scale of investment requires political will and well-designed and stable policies to overcome many of the barriers facing business action.
- The publication recommends that policymakers need to focus on prioritizing energy access in national development planning, improving the investment climate and implementing enabling measures to promote the primary energy access solutions.
- Meeting universal energy access targets will also require mobilization of significant additional financial resources.
- Public and development finance mechanisms should be specifically designed to leverage additional private investment.
- The broader financing architecture must give appropriate consideration to the quality of the regulatory and investment climate, which impact risks and returns associated with private investment.
- Finally the publication highlights that partnerships and cross-sector approaches are essential to make these opportunity areas successful and all the WBCSD member company case studies featured in the document involve partnerships of some form.
- Effective public-private partnerships will be particularly important drivers of progress toward universal access to energy.

5.8 Humanitarian Aid and Disaster Preparedness

5.8.1 Business and Disaster Preparedness Helping Communities Prepare for Effective Response

Author(s): CSR Asia

Commissioned by Prudential Corporation Asia, CSR Asia prepared an analysis of the risks and vulnerabilities faced by communities in disaster-prone areas of the Asia-Pacific region. The 'Business and Disaster Preparedness Helping Communities Prepare for Effective Response' report highlights the need for business engagement in disaster preparedness at the community level, and outlines opportunities for strategic engagement that help support business objectives.

Key findings

The human and economic losses from disasters in the Asia-Pacific region are immense.

- Rapid economic growth has not contributed to the reduction of these losses. In fact, it has spurred risk exposure and vulnerabilities. Those most vulnerable to the potential impacts of the region's manifold disaster events are the poor and marginalised.
- Disaster preparedness activities can help reduce losses from disasters and the costs of response and recovery.
- There is an evident need to help build response capacity and coping mechanisms of local communities. Business can play a vital role in helping communities prepare for disasters and in meeting the specific needs of vulnerable groups in society.
- The strategic engagement of businesses in building community capacity for effective response holds the potential for supporting business objectives. These can include enhanced reputation and brand visibility, enhanced government relationships and stakeholder perceptions, positive effects on staff motivation and retention, and new business opportunities.
- A strategic approach to business engagement on community preparedness efforts requires looking beyond one-off financial and in-kind contributions. There is a great opportunity for business to engage through employee volunteering, leveraging business assets and networks, supporting adoption of new technologies and innovative solutions, and helping advance advocacy efforts.
- Case studies showcase successful examples of strategic business engagements that have addressed community needs in disaster preparedness and supported business objectives.

Source: Social Research Digest, Mar. 2014 (Vol. 5, No. 3)

5.8.2 Global Estimates 2014: People Displaced by Disasters

Author(s): The Norwegian Refugee Council's Internal Displacement Monitoring Centre

The Norwegian Refugee Council's Internal Displacement Monitoring Centre launched a report that helps us understand some of the most pressing global challenges, that is: how we better prevent, how we prepare for and, finally, find solutions to the displacement of millions of people caused by natural disasters each year. The report, entitled "Global Estimates 2014: people displaced by disasters" also looks at those countries experiencing displacement caused by both conflict and natural hazards, which creates military and environmental obstacles to population movements, isolates communities and limits people's options in terms of migration and destinations.

Key findings

22 million people were displaced in 2013 by disasters brought on by natural hazard events.

- As in previous years, the worst affected region is Asia, where 19 million people, or 87.1% of the global total, were displaced during the year.
- Although both wealthy and poorer countries are affected, developing countries bear the brunt, accounting for more than 85% of displacement.
- In the Philippines, typhoon Haiyan alone displaced 4.1 million people, a million more than in Africa, the Americas, Europe and Oceania combined.
- Viewed relative to population size, seasonal floods also caused significant displacement in sub-Saharan Africa, most notably in Niger, Chad, Sudan and South Sudan – countries with highly vulnerable populations who are also affected by conflict and drought.

Source: Social Research Digest, Nov. 2014 (Vol. 5, No. 11)

5.8.3　Global Humanitarian Assistance (GHA) Report 2014

Author(s): Global Humanitarian Assistance

Global Humanitarian Assistance released their 2014 report that provides a shared and independent evidence base for anyone engaged in providing, using and understanding assistance in crisis settings. The Global Humanitarian Assistance (GHA) Report 2014 looks back on an extraordinary year – in terms of both the scale of high-level crises and in the levels of response – and sets it in the context of trends in humanitarian assistance.

Key findings

2013 was marked by high-profile crises in Syria, the Philippines and the Central African Republic, as well as high levels of need both on and off the international radar including in South Sudan, Yemen and the Sahel.

- The level of international humanitarian response rose to a record US$22 billion in 2013. Government donors accounted for three quarters of this, contributing US$16.4 billion – a rise of 24% from 2012. Private sources provided an estimated US$5.6 billion – a 35% increase from 2012)
- Despite this, over a third of estimated humanitarian needs went unmet: UN-coordinated appeals targeted 78 million people for assistance in 2013 and called for US$13.2 billion in funding. 65% of this funding appeal was met
- 78% of humanitarian spending from OECD DAC donors went to protracted emergencies in long- and medium-term recipient countries. Most long-term assistance is also spent in countries with high levels of poverty and low levels of government spending.

Source: Social Research Digest, Nov. 2014 (Vol. 5, No. 11)

VI.   COMMUNITY DEVELOPMENT

6.1   Development Trends

6.1.1   Arab Millennium Development Goals Report

Author(s): League of Arab States / ESCWA (Economic and Social Commission for Western Asia) / UNDP (United Nations Development Programme)

The report provides detailed information on where the Arab region stands in terms of achieving the MDGs by 2015. It proposes the necessary policies and actions that should be undertaken to enable the region to attain the MDGs and move forward on the promises of the Millennium Declaration.

Key findings

The Arab region has achieved progress in many MDGs, including significant strides in health and education.

- However, there have been setbacks and constraints attributable to several factors, including the relatively poor economic performance in the 1990s and early 2000s, inadequate financing of social policies, and increasing political tensions and conflicts.
- The Arab region continues to be characterized by sharp disparities between the different subregions, particularly between the high-income countries of the Gulf Cooperation Council (GCC) and the Least Developed Countries (LDCs).
- These disparities to the overall levels of development and progress made towards achieving the MDGs.
- Indeed, while the GCC countries are on-track to achieving most of the MDG targets, the Arab LDCs, most of which suffer from conflict, together with Iraq and the Occupied Palestinian Territory, lag significantly behind, making it unlikely that they will be able to meet the majority of the targets by 2015.
- Within this context, supporting the achievement of MDGs and reducing human poverty constitute key pillars of UNDP's work in the Arab States

region.

- As far as the MDG progress is concerned, Arab countries can be classified into three main groups:
  - countries that are likely to achieve MDGs targets (mainly GCC countries);
  - countries with mixed progress and mixed opportunities, which constitute the bulk of Arab middle-income countries (MICs);
  - and countries that are unlikely to achieve MDGs targets (mainly LDCs).

Source: CSR Research Digest, Jan. 2011 (Vol. 3, No. 1)

6.1.2 Egypt at Cross-Roads Report

Author(s): Maplecroft

Risk analysis and mapping firm Maplecroft has released an in-depth country report on Egypt. The report is specifically aimed at companies with interests in Egypt and can be adjusted to cover any specific sector or industry.

<u>Key findings</u>

The analysis cover political violence and conflict, the governance framework, corruption, the regulatory and business environment, the environment, energy and natural resources, and human rights.

- Events since protests were first launched on 25 January have mobilised the population in a hitherto unseen way.
- In the long run, a drive against corruption and improved democracy will benefit Egyptian citizens and reduce the risks to businesses looking to operate in Egypt.
- The economic risks to Egypt (food price inflation, unemployment, widespread poverty) still remain significant and a trigger for further unrest.

Source: CSR Research Digest, Feb. 2011 (Vol. 3, No. 2)

6.1.3 Independent Insights From Vulnerable Developing Countries

Author(s): Adaptation Fund NGO Network

The Adaptation Fund NGO Network, established under the Kyoto Protocol, has reached the implementation of adaption project in developing countries and has issued a report that provides insight into the implementation of adaptation projects. The "Independent Insights From Vulnerable Developing Countries" Report relies on illustrative case studies that address key elements of the Adaptation Fund Provisions for project proposals and focuses on seven developing countries, which are Benin, Jamaica, Senegal, South Africa, Honduras, Nicaragua and Pakistan.

Key findings

There have been 27 projects approved since the first call for proposals two and a half years ago with funding amounting to US$175 million and it clear that the AF is delivering on implementation. However, the overall performance of these projects needs to be continuously observed in order to help the most vulnerable communities build resilience to climate change.

- Local stakeholders must be involved from the outset of the project design until its completion and last stage of evaluation.
- The projects provide a useful opportunity to promote transparency and the free flow of information between institutions and communities.
- The establishment of interaction between government, beneficiaries, universities and NGOs is the main route towards simplifying processes and enhancing outcomes.
- Mainstreaming climate change adaptation projects and involving the most vulnerable groups are critical and require a more holistic approach.
- Direct Access is an important tool for enhancing dialogue between responsible agencies and civil society.
- It is can be difficult to successfully engage local communities in projects with stronger capacitybuilding elements, therefore, ownership by targeted communities because easier to secure when the projects constraints some infrastructure components.

Source: Social Research Digest, May 2013 (Vol. 4, No. 5)

6.1.4 The 2013 Human Development Report-The Rise of the South: The Human Progress in a Diverse World

Author(s): United Nations Development Programme

The UNDP released a report that investigates the fundamental shift in global dynamics propelled by the emergence of new powers from the developing world and its long-term ramifications. The "2013 Human Development Report-The Rise of the South: The Human Progress in a Diverse World" identifies more than 40 countries in the developing world that have done better than expected in human development terms in the past decade and analyses the causes and consequences of these countries' achievements and challenges today and in the future.

Key findings

The Report calls for a far better representation of the South in global governance systems and points to potential new sources of financing within the South for essential public goods.

- Countries from the south have been able to transform their human development as a result of three notable drivers of development: a proactive developmental state, tapping of global markets, and determined social policy innovations.
- All intergovernmental processes would be invigorated by greater participation from the South, which can bring substantial financial, technological and human resources as well as valuable solutions to critical world problems.
- Rising economic strength of development countries from the South must be matched by a full commitment to human development.
- New institutions can facilitate regional integration and South-South relationships.
- Greater representations for the South and civil society can accelerate progress on major global challenges
- The rise of the South presents new opportunities for generating a greater supply of public goods.

Source: Social Research Digest, May 2013 (Vol. 4, No. 5)

6.1.5   2012 Global Retail Development Index

Author(s): AT Kearney

The A.T. Kearney Global Retail Development Index (GRDI) ranks the top 30 emerging countries for retail development. It identifies opportunities for global retailers to invest in developing markets.

Key findings

Brazil, Chile and China top the index for retail opportunities in developing markets.

- The 2012 GRDI shows an increasingly global world.
- While the BRIC nations still have an impact, there are many opportunities in some of the smaller markets around the globe.
- The annual index is based on 25 indicators and helps mass merchant and food retailers evaluate expansion opportunities in emerging countries.
- The GRDI indicates many opportunities for retailers – not only in BRIC countries but also in small untapped markets such as Oman, Mongolia and Georgia.
- Brazil tops the index, and market made attractive by reduced political and economic risk and high per capita spending.
- Chile, ranked second, has one of the most sophisticated and competitive markets in Latin America.
- It also has high per capita spending, making it a potential market for luxury goods.
- Although China is third due to high expected sales growth, it faces many challenges including increasing inflation and labour costs.
- Botswana is the Best New Market for Global Retailers, driven by long-term growth prospects and increasing investment in the private retail sector.
- South Africa dropped from the rankings this year due to saturation of international retailers.
- Trends in the Middle East include growth of private labels and on-line shopping.
- Oman and the UAE both show strong retail prospects.

- Malaysia tops the Retail Talent Index due to low-cost labour, favourable regulations and a well-educated population; China ranks second.

Source: Social Research Digest, Jul. 2012 (Vol. 3, No. 7)

6.1.6 Time to Reimagine Development?

Author(s): Institute of Development Studies

'Time to Reimagine Development?' is the latest issue of the IDS Bulletin, the flagship journal from the Institute of Development Studies (IDS), published by Wiley-Blackwell. The report draws on 20 case studies from around the world, ranging from the experience of indigenous people in Brazil, to feedback from charities, researchers and academics at a workshop in Ethiopia.

<u>Key findings</u>

Economic growth is not always a force for good – while there is no alternative to growth, there are alternative forms of growth and as with technology, it is how it is governed that matters.

- Civil society did not deal well enough with mega-shocks – case studies found that civil society did not sufficiently rise to the challenge or opportunity afforded by the crises.
- The nation state is more relevant than multilateral mechanisms – global agreements on climate, trade and drugs do not drive national behaviour but national alliances supply oxygen and credibility to global agreements.
- Several case studies showed how national self interest will continue to undermine collective action that is in the long term interest of all.
- The global crises of the past four years and the slow burn of climate change have called into question the way we live, and have had fundamental impacts on international development.
- But this research shows that although some new ideas have emerged, they have struggled to dislodge established concepts and become embedded in development thinking.
- It is clear that the emerging powers – such as China, India and Brazil – and the new aid donors and philanthropists are not necessarily going to forge different paths.

- And it remains debatable whether development thinking is any better suited now for coping with unforeseen crises than it was before 2008.

Source: CSR Research Digest, Oct. 2011 (Vol. 3, No. 10)

6.1.7   The Bertelsmann Transformation Index 2014

Author(s): Bertelsmann Stiftung (Foundation)

The Bertelsmann Stiftung (Foundation) published its 2014 Transformation Index, ranking 129 developing and transition countries' progress in consolidating democracy, economic development and political management. The Bertelsmann Transformation Index (BTI) measures successes and setbacks on the path toward a democracy based on the rule of law and a socially responsible market economy and in-depth country reports provide the basis for assessing the state of transformation and persistent challenges, and to evaluate the ability of policymakers to carry out consistent and targeted reforms.

<u>Key findings</u>

Poverty and inequality remain structurally engrained in more than half of all countries analyzed.

- In reaction to these developments, a better-networked and more self-confident civil society is increasing its resistance to mismanagement, autocratic trends and corruption."
- Uruguay, last year's "Country of the Year" and the top-ranked country in the 2013 AQ Social Inclusion Index, led the BTI 2014's ranking on political transformation—followed by Estonia and Taiwan. Costa Rica (tied for 6th) and Chile (9th) also appeared in the top ten for political transformation.
- Taiwan ranked first for economic transformation in the BTI 2014, with Uruguay (tied for 7th) and Chile (10th) in the top ten for economic transformation. Taiwan also led the management ranking, with Uruguay runner-up, followed by Brazil (3rd) and Chile (5th).
- The lowest-ranking countries in all categories included Somalia, Eritrea, North Korea, Syria and Myanmar.
- The worldwide wave of civil protests and revolts from North Africa to Ukraine and Thailand will continue in the years ahead.

- High levels of poverty and social exclusion remain despite all the gains associated with growth. At the same time, a better-networked and more confident civil society is gaining traction in resistance to the persistent abuses of political power.

- In many countries, economic and social exclusion has led to a fundamental questioning of the quality and legitimacy of the governing elites. To be sure, economic performance and average per-capita incomes have risen significantly in the last 10 years.

- However, many countries have not benefited from this development, and within most states, welfare gains have gone primarily to small, urban middle classes. Particularly in sub-Saharan Africa, mass poverty and social discrimination remain prevalent in virtually all countries.

- A continuing abuse of political power has been evident in many countries, an issue that is not limited solely to authoritarian states. In 59 of 75 surveyed democracies, setbacks have been observed in the last eight years with respect to democratic standards such as fair elections, press freedom, legal certainty and the separation of powers. In Europe, for example, this includes Albania, Bulgaria, Hungary and Romania.

- A number of states have shown such substantial setbacks that they no longer meet basic democratic standards. For the first time, the BTI categorizes Russia as an autocracy.

Source: Social Research Digest, Jun. 2014 (Vol. 5, No. 6)

6.1.8   The Outlook on the Global Agenda 2014

Author(s): World Economic Forum (WEF)

World Economic Forum produced a comprehensive overview of the world, drawing upon the foremost global intelligence network and its collective brainpower to explore the most important issues we all face this year. To better understand the complexity of these issues, The Outlook on the Global Agenda 2014 provides deep insights into specific regional challenges, highlighting the perspectives of different stakeholders and those of the next generation.

Key findings

The Top 10 trends in the Outlook on the Global Agenda for 2014 are:

1. Societal tension in the Middle East and North Africa: war in Syria, political instability and unemployment in North Africa.
2. Widening income gap: ramifications for health, education and social mobility across all regions of the world.
3. Structural unemployment: a global issue demanding a global solution
4. Intensifying cyber threats: electronic armies and government agencies are threatening the fabric of the Internet
5. Inaction on climate change: extreme weather events may be occurring more frequently, but there has been no breakthrough on action to tackle the problem
6. Diminishing confidence in economic policies: the scale of the global downturn and the pace of recovery have left deep scars, particularly among the young
7. Lack of values in leadership: this has led to a crisis of legitimacy in governments and other institutions
8. Asia's expanding middle class: greater hope for increased prosperity – but also environmental and resource challenges
9. Growing importance of megacities: these original social networks are home to more and more people, yet we still understand surprising little about how they grow and evolve
10. Rapid spread of misinformation online: the speed of social media – and the scale of big data – is making it harder for people to know that information received is real

Emerging trends that experts believe will grow in the coming 12 months include the implications of shale gas extraction, the failure or inadequacy of democratic institutions, the rise of emerging market multinational companies and the role of space in improving our world.

Source: CSR Research Digest, Feb. 2014 (Vol. 6, No. 2)

6.1.9 Foresight Africa: Top Priorities for the Continent in 2014

Author(s): The Brookings Africa Growth Initiative (AGI)

The Brookings Africa Growth Initiative (AGI) identified the key issues for Africa's development and stability in the coming year. The briefs included in the Foresight Africa: Top Priorities for the Continent in 2014 collection are meant to create a dialogue on what critical issues Africa must pay attention to in the coming 12 months.

Key findings

Africa's position in the world is changing and will continue to evolve in 2014 and beyond.

- With new development and commercial partners like China and India, recent discoveries of additional natural resources, and millions of young people entering the labor force, Africa has the opportunity to take charge of its own development path.
- Despite these opportunities, African countries still face several challenges to sustainable growth and development.
- African countries continue to play a marginal role in international climate change negotiations, parts of the region continue to grapple with conflict, violence and instability, and tensions between the International Criminal Court and the African Union have recently increased.
- A top priority for African policymakers should be to leverage the continent's growing youth population since the absolute number of working age Africans will grow by around 14 million next year alone, leaving many low- and high-skilled workers without any source of income on an increasingly difficult labor market.
- Access to international capital markets shows great potential for Africa's growth, but big obstacles such as growing deficits and a lack of transparency could stand in the way.
- Biotechnology has the potential to exponentially raise Africa's agricultural production, increase food security, drive economic growth and save African farmers millions of dollars.

Source: CSR Research Digest, Apr. 2014 (Vol. 6, No. 4)

6.1.10 Future Proofing your Business in the Asian Century

Author(s): Deloitte

Deloitte issued a report that draws on insights from Asian leaders and emerging leaders to generate evidence-based guidance for Australian organisations on how they can address the critical issue of the 'bamboo ceiling.' The research, Cracking the Cultural Ceiling: Future proofing your business in the Asian century was initiated to: • Generate a collective understanding of the value workers from Asian cultural backgrounds bring to Australian organisations; • Promote the importance of Australian organisations effectively attracting, engaging and retaining Asian leaders and emerging leaders in today's 'Asian Century'; and • Provide evidence-based guidance on how Australian organisations can achieve this.

Key findings

For Australian organisations operating in today's Asian century, developing an Asia capable workforce and addressing the 'bamboo ceiling' is now a strategic business and talent management issue.

- Asian talent is ambitious, motivated and capable
- Asian talent is under leveraged, undervalued and likely to leave
- Key barriers are locking out Asian talent in Australian organisations
  - o Cultural bias and stereotyping
  - o Westernised leadership models
  - o Lack of relationship capital
  - o The case for culture not understood.

Source: CSR Research Digest, Sep. 2014 (Vol. 6, No. 9)

6.1.11 Hot Spots: The Global City Competitiveness Index

Author(s): Economist Intelligence Unit

Hot Spots is an Economist Intelligence Unit research programme, commissioned by Citigroup, which ranks the competitiveness of 120 of the world's major cities. It is a unique Index that compares 120 of the world's major urban agglomerations across eight distinct categories of competitiveness and 31 individual indicators.

Key findings

US and European cities are the world's most competitive today, despite concerns over ageing infrastructure and large budget deficits.

- While there is much concern in the West about the impact of the financial crisis, which has slowed plans for urban renewal, this has not reduced the ability of US and European cities to attract capital, businesses, talent and tourists, which is ultimately what this index seeks to measure.

- New York (1st) and London (2nd) are rated as the world's two most competitive cities, while cities from the United States and Western Europe account for 24 of the top 30 cities.
- All these cities perform relatively well across all eight pillars of competitiveness measured in the index, making them good all-round performers.
- Although many Western countries have sombre growth outlooks over the next decade, some of their leading cities may be able to harness their legacy advantages and global connectivity to continue to compete and succeed against fast-growing emerging market cities.
- Asia's economic rise is reflected in the economic competitiveness of its cities.
- Asian cities dominate the "economic strength" category of the competitiveness Index—the most highly weighted category.
- All but five of the top 20 cities on this measure are Asian.
- Tianjin, Shenzhen and Dalian top the list, while nine other Chinese cities rank in the top 20.
- Singapore (15th), Bangalore (16th), Ahmedabad (19th) and Hanoi (joint 20th) round off the list.
- The top 32 Asian cities are all forecast to grow by at least 5% annually between now an 2016.
- Twelve of them will grow by at least 10%.
- This is in stark contrast to the low single-digit growth of most developed market cities in Europe and the United States.
- The most significant advantage that developed country cities hold is their ability to develop and attract the world's top talent.
- European and American cities dominate the human capital category of the index.
- This stems primarily from the quality of their educational systems and the entrepreneurial mindset of their citizens (the two largest indicators within the category).
- But other factors bolster their performance too, such as cultural activities and a generally good quality of life.
- New York Mayor Michael Bloomberg says such factors are a key part of maintaining competitiveness: "I've always believed that talent attracts capital more effectively and consistently than capital attracts talent."

- Infrastructure investments will drive emerging market growth, but more will be needed to secure their attractiveness to tomorrow's talent.
- One of the most pressing challenges for emerging market cities in the decades ahead will be whether they can focus their development not just on skyscrapers, rail links and other infrastructure, but also on the softer aspects that will be crucial to their ability to attract and develop tomorrow's talent— including education, quality of life, and personal freedoms, among other things.
- Another, more basic factor will be the ability, especially within China's cities, to grapple with the pollution challenges that threaten the health of their citizens.

Source: Governance Research Digest, Apr. 2012 (Vol. 3, No. 4)

6.1.12 Rural-Urban Dynamics Report

Author(s): The World Bank & International Monetary Fund

The World Bank and International Monetary Fund released a report that starkly compares the well-being in the countryside versus the city. The "Global Monitoring Report 2013: Rural-Urban Dynamics and the Millenium Development Goals" provides an in-depth analysis on urbanization as a force for poverty reduction and progress towards the MGs in the developing world.

Key findings

Urbanization helps pull people out of poverty and advances progress towards Millennium Development Goals (MDGs), but, if not managed well, can also lead to burgeoning growth of slums, pollution, and crime.

- Poverty is located along a continuous rural-urban spectrum, with the vast majority of the world's 1.2 billion poor living in rural areas with less favorable access to basic amenities than people living in urban centers.
- With the 2015 deadline set by the international development community to attain the MDGs just over two years away, only 4 of the 21 MDG targets or sub-targets have been met worldwide: MDG 1.a (halving extreme poverty), two parts of MDG 7 (access to safe water

and improved lives of slum dwellers, and part of MDG 3.a (gender parity in primary education).

- Progress on the remaining MDGs is limited, except for MDG 3.a (gender parity in primary and secondary education), which is close to being on target

Source: Social Research Digest, May 2013 (Vol. 4, No. 5)

6.1.13 Planning, Connecting, and Financing Cities – Now: Priorities for City

Author(s): World Bank

The World Bank issued a report that provides a policy guide local officials can use to create the jobs, housing, and infrastructure needed to turn their cities into hubs of prosperity for current and future residents. "Planning, Connecting, and Financing Cities – Now: Priorities for City" distills lessons learned from 12 countries across all geographic regions and stages of urbanization—from Korea, to India, to Colombia, to Uganda and then translates these global lessons into practical policy advice.

Key findings

Rapid urbanization can hold long-term economic, social and environmental promise for developing countries if investments made now in infrastructure, housing and public services are efficient and sustainable.

- In the next two decades, cities are expected to expand by another two billion residents, as people move in unprecedented numbers from rural areas to pursue hopes and aspirations in cities.
- More than 90% of this urban population growth is expected to occur in the developing world, where many cities are already struggling to provide basic needs such as water, electricity, transport, health services and education.
- Most new urban growth will not take place in the "megacities" of the world e.g. Rio de Janeiro, Jakarta or New Delhi but rather in less commonly recognized "secondary" cities—places like Huambo in Angola, Fushun in China, and Surat in India.
- Planning is fundamental to agglomeration economies in three ways.
  (1) First, land use requires effective systems for land valuation.

(2) Second, land use must be allocated in a way that allows for infrastructure improvements.

(3) Third, the most basic infrastructure services—water, energy, sanitation, and solid waste management—need to be provided for all residents, urban and peri-urban alike.

Source: Social Research Digest, Nov. 2013 (Vol. 4, No. 11)

6.2 Social Entrepreneurship

6.2.1 Social Entrepreneurship: A Critique and Future Directions

Author(s): M. T. Dacin, P. A. Dacin and P. Tracey

The article addresses work on social entrepreneurship constituting a field that intersects a number of domains, including entrepreneurial studies, social innovation, and nonprofit management. This paper examines the promise of social entrepreneurship as a domain of inquiry and suggests a number of research areas and research questions for future study.

Key findings

Scholars are beginning to contribute to the development of this new discipline through efforts that attempt to trace the emergence of social entrepreneurship as well as by comparing it to other organizational activities such as conventional entrepreneurship.

- However, as a nascent field, social entrepreneurship scholars are in the midst of a number of debates involving definitional and conceptual clarity, boundaries of the field, and a struggle to arrive at a set of relevant and meaningful research questions.

Source: Governance Research Digest, Oct. 2011 (Vol. 2, No. 6)

6.2.2 UK State of Social Enterprise Survey 2013 – The People's Business

Author(s): Social Enterprise UK

Social Enterprise UK produced their 2013 edition of the largest survey of social enterprises in the UK. Close to a third of all social enterprises are three years old or younger, with three times the start-up proportion of traditional SMEs.

Key findings

Close to a third of all social enterprises are three years old or younger, with three times the start-up proportion of traditional SMEs.

- Start-ups are three times more likely than older social enterprises to be operating in healthcare (15% vs 5%), twice as likely to be operating in social care (16% vs 8%) and more likely to be operating in education (23% vs 14%).

- Social enterprises are very heavily concentrated in the UK's most deprived communities. 38% of all social enterprises work in the most deprived 20% of communities in the UK, compared with 12% of traditional SMEs.

- Social enterprises are far more likely to be led by women than mainstream businesses. 38% of social enterprises have a female leader, compared with 19% of SMEs and 3% of FTSE

- 100 companies. 91% of social enterprises have at least one woman on their leadership team. 49% of mainstream SMEs have all-male directors.

- 56% of social enterprises developed a new product or service in the last 12 months compared with 43% of SMEs. New product or service development is often used as a proxy- indicator of business innovation.

- 15% of social enterprise leaders are from Black, Asian and Minority Ethnic (BAME) communities. 28% of social enterprise leadership teams have BAME directors. Only 11% of SMEs report having directors from a BAME background.

- Business optimism has improved since the 2011 survey, with 63% of respondents expecting their turnover to increase in the next two to three years – compared with 57% two years ago. Only 37% of SMEs expect their turnover to grow.

- 11% of social enterprises export or licence abroad – and the newer start-up social enterprises are more likely to export than established social enterprises.

- 38% of social enterprises saw an increase in turnover compared with

29% of SMEs, in the last year. This means that proportionally, almost a third more social enterprises grew based on turnover last year than SMEs.

- 22% of social enterprises experienced a decrease in turnover in the last year compared with 31% of SMEs

Source: Social Research Digest, Feb. 2014 (Vol. 5, No. 2)

6.2.3   Sustaining Competitive and Responsible Enterprise

Author(s): International Labour Organization, Swiss State Secretariat for Economic Affairs and Norwegian Agency for Development Cooperation

The International Labour Organization, Swiss State Secretariat for Economic Affairs and Norwegian Agency for Development Cooperation published the report of the first project phase of their project aiming to support small and medium-sized enterprises in creating good jobs and economic growth. 'Sustaining Competitive and Responsible Enterprise' (SCORE) training helps SMEs attain a win-win scenario: improved productivity for enterprises and better working conditions for those who work there.

<u>Key findings</u>

30 partner institutions embed SCORE training into their SME service portfolios.

- SCORE is a practical training and in-factory counselling programme that improves the productivity and working conditions of small and medium enterprises (SMEs). The programme demonstrates best international practice in the manufacturing and service sectors, and helps SMEs to participate in global supply chains.
- The SCORE training programme is modular and focuses on developing cooperative relations in the workplace. There are five training module, which provide training on workplace cooperation, quality management, human resource management, clean production and occupational safety and health. The training module on cleaner production was developed in collaboration with the United Nations Industrial Development Organization (UNIDO).

- For each module workers and managers participate together in a two-day classroom training. After this training, local experts follow up with on-site visits, to help enterprises to implement what they have learnt. SCORE trainers train 800 SMEs, 3,200 workers and managers, on SCORE modules in eight countries;
- 75% of participants rate training and counseling as good or excellent;
- 30% of SMEs take additional modules;
- 80% of SMEs report costs savings, plus monthly reductions in absenteeism, employee turnover, defects, and waste;
- Social marketing campaigns effect positive change in attitudes among SME owners to workplace cooperation and working conditions, in collaboration with labour inspectorates;
- There is a change in attitudes among the target groups to workplace collaboration and competitiveness.

Source: Social Research Digest, May 2014 (Vol. 5, No. 5)

6.2.4   Enhancing Europe's Competitiveness: Fostering Innovation-Driven Entrepreneurship in Europe

Author(s): *World Economic Forum and A.T. Kearney*

World Economic Forum in collaboration with A. T. Kearney published a report that analyses Europe's lagging innovation capabilities, the challenges associated with scaling entrepreneurship in the region and the conditions needed to create an enabling environment for ambitious, serial entrepreneurs. Enhancing Europe's Competitiveness: Fostering Innovation-Driven Entrepreneurship in Europe is based on data gathered in an online survey of over 1,000 entrepreneurs across Europe, as well as intelligence gathered from 60 structured interviews and interactive workshops that took place across Europe and China.

Key findings

Fostering innovation-driven entrepreneurship in Europe requires a comprehensive view of the entire entrepreneurial life cycle.

- Policy-makers, business leaders and individuals are significantly motivated to improve the conditions for entrepreneurship in Europe.
- To more effectively and efficiently support innovation-driven

entrepreneurship in Europe, stakeholders need to focus, connect and partner.

- Supporting the innovations of today in isolated sectors is not enough – Europe needs to create ecosystems that will support innovations emerging in unconventional ways across government and business.
- Entrepreneurial ecosystems are deeply affected by technological and cultural developments. As digital infrastructure and its applications for enterprises continue to develop, the transaction costs of collaborations will decrease and the ability of different sectors to adopt new ways of working will increase.

Source: CSR Research Digest, Aug. 2014 (Vol. 6, No. 8)

6.3 Education and Human Capital

6.3.1 Sustainability Education: A Student Perspective

Author(s): University of British Columbia

This study examining student interest in sustainability education is one of three reports detailing employer, industry and thought leader perspectives on sustainability knowledge and skills within the labour market. 635 students at the University of British Columbia responded to a survey carried out in the spring of 2009.

Key findings

The majority of respondents believe that sustainability should be a component of their degree.

- Clean/renewable energy and energy efficiency rank as the subjects of highest interest. Applied scientists were the most interested.
- Sustainable transportation and sustainable community development rank next highest as subjects of greatest interest, regardless of student type.
- For the most part, students prefer to take specific courses in sustainability, rather than pursue degree options in sustainability.
- Subject areas with 'sustainability' in the title tended to be more popular than subject areas with 'environment' in the title.

- There was near universal agreement that there is a medium to large added benefit in taking integrated classes with students from other departments, programmes or faculties.
- Graduate students were less interested in business, sustainability and corporate social responsibility, and globalization and international trade as their undergraduate counterparts.

Source: Social Research Digest, Nov. 2009 (Vol. 1, No. 11)

6.3.2 2011 Higher Education Sustainability Review

Author(s): AASHE

Since 2006, AASHE has produced an annual review of higher education sustainability efforts over the previous year. The goal of the report is to serve as a standard Author(s) for who is doing what to advance sustainability in higher education.

<u>Key findings</u>

Nearly 60% of all new higher-education programs or training opportunities in 2011 focused on renewable energy and green careers, with $543 million recorded toward the effort.

- Colleges and universities developed a total of 137 academic programs on sustainability in 2011, compared to 146 in 2010.
- Popular non-degree training opportunities included sustainable agriculture, green business and, with the largest percentage (83%), green job training.
- Compared to 2009, green job training efforts increased 142%.
- Campuses announced 284 energy-related initiatives (including 97 new or planned solar installations and 34 completed or planned campus energy overhauls).
- This represents a 28% increase from 2010.
- Food security efforts on higher education campuses made up the largest percentage of the Bulletin's "Public Engagement" (33%) and "Dining Services" (64%) categories.
- Together with "Funding" and "Grounds" categories, these four categories yielded 79 food security initiatives.

- With 191 environmentally friendly building stories, there were more green building efforts on campus reported in the AASHE Bulletin in 2011 than ever before.
- Solar energy research projects were the most widely reported item in the Bulletin's "Research" category, with nearly $1.8 million in total investment.

Source: Social Research Digest, May 2012 (Vol. 3, No. 5)

6.3.3 National Journeys Towards Education for Sustainable Development

Author(s): *United Nations Educational, Scientific and Cultural Organization (UNESCO)*

The United Nations Educational, Scientific and Cultural Organization (UNESCO) published a report that aims to chronicle how societies use learning and education to address sustainability challenges. "The National Journeys towards Education for Sustainable Development" Report focuses on case studies from Costa Rica, Morocco, South Africa, Sweden and Viet Nam and identifies lessons learnt to support other countries on their journey towards ESD.

Key findings

Political support from the national government is important for driving Education for Sustainable Development (ESD) process.

- Having an institutional and legal framework and a national strategy to implement ESD is also necessary for an efficient implementation of ESD at the country level.
- A central coordinating body that can ensure the collaboration of all stakeholders and oversee a coherent ESD stretegy is vital for effective ESD implementation.
- Participatory approaches to ESD are important for fostering ESD, particularly approaches that include teachers, teacher trainers, researchers and various stakeholders ranging from the smallest communities up to the national level have proven to be successful.

- ESD is a multi-stakeholder initiative. The extension of ESD to all levels of education requires the partnership of different stakeholders, including from non educational sector and civil society.
- An important recommendation for the way forward in successful ESD implementation is allocating sufficient financial resources.
- ESD should be further integrated into teacher education to foster quality education and ESD.
- In order for teachers to effecitvely teach ESD, they need to understand the multidimensional character of local and global SD and learn the basic methods for teaching ESD and evaluating, prioritising, and deciding SD issues.
- More effort is needed in designing learning opportunities for ESD, and integrating and mainstreaming ESD across sectos and disciplines, more attention now needs to be paid to developing monitoring and assessment processes for ESD learning.
- Information and communication technologies (ICT), social networking, mobile communications should be explored as platforms for ESD learning.
- The case studies highlight the importance of promoting partnerships for ESD, involving active NGOs further and supporting university networks for the development of ESD

Source: Social Research Digest, Sep. 2013 (Vol. 4, No. 9)

6.3.4 Financing for Global Education – Opportunities for Multilateral action

Author(s): The Center for Universal Education at the Brookings Institution, Education for All Global Monitoring Report, Pauline Rose, Liesbet Steer with Katie Smith & Asma Zubairi

UNESCO published a report that focuses on how the international community, and multilateral agencies in particular, can contribute to meeting the existing global commitments to a quality basic education for all. The report, 'Financing for Global Education – Opportunities for multilateral action' analyzes the role that multilateral agencies can play, either through their own resources or by mobilizing others.

Key findings

Worldwide, there are still 57 million children out of primary school, largely from marginalized populations such as boys—but especially girls—who are affected by armed conflict, extreme poverty and disability.

- While total aid levels declined by 3% between 2010 and 2011, aid to basic education aid fell, for the first time since 2002, by 6%—from $6.2 billion in 2010 to $5.8 billion in 2011.
- Multilaterals play a significant role in the education sector.
- The five largest institutions contributed 25% of total ODA to education over the past decade.
- But despite significant efforts, education remains highly fragmented, leaving some countries with too many donors and high transaction costs and others with too few donors to generate a minimum level of support to meet needs.
- The report suggests five opportunities for action which could make a major contribution in enhancing the role that multilateral agencies can play. #1: Inspire demand for more support for basic education, #2: Organize high level dialogue to target countries in need, #3: Improve information and financial data, #4: Catalyze domestic resources and #5: Crowd in innovative finance.

Source: Social Research Digest, Dec. 2013 (Vol. 4, No. 12)

6.3.5   Education Under Attack 2014

Author(s): The Global Coalition to Protect Education from Attack

The Global Coalition to Protect Education from Attack released a global study that charts the scale and nature of attacks on education; highlights their impact on education – including on students, teachers and facilities; and documents the ways that governments, local communities, non-governmental organizations (NGOs) and UN agencies try to reduce the impact of such violence and prevent future attacks. In doing so, the study, Education Under Attack 2014 provides the most extensive documentation of attacks on education to date and reports in detail on 30 countries where there was a significant pattern of attacks in the five-year reporting period and lists 40 other countries where isolated attacks took place.

Key findings

Over the past five years, armed non-state groups, state military and security forces, and armed criminal groups have attacked thousands of schoolchildren, university students, teachers, academics and education establishments in at least 70 countries worldwide.

- "Education Under Attack 2014" identifies 70 countries where attacks occurred between 2009 and 2013, including 30 where there was a pattern of deliberate attacks.
- Targeted attacks on education and incidents of military use of schools and universities are occurring in far more countries and far more extensively than previously documented. It is not known whether this reflects growing awareness of the problem and more and better reporting of such attacks since the earlier studies were published or an actual increase in the number of attacks.
- Many attacks involve bombing or burning schools or universities, or killing, injuring, kidnapping, or illegally arresting, detaining or torturing students, teachers and academics. Hundreds have died as a result and hundreds of thousands more have missed out on the right to an education. In many places, children and young people, and those who teach them, live in fear of attacks.

Source: Social Research Digest, Jun. 2014 (Vol. 5, No. 6)

6.3.6 E-Learning Market Trends & Forecast 2014 – 2016 Report

Author(s): Docebo

Docebo issued a report that analyzes the global value of e-Learning, market trends and predictions by continent and sector, and tells you why it is important to embrace innovative training strategies to serve corporate objectives. The E-Learning Market Trends & Forecast 2014 – 2016 Report provides a detailed segmentation on business opportunities in Africa, Asia, Australia, Europe, North America and South America and gives a comprehensive overview on the international e-Learning Market.

Key findings

Employees need to be trained continuously in order for Companies to avoid the dangers of being out-thought and out-maneuvered by competitors.

- The worldwide market for self-paced e-Learning reached $35.6 billion in 2011.
- The five-year compound annual growth rate is estimated at around 7.6% so revenues should reach some $51.5 billion by 2016.
- While the aggregate growth rate is 7.6%, several world regions appear to have significantly higher growth rates.
- The highest growth rate is in Asia at 17.3%, followed by Eastern Europe, Africa, and Latin America at 16.9%, 15.2%, and 14.6%, respectively.
- Each of the world's regions has its idiosyncrasies n terms of the factors that drive this market. The U.S. and Western Europe markets are the most mature. The U.S.A. spent more on Self-Paced E-Learning than anywhere else in the world. Western Europe is the world's second largest buying region for E-Learning products and services but Asia is predicted to outspend Western Europe in E-Learning terms by 2016.
- The Cloud is changing the way Organizations, Employees and Partners interact and collaborate. Within the Cloud solutions universe, Software-as-a-Service (SaaS) is playing a major role. According to Gartner, SaaS will continue to experience healthy growth through 2014 and 2015, when worldwide revenue is projected to reach around $22 billion. Many Enterprises are now replacing their legacy systems with SaaS-based CRM systems. Enterprise clients also report that SaaS-based CRM systems are delivering new applications that deliver complementary functions which are not possible with older, legacy CRM platforms.
- The new frontier to address is the trend towards Bring Your Own Device (BYOD) — where individuals take their personal (usually mobile) devices to workplaces. Increasingly, these seem to be being used to help their owners perform work activities (including formal training), both in and out of the workplace. Smartphones are the most common examples of these devices but employees often also use their tablets or laptops in the workplace.

Source: Social Research Digest, Jul. 2014 (Vol. 5, No. 7)

6.3.7 OECD Survey of Adult Skills

Author(s): OECD

OECD conducted a survey that measured the level of skills within the adult population –

testing actual ability in literacy, numeracy and digital skills, rather than looking at qualifications. 'The Survey of Adult Skills 2013' involved 166,000 adults taking tests in 24 education systems, representing populations of 724 million people.

Key findings

The highest-performing countries among this younger age group were Japan, Finland and the Netherlands.

- The country with the lowest numeracy skills was the United States, plummeting from once being one of the strongest education systems.
- England and Northern Ireland are below average for both literacy and numeracy, in league tables headed by Japan and Finland.
- For most industrialised countries the younger population are much better at such tests than the older generations.
- For England, when the results are separated from Northern Ireland, there was a different and unusual pattern, with almost no advance in test results between the 55 to 65-year-olds and those aged 16 to 24.

Source: Social Research Digest, Nov. 2013 (Vol. 4, No. 11)

6.3.8 Human Capital Report

Author(s): World Economic Forum in collaboration with Mercer

World Economic Forum in collaboration with Mercer issued a report which identifies the countries that are best positioned to contribute to effective workforce development, growth potential, and economic success. In 'The Human Capital Report' each country was measured against 51 factors in four distinct categories: Education; Health and Wellness; Workforce and Employment; and Enabling Environment.

Key findings

Talent, the economic potential of people, is one of the most critical drivers of growth in today's global environment.

- According to the Human Capital Index, countries in Northern and Western Europe account for eight of the ten top positions.

- Switzerland heads the overall global ranking followed by Finland (2), Netherlands (4), and Sweden (5). Singapore, which ranks in third place, and Canada (10) round out the list.

- Aside from those European countries in the top 10, France (21) and Spain (29) received high marks in Health and Wellness, but both countries did less well in their Workforce and Employment ratings. Regardless, both rank ahead of Italy (37), Greece (55), and Serbia (85).

- In North America, the United States ranks 16 because of its strong workforce and ability to attract talent. Canada (10) ranks even higher because of its solid rating in Education, where it ranks second in the world. Among Latin American and Caribbean countries, Barbados (26) is the highest-ranked followed by Chile (36) and Panama (42). Mexico ranks 58.

- Within Asia, Japan (15) ranks the next-highest after Singapore because of high marks in Health and Wellness and Workforce and Employment. These countries are followed by Malaysia (22) and Korea (23). Both China (43) and India (78) received lower marks in Health and Wellness and Education.

- Among the Middle Eastern and African countries, Qatar (18) ranks the highest followed by UAE (24), Israel (25), and Saudi Arabia (39). Other countries ranking favorably include Mauritius (47), Botswana (79), and Kenya (81). Nigeria, a more populous country in Africa, ranks 114.

Source: Social Research Digest, Jan. 2014 (Vol. 5, No. 1)

6.3.9   Human Capital Trends

Author(s): Deloitte

Deloitte released a report that provides human resources executives with the roadmap they can use to help them address critical talent issues that could directly impact an organization's performance going forward. The seven Human Capital Trends for 2013 provide a solid checklist for getting started with the crucial conversations important to helping your organization actively engage with one another.

Key findings

The open talent economy – An organization that embraces the emerging concept of the open talent economy – a collaborative, technology-driven, rapid-cycle way of doing business – can be poised to exploit its opportunities and immerse itself more effectively in the global talent market.

- Creating an elastic workplace – Leading organizations are taking a fresh look at workplace flexibility through the lens of business strategy as the issue evolves into an opportunity that impacts all employees.

- Innovating the talent brand – In order to effectively retain and attract the best talent, companies should focus on their talent brand by building leading talent practices and communicating them in innovative ways.

- Finding the silver lining in the talent gap – The nature of retirement along with the changing ability of a generation to retire early is shifting the demographics of the workforce again. In fact, Deloitte found in a previous study that 34% of U.S. employees plan on delaying their retirement age. The combination of an aging workforce remaining actively employed, even when facing retirement age to an influx of talent from Generation Y, means that organizations need to determine the best way to continue to get value from older workers without holding younger workers back.

- Debunking the Superman myth – Given the ever-changing pressures on businesses today, including adopting new technologies, entering an emerging market country or adapting to new regulatory environments, companies need a bench of leaders who can operate across different environments and adapt to the unexpected.

- The performance management puzzle – To effectively motivate employees, some leading organizations are considering new performance management tools with social media characteristics that incorporate peer, customer and other stakeholder feedback.

- Thinking like an economist – HR and talent leaders should adopt an economist's mindset and expand their use of economic data to make fact-based decisions, which not only increases their alignment with the other business leaders in their organization, but also helps put people in the right positions to unlock their most valuable talents.

Source: Social Research Digest, Feb. 2014 (Vol. 5, No. 2)

6.3.10 The Global Workforce Crisis: $10 Trillion at Risk

Author(s): Boston Consulting Group

Boston Consulting Group released a report that examines workforce supply-and-demand dynamics in 25 major economies—including the G20—to forecast the extent of labor shortages and surpluses for 2020 and 2030. The Global Workforce Crisis: $10 Trillion at Risk is the first in a series of reports on this issue and subsequent reports will break down the surplus and shortage numbers by education levels to reveal in greater detail the severity of global labor imbalances.

Key findings

Workforce shortages and surpluses worldwide are becoming so acute that they threaten $10 trillion of world GDP over the next one to two decades.

- This projected value loss stems from acute shortages and unrelenting surpluses that are being exacerbated by a range of factors, from anemic economic growth and aging populations to low birth rates and restrictive immigration policies.
- Overall, by 2020, many countries will still be experiencing a surplus. But by 2030, this surplus will for most have turned into a massive shortfall.
- The impact of the labor imbalances worldwide will be neither simultaneous nor uniform.
- Germany will see a shortage of up to 2.4 million workers by 2020 and up to 10 million by 2030—23% of the labor supply. The country will not reach its historical GDP growth rates unless it takes action soon.
- Brazil will have a shortage of up to 8.5 million workers in 2020; by 2030, that figure could increase nearly fivefold to 40.9 million people—at 33% of the labor supply, more than 10% worse than Germany's and the highest projected 2030 shortage of the 25 nations studied.
- China is expected to have a surplus of 55.2 million to 75.3 million workers by 2020. By 2030, that surplus could reverse sharply, turning into a shortage of up to 24.5 million people.
- The U.S. is expected to have a surplus of between 17.1 million and 22 million people in 2020. By 2030, it will still face a surplus—at a minimum, 7.4 million.

- France, Italy, and the UK, all projected to have single-digit surpluses in 2020, face labor shortages by the subsequent decade.
- South Africa faces the gloomiest prospects, with a projected surplus of 36% in 2020 that's expected to grow to 39% by 2030.

Source: Social Research Digest, Jul. 2014 (Vol. 5, No. 7)

6.3.11 Education to Employment: Designing a System that Works

Author(s): The McKinsey Centre for Government

The McKinsey Centre for Government released a study that considers the journey from education to employment and to investigate what can be done to improve it. The "Education to Employment: Designing a System that Works" Report provides analysis of more than 100 education-to-employment initiatives from 25 countries and provides a survey of youth, education providers, and employers in nine geographically and socio-economically diverse countries.

Key Findings

Employers need to work with education providers so that students learn the skills they need to succeed at work, and governments also have a crucial role to play.

- In Greece, Spain, and South Africa, more than half of young people are unemployed, and jobless levels of 25% or more are common in Europe, the Middle East, and Northern Africa.
- Around the world, the International Labour Organization estimates that 75 million young people are unemployed.
- If young people who have worked hard to graduate from school and university cannot secure decent jobs and the sense of respect that comes with them, society will have to be prepared for outbreaks of anger or even violence.
- The gap between the haves and the have-nots in the OECD is at a 30-year high, with income among the top 10% nine times higher than that of the bottom 10%.
- In order to address youth unemployment, two fundamentals need to be in place: skill development and job creation.

- This report focuses on skill development, with special attention to the mechanisms that connect education to employment.
- The report's findings include the following six highlights:
  (1) Employers, education providers, and youth have a different understanding of the same situation and it's a result of not being engaged with one another.
  (2) the education-to-employment journey is fraught with obstacles.
  (3) the education-to-employment system fails for most employers and young people
  (4) Innovative and effective programs around the world have important elements in common
  (5) creating a successful education-to-employment system requires new incentives and structures
  (6) Education-to-employment solutions need to scale up.

Source: Social Research Digest, Aug. 2013 (Vol. 4, No. 8)

6.4 Employment and Retirement

6.4.1 Africa at Work: Job Creation and Inclusive Growth

Author(s): McKinsey Global Institute

The report by McKinsey Global Institute examines the employment landscape on the African continent. It identifies five key steps policy makers and business leaders can take to accelerate job creation.

Key findings

Africa must create wage-paying jobs more quickly to sustain achieved successes and ensure that growth benefits the majority of its people.

- Despite the creation of 37 million new and stable wage-paying jobs over the past decade, only 28% of Africa's labor force holds such positions.
- Instead, some 63% of the total labor force engages in some form of selfemployment or "vulnerable" employment, such as subsistence farming or urban street hawking.

- If the trends of the past decade continue, Africa will create 54 million new, stable wagepaying jobs over the next ten years—but this will not be enough to absorb the 122 million new entrants into the labor force expected over the same period.
- However, by implementing a five-part strategy to accelerate the pace of job creation, it is estimated that Africa could add as many as 72 million new wage-paying jobs over the next decade, raising the wage-earning share of the labor force to 36%.
- The five key steps for policy makers:
  - identify one or more labor-intensive subsectors in which an African country has a global competitive advantage or could fill strong domestic demand;
  - improve access to finance in target sectors;
  - build a suitable infrastructure: countries that remove infrastructure constraints in target subsectors, particularly in export-oriented industries, can reap sizable benefits;
  - cut unnecessary regulations; removing needless red tape in certain sectors is also important;
  - develop skills in target sectors: around 40% of African workers now have at least some secondary education, and that share will rise to 48% by 2020.

Source: Social Research Digest, Dec. 2012 (Vol. 3, No. 12)

6.4.2 IFC Jobs Study: Assessing Private Sector Contributions to Job Creation and Poverty Reduction

Author(s): *International Finance Corporation*

International Financial Corporation in partnership with the ministry of Foreign Affairs of the Netherlands and World Bank Group released a report that examines how and under what conditions the private sector can best contribute to job creation and poverty reduction. The "IFC Jobs Study: Assessing Private Sector Contributions to Job Creation and Poverty Reduction" is a result of an open-course study to assess the direct and indirect effects of private sector activity on job creation and it relies on surveys of more than 45,000 businesses in over 100 countries.

Key findings

There are various useful insights into how IFC and World Bank Group can strengthen employment creation effects of private sector activities and contribute to improving the quality of jobs created.

- The world is facing a jobs challenge where 600 million job must be created by 2010 within the context of where informality and working poverty are rampant.
- Private sector, which provides nine out of 10 jobs in developing countries, holds the answer to this challenge.
- There are four constraints to job creation:
  o Poor investment climate
  o Inadequate infrastructure structure
  o Lack of access to finance
  o Insufficient skills and training
- There are specific types of interventions that are the most successful in removing the main obstacles to job creation:
- Establishing a friendly investment climate to promote job creation by the private sector
- Improved services that result form the new infrastructure can generate far larger number of jobs
- One of the ways to improve private companies' access to finance and financial services, and it depends on the degree of development of the local financial sector.
- Some reforms or programs and the jobs created have a transformational impact on an economy
- Example: the strengthening of local suppliers and distributors in agribusiness and manufacturing can reduce poverty.
- A comprehensive approach is needed to tackle the lack of more advanced skills and future employment needs

Source: Social Research Digest, Apr. 2013 (Vol. 4, No. 4)

6.4.3   The World Development Report 2013: Jobs

Author(s): The World Bank

The World Bank released a report that highlights the role of strong private sector led growth in creating jobs and outlines how jobs that do the most for development can ignite a virtuous cycle. The "The World Development Report 2013: Jobs" Report advances a three-stage approach to help government to meet objectives.

Key findings

The Report finds that jobs with the greatest development payoffs are those that make cities function better, connect the economy to global markets, protect the environment, foster trust and civic engagement, or reduce poverty.

- A vast majority of jobs are created by the private sector.
- Government policies should remove obstacles that prevent the private sector from creating jobs.
- 1.6 billion people are working for a wage or salary.
- 600 million jobs needed over 15 years to keep current employment levels.
- 39% of the manufacturing jobs are microenterprises in Chile.
- 97% of the manufacturing jobs are in microenterprises in Ethiopia.
- The country's level of development, institutional strength, endowments, and demography
- The country's level of development, institutional strength, endowments, and demography define where the development payoff from jobs is greatest.
- The challenges facing countries as they move along agrarian, urbanizing and formalizing cases, illustrates the development path.
- 1.5 billion people are working in farming and self-employment.
- 77% of the labor force is the participation of women in Vietnam.
- 28% of the labor force participation is by women in Pakistan.
- 115 million children are working in hazardous conditions.
- 21 million are victims of forced labor.

Source: Social Research Digest, May 2013 (Vol. 4, No. 5)

6.4.4   Infrastructure and Employment Creation in the Middle East and North Africa

Author(s): The World Bank

The World Bank released a study that capitalizes on its longstanding knowledge on infrastructure, employment, and growth and applies it to the case of Middle East and North Africa (MENA) to assess the employment creation potential of infrastructure investment. The "Infrastructure and Employment Creation in the Middle East and North Africa (MENA)" Report uses the infrastructure- and employment-growth elasticities for the purpose of estimating the potential benefits of infrastructure investments for employment creation between 2010 and 2010.

Key findings

The Report concludes while there have been many gains with infrastructure; it alone cannot resolve the substantial employment challenges in the region. As a complement to labor-intensive public works, subsidized employment programs combined with training and counseling can be used to create jobs.

- Ever since the Arab Spring, unemployment rates have soared in many transition economies while private investment and economic growth have declined and government finances have deteriorated.
- Important question for the MENA region is how to stimulate employment creation in the immediate future while building foundations for sustainable growth and job creation.
- Infrastructure investment can be part of the solution to the problem of employment creation in MENA.
- The data suggests that potential of infrastructure investments to create jobs is significant, with some countries and some sectors with more potential than others.
- Policy makers can make infrastructure investment an effective instrument of job creation in the face of fiscal pressures to reduce spending.
- Infrastructure project will need to be prioritized based on a country's employment and infrastructure needs to boost short-term jobcreation impact of public investment programs, while building the foundation for long-run growth.
- Strengthening governance and efficiency of investment spending is fundamental for delivering results through infrastructure investments.

- The report offers a few conclusions: o In the short-run, every US$1 billion invested in infrastructure has the potential to general about 110,000 infrastructure-related jobs in the oil importing countries
- Estimated annual infrastructure needs of about US$106 billion, the region could generated 2.5 million jobs by meeting these needs
- Jobs could be lost if countries decide to trim their public investment rates going forward.

Source: Social Research Digest, Jun. 2013 (Vol. 4, No. 6)

6.4.5   Investing in Women's Employment: Good for Business, Good for Development

Author(s): International Finance Corporation

International Finance Corporation published a report that outlines how investing in women's employment has led to enhanced business performance and productivity for companies in diverse countries and sectors. The report, 'Investing in Women's Employment: Good for Business, Good for Development' presents specific examples of how initiatives tailored to women—such as training, childcare support, health services, and alternative work arrangements—can enhance business performance while improving working conditions for women and men.

<u>Key findings</u>

Investing in women's employment is key to unlocking growth in emerging and developing economies.

- Women workers constitute 40% of the world's workforce, yet in many sectors, such as mining, construction and energy, women represent only a small minority of workers, and in almost all sectors women are less likely than men to be in management positions.
- Women continue to face many barriers to full and productive participation in the labor market, including discrimination and culturally entrenched ideas about gender roles, and their contribution is not always equally valued.
- It makes business sense to support better employment opportunities for women beyond minimum statutory compliance.

- Inclusive recruitment and training policies have helped companies in diverse locations like Anglo American in Chile, Chindex healthcare provider in China, Finlays in Kenya, Mariya in Ukraine, and Odebrecht in Brazil to expand the pool of job candidates at all levels, from entrylevel to the boardroom, and become an "employer of choice".

- Programs that improve work-life balance for parents or health outcomes for women can lead to potentially significant returns.

Source: Social Research Digest, Nov. 2013 (Vol. 4, No. 11)

6.4.6   Global Employment Trends 2014: The Risk of a Jobless Recovery

Author(s): International Labour Organization

International Labour Organization launched a study that offers the latest global and regional information and projections on several indicators of the labour market, including employment, unemployment, working poverty and vulnerable employment. The 'Global Employment Trends 2014: The risk of a jobless recovery' report highlights the role of a strategy that combines short-term measures (job-friendly macroeconomic and labour market policies) with further action to tackle long-standing imbalances.

<u>Key findings</u>

The weak global economic recovery has failed to lead to an improvement in global labour markets, with global unemployment in 2013 reaching almost 202 million.

- Employment growth remains weak, unemployment continues to rise, especially among young people, and large numbers of discouraged potential workers are still outside the labour market.

- On current trends, around 40 million new jobs could be created every year until 2018, which is less than what is required to absorb the growing number of new entrants into the labour market each year.

- The number of unemployed worldwide rose by 5 million in 2013 to over 202 million, a 6% unemployment rate.

- Some 23 million workers have dropped out of the labour market.

- The number of jobseekers is expected to rise by more than 13 million by 2018.

- Some 74.5 million people in the 15 to 24 age group were unemployed in 2013, a 13.1% youth unemployment rate.
- Around 839 million workers lived with their families on less than US$ 2 in 2013.
- Some 375 million workers lived with their families on less than $1.25 a day in 2013.

Source: Social Research Digest, Mar. 2014 (Vol. 5, No. 3)

6.4.7 The Longevity Economy

Author(s): Oxford Economics in cooperation with AARP

Oxford Economics in cooperation with AARP produced a report that combines available data with new economic modeling to show the growing Longevity Economy's contribution to the workforce and unprecedented consumer power. 'The Longevity Economy – Generating economic growth and new opportunities for business' sums all economic activity serving the needs of Americans over 50 and including both the products and services they purchase directly and the further economic activity this spending generate.

Key findings

By any measure, the Longevity Economy is already one of the most significant contributors to overall US economic activity.

- By 2032, it is projected to make up about 52% of US GDP.
- Already, it accounts for roughly two-thirds of employment as well as wages and salaries in the US.
- The economic clout of the over-50 population, in fact, is enormous. As a group, they control almost 80% of US aggregate net worth.
- The average wealth of households headed by people over 50 is nearly $765,000, compared with $225,000 for those headed by 25–to-50-year-olds.
- The Longevity Economy is driving the growth and direction of the health care industry.
- In real terms, its health care consumption is forecast to increase 158% by 2032, to $4.0 trillion, accounting for nearly 79% of the US total.
- This vast expansion is likely to translate into a large increase in the

demand for particular types of services, such as home health services and aging-in-place technology.

- The Longevity Economy also has an outsized impact on technology spending.
- According to Forrester Research, in 2010, people aged 46-64 comprised approximately 25% of the total population, but accounted for over 40% of technology purchases.
- The Longevity Economy is refuting the conventional wisdom that consumers over 50 spend less.
- In fact, they spend more than any other age group, and will increasingly challenge businesses to win their attention.
- People over 50 outspend the average consumer across most categories, and the economic activity they generate affects all sectors of the US economy. They dominate spending in 119 of 123 consumer packaged goods segments

Source: Social Research Digest, Jan. 2014 (Vol. 5, No. 1)

6.4.8 Future of Retirement: Life after work

Author(s): Hongkong and Shanghai Banking Corporation (HSBC)

The Hongkong and Shanghai Banking Corporation (HSBC) published its ninth report in The Future of Retirement series of independent global research studies, that compares the real-life experience of today's retirees with the views and expectations of those still working towards retirement. With the benefit of this hindsight, the report, Future of Retirement: Life after Work explores key retirement issues including transitioning into retirement, ensuring an adequate post-retirement income, leaving a legacy for future generations and achieving later life aspirations. It also includes some practical steps that people can take to help secure a more comfortable retirement.

Key findings

People are not saving enough for their retirement years.

- One in five Britons expect they will never stop working. One in five workers (19%) in the UK expect that they will never be able to afford to retire fully. Brits topped the league table of the countries with the highest proportion (36%) of those who are divorced or separated expecting to work indefinitely – compared to just 20% globally. 31% of those who are widowed had the same expectation – compared to 23% globally.

- Whilst many will be forced to work longer than they had planned, a significant proportion of people around the world looked forward to working in later life. However, while 27% globally said they intended to start a business in retirement, a remarkably smaller 7% of those questioned in UK felt the same, with Brits seemingly lacking the same entrepreneurial spirit. This attitude changed with age, as 37% of UK respondents between 55-64 years of age said it was actually an aspiration to continue working (compared to 44% globally).

- Even those who do eventually retire might not be able to achieve the retirement they want. Half (49%) of retired people surveyed in the UK who said they have been unable to realise their plans for retirement, believed this was because they have less money to live on than they had envisaged.

- People's expectations of a work-free retirement dwindle as they enter old age, with 20% of people between 55-64 years of age saying they expect they will have to continue working indefinitely, compared to just 15% of 25-34 year-olds.

- HSBC's research summarised four actions, which can help today's retirement savers plan a better future for themselves:

- Action 1. Don't rush into retirement. There is a view among retired people that they might have been too hasty in giving up paid employment. Nearly two-thirds (64%) who entered semi-retirement wished that they had stayed in full time employment longer. This regret is largely for positive reasons, with many retired people seeing work as an important means of keeping the body and mind active.

- Action 2. Don't rely on one source of retirement income. Current retirees have three different sources of retirement income on average, wisely choosing not to generate all of their income from one place. Spreading their sources of retirement income and associated risks means that not all their eggs are in one basket.

- Action 3. Plan your retirement with family in mind. Rather than family ties loosening in future, the family will continue to be a major consideration in retirement planning, and may even grow in importance for the next generation. While many people (40%) aspire to travel extensively during their retirement, nearly half (49%) of current workers expect to have some financial responsibilities towards others even when they are themselves retired.

- Action 4. Be realistic about your retirement outgoings. Many working people assume that their income needs will fall once they enter retirement. Yet 52% of people in retirement have seen no reduction in their outgoings, and 17% have seen their outgoings increase. Although people are familiar with the concept of increasing life expectancy, the consequent increase in later life medical and nursing care costs may not be well understood as people are still not doing enough to prepare themselves for these potential costs.

Source: Social Research Digest, May 2014 (Vol. 5, No. 5)

6.4.9   Financial Resilience in Later Life

Author(s): Age UK

Age UK launched a new report that calls for regular financial check-ups for the retired and people approaching pension age, which Age UK deems critical to help the growing number of people aged 60 and over navigate later life. The report, Financial resilience in later life, is the culmination of Age UK's Financial Services Commission, a series of three summits involving industry leaders, Government, consumer advocates and older people.

<u>Key findings</u>

Many older people lack financial resilience. The financial provision for people in later life is poor.

- It's a myth that the entire generation of so-called 'baby boomers' is financially prepared for retirement – up to 20% show very low readiness for ageing, having little or no private pension, housing wealth nor material wealth. All but the most affluent face challenges.
- People aged 85 and over represent the fastest growing segment of the population but are arguably the poorest served by the financial services industry.
- Over the long term there is much to be positive about. Automatic

enrolment is moving more and more people into pensions saving and the new single-tier state pension will provide much needed clarity around which people can save. But these initiatives have no impact on existing pensioners and the majority of those within twenty years of retirement will only be marginally affected.

- And increasing the State Pension Age certainly doesn't benefit people coming up to retirement in the next 15 years who haven't proactively built up enough funds for retirement or who are struggling to stay within the labour market.

- There is more to do to encourage long term savings. The advent of automatic enrolment, together with the abolition of compulsory annuitisation could significantly change the landscape, e.g. with the introduction of pensioner bonds and New Individual Savings Accounts (NISAs) with more generous allowances.

- After 2015, Age UK would welcome a cross-government commissioned review into long-term savings and retirement products, to develop a more coherent policy for annuities, pensions, tax relief, NISAs and other savings products. It would also serve as an opportunity to review the impact of the reforms on industry behaviour and assess whether the reforms protect consumer interests.

- Whilst retirement may follow a 'u-shaped' spending curve, individuals don't tend to plan for it and financial products and services don't necessarily cater for this pattern of spending. Generally, people tend to spend more in the early, more active years of retirement, with spending decreasing in the middle years and then increasing again with additional care and medical expenses. At the very least, everyone retiring should be encouraged to think about how their spending patterns may vary over the course of their retirement, including what they may need to contribute towards the cost of care.

Source: Social Research Digest, Jul. 2014 (Vol. 5, No. 7)

6.5 Technology Development and Access

6.5.1 Global Innovation 1000 Navigating the Digital Future

Author(s): Booz & Co

Booz & Co published the ninth annual study of the world's 1,000 largest publicly listed corporate R&D spenders. 'The Global Innovation 1000 Navigating the Digital Future' focuses on the digital enablers of the innovation process, how the most successful companies are and are not using digital tools and processes to improve speed, decrease cost, enhance quality, reduce complexity, and sharpen insight into customer and market needs to improve their innovation efforts.

Key findings

Yearly R&D spending among the world's 1,000 largest public corporate R&D spenders has hit a record high of US$638 billion.

- Companies are spending 8.1% of their R&D budgets on digital tools to enable their innovation process—either to boost productivity or to improve their ability to gain better insight into customer needs.
- Apple and Google took top honors for the fourth consecutive year. Samsung displaced 3M from the number three spot for the first time, capping its steady rise in the rankings, and Amazon also made a significant move up, jumping six spots into fourth place.
- New to the list this year was Tesla, making its debut in the number nine slot, and Facebook returned at number 10 after a hiatus last year.
- Higher R&D spending is no guarantee of better financial performance. This year's 10 most innovative companies outperformed the top 10 spenders on both five-year revenue and market-cap growth averages.
- R&D spending in 2013 rose by 5.8% from the previous year, signaling a return to the long-term growth trend after two years of faster growth following the recession.
- Ninety percent of R&D spending worldwide in 2013 was from companies headquartered in North America, Europe, and Japan.
- Computers & electronics, healthcare, and automotive remained the three largest industries in terms of total R&D spend in 2013, representing 65% of the global total.

Source: CSR Research Digest, Dec. 2013 (Vol. 5, No. 12)

6.5.2 Leveraging Information and Communication Technology for the Base of the Pyramid

Author(s): Hystra / Ashoka

This study aimed to learn from "what works" in terms of full projects (as opposed to technologies) combining both an economically viable model and socio-economic impacts on their end-users, in the field of ICT for development. The study was sponsored by AFD-Proparco, Ericsson, ICCO, France Telecom-Orange, and TNO and conducted by Hystra and Ashoka from October 2010 to June 2011.

Key findings

This work is based on the screening of existing projects led by various types of actors (social entrepreneurs, NGOs, private companies).

- It encompasses 4 sectors of "development" where ICT has already shown it could play a key role: healthcare, education, agriculture, and financial services.
- 15 of the most ground breaking market-based business models, with a proven scale and results on the ground showing that ICT can be a lever improving the living standards of the BoP, are analysed in depth in the report to support the main conclusions.

Source: Social Research Digest, Oct. 2011 (Vol. 2, No. 6)

6.5.3 IBM Five in Five

Author(s): IBM

IBM has unveiled the sixth annual "IBM Five in Five" – a list of innovations that have the potential to change the way people work, live and play over the next five years. The IBM 5 in 5 is based on market and societal trends as well as emerging technologies from IBM's research labs around the world that can make these transformations possible.

Key findings

The 5 future trends are: People power will come to life, You will never need a password again, Mind reading is no longer science fiction, The digital divide will cease to exist, Junk mail will become priority mail.

- Anything that moves or produces heat has the potential to create energy that can be captured.
- Advances in renewable energy technology will allow individuals to collect this kinetic energy, which now goes to waste, and use it to help power our homes, offices and cities.
- Your biological makeup is the key to your individual identity, and soon, it will become the key to safeguarding it.
- You will no longer need to create, track or remember multiple passwords for various logins.
- From Houdini to Skywalker to X-Men, mind reading has merely been "wishful thinking" for science fiction fans for decades, but their wish may soon come true.
- Scientists in the field of bioinformatics have designed headsets with advanced sensors to read electrical brain activity that can recognize facial expressions, excitement and concentration levels, and thoughts of a person without them physically taking any actions.
- In our global society, growth and wealth of economies are increasingly decided by the level of access to information.
- And in five years, the gap between information haves and have-nots will narrow considerably due to advances in mobile technology.
- In five years, unsolicited advertisements may feel so personalized and relevant it may seem spam is dead.
- At the same time, spam filters will be so precise you'll never be bothered by unwanted sales pitches again.

Source: Social Research Digest, Jan. 2012 (Vol. 3, No. 1)

6.5.4   Socioeconomic Impacts of Wireless Technology

Author(s): BSR

Building on BSR's review of wireless and the environment, this follow-up report explores the opportunities and challenges for society from the use of wireless (licensed spectrum) technology. The report has a particular focus on the areas of health care, finance, education, and community empowerment.

Key findings

Wireless products and services are a powerful agent of social change that provide billions of people around the world with anytime, anywhere access.

- Around the world, there are billions of "underbanked" or "unbanked" people, but thanks to wireless technology, they have access to market information and banking services so they receive a fair price for their goods and services and protect their money.
- From remote monitoring to disease management, wireless technology is helping improve healthcare outcomes and address the healthcare worker shortage.
- In the United States, chronic disease treatment costs more than US$1.4 trillion each year, but using mHealth could mean a savings of more than US$21.1 billion per year.
- By using mobile technology, interactive learning may happen at any time and virtually anywhere.
- Technology-based instruction can reduce the time it takes students to reach learning objectives by 30 to 80%.
- Wireless technology empowers citizens around the world to create and interact with their communities and the world, hold their political leaders accountable, and organize for social, political, and economic change.
- The report also highlights the role that licensed spectrum availability and the world's 6 billion mobile connections have played in encouraging innovators to develop a range of applications.

Source: Social Research Digest, May 2012 (Vol. 3, No. 5)

6.5.5 Information and Communication Technology: An Enabler for Inclusive Business Solutions

Author(s): WBCSD

A WBCSD issue brief looks at the opportunities for information and communication technology (ICT) to facilitate and scale the private sector'scontribution to development. The report displays best practice cases and highlights opportunities for, and barriers to, achieving further scale.

Key findings

ICT-enabled services deliver a wide range of benefits for low-income communities, local businesses, and large companies alike.

- Potential benefits of ICT enabled services include: better, faster and easier access to information, improved interaction and two-way communication, cost efficiency and lower transaction costs, automation and standardization, economic and other opportunities, and improved data visibility or transparency.
- To date, lessons from the implementation of ICT-enabled ventures point to a number of factors that still need to be addressed to further increase the benefits:
  - Infrastructure: ICT cannot replace investment in other types of infrastructure, and in some cases new, innovative ventures are less effective as a consequence of poor infrastructure. For example, ICT can be used to access more accurate price information, but goods cannot be transported to market without a functioning road system.
  - Legislation and public policy: Regulatory frameworks can play a significant role in supporting ICT as a development tool and in fostering innovation, for example by encouraging a competitive telecommunication environment or by incentivizing convergence of services toward a single network. Appropriate license prices and taxation levels are also important factors in fostering investment and rapid spread of ICT networks.
  - Inertia and resistance from traditional models: It is important for other industry sectors to familiarize themselves with examples of business opportunities that can be developed by leveraging technology in emerging markets. At the same time, new technologies and business models often threaten incumbents in the market by providing better value or even making existing solutions redundant. Mobile money services, for instance, compete with traditional financial services offered by the banking sector.
  - User interfaces: If users are not able to use ICT at a level that allows them to benefit, the impact on development will be undermined. Examples of solutions addressing this challenge include voicebased systems and iconic user interfaces.

Source: Social Research Digest, Oct. 2012 (Vol. 3, No. 10)

6.5.6 Disruptive Technologies: Advances that will Transform Life, Business and the Global Economy

Author(s): McKinsey Global Institute

The McKinsey Global Institute (MGI) released a report that assesses the potential disruptive technologies, as well as the potential economic impact and sorption of major rapidly advancing technology areas. The "Disruptive Technolgies: Advances that will transform life, business and the global economy" Report aims to identify 12 technology areas with potential for massive impact on how people live and work, and on industries and economies. Also, the Report attempts to quantify the potential economic impact of each technology across a set of promising applications in 2025.

Key findings

Important technologies can come in any field or emerge from any scientific discipline, but they share four characteristics: high rate of technology change, broad potential scope of impact, large economic value that could be affected, and substantial potential for disruptive economic impact.

- The future seems bright for entrepreneurs and innovators.
- 3D printing, the mobile Internet, cloud technology, and even next-generation genomics could provide the opportunities and the tools to allow small enterprises to compete on a meaningful scale and advance into new markets rapidly.
- There are a set of overarching implications for stakeholders to consider as they plan for the coming decade of economically disruptive technology:
  o Information technology is pervasive
  o Combinations of technologies could multiply impact
  o Consumers could win big, particularly in the long run
  o The nature of work will change, and millions of people will require new skills
  o The future for innovators and entrepreneurs looks bright;
  o Technology impact differs between davanced and developing economies
  o Benefits of technologies may not be evenly distributed
  o The link between hype and potential is not clear

- o Scientific discovery and innovation will surprise us
- o There are some troubling challenges
- The scope of impact of the technologies in this report makes clear that policy makers could benefit from an informed and comprehensive view of how they can help their economies benefit from new technologies.

Source: Social Research Digest, Jul. 2013 (Vol. 4, No. 7)

6.5.7   Measuring Information Society

Author(s): International Telecommunication Union (ITU)

International Telecommunication Union (ITU) published a report that captures the level of ICT developments in 157 economies worldwide and compares progress made during the last year. The "Measuring Information Society 2013" report also presents the first comprehensive mobile-broadband price data set for almost 130 economies and features key ICT data and benchmarking tools to measure the information society, including the ICT Development Index (IDI).

Key findings

250 million additional people came online in 2012.

- Republic of Korea tops ICT ranking for 3rd year in a row
- By end 2013 40% of the world will be online – but 1.1 billion households – or 4.4 billion people – remain unconnected.
- Mobile broadband is now more affordable than fixed broadband.
- Mobile broadband over smartphones and tablets has become the fastest growing segment of the global ICT market.
- Almost the whole world is now within reach of mobile cellular service.
- 30% of the world's young population are 'digital natives'.
- Broadband is getting faster; 2Mbps now most popular basic package.
- Telco operator CAPEX peaked in 2008; despite economic upturn investment levels have not returned.
- By end 2013 there will be 6.8 billion total mobile-cellular subscriptions – almost as many as there are people on the planet.
- An estimated 2.7 billion people will also be connected to the Internet – though speeds and prices vary widely, both across and within regions.

- Mobile broadband connections over 3G and 3G+ networks are growing at an average annual rate of 40%, equating to 2.1 billion mobile-broadband subscriptions and a global penetration rate of almost 30%. Almost 50% of all people worldwide are now covered by a 3G network.

Source: Social Research Digest, Oct. 2013 (Vol. 4, No. 10)

6.5.8 The Global Information Technology Report 2014: Rewards and Risks of Big Data

Author(s): The World Economic Forum in collaboration with McKinsey & Company

The World Economic Forum in collaboration with INSEAD and Johnson Cornell University issued the 13th edition of the Global Information Technology Report, which provides a comprehensive assessment of networked readiness, or how prepared an economy is to apply the benefits of information and communications technologies (ICTs) to promote economic growth and well-being. Using updated methodology that was introduced in 2012, this year's report ranks the progress of 148 economies in leveraging ICTs to increase productivity, economic growth and the number of quality jobs.

<u>Key findings</u>

Information and communication technologies (ICTs) continue to rank high on the list as one of the key sources of new opportunities to foster innovation and boost economic and social prosperity, for both advanced and emerging economies.

- Data have always had strategic value, but with the magnitude of data available today—and our capability to process them—they have become a new form of asset class. In a very real sense, data are now the equivalent of oil or gold.
- This new asset class of big data is commonly described by what we call the "three Vs." Big data is high volume, high velocity, and includes a high variety of sources of information. Next to those traditional three Vs we could add a fourth: value.
- Big data can take the form of structured data such as financial transactions or unstructured data such as photographs or blog posts. It

can be crowd-sourced or obtained from proprietary data sources. Big data has been fuelled by both technological advances (such as the spread of radio-frequency identification, or RFID, chips) and social trends (such as the widespread adoption of social media).

- Big data is changing our lives and changing the way we do business. But succeeding with big data requires more than just data. Data-based value creation requires the identification of patterns from which predictions can be inferred and decisions made.

- Businesses need to decide which data to use. The data each business owns might be as different as the businesses themselves; these data range from log files and GPS data to customer- or machine-to-machine data. Each business will need to select the data source it will use to create value. Moreover, creating this value will require the right way of dissecting and then analyzing those data with the right analytics. It will require knowing how to separate valuable information from hype.

- This world of big data has also become a source of concern. The consequences of big data for issues of privacy and other areas of society are not yet fully understood.

Source: Social Research Digest, Sep. 2014 (Vol. 5, No. 9)

6.5.9   Digital Shopper Relevancy Report

Author(s): CapGemini

CapGemini released its second edition of the global "Digital Shopper Relevancy Report" which surveyed over 18,000 digital shoppers from 18 countries to provide insight into the changing nature of shoppers' online retail habits. The study was focused on on five product categories: food, health and personal care, fashion (clothing, footwear, and accessories), do-it-yourself home improvement (DIY) and electronics to provide a broad picture of the retail market as a whole.

Key findings

- Social media as part of the shopping journey has shown a comparative decline since 2012. Less importance is being placed on following retailers on social media (such as Twitter and Facebook), finding out about new products through blogs, and participating in online retail customer communities.

- Conventional retail store experience, Internet, email, smartphone apps, or the use of technologies in-store are rated significantly higher. Fewer shoppers expect the use of social media will change their shopping in the future.

- Physical store reigns – for now. For point-of-sale, the physical store is still the favoured destination for global shoppers, particularly in mature markets. For transactions, 72% of respondents, in all categories except for electronics, see the store as important or very important, compared to 67% for the Internet.

- High-growth markets show a significantly stronger appetites for digital technologies – smartphone, social media and in-store technology – than all the thirteen mature markets polled, particularly for sourcing product information, price-comparisons and purchasing. They are also more interested in receiving personalized offers and recommendations, compared to low interest in Western Europe.

Source: Social Research Digest, Oct. 2014 (Vol. 5, No. 10)

6.5.10 World Quality Report 2014-15

Author(s): HP, Sogeti, and Capgemini

HP, Sogeti, and Capgemini released the 6th edition of the World Quality Report, the largest global research study and expert commentary on enterprise application quality and testing. The report is based on findings from a global research study conducted via telephone interviews with 1,543 CIOs, IT directors/managers, VP of applications and quality assurance directors/managers across 25 countries.

Key findings

Transformational programs using social, mobile, analytics, cloud and the Internet of things (IoT) change the focus and increase the importance of QA and testing.

- QA and testing budgets continue to increase – to levels not seen previously, in part driven by digital transformation initiatives.

- Many businesses prefer to organize QA and testing functions with a combination of centralized and decentralized approaches.

- Many organizations increasingly engage external service providers in a co-managed approach.

- Non-functional requirements – specifically security and performance – and customer experience testing represent increasingly important focus areas for QA and testing.
- Most organizations require fast and responsive QA and testing solutions that are integrated with agile development methods.
- The adoption of cloud-based solutions for testing is growing.
- Many organizations' maturity in the field of test environment, data management and test automation is increasing.

Source: Social Research Digest, Oct. 2014 (Vol. 5, No. 10)

6.5.11 Digital Transformation Report

Author(s): MIT Sloan Management Review and Capgemini Consulting

To better understand how businesses succeed or fail in using digital technology to improve business performance, MIT Sloan Management Review and Capgemini Consulting conducted a survey in 2013 that garnered responses from 1,559 executives and managers in a wide range of industries. The Digital Transformation Report (as well as the survey) focuses on digital transformation, which are defined as the use of new digital technologies (social media, mobile, analytics or embedded devices) to enable major business improvements (such as enhancing customer experience, streamlining operations or creating new business models).

Key findings

Managers believe in the ability of technology to bring transformative change to business. But they also feel frustrated with how hard it is to get great results from new technology.

- According to 78% of respondents, achieving digital transformation will become critical to their organizations within the next two years.
- However, 63% said the pace of technology change in their organization is too slow.
- The most frequently cited obstacle to digital transformation was "lack of urgency."
- Only 38% of respondents said that digital transformation was a permanent fixture on their CEO's agenda.

- Where CEOs have shared their vision for digital transformation, 93% of employees feel that it is the right thing for the organization. But, a mere 36% of CEOs have shared such a vision.

Source: CSR Research Digest, Jan. 2014 (Vol. 6, No. 1)

6.6   Health and Wellbeing

6.6.1   HIV/AIDS as Business Risk: A South African Case Study

Author(s): J. van Wyk

This article utilizes a political system framework to trace the political sources of business risk stemming from the unfolding HIV/AIDS generalized epidemic in South Africa. The conditions from which business risk emerges, the politicization of the generalized (i.e., widespread) epidemic through boundarycrossing activities, and "inputs" are explored.

Key findings

The transformation of HIV/AIDS from an epidemic to a business threat is underscored by the South African government's tendency to view the issue as part of the public agenda rather than part of its formal agenda.

- Governmental inaction, as well as action, led to an array of risks for firms operating in South Africa (e.g., operations, asset impairment, competitive, franchise).
- Mitigating strategies for managers are discussed, including avoidance, offsetting, transference, sharing, remedy, and anticipation.

Source: Social Research Digest, May 2012 (Vol. 3, No. 5)

6.6.2   Health for the EU in 20 Success Stories: A Selection of Successful Projects Funded by the EU Health Programmes

Author(s): European Commission

The European Commission has recently issued a new publication outlining a series of best projects funded under the second Health Programme. The report provides an overview of 20 successful projects funded by the EU health programmes, programmes developed to support EU member states in their efforts to improve health and lifestyles throughout Europe.

Key findings

Since 2008, the Health Programme has financed projects worth close to 237 million EUR and aims to contribute to support the Europe 2020 strategy by delivering the growth agenda for a smarter, inclusive and more sustainable Europe.

- These projects show, for example, how the Health Programme has helped:
  o to raise awareness on cardiovascular disease and diabetes;
  o to implement cervical cancer screening for women;
  o or to develop the worldwide online source of information on rare diseases – ORPHANET.
- Amongst the series of projects outlined the 'FOOD' ('Fighting Obesity through Offer and Demand') by Edenred aimed to promote a healthy diet at work.
- The aim of the project is two-fold:
  o firstly, it wants to improve the nutritional habits of employees by raising their awareness of health issues and;
  o secondly, by working with restaurants it aims to improve the nutritional quality of the food on offer.

Source: Social Research Digest, Sep. 2012 (Vol. 3, No. 9)

6.6.3   The Role of Business in Health and Wellness

Author(s): U.S Chamber of Commerce Foundation/Business Civic Leadership Center

This report aims to uncover how business interacts with key social and environmental issues. The report highlights what is succeeding in the health sector and shares case studies of business solutions for wellness and prevention, systems innovation, disease management, and market mechanisms.

Key findings

Based on illustrative case studies it can be concluded that business generates excellent ideas and solutions for health and wellness challenges.

- Businesses are motivated to innovate and create products and service to meeting the challenging climate of health and wellness.
- The impact of business on health and wellness innovation is diverse and robust.
- The health sector is embedded with business solutions that have achieved:
  o better disease management;
  o reliable organ transplants;
  o precision in surgery;
  o innovations in prosthetics and other medical equipment;
  o more knowledge and insight into good fitness and nutrition habits.
- There are various illustrative case studies that spotlight business solutions for wellness and prevention, systems innovation, disease management, and market mechanism. Case studies include:
  o A prevention program at Accenture that combines work-life balance, wellness solutions, and health benefits into one portfolio to provide employees a comprehensive menu of health programs.
  o GlaxoSmithKline designing a medicine adherence program to develop an in depth understanding of patient needs.
  o Medtronic's commitment to increasing patient access to appropriate healthcare, which in effect increase availability of its life-enhancing therapies globally to patients who could benefit.
- Based on the aforementioned case studies and others, business develops excellent ideas and solutions to health and wellness challenges.

Source: Social Research Digest, Feb. 2013 (Vol. 4, No. 2)

6.6.4   World Health Statistics 2013

Author(s): The World Health Organization

The World Health Organization Department of Health Statistics and Information Systems of the Health Systems and Innivation Cluster published a report that highlights summaries on topics of reducing the health gaps between the world's most-advantaged and least-advantaged countries, and on current trends in official development assistance (ODA) for health. The "World Health Statistics 2013" Report is has been compiled using publications and databases produced and maintained by WHO technical programmes and regional offices.

Key findings

This report finds that the current trends provide grounds for intensified collective action and the expansion of successful approaches to overcome the challenges posed by multiple crises and large inequalities.

- Between 1990 and 2011, under-five mortality declined by 41% from an estimated rate of 87 to 51 deaths per 1000 live births.
- The proportion of underweight children in developing countries declined from 28% to 17% between 1990 and 2011.
- The total number of neonatal deaths decreased from 4.4 million in 1990 to 3.0 million in 2011.
- In 2011, global measles immunization coverage was 84% among children aged 12-23 months with 64% of WHO Member States reaching at least 90% coverage.
- Between 2000 and 2011, the estimated number of measles deaths decreased by 71% as more countries achieved high levels of immunization coverage.
- The WHO African Region remains the region with the highest maternal mortality ratio.
- In order to reduce maternal deaths, women need access to good-quality reproductive health services.
- In 2010, 63% of women aged 15-49 years who were married or in a consensual union were using some form of contraception.
- The proportion of births by skilled personnelcrucial for reducing perinatal, neonatal and maternal deaths—was above 90% in three of the six WHO regions for the period 2005-2012.
- About half of the world's population is at risk of contracting malaria, and an estimated 219 million cases of malaria led to 660,000 deaths in 2010.
- The 2011 global estimate of 34 million people living with HIV represents an increase on previous years.
- In 2011, an estimated 1.7 million people died from AIDS-related causes worldwide-24% less than 2005.

- Approximately 69% of all those living with HIV are in sub-Saharan Africa with the same region accounting for 70% of all deaths from AIDS-related causes in 2011.
- "Neglected tropical disease" is a term that refers to a group of 17 diseases that affect more than one billion people worldwide.
- Analysis of data from 35 countries in sub- Saharan Africa has shown that over 90% of the richest quintile in urban areas uses improved drinking-water sources compared with just over 60% of the poorest household quintile.
- In rural areas, the situation is even worse with improved sources only available to one third of the poorest households.
- Surveys undertaken from 2007 and 2012 indicated that the average availability of selected generic medicines in the public sector in low-and middle-income countries was only 57%
- It is apparent that despite significant progress made, much will be needed to be done if the health-related MDGs are to be achieved.

Source: Social Research Digest, May 2013 (Vol. 4, No. 5)

6.6.5 2013 Progress Update on the 2012 Sanitation and Water for All High Level Meeting Commitments

Author(s): The Sanitation and Water for All (SWA) Partners

The Sanitation and Water for All (SWA) Partners released a progress report that synthesizes the status of 2012 commitments to address barriers to delivering sustainable water and sanitation services. The "2013 Progress Update on the 2012 Sanitation and Water for All High Level Meeting Commitments" Report relies on information provided by self-reporting by partners.

Key findings

Significant progress has been achieved such as the increased budget allocation, strengthened relationships among key ministries, and better evidence and concrete results; however; additional time, effort and support is still required to carry out structural changes that will improve the effectiveness.

- Although there has been positive progress, additional effort is needed to fulfill commitments by 2014.
- Only 44% of country commitments and 42% of donor commitments are on track to be achieved by April 2014.
- 'Quick-win' budget allocations have been made; however, progress towards stuctural changes in overall financing systems has been slower.
- Longer-term structural changes such as the creation of dedicated budget lines, are reported to be progressing significantly more slowly although 9 countries have reported increased budget allocations.
- Major progress has been made in reducing open defecation however more effort is needed to achieve elimination
- 15 countries reported achieving good progress in tackling open defecation with community-based approaches; however, additional funds and efforts of all partners are still required.
- Although partners have taken mutual accountability seriously; inclusion of multiple stakeholders in the review should be enhanced.
- All of the developing country governments and donors that made commitments at the 2012 SWA High Level Meeting submitted reports; but only two-thirds consulted with development partners and only ten percent included civil society and ministry of finance.
- The SWA and High Level Meeting (HLM) positively influenced progress in sector visibility, financing and sanitation
- Developing countries reported better relationship between sector ministries and finance ministries; sector dialogue is stronger and donors report that there is increased political support and visibility for water, sanitation and hygiene (WASH).

Source: Social Research Digest, Aug. 2013 (Vol. 4, No. 8)

6.6.6 US Oral Health Report

Author(s): Robert Wood Johnson Foundation (RWJF)

The Robert Wood Johnson Foundation (RWJF) released a series of oral health reports examining 25 programs that addressed barriers to preventive oral health services with solutions in non-traditional, community, and mobile settings. The reports point to solutions that are applicable to other oral health programs and address socioeconomic, cultural, and geographic barriers to care; provide care in schools, Head Start sites, and senior centers; and offer preventive oral health care for infants and toddlers.

<u>Key findings</u>

A key to improving the US oral health may rest with innovative programs that already exist.

- Nine of the 25 programs studied work to bridge socioeconomic, cultural, and geographic barriers.
- In response to barriers to care, the nine programs offered the following successful strategies:
  (1) Implement cost-effective strategies to expand services;
  (2) Provide training and technical assistance to increase competence in delivering oral health education and care for children;
  (3) Develop creative service delivery models that address transportation and cultural barriers.
- Five programs provided or arranged transportation to obtain care, and nearly all used strategies such as staff training and childfriendly, culturally welcoming clinics and materials to engage patients, families, and communities in preventive oral health behavior.
- The assessment team examined seven programs providing preventive oral health care to infants and young children in Women, Infants, and Children (WIC), Early Head Start, and primary care settings.
- Four of the programs prioritized integrating oral health into primary care settings, and four pushed integration of oral health within WIC and Early Head Start.
- Most of the programs created an expanded role in community settings for workforce providers from primary care, public health, and childhood development professionals to play an essential role in access to preventive oral health care.

Source: Social Research Digest, Sep. 2013 (Vol. 4, No. 9)

6.6.7 State of Preventive Health

Author(s): Australian Government

The Australian Government released a comprehensive overview of the current health challenges facing Australians in relation to chronic disease. The first ever 'State of Preventive Health' report highlights the substantial leadership and effort that is underway in Australia to reduce the key risk factors for chronic disease, including obesity and physical inactivity, tobacco use and the harmful use of alcohol.

Key findings

In many areas of preventive health practice Australia is a global leader.

- The reduction in road trauma-related mortality with alcohol-related measures, laws and community education; the response to the emergence of the human-immunodeficiency virus (HIV) involving affected and at-risk communities; and, the multi-faceted response to tobacco control which has Australian smoking rates amongst the lowest in the world, are a few key examples.
- The health risk behaviours are being obese or overweight; smoking tobacco; and consuming alcohol at levels harmful to health.
  (1) Australia is one of the most overweight of the developed nations, with overweight and obesity affecting almost two in three adults and around one in four children.
  (2) Tobacco smoking is recognised as one of the largest preventable causes of death and disease in Australia.
  (3) Alcohol is consumed widely in Australia and, as a health issue, harmful levels of consumption are associated with increased risk of chronic disease, including certain forms of cancer, injury and premature death.

Source: Social Research Digest, Nov. 2013 (Vol. 4, No. 11)

6.6.8   World Malaria Report 2013

Author(s): World Health Organization (WHO)

World Health Organization issued a report that summarizes information received from malaria-endemic countries and other sources, and updates the analyses presented in the 2012 report. The World Malaria Report 2013 highlights the progress made towards global malaria targets set for 2015, and describes current challenges for global malaria control and elimination.

Key findings

Global efforts to control and eliminate malaria have saved an estimated 3.3 million lives since 2000, reducing malaria mortality rates by 45% globally and by 49% in Africa.

- An expansion of prevention and control measures has been mirrored by a consistent decline in malaria deaths and illness, despite an increase in the global population at risk of malaria between 2000 and 2012.
- Increased political commitment and expanded funding have helped to reduce incidence of malaria by 29% globally, and by 31% in Africa.
- The large majority of the 3.3 million lives saved between 2000 and 2012 were in the 10 countries with the highest malaria burden, and among children aged less than 5 years – the group most affected by the disease.
- Over the same period, malaria mortality rates in children in Africa were reduced by an estimated 54%.
- In 2012, there were an estimated 207 million cases of malaria (uncertainty interval: 135 – 287 million), which caused approximately 627 000 malaria deaths (uncertainty interval 473 000 – 789 000). An estimated 3.4 billion people continue to be at risk of malaria, mostly in Africa and south-east Asia. Around 80% of malaria cases occur in Africa.
- In sub-Saharan Africa, the proportion of the population with access to an insecticide-treated bed net remained well under 50% in 2013.

Source: Social Research Digest, Dec. 2013 (Vol. 4, No. 12)

6.6.9 Risking your Health: Causes, Consequences and Interventions to Prevent Risky Behaviors

Author(s): World Bank

World Bank released a report that looks at how individual choices that led to five risky behaviors –smoking, using illicit drugs, alcohol abuse, unhealthy diets, and risky sex— are formed. The report, 'Risking your Health: Causes, Consequences and Interventions to Prevent Risky Behaviors', uses empirical evidence to examine what works and what doesn't.

Key findings

Engaging in risky behaviors exerts a significant toll on the individual's productivity in the long run.

- Society also loses as immediate peers of those who engage in risky behaviors also experience declines in their productivity.
- Children are at particular risk, for example if they have to stop schooling due to a sick parent or if development of their cognitive abilities is compromised due to early exposure to harmful substances.
- Costs and spillovers associated with risky behaviors justify public interventions and that certain policy interventions, when done properly, can improve overall welfare.
- Evidence suggests that legislation tends to be effective, especially when enforcement mechanisms are strong.
- Tax policies can be efficient mechanisms to prevent smoking and alcohol consumption. Most of the evidence comes from developed countries, but emerging evidence from developing countries – for example from China and Indonesia for tobacco taxes and from Kenya for alcohol prices – points in the same direction.

Source: Social Research Digest, Jan. 2014 (Vol. 5, No. 1)

6.6.10 Progress on Sanitation and Drinking Water 2013 Update: Joint Monitoring Programme for Water Supply and Sanitation

Author(s): *World Health Organization and UNICEF*

World Health Organization and UNICEF launched a 2013 update of the Joint Monitoring Programme (JMP) for Water Supply and Sanitation, presenting country, regional and global estimates for the year 2011. The 'Progress on sanitation and drinking-water' report covers the following chapters: Global sanitation trends 1990-2011, Trends in open defecation 1990-2011, Global drinking-water trends 1990-2011, Towards a post-2015 development agenda and the JMP method.

Key findings

Drinking-water coverage in 2011 remains at 89% – which is 1% above the MDG drinking-water target. In 2011, 768 million people relied on unimproved drinking-water sources.

- Sanitation coverage in 2011 was 64%. The world remains off track to meet the MDG sanitation target of 75% and if current trends continue, it is set to miss the target by more than half a billion people.
- By the end of 2011, there were 2.5 billion people who still did not use an improved sanitation facility.
- The number of people practising open defecation decreased to a little over 1 billion, but this still represents 15% of the global population.
- Since 2011, the JMP has facilitated broad discussions among more than 200 representatives from the water, sanitation and hygiene (WASH) sector, academia and the human rights and global monitoring communities to formulate new global WASH targets and indicators for consideration under the post-2015 development agenda.
- With less than three years to go, a final push is needed to meet the MDG sanitation target. This requires providing around 1 billion people with access to sanitation – a daunting task that can only be accomplished through the concerted efforts of many partners.
- In March 2013, the Deputy Secretary-General of the United Nations called upon the world to increase global efforts to accelerate progress towards the MDG sanitation target, which is among the targets for which progress has fallen furthest behind. In particular, he called upon governments, civil society, the private sector and UN agencies to pull together and help end the practice of open defecation by the year 2025.

Source: Social Research Digest, Feb. 2014 (Vol. 5, No. 2)

6.6.11 Addressing Diseases of Poverty

Author(s): The Asian Development Bank, the Global Network for Neglected Tropical Diseases at the Sabin Vaccine Institute and the WHO Regional Office for the Western Pacific

The Malaria and other Vectorborne and Parasitic diseases unit of the WHO Regional Office for the Western Pacific developed a publication that presents an overview of the burden of neglected tropical diseases in the

Asia Pacific region and suggests a way forward. 'Addressing Diseases of Poverty – An Initiative to Reduce the Unacceptable Burden of Neglected Tropical Diseases in the Asia Pacific' outlines how, with renewed commitment and investment, the Asia Pacific region can achieve the goals of neglected tropical diseases control and elimination and contribute to poverty reduction and development among its most vulnerable populations.

<u>Key findings</u>

Caused by several different organisms, neglected tropical diseases (NTDs) are present in at least 39 countries and areas in the Asia Pacific, and more than 1 billion people are at risk of infection with at least one of them.

- Some NTDs, such as soil-transmitted helminthiases (intestinal worms) and foodborne trematodiases (liver and lung flukes), can be controlled easily at low cost, while others, such as leprosy, lymphatic filariasis (elephantiasis), schistosomiasis (snail fever), trachoma and yaws can even be eliminated.
- Left untreated, NTD infections can cause blindness, cognitive impairments, limitations in psychomotor development and disfigurement.
- Families suffer as those affected members lose their ability to work and take part in social life. Entire communities bear the economic burden from increased health-care costs and reduced productivity.
- However, proven strategies exist to prevent and treat NTDs. Five of these diseases can be treated properly for less than $0.25 per person through mass distribution of donated medicines to communities at risk; others require diagnosis and treatment delivered through primary health-care services.
- With the support of WHO and donors, the Asia Pacific NTD Initiative signifies a call to action for reducing the disproportionate burden of NTDs in the Asia and Pacific region and therefore contributing to poverty reduction in the region.
- The five-year Asia Pacific NTD Initiative for the control and elimination of NTDs, which highlights successes, priorities and needs, has been costed at $243 million.
- Significant government ownership through budgetary and policy

commitments and donor contributions account for nearly 50% of the total budget.

- The support of pharmaceutical companies and other partners, which donate a substantial proportion of the drugs for these efforts, is key to achieving success.

- These contributions are appreciated as a shining example of public–private partnerships for development. Yet a gap remains in achieving full access, highlighting yet again the regional health inequities.

Source: Social Research Digest, Mar. 2014 (Vol. 5, No. 3)

6.6.12 Responses to NCDs in the Caribbean Community

Author(s): Healthy Caribbean Coalition

Healthy Caribbean Coalition produced a report that seeks to understand and assess the Caribbean response to non-communicable diseases (NCDs), from a civil society perspective. The 'Responses to NCDs in the Caribbean Community' report highlights best practices and identifies areas for further action and provides an evidence-based platform, from which civil society can monitor progress as well as complement regional and national NCD policies and programmes.

Key findings

The NCD response, regionally and nationally, is overall a satisfactory response, led by regional public health institutions (PAHO/WHO, CARPHA), CARICOM Secretariat, National Governments and their Ministries of Health, with the support of the University of the West Indies, and in-country health non-governmental organisations and the recently formed civil society NCD Alliance, the HCC.

- The response may be characterised as being strong on statements of support, agreements and policy positions but less so with respect to implementation, monitoring and evaluation. The Region has played a significant role globally in advancing the response to NCDs.

- Governments of the Region have theoretically accepted the concept of a 'whole of Government' response, but for the most part have not put this into practice and NCDs have not been inserted into national development plans in the majority of CARICOM countries.

- Fledgling multi-sectoral activity has been embraced by quite a few CARICOM countries, led by NCD Commissions in the larger CARICOM countries where these have been established.

- In other CARICOM countries, particularly those with small populations, the multi-sector approach to NCDs has mostly been in the form of NCD meetings. However, in all CARICOM countries Caribbean Wellness Day has contributed to wide stakeholder involvement in the NCD response.

- Civil Society, especially health NGOs, play a major role in the Caribbean especially in provision of services, provision of financial support, outreach and education and consider these to be important advocacy efforts. They are less engaged in advanced advocacy efforts such as in the drafting and enactment of national legislation and policies.

- Almost all CARICOM countries have ratified the Framework Convention on Tobacco Control (FCTC) but few have implemented the provisions of the Treaty, with for example only four of them enacting legislation banning smoking in public places, very few having programmes in place for treatment of tobacco dependency and only very few having enacted legislation against tobacco company sponsorship and advertising of tobacco products.

- There are no national policies against advertising of unhealthy foods to children, none against the harmful use of alcohol and national population salt reduction initiatives in only a single country. Community based physical activity is encouraged and supported, and some countries have put specific policies in place to this end.

- Fairly robust health systems provide services for NCDs in most CARICOM countries, with the majority providing medications for NCDs at highly subsidised cost at point of delivery.

- Some gaps identified in health systems included lack of equipment for management of certain lung conditions, absence of some drugs such as tamoxifen for breast cancer treatment, lack of well-established rehabilitative services, inadequate uptake of guidelines, many of which are outdated, lack of accountability in delivery of health services, and absence of widespread use of the chronic care delivery model.

Source: Social Research Digest, Mar. 2014 (Vol. 5, No. 3)

6.6.13 World Cancer Report 2014

Author(s): The International Agency for Research on Cancer (IARC)

The International Agency for Research on Cancer (IARC) launched a report that provides a professional, multidisciplinary assessment of all aspects of the geographical distribution, biology, etiology, prevention, and control of cancer, predicated on research. World Cancer Report is designed to provide non-specialist health professionals and policy-makers with a balanced understanding of cancer control and to provide established cancer professionals with insights about recent development.

<u>Key findings</u>

Cancer is now the world's biggest killer – with the number of cases set to explode in coming years.

- As a single entity, cancer is the biggest cause of mortality worldwide2 – there were an estimated 8.2 million deaths from cancer in 2012.
- Global cancer incidence over four years increased by 11% to an estimated 14.1 million cases in 2012 – equal to the population of India's largest city (Mumbai).
- Cancer cases worldwide are forecast to rise by 75% and reach close to 25 million over the next two decades.
- The number of deaths due to the disease amongst the world's poor is growing at a faster rate than previously expected. Specifically, by 2025 almost 80% of the increase in the number of all cancer deaths will occur in less developed regions.
- Unlike the developed countries, a large proportion of cancers in developing nations are caused by infections, such as the human papillomavirus (HPV), which accounts for more than 85% of all HPV-related cancer cases.
- Low- and middle-income countries are most at risk of cancer overwhelming their health systems and hindering economic growth, as they have the least resources and infrastructure to cope with the predicted levels of disease escalation.
- Worryingly, according to the World Health Organisation, only 50% of low- and middle-income countries have operational National Cancer Control Plans.

Source: Social Research Digest, Mar. 2014 (Vol. 5, No. 3)

6.6.14 World Health Statistics 2014

Author(s): *World Health Organisation*

World Health Organization released its annual compilation of health-related data for its 194 Member States including a summary of the progress made towards achieving the health-related Millennium Development Goals (MDGs) and associated targets. World Health Statistics 2014 highlights summaries on the ongoing commitment to end preventable maternal deaths; on the need to act now to combat rising levels of childhood obesity; on recent trends in both life expectancy and premature deaths; and on the crucial role of civil registration and vital statistics systems in national and global advancement.

<u>Key findings</u>

People everywhere are living longer.

- Low-income countries have made the greatest progress, with an average increase in life expectancy by 9 years from 1990 to 2012. The top six countries where life expectancy increased the most were Liberia which saw a 20-year increase (from 42 years in 1990 to 62 years in 2012) followed by Ethiopia (from 45 to 64 years), Maldives (58 to 77 years), Cambodia (54 to 72 years), Timor-Leste (50 to 66 years) and Rwanda (48 to 65 years).
- Wherever they live in the world, women live longer than men. The gap between male and female life expectancy is greater in high-income countries where women live around six years longer than men. In low-income countries, the difference is around three years.
- Women in Japan have the longest life expectancy in the world at 87 years, followed by Spain, Switzerland and Singapore. Female life expectancy in all the top 10 countries was 84 years or longer. Life expectancy among men is 80 years or more in nine countries, with the longest male life expectancy in Iceland, Switzerland and Australia.
- The top three causes of years of life lost due to premature death are coronary heart disease, lower respiratory infections (such as pneumonia) and stroke.
- Worldwide, a major shift is occurring in the causes and ages of death. In

22 countries (all in Africa), 70% or more of years of life lost (due to premature deaths) are still caused by infectious diseases and related conditions. Meanwhile, in 47 countries (mostly high-income), noncommunicable diseases and injuries cause more than 90% of years of life lost. More than 100 countries are transitioning rapidly towards a greater proportion of deaths from noncommunicable diseases and injuries.

- Around 44 million (6.7%) of the world's children aged less than five years were overweight or obese in 2012. Ten million of these children were in the WHO African Region where levels of child obesity have increased rapidly.
- Most deaths among under-fives occur among children born prematurely (17.3%); pneumonia is responsible for the second highest number of deaths (15.2%).
- Between 1995 and 2012, 56 million people were successfully treated for tuberculosis and 22 million lives were saved. In 2012, an estimated 450 000 people worldwide developed multi-drug resistant tuberculosis.
- Only one-third of all deaths worldwide are recorded in civil registries along with cause-of-death information

Source: Social Research Digest, Jun. 2014 (Vol. 5, No. 6)

6.6.15 Global Health Care Outlook: Shared Challenges, Shared Opportunities

Deloitte Touche Tohmatsu Limited's (DTTL) released a report that examines the current state of the global health care sector and provides a snapshot of activity in a number of geographic markets. The report, Global health care outlook: Shared challenges, shared opportunities, suggests considerations for stakeholders as they address funding, cost, and other issues while seeking to grow revenue and market share in 2014 and beyond.

Key findings

Rising demand of health care services coupled with technological advances will create new business opportunities for the health care industry.

However, continued pressures on cost, lack of access, and market conditions will present serious industry challenges in 2014.

- Among drivers for growth in the global health care sector are spending increases in emerging markets, expected population growth, increasing consumer wealth, and government programs to expand access to health care.
- Yet stakeholders also face four major issues in 2014:
  1. Aging population and chronic diseases. The shared, long-term trends of an aging population and an increase in people inflicted with chronic diseases are expected to drive demand for health care services in both developed and emerging economies in 2014 and beyond. Aging populations and increasing life expectancies are anticipated to place a huge burden on the health care system in many markets. The treatment cost of chronic diseases is expected to compel a more intense focus on disease education and prevention by governments and health care practitioners while life sciences companies continue to develop innovative new medicines.
  2. Cost and quality. Public and private health care funding systems are economically stressed – across the globe rising health care costs are unaffordable and unsustainable. And higher costs do not necessarily correlate to better results or higher-quality care, even in developed countries.
  3. Access to care. Improving health care access appears to be a major goal of governments around the world, and a centerpiece of many reform efforts. While facilitating increased health care access is an important and worthy endeavor, more people in the system means more demand for services that numerous health care systems are unable to accommodate due to workforce shortages, patient locations, and infrastructure limitations, in addition to cost issues.
  4. Technology. Advances in health technologies and data management are helping facilitate innovation through new diagnostic and treatment options; however, these same advances are likely to increase overall costs, prompting widespread efforts by public and private health care providers and insurers to contain expenditures by restructuring care delivery models and promoting more efficient use of resources. Also, the technology-enabled, transforming health

care system is producing an immense volume of information; how to interpret and use that data will be important. Organizations must also address patient safety, economic, and reputational issues that may arise if they lack appropriate security and privacy controls.

Author(s): Deloitte Touche Tohmatsu Limited's (DTTL)

Source: Social Research Digest, Jul. 2014 (Vol. 5, No. 7)

6.6.16 The Gap Report

Author(s): UNAIDS

UNAIDS launched a first of its kind report that emphasizes the importance of location and population through an in-depth regional analysis of HIV epidemics and through analysis of 12 populations at higher risk of HIV. The Gap report analyses the reasons for the widening gap between people gaining access to HIV prevention, treatment, care and support, and people being left behind.

Key findings

19 million of the 35 million people living with HIV today do not know that they have the virus.

- In sub-Saharan Africa, nearly 90% of people who know their HIV-positive status are on antiretroviral therapy (ART) —ending the AIDS epidemic by 2030 will require smart scale-up to close the gap.
- In 2013, an additional 2.3 million people gained access to the life-saving medicines. This brings the global number of people accessing ART to nearly 13 million by the end of 2013. Based on past scale-up, UNAIDS projects that as of July 2014 as many as 13 950 296 people were accessing ART.
- By ending the epidemic by 2030, the world would avert 18 million new HIV infections and 11.2 million AIDS-related deaths between 2013 and 2030.
- Just 15 countries* account for more than 75% of the 2.1 million new HIV infections that occurred in 2013. In every region of the world the report finds that there are three or four countries that bear the burden of the epidemic. In sub-Saharan Africa, just three countries—Nigeria, South Africa and Uganda—account for 48% of all new HIV infections.

- Entire countries are being left behind—for example, six nations—Central African Republic, Democratic Republic of the Congo, Indonesia, Nigeria, Russian Federation and South Sudan—are facing the triple threat of high HIV burden, low treatment coverage and no or little decline in new HIV infections.
- HIV prevalence is estimated to be 28 times higher among people who inject drugs, 12 times higher among sex workers, 19 times higher among gay men and other men who have sex with men and up to 49 times higher among transgender women than among the rest of the adult population.
- A lack of data on people most affected by HIV, coupled with widespread stigma and discrimination, punitive legal environments, barriers to civil society engagement and lack of investment in tailored programmes are holding back results.
- It confirms that countries that ignore discrimination and condone inequalities will not reach their full potential, and face serious public health and financial consequences of inaction.
- The report emphasizes the need for equal access to quality HIV services as both a human rights and public health imperative.

Source: Social Research Digest, Oct. 2014 (Vol. 5, No. 10)

6.6.17 World Drug Report 2014

Author(s): UNDOC

The United Nations Office of Drugs and Crime (UNODC) published its annual overview of the major developments in drug markets for the various drug categories, ranging from production to trafficking, including development of new routes and modalities, as well as consumption. Chapter one of the World Drug Report 2014 provides a global overview of the latest developments with respect to opiates, cocaine, cannabis and amphetamines (including "ecstasy") and the health impact of drug use and chapter two zeroes in on the control of precursor chemicals used in the manufacture of illicit drugs.

Key findings

Drug use continues to exact a significant toll, with valuable human lives and productive years of many persons being lost.

- An estimated 183,000 (range: 95,000-226,000) drug-related deaths were reported in 2012. That figure corresponds to a mortality rate of 40.0 (range: 20.8-49.3) deaths per million among the population aged 15-64.
- While that estimate is lower than for 2011, the reduction can be ascribed to the lower number of deaths reported in a few countries in Asia.
- Globally, it is estimated that in 2012, between 162 million and 324 million people, corresponding to between 3.5% and 7.0% of the world population aged 15-64, had used an illicit drug — mainly a substance belonging to the cannabis, opioid, cocaine or amphetamine-type stimulants group — at least once in the previous year.
- The extent of problem drug use - by regular drug users and those with drug use disorders or dependence - remains stable at between 16 million and 39 million people.
- However, there continues to be a gap in service provision, as in recent years, only one in six problem drug users globally have had access to or received drug dependence treatment services each year.
- Although the general public may perceive cannabis to be the least harmful illicit drug, there has been a noticeable increase in the number of persons seeking treatment for cannabis use disorders over the past decade, particularly in the Americas, Oceania and Europe.
- Nonetheless, opiates remained the most prevalent primary drug of abuse among those seeking treatment in Asia and in Europe, as did cocaine in the Americas.

Source: Social Research Digest, Dec. 2014 (Vol. 5, No. 12)

6.6.18 Economics of Non-Communicable Diseases in India

Author(s): World Economic Forum and the Harvard School of Public Health

The World Economic Forum and the Harvard School of Public Health developed a report that provides new data on the costs of NCDs in India, the views of business leaders on the impact of NCDs and estimations of the ROI of specific India-based interventions. The "Economics of Non-Communicable Diseases in India" report aims to reorient dialogue about investing in healthy living and NCD prevention in India, with the view that a healthy population is an important factor for sustainable growth.

<u>Key findings</u>

India stands to lose a whopping USD 4.58 trillion to non-communicable diseases and mental disorders between 2012 and 2030.

- Non-communicable diseases (NCDs) such as cardiovascular diseases (CVDs), chronic respiratory diseases, diabetes and cancer are a major threat to human health, economic growth and national development.
- Of this amount, CVDs (USD 2.17 trillion) and mental health conditions (USD 1.03 trillion) will account for the majority of the economic loss.
- Interventions such as screening (in the case of hypertension); vaccination (in the case of human papillomavirus); reduced tobacco use (in the case of public policy prevention and mobilising youth) and stepped care intervention (in the case of depressive and anxiety disorders) can reverse this trend with a return on investment of at least 15%.
- The most prevalent NCDs in the country are cardiovascular disease (cause of 26% of deaths in India, 2014), chronic respiratory disease (13%), cancer (7%) and diabetes (2%).

Source: Social Research Digest, Dec. 2014 (Vol. 5, No. 12)

6.8   Crime and Incarceration

6.8.1   Ten Economic Facts about Crime and Incarceration in the United States

Author(s): The Hamilton Project

The Hamilton Project released a policy memo that provides ten economic facts highlighting recent trends in crime and incarceration in the United States. Specifically, it explores the characteristics of criminal offenders and victims; the historically unprecedented level of incarceration in the United States; and evidence on both the fiscal and social implications of current policy on taxpayers and those imprisoned.

Key findings

The incarceration rate in the United States is now at a historically unprecedented level and is far above the typical rate in other developed countries. As a result, imprisonment has become an inevitable reality for subsets of the American population.

- Low-income individuals are more likely than higher-income individuals to be victims of crime.
- The majority of criminal offenders are younger than age thirty.
- Disadvantaged youths engage in riskier criminal behavior.
- Crime rates in the United States have been on a steady decline since the 1990s. Despite this improvement, particular demographic groups still exhibit high rates of criminal activity while others remain especially likely to be victims of crime.
  - Federal and state policies have driven up the incarceration rate over the past thirty years.
  - The U.S. incarceration rate is more than six times that of the typical OECD nation.
  - There is nearly a 70% chance that an African American man without a high school diploma will be imprisoned by his mid-thirties.
- Today's high rate of incarceration is considerably costly to American taxpayers, with state governments bearing the bulk of the fiscal burden. In addition to these budgetary costs, current incarceration policy generates economic and social costs for both those imprisoned and their families.
  - Per capita expenditures on corrections more than tripled over the past thirty years.
  - By their fourteenth birthday, African American children whose fathers do not have a high school diploma are more likely than not to see their fathers incarcerated.
  - Juvenile incarceration can have lasting impacts on a young person's future.

Source: Social Research Digest, Aug. 2014 (Vol. 5, No. 8)

6.8.2   The Treatment of Persons with Mental Illness in Prisons and Jails

Author(s): The Treatment Advocacy Center

The Treatment Advocacy Center released a report that condemns the widespread "criminalization of mental illness" in the United States, and the existence of "new asylums" within the prison system. The report, titled "The Treatment of Persons with Mental Illness in Prisons and Jails," surveyed professional staff members at correctional facilities and hospitals throughout the country.

Key findings

There are now 10 times as many individuals with severe and persistent mental disorders in state and county prisons than in state psychiatric institutions. The ratio may be even larger than 10 to 1, since mentally ill inmates in federal prisons were excluded from the report, as were those in private prisons utilized by states such as Alaska and Hawaii.

- In 2012, prisons and jails housed 365,000 people suffering from chronic psychotic disorders such as schizophrenia and bipolar disorder, while the number of such patients at state medical facilities was just 35,000. Forty-four states and the District of Columbia have a prison or jail that holds more individuals with serious mental illness than the largest psychiatric hospital in the area. In several states, such as Illinois and Iowa, a number of county jails hold more mentally ill patients than all of the psychiatric hospitals in the state combined.
- The report also describes a trend in which both the number of inmates with mental disorders and the severity of the disorders themselves have steadily increased over the last 40 years, while prison administrators and guards lack the resources, training, or legal basis to provide such prisoners with adequate treatment.
- Officials and health care workers in prisons are often legally barred from treating mentally ill inmates with psychiatric medications or sedatives. The District of Columbia and 18 states require either a formal judicial review or transfer to a state psychiatric hospital in order to involuntarily administer medication. Many county jails have involuntary commitment guidelines requiring transfer to a state

hospital as well.

- However, because state hospitals are scarce and overcrowded, these laws usually render such methods of treatment impossible. Solitary confinement and the use of restraining devices are therefore used as common alternatives.

- Lack of treatment and the hostile nature of the criminal justice system itself usually combine to worsen the prisoners' disorders, with most prisoners being in poorer psychological health when they leave than when they first entered. In some cases, prisoners denied proper treatment act out violently, or even commit suicide.

- The Treatment Advocacy Center report attributes such events to the historical effects of deinstitutionalization, a nationwide process of systematically closing state psychiatric hospitals. In its list of recommendations, the organization calls for various legal measures to reverse this trend and remove restrictions surrounding involuntary commitment of the mentally ill.

- The deinstitutionalization movement arose in the 1960s during the Kennedy administration as the combined effect of the efforts of patients' rights activists, profiteering by the pharmaceutical industry, and state officials seeking to shift mental health care costs to the federal government.

Source: Social Research Digest, Jun. 2014 (Vol. 5, No. 6)

6.9   Wealth and Income Creation

6.9.1   Global Economic Prospects 2013

Author(s): The World Bank

The Prospects Group in the Development Economics Vice Presidency of the World Bank released a report that examines trends for the Global economy and how they affect developing countries. The "The Global Economic Prospects: 2013 " Report includes three-year forecast for the global economy, topical annexes, which cover industrial production, inflation, financial markets, trade, exchange rates and commodity markets.

Key findings

For high-income countries, fiscal consolidation, high unemployment and still weak consumer and business confidence will continue to inhibit growth in 2013, while growth in the developing world will be solid but weaker than during the pre-crisis boom period

- Global GDP is expected to expand about 2.2% in 2013 and strengthen to 3.0% and 3.3% in 2014 and 2015.
- For high-income countries, growth this year will be a modest 1.2%, firming to 2.0% in 2014 and 2.3% by 2015.
- Developing economies have almost recovered completely recovered from the 2008 crisis and less volatile external conditions are expected to yield a gradual acceleration of activity in developing regions.
- Developing-country GDP is now projected to be around 5.1% in 2013, strengthening to 5.6% and 5.7% in 2014 and 2015, respectively.
- In China also, growth has slowed as authorities seek to rebalance the economy.
- East Asia is expected to grow by 7.3% in 2013.
- Developing Europe and Central Asia by 2.8%; Latin America by 3.3%; Middle East & North Africa (MENA) by 2.5%; South Asia by 5.2% and Sub-Saharan Africa by 4.9%.
- Several fast growing economies in East Asia, Sub-Saharan Africa and a few in Latin America, are at risk of overheating. Therefore, tighter macroeconomic policy stances are warranted to reduce vulnerabilities in these economies.
- Developing countries face new risks:
  o The potential effects of the radical relaxation of both fiscal and monetary policy in Japan.
  o A faster than expected decline in commodity prices
  o Domestic challenges, including inflationary pressures and asset price bubbles, and weaker than pre-crisis growth rates.
  o The challenges of the withdrawal of quantitative easing in the United States
  o To achieve higher growth on a sustained basis, all developing countries will need to redouble efforts to restore and preserve macroeconomic stability, improve governance, simplify regulations,

opening up to trade and foreign investment and investing in infrastructure and human capital.

Source: Social Research Digest, Jul. 2013 (Vol. 4, No. 7)

6.9.2   World Bank Remittance Flows: 2013-2016 Outlook

Author(s): World Bank

World Bank issued revised estimates and forecasts of the remittances to the developing world. The estimates reflect recent changes to The World Bank Group's country classifications, with several large remittance recipient countries, such as Russia, Latvia, Lithuania and Uruguay no longer considered developing countries and, in addition, the data on remittances also reflects the International Monetary Fund's changes to the definition of remittances that now exclude some capital transfers, affecting numbers for a few large developing countries like Brazil.

Key findings

Remittances to the developing world are expected to grow by 6.3% this year to $414 billion and are projected to cross the half-trillion mark by 2016.

- India and China alone will represent nearly a third of total remittances to the developing world this year. Remittance volumes to developing countries, as a whole, are projected to continue growing strongly over the medium term, averaging an annual growth rate of 9% to reach $540 billion in 2016.
- Global remittances, including those to highincome countries, are estimated to touch $550 billion this year, and reach a record $707 billion by 2016.
- The top recipients of officially recorded remittances for 2013 are India (with an estimated $71 billion), China ($60 billion), the Philippines ($26 billion), Mexico ($22 billion), Nigeria ($21 billion), and Egypt ($20 billion). Other large recipients include Pakistan, Bangladesh, Vietnam, and Ukraine.
- As a percentage of GDP, the top recipients of remittances, in 2012, were Tajikistan (48%), Kyrgyz Republic (31%), Lesotho and Nepal (25% each), and Moldova (24%).

- Growth of remittances has been robust in all regions of the world, except for Latin America and the Caribbean, where growth decelerated due to economic weakness in the United States.

Source: Social Research Digest, Oct. 2013 (Vol. 4, No. 10)

6.9.3 How Banks are Supporting Local Economies Facing the Current Financial Crisis?

Author(s): L. Condosta

This paper aims to understand how Italian banks are supporting the context in facing the current financial crisis through CSR strategies. This paper presents shows example of how banks can integrate societal need in their daily business, improving the context and by that improving also their reputation.

Key findings

The current financial crisis offers to banks the possibility to rethink to their societal role and move from a compliance approach to CSR to a more strategic one.

- Banks are working in the CSR field, not only with a compliance approach, but trying to support also local economies where they operate.
- This answers to the societal function they have, but allow them to get also a wider social acceptance and stimulate the context in area which are no more supported by local authorities (i.e. renewables energies, students, etc.).
- To work properly, banks should identify effective partners (NGO, local representatives) able to help them in integrating in ordinary model of access to credit other variables to define the credit risk of a beneficiary.
- The great opportunity banks can take from the crisis is to enlarge their presence in local economies, and supporting them, gain a better reputation that will be of great value when the crisis will be gone.
- Customers involved in microcredit programs today, can become ordinary customers tomorrow and for sure will be very proud to continue working with the bank who supported them in crisis time.

Source: Social Research Digest, Aug. 2012 (Vol. 3, No. 8)

6.9.4 Willful Blindness: How the World Bank's Doing Business Rankings Impoverish Smallholder Farmers

Author(s): The Oakland Institute and /The Rules

The Oakland Institute, an independent policy think tank, and /The Rules, global network of organizers and activists, issued a report that raises questions about the harmful effects on smallholders and traditional farmers by the World Bank's country ranking system, which is claimed to lead to corporate land grabs, which further impoverishes the poor. The report, Willful Blindness: How the World Bank's Doing Business Rankings Impoverish Smallholder Farmers, is a product of a campaign, Our Land Our Business, aiming to hold the World Bank accountable for its role in the rampant theft of land and resources from some of the world's poorest people–farmers, pastoralists, and indigenous communities, many of whom are essential food producers for the entire planet.

Key findings

180 organizations, including NGOs, unions, and farmer and consumer groups from over 80 countries, demand that the World Bank end its Doing Business rankings and its support of the rampant theft of land and resources from some of the world's poorest people — farmers, pastoralists, and indigenous communities, many of whom are essential food producers for the entire planet

- The Bank's "Doing Business" rankings, which score countries according to how Washington officials perceive the "ease of doing business" there, have caused many developing-country leaders to deregulate their economies in hopes of attracting foreign investment. But what the Bank considers beneficial for foreign business is very often the exact opposite for the local communities.
- In the agricultural sector, the rankings encourage governments to commoditize their land — and to sell or lease it to foreign investors, regardless of environmental or social impact. Smallholder farmers, pastoralists, and the indigenous peoples are casualties of this approach, as governments and foreign corporations work hand-in-hand to dispossess them of their land — and gain World Bank's approval in the process.

- The results have been devastating. Thanks to reforms and policies guided by the Bank, 20% of the arable land in Sierra Leone taken from rural populations has been leased to foreign sugar cane and palm oil producers. In Liberia, British, Malaysian, and Indonesian palm-oil giants have secured long-term leases for over 1.5 million acres of land formerly held by local communities. In the Philippines, world's third most popular destination for foreign investment in land, 5.2 million hectares have been acquired by corporations since 2006.

- The land-grab problem is about to get worse. Under pressure from the G8 and with funding from the Gates Foundation, the Bank is doubling down on its fetish for rankings by introducing a new program called "Benchmarking the Business of Agriculture" (BBA). The BBA's explicit goal is to promote "the emergence of a stronger commercial agriculture sector."

- The Bank's 1980s structural adjustments programs (SAPs), impoverished millions in developing countries after imposing the withdrawal of state intervention and sweeping liberalization of economies as conditions to receive loans. The SAPs came under heavy attack from all quarters of civil society until they were officially withdrawn in 2002.

Source: Social Research Digest, Jun. 2014 (Vol. 5, No. 6)

6.9.5 World Payments Report 2014

Author(s): CapGemini and Royal Bank of Scotland (RBS)

CapGemini and Royal Bank of Scotland released their tenth edition of World Payments Report that tracks the state and evolution of the global non-cash payments market. WPR 2014 examines the need for traditional payments processors to transform their payments processing operations.

Key findings

Overall, more than 50% of global non-cash payment growth comes from developing countries despite them only making up one quarter (25.5%) of the market size at 93 billion transactions.

- China remains a relatively underdeveloped market for non-cash transactions but its population and growth rate suggest in certain conditions that it could soon outstrip the US and Eurozone within the next five years. Currently, one in five people in the world that are using mobile banking, lives in China.

- Alongside China, growth rates for Central Europe, Middle East & Africa (CEMEA) followed closely at 23.8%, emerging Asia at 22.8%, and Latin America at 11.0%.

- Despite high growth in developing markets, the U.S. and the Eurozone are still ahead in the number of non-cash transactions made per inhabitant. Finland, with 448 transactions per person per annum, continues to be a clear leader and recorded growth of 10.6% during 2012, outstripping other nations in Europe and North America. The U.S. has the second highest number of non-cash transactions per inhabitant, at 376, but grew by only 2.6% for 2012.

- Increased use of tablets and smartphones is creating a convergence of e- and m- payments, posing new challenges for Payments Services Providers (PSPs). In 2015, m-payments are projected to grow at 60.8% while e-payments growth is forecast to decelerate to 15.9% annually over the next year, as more people use mobile devices to make payments. This trend is adding to the pressure on PSPs to modernize their payments processing infrastructures to support the wide-range of customer-facing innovations.

- The growth of the industry coupled with the fast pace of new regulation requires flexibility from PSPs to adapt. More than 50% of new Key Regulatory and Industry Initiatives (KRIIs) are focusing on innovation and some of which also play a significant role to reduce risk, improve transparency and competition and facilitate standardization. As these new KRIIs are created, there is a tendency for them to cascade across the globe spreading regulatory initiatives across regions. Initiatives such as real-time payments, pressure on card interchange fees and improved payments governance are examples of cascading regulation.

Source: Social Research Digest, Nov. 2014 (Vol. 5, No. 11)

6.10   Prosperity and Happiness

6.10.1   World Happiness Report

Author(s): John Helliwell, Richard Layard and Jeffrey Sachs

A group of independent experts wrote a report that assembles the available international happiness data on how people rate both their emotions and their lives as a whole. The 'World Happiness Report' provides guidance for policy makers on how to effectively incorporate wellbeing into their decision making processes.

<u>Key findings</u>

The countries with the highest levels of happiness are as follows: 1. Denmark, 2. Norway, 3. Switzerland, 4. Netherlands, 5. Sweden.

- On a scale running from 0 to 10, people in over 150 countries, surveyed by Gallup over the period 2010-12, reveal a population-weighted average score of 5.1 (out of 10).
- Six key variables explain three-quarters of the variation in annual national average scores over time and among countries.
- These six factors include: real GDP per capita, healthy life expectancy, having someone to count on, perceived freedom to make life choices, freedom from corruption, and generosity.
- There is some evidence of global convergence of happiness levels, with happiness gains more common in Sub-Saharan Africa and Latin America, and losses more common among the industrial countries.
- For the 130 countries with data available, happiness (as measured by people's own evaluations of their lives) significantly improved in 60 countries and worsened in 41.

Source: Social Research Digest, Nov. 2013 (Vol. 4, No. 11)

6.10.2   Legatum Prosperity Index

Author(s): Legatum Institute

Legatum Institute published their assessment of global wealth and wellbeing, which benchmarks 142 countries around the world in eight distinct categories: Economy; Education; Entrepreneurship & Opportunity;

Governance; Health; Personal Freedom; Safety & Security; and Social Capital. The Legatum Prosperity Index offers a unique insight into how prosperity is forming and changing across the world.

Key findings

US drops out of top 20 in the Economy sub-index.

- Latin America and the Caribbean rise above the world average in the Economy sub-index for the first time in 2013.
- Bangladesh overtakes India in overall Prosperity.
- Norway tops the Index for the fifth consecutive year.
- Botswana is the highest ranking Sub-Saharan country for the fifth consecutive year.
- Since 2009 Global prosperity is increasing, and this year for the first time, all sub-indices are higher than they were five years ago.
- All the sub-regions, except for Northern Europe, are also more prosperous than they were in 2009. The sub-region that has improved the most is Central Asia, followed by sub-Saharan Africa.
- Despite prosperity increasing across the globe, Europe remains below its peak on the Economy sub-index; not yet fully recovering from the financial crisis and ensuing recession. As a result many European countries have dropped out of the top 20 of the Economy sub-index, including France (22nd), Denmark (23rd), Belgium (25th), Finland (26th), and Ireland (33rd). They have been replaced by rapidly growing Asian economies, including China (7th), Thailand (12th), Taiwan (16th) and South Korea (19th)

Source: Social Research Digest, Apr. 2014 (Vol. 5, No. 4)

6.10.3 Hunger Report 2014: Ending Hunger in America

Author(s): Bread for the World Institute

Bread for the World Institute released a report that proposes bold steps to end hunger in the United States by 2030. Hunger Report 2014: Ending Hunger in America calls on the U.S. government to work with the international community to establish a universal set of goals to succeed the Millennium Development Goals (MDGs), which expire in December 2015.

Key findings

Reducing funding for food stamps by $39 billion, as the House of Representatives is pushing to do, would increase hunger for six million Americans.

- Ending hunger in the the United States can be achieved by improving job quality, strengthening the safety net, and investing in human capital development.

- In order to make economic mobility a real possibility for children born to low-income families, human capital development needs to start with early education and go all the way through college.

- To end hunger altogether, social issues, such as racism and other forms of discrimination that drive too many people to the margins of society must be tackled.

- Social exclusion is a problem in countries around the world as well as in the United States. Per capita incomes are on the rise in many nations, but not everyone is sharing the gains—particularly people at the very bottom, a group sometimes referred to as the ultra-poor. The USA has its own group of ultra-poor people, including more than a million households with children and with incomes below $2 a person a day.

- Ending hunger in the United States will require leadership not only at the federal level but also at the state and local levels. There are countless examples of locally-led initiatives that are achieving great success in their communities. At their core, these initiatives are formed around the belief that to end hunger in a community, a broad range of stakeholders must unite behind a common vision and strategy. Partnerships at the local level, and between local initiatives and state and federal government, build that ownership. Local partners do more than feed people; they feed information to leaders in government, and they make informed suggestions as to how partners can work together to fight hunger more effectively.

- Setting a national goal to end hunger would place independent local efforts within a wider framework. Connecting the many community-led anti-hunger efforts will enable them to develop a broadly shared narrative—the story of ending hunger in America

Source: Social Research Digest, May 2014 (Vol. 5, No. 5)

6.10.4 The Hope Index

Author(s):The GlobeScan Foundation

The GlobeScan Foundation launched the first index that reflects the degree of hope that people have for their future. The Hope Index is based on perspectives from 12,000 citizens across the United States, the United Kingdom, Mexico, Pakistan, Nigeria, Russia, Poland, Panama, India, Turkey, Kenya and Indonesia.

Key findings

A majority of citizens (59%) in a 12-country public opinion poll believe "the social, environmental and economic challenges the world faces today are more difficult than the ones we have faced in human history.

- Only one in four (25%) believe our challenges are less difficult.
- In spite of this, a similar majority (63%) believe that "humanity will find a way to overcome our current challenges."
- However, almost a third of citizens (31%) think it is "very or somewhat unlikely" that we will be successful.
- One in two (53%) disagree that "the world is going in the right direction."
- A similar one in two (52%) disagree that their "country is going in the right direction."
- Majorities believe that global conflict is getting worse (60%), along with the world economy (52% worse) and the global environment (51%).
- Citizen opinion is split on whether personal freedoms are getting better (42%) or worse (43%) in the world.

Source: Social Research Digest, Dec. 2014 (Vol. 5, No. 12)

List of Organisations

3BL Associates
AARP
AASHE
Accenture
Acona
Acre Resources
Adaptation Fund NGO Network
Adessy Associates
Advocates for International
Development
Age UK
Allen & York
Alliance for Inclusive Business
Alliance for the Control of
Tobacco Use
Amnesty International
Angus Reid Public Opinion
Ashoka
Asian Development Bank
Asian Development Bank (ADB)
Aspen Institute
AT Kearney
Australian Government
Aviva
Bain & Co.
Banking on Change (a
partnership between Plan UK,
CARE International UK and
Barclays)
BBMG
Bertelsmann Stiftung
(Foundation)
Booz & Co

BoP Innovation Center
Boston College Center for
Corporate Responsibility
Boston Consulting Group
BRANDfog
Brandlogic
Bread for the World Institute
Brookings Africa Growth
Initiative (AGI)
BSR
Buck Consultants
Business & Human Rights
Resource Centre
Business Action for Africa
Business Call to Action
Business Civic Leadership Center
Business For Social
Responsibility
Business in the Community
C&E
Campaign for Tobacco-Free Kids
Capgemini Consulting
Carbon Trust
CBI
Center for Australian Ethical
Research
Center for Resource Solutions
Center for Science and
Democracy at the Union of
Concerned Scientists (UCS)
Center for Universal Education at
the Brookings Institution

Chronic Poverty Advisory
Network (CPAN)
City Food Lecture
Climate Counts
Cohn & Wolfe
Committee Encouraging
Corporate Philanthropy
CompassPoint
Cone Communications
Consumer Electronics Association
Cornucopia Institute
Corporate Accountability
International
Corporate Accountability
International
Corporate Citizenship
Corporate Responsibility
Magazine
Corporate Responsibility Officers
Association (CROA)
CRD Analytics
Crowdfund Capital Advisors
(CCA)
CSR Asia
CSR Europe
CSR Europe and Econsense
Datamonitor
Deloitte
Deloitte Touche Tohmatsu
Limited's (DTTL)
Docebo
Echo Research
Ecole Polytechnique de Lausanne
Economist Intelligence Unit
Edelman
Education for All Global
Monitoring Report

EIRIS
EnviroMedia
Environmental Analyst
ESCWA (Economic and Social
Commission for Western Asia)
Esty Environmental Partners
Ethical Corporation
Ethical Performance
Eurobarometer
EuroCharity
European Commissionon
European Union Agency for
Fundamental Rights
Fair Trade Foundation (DTTL)
Fenton
First Peoples Worldwide
Flag and Ethical Performance
Food Standards Agency
Forbes
Forum for the Future
FRA
Framework Convention Alliance
FSG Social Impact Advisors
Futerra Sustainability
Communications
Generate Insight
George Mason University Center
on Climate Change
Communication
GfK
GfK Roper Consulting
Gibbs & Soell
Global Compact
Global Humanitarian Assistance
Global Impact
Global Network for Neglected

Tropical Diseases at the Sabin
Vaccine Institute
Global Witness
GlobeScan
GlobeScan
Grail Research
Green Research
GreenBiz
Grocery Manufacturers
Association
Harris Interactive
Harvard Food Law & Policy Clinic
Harvard School of Public Health
Havas Media Group
Headstream
Healthy Caribbean Coalition
Hongkong and Shanghai Banking
Corporation (HSBC)
HP
Human Rights Campaign
Foundation
Human Rights in Latin America
Hystra
IBE
IBM
ICCR
IFC
Indiana University
infoDev
Institute for Global Labour and
Human Rights
Institute for Public Policy
Research (IPPR)
Institute of Business Ethics
Institute of Development Studies
Institute of Fiscal Studies
InterAmerican Heart Foundation

Interbrand
Interchurch Organisation for
Development Cooperation (ICCO)
International Centre for
Corporate Social Responsibility
International Federation for
Human Rights
International Finance
Corporation
International Institute for
Management Development
International Labor Rights Forum
International Labour
Organisation (ILO)
International Monetary Fund
International Telecommunication
Union (ITU)
International Textile Garment
InterOrganization Network
ISSP
J.D. Power and Associates
Japan For Sustainability
Justmeans
Kav LaOved
KMPG International
Labour Behind the Label
Landor Associates
LBG
League of Arab States
Leather Workers' Federation
Legatum Institute
Lipscomb University
Luxury Institute
ManpowerGroup
Maplecroft
McKinsey & Company
McKinsey Global Institute

McKinsey Quarterly
Media Alliance
Mercer
Miller Zell
Minority Rights Group
International (MRG)
MIT Sloan Management Review
Mitch Baranowski
Monitor Group
National Environmental
Education Foundation
National Geographic
Natural Marketing Institute
Net Impact
Network for Business
Sustainability
Network for Good
Norwegian Agency for
Development Cooperation
OECD
Ogilvy & Mather
ORC Guideline
Overseas Development Institute
(ODI)
Oxfam
Oxfam International
Oxford Economics
Penn Schoen Berland
Play Fair
Poverty-Environment
Partnership
PR News
Publish What You Fund (The
Global Campaign for Aid
Transparency)
PwC

Regeneration Roadmap, BBMG,
GlobeScan and SustainAbility
Resource Innovation Group's
Social Capital Project
Restaurant Opportunities Center
(ROC) United
Reuters
Robert Wood Johnson
Foundation (RWJF)
Royal Bank of Scotland (RBS)
RT Strategies
Saatchi & Saatchi
Sainsbury's
Seyfarth
Sheffield University
Sigmund Wagner-Tsukamoto
SJF Institute
Small Planet Fund
Social Accountability
International (SAI)
Social Enterprise UK
Sogeti
Southeast Asia Tobacco Control
Alliance
St. Paul's Institute
Standard Chartered
Strandberg Consulting
SustainAbility
Sustainable Plant
Swiss State Secretariat for
Economic Affairs
Tellus Institute and Sustainalytics
texSture
The Co-operative Group
The Coalition for the Homeless
The Conference Board
The Consumer Goods Forum

The Global Coalition to Protect Education from Attack
The GlobeScan Foundation
The Hamilton Project
The Hartman Group
The International Agency for Research on Cancer (IARC)
The International Trade Union Confederation
The McKinsey Centre for Government
The MDG Gap Task Force
The Natural Resources Defence Council (NRDC)
The Nielsen Company
The Norwegian Refugee Council's Internal Displacement Monitoring Centre
The Oakland Institute
The OSCE Office for Democratic Institutions and Human Rights (ODIHR)
The Regeneration Project
The Rules
The Sanitation and Water for All (SWA) Partners
The Shared Value Initiative and FSG
The Treatment Advocacy Center
The United Nations Human Rights
The US Institute of Peace
The Women's World Banking
The World Bank
The World Economic Forum
The World Health Organization

The Yale Project on Climate Change Communication
Tobacco Control Alliance
Turkish Philanthropy Funds
Two Tomorrows
U.S Chamber of Commerce Foundation
U.S. State Department
UN Human Rights Council
UN Volunteers
UN Women and V.V Giri Labour Institute
UNAIDS
Underwriters Laboratories
UNDOC
UNDP (United Nations Development Programme)
UNESCO
UNICEF
Unilever
United Nations Development Programme
United Nations Educational, Scientific and Cultural Organization (UNESCO)
United States Citizenship and Immigration Services (USCIS)
University of British Columbia
University of Michigan's Ross School of Business
Verdantix
Verite
Verité Works
Waggener Edstrom
Walden University
WBCSD
Weinreb Group

WHO Regional Office for the
Western Pacific
Work Group on Mining
World Bank Institute
World Business Council for
Sustainable Development
World Economic Forum (WEF)
World Federation of Advertisers
(WFA)
World Health Organisation
Yahoo
Yale University

List of Authors

A. Argandoña

A. Calabrò

A. Crane

A. D. Boss

A. Douglas

A. J. S. Stanaland

A. Muller

A. Ralston

A. Shome

A. Tencati

A.E. Dembe

Amanda Lenhardt

Andrew Shepherd

Asma Zubairi

B. B. Dunford

B. Doherty

B. Lowry

B. Ramasamay

B. Seaton

B. Victor

B.A. Kazmi

B.A. Lubbe

Bandita Sijapati

Binayak Sen

Brock

C-M. Alcover

C. Kuo

C. Liston-Heyes

C. P. Egri

C.J. Doran

C.J. Oates

Charles Lwanga-Ntale

Chiara Mariotti

Christian N. Thoroughgood

Ciara Kelly

D. A. Ralston

D. Arenas

D. B. Lowry

D. Baur

D. Brock

D.P. Skarlicki

E. A. Veral

E. C. Elise

E. Daspro

E. Davenport

E. Hawkins

E. Reynaud

E. Rubaltelli

E. Wallace

Evelyn and Walter Haas

F. Gil.

F. L. Darder

F. MacPhail

F. Perrini

F. Prior

F. Wangenheim

Flora Kessy

G. Eweje

G. Hastings

G. Hills

G. Liu

G. Whiteman

Ganesh Thapa

H. J. Shapiro

H. P. Schmitz

H. Park

H.-H. Hsieh

Helen Underhill

I. A. Davies

I. Ahonkhai

I. Angermeier

I. Baghi

I. Buil

I.A. Davies

J. Barling

J. H. Michael

J. J. Singh

J. M. Batista-Foguet

J. M. Twenge

J. Moon

J. N. Muthuri

J. P. Stites

J. Sandstrom

J. Tsalikis

J. van Wyk

J.M. Stansbury

Jeffrey Sachs

Johan De Herdt

John Helliwell

Jr. Fund

Jung E. Ha-Brookshire

K-T. Hsu

K. Hwang

K. M. Sheldon

K. P. Winterich

K.T. Dirks

Katharina Hanifnia

Katie Smith

Katina B. Sawyer

L. Chernatony

L. Condosta

L. Schmeltz

L. Stott

L.T. Raynolds

Leni Wild

Liesbet Steer

Lucia da Corta

Lucy Scott

M. Baranowski

M. E. Porter

M. Frostenson

M. Huse

M. J. Barone

M. O. Lwin

M. Pfitzer

M. Rein

M. Sánchez-
Manzanares

M. T. Dacin

M. Tedeschi

M. Torchia

M. Yeung

M.R. Greenberg

Malcolm Patterson

Michele Simon

N. Craig Smith

N. Misani

N. Palakshappa

N. Srinivasan

N. Turner

N. van Quaquebeke

Nidhi Kaicker

O. Emelianova

O. Furrer

O. Iglesias

P. A. Dacin

P. Dunn

P. E. Murphy

P. Egri

P. Rodrigo

P. Tracey

P.Bowles

Pamela S. Norum

Pauline Rose

R. Abraham

R. Alas

R. Kräussl

R. Rico

R. W. Boss

R.E. Kidwell

Raghav Gaiha

Richard Layard

S-Y. Kim

S. Castaldo

S. D. Hansen

S. Helin

S. Knox.

S. McDonald

S. P. Sethi

S. Patscheke

S. Simola

S. Unathi Ngcwangu

S. Zhang

S.R. Valentine

Samuel T. Hunter

Schmeltz

Sri W. Handayani

Sushil Vachani

T. Bondy

T. Eckloff

T. Kasser

Terry McKinley

Tim Strawson

Torchia

U. Idemudia

Ute Stephan

V. Talwar

W-W. Ko.

W. D. Davis

W. K. Campbell

W. Lassar.

W. Liu

W. Low

W. R. Evans

W. Young

Weber Shandwick

X. Liu

Y.-D. Wand

Z. Lee

About the Editors

Wayne Visser

Dr Wayne Visser is Director of the think tank Kaleidoscope Futures, Founder of CSR International and Vice President of Sustainability Services for Omnex Inc. Wayne is also Chair of Sustainable Business at the Gordon Institute of Business Science in South Africa, Adjunct Professor of Sustainable Development at Deakin Business School in Australia and Senior Associate at the University of Cambridge Programme for Sustainability Leadership in the UK. Wayne is the author of twenty one books and has been listed as one of the Top 100 Thought Leaders in Trustworthy Business Behavior. Before getting his PhD in Corporate Social Responsibility (Nottingham University, UK), Wayne was Director of Sustainability Services for KPMG and Strategy Analyst for Cap Gemini in South Africa. His work has taken him to 70 countries in the last 20 years. Wayne lives in Cambridge, UK, and enjoys art, nature, writing poetry and travel. Much of his writing and art is on www.waynevisser.com.

Ileana Magureanu

Ileana is currently the research director for CSR International. She began her career as a researcher at the Romanian Institute of Soil Science and Environment Protection before working as an environmental journalist for Green Report, the first magazine in Romania dedicated to environmental issues. In 2010 she became an environmental assessor for the Green Revolution Association, an urban ecology NGO. Ileana has successful prepared applications for community projects that aim to promote a low-carbon economy and was also a key expert in the Green Business Index project, the barometer of corporate environmental responsibility in Romania. She is a certified CSR 2.0 assessor and advisor, currently managing Green Citadel, her own environmental NGO, which aspires to catalyse the transformation of resource-dependent human settlements into self-sufficient and nature-harmonious green citadels. She also speaks five foreign languages: English, French, Spanish, Portuguese and German.

Karina Yadav

Karina Yadav is a corporate sustainability and responsibility (CSR) professional focusing on sustainability agenda in Asia and Europe. Her main research area comprises of the state of CSR in India, including the role of the government to institutionalise CSR. Besides her research interest, Karina is managing India Business & Biodiversity Initaitive (IBBI), hosted by the Confederation of Indian Industry (CII). IBBI is a multi-stakeholder national platform for dialogue, sharing and learning on conservation amd sustainable use of biodiversity. Karina is Founder of an advisory firm CSRway. Prior she has served as Managing Director of the think-tank CSR International. She holds MSc in CSR from Nottingham University Business School's (UK) International Centre for Corporate Social Responsibility (ICCSR). Additionally, she has been a scholar at Blekinge Institute of Techology (Sweden) in strategic sustainable development.

www.ingramcontent.com/pod-product-compliance
Lightning Source LLC
Chambersburg PA
CBHW082121210326
41599CB00031B/5835